National Narratives in Mexico

National Narratives in Mexico: A History

ENRIQUE FLORESCANO

TRANSLATED BY NANCY T. HANCOCK

DRAWINGS BY RAÚL VELÁZQUEZ

UNIVERSITY OF OKLAHOMA PRESS : NORMAN

Also by Enrique Florescano

(with Lysa Hochroth, trans.) *The Myth of Quetzalcoatl* (Baltimore, 2002)
(with Albert G. Bork, Kathryn R. Bork, trans.) *Memory, Myth, and Time in Mexico: From the Aztecs to Independence* (Austin, Tex., 1994)

This work was translated with the support of the Programa de Apoyo a la Traducción de Obras Mexicanas a Lenguas Extranjeras (ProTrad), of the Fondo Nacional para la Cultura y las Artes.

Library of Congress Cataloging-in-Publication Data

Florescano, Enrique.
    [Historia de las historias de la nación mexicana. English]
    National Narratives in Mexico: a history / Enrique Florescano ; translated by Nancy T. Hancock ; drawings by Raúl Velázquez.
    p. cm.
    Includes bibliographical references and index.
    ISBN 0-8061-3701-0 (hc : alk. paper)
    1. Mexico—Historiography. 2. Mexico—History—Philosophy. I. Title.

F1224.F5213 2006
972.0072'2—dc22

                                2005046748

Originally published as *Historia de las historias de la nación mexicana*, copyright © 2002 by Enrique Florescano. Published by Taurus, Mexico.

1 2 3 4 5 6 7 8 9 10

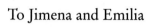

To Jimena and Emilia

CONTENTS

Preface

In the course of their lives, all people develop their own ideas about the past. We know that the origin of that irrepressible compulsion is their desire to settle their sense of themselves in the past and to project the future. The interpretation of the past is one of the most deeply engrained habits of nations. It has been a daily practice of the majority of people in every population throughout history, an imperative related to matters of state and the special offices of scribes, bards, chroniclers, and historians. Mexico is a country steeped in memories, but it has lacked a summary cataloging the interpretations that have been made of its past.

This book is concerned with the interpretations of history that in different periods have attempted to explain the Mexican past. By interpretations of history, I mean not only the stories elaborated by chroniclers and historians but also the conceptions of the past sustained by those who have had in their hands the administration of the State and those perceptions of the past in the imaginations of the common people. In studies dedicated to the investigation of historical thought, the usual approach has been to look to the individual works of historians for conceptions of the past that had been entered there.

I am proposing an approach to historical thought that differs from that tradition. As I have gone through the long stretches that comprise Mexican history, I have observed the presence of interpretations of the past that lasted for a long time, sometimes for hundreds of years. I have noticed that, independent of individual creativity, at certain moments in our historical development one interpretation of the past predominated and absorbed the others that coexisted with it, spreading to far-flung territories, being taken over by successive generations, and finally imposing itself on the most original of individual ideas. It was, in other words, a vision of the world that at a given time encompassed the origin of human beings and their development. This metanarrative contained the values that gave people their identity and strengthened the bonds that united past with present, this framework giving meaning to the collective undertaking of building the nation. In different phases of the development of Mexico, we can discover this cosmovision summed up in a historiographic canon.

The historical canon of itself that one epoch produces is like a precious jewel box. Its interior contains both the substance that gives life to the nation and the forces that drive it toward the future. And its outward appearance is almost always brightly colored and attractive, presenting a brief, clear, and effective message. When historical memory is able to reconcile the substance of an epoch with the best messenger for transmitting that legacy, it is consistently imperishable; it becomes a canon, an unsurpassable rendition of the past in an original synthesis of the totality of one moment in history.

A canon is a model, a work that harmonizes content and form into a virtuous, exemplary ensemble. Such were the stories that in the pre-Hispanic epoch encompassed the creation of the cosmos, the origin of human beings, the foundation of the kingdom, and the beginning of civilized life. For more than fifteen hundred years, the numerous peoples of Mesoamerica encapsulated their past in this narrative structure and used oral discourse, myths, rites, architectural images, and the codices to transmit it to their descendents. When the Viceroyalty was installed, this millennial canon was violently displaced by the Christian interpretation of history, which based human existence on religious values, the ultimate salvation of the soul, and the providential mission of

Spanish imperialism. Later, political independence from Spain and the founding of the Federal Republic drove the story, which concentrated on the building of the nation-state. The political process being developed by the state and the national identity became the nucleus of historical narration.

In the twentieth century two canonical interpretations dominated historical discourse. On one side, the triumph of the Revolution of 1910 led to a nationalistic ideology based on the principles generated by that movement. The Revolution of 1910 changed historical development into a process moved by successive political disruptions that drove the formation of the nation. The Revolution (with a capital R) became the historical moment par excellence, "the midwife of history," and a new conception of the national identity was constructed around it, its heroes, and its plan for the future of the nation.

Simultaneously, along with the nationalistic plan for the future, the canon elaborated by the professionals of history was taking shape, based on the academic ideals of objectivity, autonomy, analytic rigor, and freedom of thought. Unexpectedly, when economic and administrative resources joined in the academic realm with human resources (professors, researchers, students) and the means of investigation and diffusion (archives, libraries, journals, publications), the academic institution held a power comparable to that formerly exercised by the Church or the prince. With that force it produced its own historiographic canon.

Inevitably, in the trajectory of the twentieth century, the nationalistic discourse of the Revolution clashed with the discourse of professionals of history. The latter submitted the revolutionary canon to an implacable critical revisionism and demonstrated that the speeches, ceremonies, monuments, books, and heroes of the Revolution formed an ideological image of that movement, a "history in bronze" that magnified and distorted the process. The professional historians, by making academic principles the support of historical research, devalued collective memory and moved the amateur historian to the margins of history. Because of this, professional history—that is to say, history elaborated according to the precepts established by academics—was separated from collective memory, from the placenta of myths, legends, identities, and popular imagery. A great chasm was thus opened between social memory and the research practiced by specialists.

By reviewing the different interpretations of the past canonized in historiographic discourse, this book will open another window through which to look at the past and revise conceptions of the national identity. I do not claim to gather all the discourses that attained the category of canon, but I have included the most representative. When you read them, you will see that no other discourse has been so decisive in forging the idea of a Mexican nation.

National Narratives in Mexico

I. The Origin of the Story of the Creation of the Cosmos, the Beginning of the Kingdoms, and the Deeds of the Rulers

Many centuries ago, when the state emerged in Mesoamerica, the story of the creation of the cosmos, human beings, cultivated plants, the sun, and the founding of the kingdom was born. This succession of portents culminated in the remembering of the deeds of the ethnic group, related in the form of annals or chronicles. The central episodes of this narrative described the appearance of fertile land, the birth of human beings out of a cave in the underworld, the founding of the kingdom, and the recording of the notable deeds accomplished by the rulers.

I made an effort to test whether the story of the creation of the cosmos and the beginning of the kingdoms came into being at the time of the establishment of the state. According to this hypothesis, the founding of the kingdom gave the group a territory and a common identity and led to the creation of writing and the computation of time, which allowed the people to record the past in a continuous form and to share collective memories. The historical canon that appeared then united the origins of the kingdom with the ethnic group memory and brought into play various artifacts of memory to transmit that past, including the codices, myths, songs, the calendar, and the rituals that periodically recalled those founding events.[1]

In this chapter I propose to show that later stories intended to tell the history of the ancient peoples of Mesoamerica descend from that fundamental canon, whose Classic version was constructed between A.D. 200 and 640.

The Origins of the Story of the Founding of the Kingdom

The recent decoding of Mayan writing gave us access to the most ancient text of the Classic Period, which tells of the creation of the cosmos, the founding of the kingdom, and the divine origin of the rulers, who, according to the story, descended from the creator gods. This great story, engraved in the ceremonial center of Palenque on the Temple of the Cross, Temple of the Foliate Cross, and Temple of the Sun in the year A.D. 692, told of the creation of the current era of the world by the First Father and the First Mother, the creator-god couple. In other Maya testimonials of the Classic Period, the First Father was the same as the maize god, Jun Nal Ye.[2]

According to the cosmogonic text of Palenque, the gods first created the heavens, the earth, the underworld, and the four corners of the cosmos, and they later founded the earthly kingdom. The text then lists the names of the successive rulers, all invested with a divine halo because they had descended from the gods who protected Palenque. In this story the supernatural and human occurrences are dated by precise days, months, and years and placed in a limited territory, the kingdom of Palenque.[3] Among the Mayas, as in other cultures of Mesoamerica, historical deeds were identified with signs of place and time. As Donald Robertson indicates in referring to the histories recorded by the Mixtecs, "Individual events are located in space with place signs and in time with calendar signs. Mixtec history, as it has come down to us, fuses two dimensions of the past. The texts form a series of events labeled as to place and time. The events are the fabric of history, and time and place are the qualifying labels."[4]

Time and place, the two ordering principles of historical reporting, were fully developed in the Maya texts of the Classic Period. Surely these concepts were born earlier, with the first Olmec states that prospered in the southern part of Veracruz and the Zapotec kingdoms established in the central valleys of Oaxaca during the so-called Formative Period (1150–500 B.C.). In Olmec monuments of La Venta, the oldest city in Mesoamerica, one can read, engraved in images or wrapped in symbols, a primitive story of the creation of the cosmos and the beginning of the kingdoms. In contrast to the earlier small villages, La Venta was planned as a city, with buildings and plazas in the central part of a size never before seen. It was the capital of the first Mesoamerican state, governed by a lineage that transmitted power through heredity. This new political organization had its own territory and symbols, which divulged the glorious moment when the kingdom was founded, the antiquity of the royal lineage, the conquests of nearby towns, and the force that emanated from that original creation. The great pyramid that was raised in the central plaza (fig. 1) and the stelae and monuments that surrounded it celebrated that founding moment and presented it as the origin of the Olmec people. At that time the banners and emblems of the state, as well as the figure of the ruler, his scepter, his royal diadem, and the throne, were converted into representations of the kingdom.

There is still discussion concerning whether the Olmecs were the first culture in Mesoamerica. What we know without the shadow of a doubt is that the Olmecs disseminated their first state emblems and the symbols of royal power throughout Mesoamerica. For the first time, visually powerful formulas appeared that integrated into the figure of the ruler the concepts of a territorial state, an ethnic identity, and political power. On the stelae that proliferated at that time, on the stone reliefs, on ceremonial axes, and in sculpture and ceramics, the image of the sovereign was immortalized in his triple role as head of the kingdom, captain of the armies, and high priest, who maintained a continuous and privileged communication with the gods and the founding ancestors (figs. 2, 3, and 4). The architecture and monuments of the ceremonial center made holy the emblems of the kingdom and the effigy of the sovereign, who appeared in these images as the archetype of the ethnic features of the group. The ubiquitous presence of the gods in the city, the villages, and the fields indicated that the place was a sacred site,

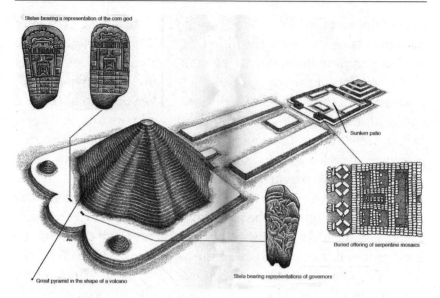

Fig. 1. Reconstruction of the ceremonial center at La Venta, with a representation of the primordial mountain, the sunken plaza, the buried offerings, and the stelae, or stone trees, with the effigies of their gods and governors. (Drawing based on Freidel, Schele, and Parker, 1993: figs. 3 and 4; and *RES* 29/30: 56.)

blessed by the powers of fertility. The city where political power and social wealth were concentrated was also the navel of the cosmos, the emblem of the kingdom, and the home of the gods.

Among the symbols most widely distributed at that time were those related to the maize plant and fertility. We know that between 1150 and 500 B.C. maize became the main crop of the Olmec people in the coastal regions of Veracruz and Tabasco.[5] The representation of maize proliferated in their cities in symbols of fertility, rebirth, abundance, plenitude, wealth, and cosmic vitality.[6]

Several objects carved in jade depicted the land surface or territory of the kingdom, with four kernels of maize representing the four corners of the cosmos. The central part of this space was occupied by the figure of the maize god or the sovereign (fig. 5).

Fig. 2. Effigy of an Olmec governor, represented with a scepter or ceremonial baton in his hands and a tall headdress with the image of the protector gods. Stela 2 at La Venta. (Drawing based on Covarrubias, 1961: 74.)

The maize plant shown in the form of a cross was an image of the four directions of the cosmos as well as vertical space, including the underworld, the land surface, and the celestial regions (fig. 6). The maize plant, the ultimate expression of fertility and of human sustenance, became the creator god of the Olmec pantheon.[7]

The Olmec maize god was a stylized representation of an ear of maize, which in Mesoamerica symbolized the attributes of the plant's growth and vitality. Most of the representations of this god assumed an anthropomorphic form (fig. 7), but the head maintained the features that defined the deity (fig. 8). As can be seen in figures 5, 6, and 8, the maize god had a head in the shape of an ear of maize, almond-shaped eyes, a mouth with jaguar features, and a brow band ornamented with four kernels of maize. Maize leaves or an ear of maize sprouted from a cleft in the back of his head.

Fig. 3. Painting in the Olmec style, which shows a character dressed in a plumed cape and a bird mask, seated on a throne in the shape of an earth monster. The image symbolizes the relationship of the governor with heavenly and terrestrial forces. (Drawing based on Joralemon, 1976: fig. 10, L.)

Fig. 4. Figure of an Olmec governor bearing a ceremonial dagger for bloodletting in the rites of sacrifice in his left hand. He wears a tall headdress, with the head of the maize god showing at the top. (Drawing based on Benson and De la Fuente, 1996: 213.)

Green was his defining color, and polished jade was the preferred stone for engraving his resplendent image.

The founders of the first Olmec kingdoms made the maize plant the creator god of their people and the absolute representation of

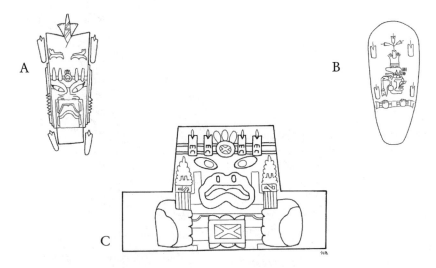

Fig. 5. (A and B) Jade axes with figures of the maize god represented as the cosmic axis. In the four corners of the central figure are maize kernels, which also spring from the head of the god. On the foreheads of these figures can be seen a band made of kernels of the maize plant. (C) The Olmec god of maize with a royal band and the symbols of maize on his forehead. Monument I of Teopantecuanitlan (Guerrero). (Drawings A and B based on Joralemon, 1976: 41; drawing C based on Martínez Donjuán, 1982: 123–31.)

fertility. It is probable that the Maya myth of the creation of the world in Palenque had its origin among the Olmecs, the first people to build a State based on the cultivation of maize.[8] For the Olmec people, the first creator of the current era of their world was the god of maize, the deity who multiplied the generations of humankind, defined the shape of the cosmos, and fixed his vital center at the place where the maize plant flourished. Earth was a field where the annual sprouting of the maize plant transformed the wrinkled dark skin of the earth, symbolized by a crocodile or a serpent, into a bright blanket of green, represented by the iridescent green plumes of the quetzal (fig. 9). The image of the Plumed Serpent

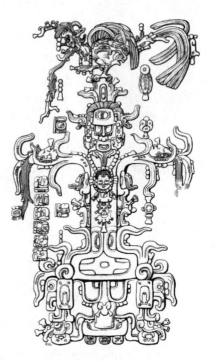

Fig. 6. The cosmic tree, in the stylized form of a maize plant, in the center of the panel of the Palenque Cross. In the bottom part, the face of the monster of the earth symbolizes the underworld. The middle part, which represents the surface of the earth, is symbolized by ears of maize in the form of human faces. The heavenly world of the upper part is represented by the figure of a bird. (Drawing based on Schele and Miller, 1992: 115.)

Fig. 7. Representation of Jun Nal Ye, the Mayan maize god, being reborn from the interior of the earth (symbolized here by the turtle's shell) in the form of a young man of extraordinary beauty. The children of the god, Xbalanqué on the right and Junajpú on the left, are helping him come out of the earth. (Drawing based on Robicsek and Hales, 1981: vase 117.)

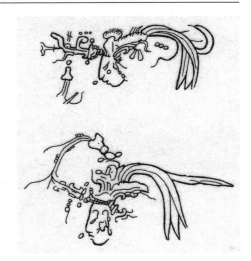

Fig. 8. Representations of the
head of the Mayan maize god
in the form of an ear of maize.
(Drawing based on Taube,
1985: fig. 1.)

was thereby a representation of earth dressed in the first green leaves of the maize plant. Thus, the cosmogonic myth of the Mesoamerican people was a hymn to fertility and agricultural abundance represented by the green maize plant, the genetic cereal that provided humans with food (fig. 10).[9]

Under the protection of this benevolent god, the first metaphors for the cosmos, the capital of the kingdom, and dynastic power were constructed. To the territory they inhabited, the Olmecs attributed the quality of a cosmic axis that connected the underworld, earth, and sky; its center was the vital point where the four directions of the universe came together. The Olmecs traced the first symbolic map of the cosmos, with its different levels, directions, colors, and meanings. During the same time that they were founding the first sedentary settlements, ruled over by hereditary governments, they imbued those advances with a sense of transcendence by relating them to a religious ceremony that periodically celebrated the advances and summoned the protection of their ancestors.

The Olmecs were the first to sanctify the effigy and the memory of their rulers, as can be seen in several sculptures (figs. 11 and 12) and the impressive group of monumental "Olmec heads" that

Fig. 9. This image from the *Códice Borgia* represents the surface of the earth as a crocodile. In the upper part, Tlaloc, the god of rain, pours fertilizing water over the earth. As can be seen, the conjunction of water and fertile earth produces the growth of ears of maize. (Drawing based on Díaz and Rodgers, 1993: plate 27.)

Fig. 10. Representation of the maize plant as nourishment and meat for human beings. In this painting from Cacaxtla, the ears of maize have human form and are the meat and the creation of the maize. (Drawing based on *Cacaxtla*: 127.)

represented the rulers (fig. 13). Since that time, the perpetuation of the figure of the sovereign and the exaltation of his works have been common elements in the political propaganda of Mesoamerica.

The Olmecs exemplified societies obsessed with the founding of stable institutions. Their leaders were able to create strong political organizations and imbue their residents with shared beliefs about

Fig. 11. Sculpture of the Young Governor from the Pacific Coast of Guatemala. He shows a rich iconography on his body, alluding to the powers that accompany the governor at the moment in which he assumes command. (Drawing based on Benson and De la Fuente, 1996: 213.)

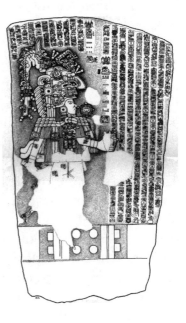

Fig. 12. Stela 1 of La Mojarra shows one of the oldest scenes of the ascension to power of a governor, dating between A.D. 143 and 156. On the right side is an extensive text, a sample of the writing of this region of southern Veracruz. The text relates the war actions and religious ceremonies accomplished by this individual before his ascent to the throne. (Drawing based on Stuart, 1993.)

themselves, the cosmos, and the outside world. The symbols they devised to indicate the kingdom, the rulers, and the gods were so attractive that other peoples adopted them as their own. The Olmecs depicted those symbols with a creativity so skillful that they became sacred objects, expressions of the divinity or the all-

Fig. 13. Monumental Olmec heads representing the governors, each of which is a portrait. They were located in front of the main monuments of the ceremonial center and in its courtyards. (Photographs from the Anthropological Museum, Jalapa, Veracruz.)

powerful ruler, and those objects acquired such prestige that years later, when their creators had all disappeared, they continued to be treasured and revered by the leaders of other states.

The Memory of the Kingdom of Teotihuacán

Perhaps it was Teotihuacán, the State that dominated the central part of Mesoamerica for more than six centuries, that canonized the symbols of power and gave them a Mesoamerican dimension. Until recently, even though the image of Teotihuacán was one of the most widely circulated in the Mesoamerican territory, its history was ignored or entangled in the threads of legend. Archaeologists affirm that from the beginning of the current era until the eighth century, Teotihuacán was the most powerful capital in Mesoamerica. But suddenly—around 750—the splendid city fell, demolished in a destructive fury, and its ceremonial center was burned. The catastrophe that destroyed the metropolis did away with the effigies of its rulers and also consumed the books and testimonials that had recorded their history. Nevertheless, the tracks this kingdom left were so deep that they survived its years of misfortune. After the disaster that ended its political organization, during the time when the foundations of the Post-Classic states were beginning to be laid, the image of Teotihuacán was reborn in the memories of the peoples of Mesoamerica with the splendor of an ideal kingdom.

This image surpassed the dimensions of the historical kingdom. Archaeological indications are that since the time it was founded Teotihuacán was planned to be a great city. Its architects tried to make the terrestrial city a copy of the balanced harmony they believed they could discern in the cosmos (fig. 14). Its outline, closely measured, followed the movement of the sun, that star which regulated the flow of time and impressed order and vitality on human endeavors.

Teotihuacán was the first city in the Central Highlands that mirrored the requisites of the ideal metropolis as conveyed by the cosmogonic myths, the universal model for Mesoamerican creations. It was an *axis mundi,* a world axis where the forces that maintained the cosmic order came together: its vertical axis united the generative powers of the underworld with the procreators of heaven, and both gave vitality to the earth, the center of the cosmos, the place where forces from the four corners of the universe came together. It was also a sanctuary where religious ceremonies were held to sanctify the earthly world, drawing pilgrims from the farthest provinces. And above all it was the city where political power, wealth, and civilization were concentrated.[10]

Around A.D. 400, Teotihuacán was the largest metropolitan center on the continent: it was twelve square miles in size and had a population of more than one hundred thousand, composed of ethnic groups coming from several parts of Mesoamerica.[11] Nevertheless, only a decade ago we were not even aware of its ancient name, the language of its residents, or the importance of these people in the Mesoamerican world of their time. Surprisingly, only a few years ago researchers found that in the Classic Period the kingdom's contemporaries the Zapotecs and Mayas knew it by the name Tollan, "the place of the reeds" (a symbol of multitudes) and called it "the city of the wise men" (Ah Puh). Other researchers affirm that the residents of this first Tollan spoke an ancient Nahua tongue, the predecessor of the language of the founders of Tula

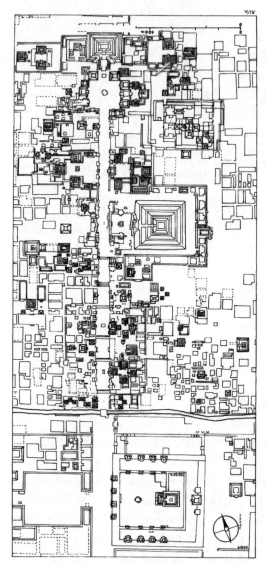

Fig. 14. A map of the city of Teotihuacán, which divides the city into four sectors. At the bottom is the great enclosure of La Ciudadela, and at the very top are the Pyramids of the Sun and the Moon. (Drawing based on Millon, 1981: 201.)

de Hidalgo and Mexico-Tenochtitlán. Likewise, inquiries into other regions of Mesoamerica indicate that Teotihuacán was an imperial city in the Classic Period—an urban center whose symbols of power fascinated the rulers of other states, who rushed to copy them and reproduce them in their own kingdoms. According to recent research, the rulers of the Maya kingdoms of Tikal and Copán claimed with pride that the founders of their dynasties descended from the royal lineage of Tollan and that their investiture and symbols of power came from that capital.[12]

But even as our understandings of historic Tollan are more numerous and dazzling day by day, our image of it is inferior to the one its descendants built after the fall of the great city. Surely with the idea of avoiding the memory of the catastrophe that had swept away the foundations of the most powerful State in Mesoamerica, the descendants of the ancient lineages built a grandiose but nostalgic vision of the fallen Tollan, an idealized image of the old kingdom. According to this image, Tollan was the encarnation of a marvelous kingdom: the core from which the new humanity had sprung, the Eden of fecundity, the home of the gods and shining temples, the archetype of military power, the cradle of arts and science, the emblem of the civilized world, the house of noble lineages, and the seat of wise government.[13]

In contrast with the cosmogonic myth of the Olmecs, which celebrated fertility and agricultural abundance, the Teotihuacán myth exalted the achievements of civilization and attributed its origin to the State, the institution that multiplied and gave permanence to the benefits of civilization. According to the songs preserved as a precious heritage by the kingdoms that followed Tollan, the civilized world and political organization first saw the light of day in that city. The State and the wise ruler were of the highest value, celebrated in the myths, songs, and images that came out of Teotihuacán.

According to one tradition retained by the Mexicas, when there were no humans nor animals, the gods met in Tollan-Teotihuacán and decided to create the cosmos. After deliberation, they agreed that two of them should sacrifice themselves in the divine oven so that life might begin on earth. Tecuciztécatl and Nanahuatzin were chosen and immediately began to make propitiatory offerings. But while Tecuciztécatl wore elegant robes and made ostentatious offerings, Nanahuatzin, poor and with sores all over his body,

Fig. 15. Reconstruction of the Temple of the Plumed Serpent in the Ciudadela of Teotihuacán. (Drawing by Raúl Velázquez.)

offered handfuls of green canes, maguey thorns, and his own scabs in place of incense. When both drew close to the flaming oven where they were to sacrifice themselves, Tecuciztécatl tried four times to throw himself into the flames but four times turned back. On the other hand, when Nanahuatzin was called, he went in the first time and was consumed in the flames. In this manner Nanahuatzin was changed into the radiant Sun of the new era of the world, and Tecuciztécatl, who immolated himself later, became the Moon.[14] The Mexicas living in Tenochtitlán in the fourteenth and fifteenth centuries considered the two great pyramids of Teotihuacán to be the monuments to the Sun and Moon.

The monuments and architecture of Teotihuacán also tell how the surface of the land rose up and how the territory was organized. The famous Templo de la Serpiente Emplumada (Temple of the Plumed Serpent) symbolized the birth of the First True Mountain, the rising up of the land from the primordial seas (fig. 15). Like the

Fig. 16. Representation of the panel and slope of the Temple of Quetzal-cóatl in Teotihuacán. In the upper part of the panel is the head of a plumed serpent that springs up out of a plumed circle. Beside it is a headdress related to Cipactli, which symbolizes the earth and the first day of the calendar in time. On the lower part of the slope is the figure of the Plumed Serpent, swimming in the primordial ocean. (Drawing by José Francisco Villaseñor, based on Fuente, 1995: 12.)

central pyramid of La Venta, in Teotihuacán the mountain-pyramid rises from a great sunken patio that was flooded in the summer to resemble the ocean of the primordial waters. The slope of this great monument (the lower part of the pyramid where it joins the earth) is covered with plumed serpents that seem to be swimming in a marine setting, represented by shells and snails (fig. 16). In this image the Plumed Serpent is a representation of the land surfaces in formation—the serpent or crocodile that, according to other cosmogonic stories, floated in the primordial seas.[15] Thus, ever since the first day of creation, the earth was seen to be located in the center of the cosmos, possessing the characteristics that distinguished it as the seat of human habitation: primordial land, fertile ground; it was the cosmic navel, the place where life was born and reproduced.

Researchers have identified the motif in the panels at the side of the Plumed Serpent heads as a coiffure that symbolized time (fig. 16). This coiffure was appropriate to the first day of the calendar, *cipactli* (lizard or crocodile), which "is the original monster, feminine and aquatic, that according to Nahua myths was divided into two parts to form the heaven and the earth."[16] According to this symbolism, *cipactli* was the earth itself and was also the first

of the twenty days of the month. So if we combine these interpretations, the Temple of the Plumed Serpent is a monument
dedicated to the appearance of fertile land, the beginning of time
and of the calendar, the first day of creation, and the beginning of
the era of the Fifth Sun and the founding lineage of the grandeur
of Tollan.[17]

Several Nahua statements coming from the Teotihuacán tradition indicate that the first humans were created in Tollan. These
texts say that after the earth was put in order, the god Quetzalcóatl received the order to create human beings. Several stories
describe how Quetzalcóatl descended to the underworld in
search of extinct humans to create the beings of the age of the
Fifth Sun out of their bones.[18] One of the texts narrates, in a form
similar to that of the K'iche' story of the *Popol Vuh*, the terrible
battle between Quetzalcóatl, the celestial deity, and Mictlantecutli,
the lord of the underworld. Quetzalcóatl was trying to take control
of the human remains that lay in the fertile regions of the underworld, while Mictlantecutli was trying to keep them there. The
most dramatic moment of the dispute occurred when Mictlantecutli
seemed to accede to the request of Quetzalcóatl, who took the
bones and started to depart from Mictlán. But then the lord of
the region of shadows sprang his trick: he opened a pit in the
road and Quetzalcóatl fell into it, which caused the bones to be
scattered and broken. Because of this mishap, the men of the Fifth
Sun were no longer as large as their ancestors, who had been the
size of giants.

As soon as Quetzalcóatl was able to pull himself together, he
gathered up the bones and went with them to Tamoanchan, where
the other creators had met. Quetzalcóatl gave the bones to the
goddess Quilaztli, who ground them up in an earthenware pot
and gave them vitality by mixing them with the germinating
dough of the maize. Then Quetzalcóatl spilled blood from his
sex organ over that substance, as did the other gods. In that
way, from the mixing of the sacrifice of the creator gods with
the nutritious dough of the maize, the first human beings, the

founders of the Fifth Sun, were born. Here, as in the myth of the *Popol Vuh,* humans are a gift, a present from the gods, and because of that, ever since their origin they have had to struggle to merit the favor of their creators.

The myths of creation related to Teotihuacán imply that human beings were born out of a cave in the interior of the country, probably the cave under the Pyramid of the Sun (fig. 17).[19] So a defining trait of the cosmogonic myth of Tollan-Teotihuacán is the claim that the appearance of the sun, the birth of fertile land, and the creation of human beings were occurrences that took place in their own land, in the marvelous Tollan.[20]

After describing these initial episodes, the myth was limited to the narration of the founding of Tollan, the kingdom that began the age of the Fifth Sun. Later creation myths, inspired by the cosmogonic myth of Tollan, after telling of the appearance of the sun and of a new humanity, also concentrated on the exaltation of Tollan. Thus, the Mexica creation myths considered Teotihuacán as the first kingdom of the Fifth Sun and presented an exaggerated image of that marvelous city, the quintessence of human creations. The Nahua songs that celebrated the appearance of the first kingdom of the Central Highlands were the most hyperbolic in Mesoamerican literature. In those stories the kingdom of Tollan was the image of civilization and of material riches. The Toltecs, as they called the residents of Tollan, were the inventors of the recording of time, of astronomy, of writing, and of the art of divination; they were experts in the knowledge of plants, religion, and painted books. The residents of Tollan were well-known craftsmen in sculpture, architecture, goldsmithing, painting, working with precious stones, feather work, weaving, and music. In those stories *Toltec* meant a master jeweler of the refined arts; the equivalent of a wise man, a knower of the secrets of civilized life. And Tollan, that opulent urban center, ornamented with monuments and magnificent buildings such as the so-called Temple of Quetzalcóatl, became the synonym for *metropolis,* the archetype of the capital of the kingdom.[21]

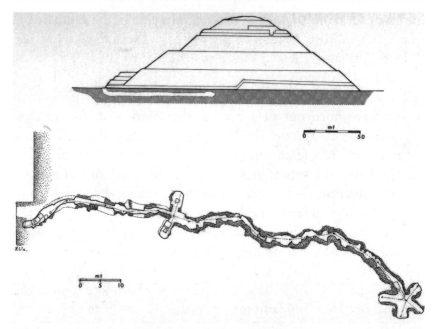

Fig. 17. Design of the Pyramid of the Sun in Teotihuacán, showing the configuration of the cave located in its lower part. (Drawing based on Millon, 1993: 23.)

That exalted description of Tollan and the Toltecs was joined to another image that described the kingdom as a place of privilege because of its material richness and agricultural abundance. One text said that Tollan had "all the wealth of the world, gold, silver, and green stones called chalchihuites, and other precious things." Another affirmed that Tollan was a prodigal orchard, where cotton grew with multicolored bolls and maize

> was very plentiful, and the squash very fat . . .
> and the ears of maize were so large that
> you had to carry them embraced in your arms . . .
> and the aforementioned Toltecs were very rich
> and lacked for nothing, nor suffered from hunger.[22]

After drawing a picture of the perfect kingdom, the myth traced the archetype of royal lineage. Two Nahua texts indicated that Tollan was founded by Ce Ácatl Topiltzin (Our Lord One Reed) Quetzalcóatl (Plumed Serpent). *La historia de los mexicanos por sus pinturas* clearly stated that "in the thirteenth sixth [year after the] flood Ce Ácatl began to wage war and became the first lord of Tula."[23] On the other hand, the *Leyenda de los soles* (Legend of the suns) stated: "The name of this Sun is Naollin [Fourth Movement] who was the same Sun as Topiltzin of Tollan, of Quetzalcóatl."[24] This and other texts described Ce Ácatl Topiltzin Quetzalcóatl as a conqueror who—thanks to his deeds of war—established the kingdom of Tollan. Other sources praised his virtues as a wise ruler, declaring that he was the inventor of specialized knowledge (writing, measuring time, astronomy), the patron of the refined arts (architecture, painting, sculpture, featherwork, music), and the supreme executor of religious services. We cannot be certain whether those texts referred to the founder of the lineage of the first Tollan (Teotihuacán) or to the hero, ruler, and god of Tula de Hidalgo, the capital that flowered from the ninth to eleventh centuries and assumed the prestige of the first Tollan. But we can say with certainty that the canonical image of the conquering leader and wise ruler was created in Teotihuacán. Several testimonials from this city attributed the highest prestige to the ruler: the founder of the royal dynasty, the seed that instilled a lasting vitality to the kingdom. An old song identified the Toltecs with the archetype of the kingdom, the place of command:

> In the place of command,
> in the place of command we govern,
> it is the mandate of my principal lord.
> The mirror who makes visible all that is.[25]

Investigations by archaeologists in the Temple of the Plumed Serpent confirm that this monument was a representation of political power. Several earlier authors had attributed a direct relationship with political power and royalty to La Ciudadela (The Citadel), the enclosure where the Temple of the Plumed Serpent was located.[26] But the burial in this monument of more than two hundred warriors sacrificed to celebrate its completion, the discovery of rich offerings dedicated to honor the mortal remains of one or more individuals, and the symbols associated with royalty that were found there led Saburo Sujiyama to maintain that this monument was built to commemorate "the sacred authority of a specific ruler who organized the building of this pyramid." According to Sujiyama, "the Plumed Serpent seems to have established himself since birth as a mythical being who legitimized the political authority of the rulers before society. And as far as available archaeological knowledge indicates, the place of origin of this singular symbolism was Teotihuacán."[27]

So it could be said that in the Teotihuacán tradition, Quetzal-cóatl was the founder of Tollan and of the lineage that governed that city for many years under the emblem of the Plumed Serpent, the symbol of the royal house that was engraved on the Temple of the Plumed Serpent as of the second century of the current era. According to my interpretation, the symbol of the Plumed Serpent represented so vigorously on that monument was not a "mythical being" or a god; it was the royal emblem of the ruler buried there, an emblem that from that time forward became the representation of the royal house of Tollan. This emblem acquired so much prestige that from that time until the fall of Tenochtitlán, it was the most widely distributed and appreciated emblem in Mesoamerica, as confirmed by its repeated and exalted appearances in Xochicalco, Cacaxtla, Tula, Chichén Itzá, Cholula, Uxmal, Mayapán, Tenochtitlán, Coixtlahuaca, and other capitals (fig. 18). In this series of images it can be seen that the rulers of those kingdoms, to make their rank clear, invariably had themselves pictured beneath the protecting halo of the emblem of the Plumed Serpent, which literally enveloped and protected their bodies. The royal personage who governed Tollan and elaborated the grandiose program of political legitimization encapsulated in the Temple of the Plumed Serpent infused so much transcendency into the exercise of power that in the future his name and his emblem acquired the meaning of dynastic foundation, royal lineage, wise government, and archetype of the political leader.

Characteristics of the Historical Canon of the Classic Period

It can be seen then that in Tollan-Teotihuacán the characteristics took shape that would define the story of the creation of the world and the beginning of civilized life in the Classic Period (A.D. 250–900). The basic components of this canon were: The Creation of the Fifth Sun, the act that imposed order on the cosmos and gave origin to the fertile earth; The Creation of Human Beings and Maize; and The Founding of the Kingdom and the Chronicles of the Deeds Accomplished by its Leaders. A later version of the Teotihuacán myth of the creation of the cosmos and the beginning of the kingdoms is found in Palenque, engraved in hieroglyphics in the year A.D. 692. The main characteristics of this founding myth are summarized in table 1.

There is every indication that in ancient Mesoamerica the most celebrated story was that which told of the marvelous ordering of the cosmos, the creation of earth, the origin of human beings, and the establishing of the kingdoms. According to my interpretation, Tollan-Teotihuacán was the first kingdom that canonized this story, wrote it into a codex that gave it uniformity and allowed it to be handed down, and converted it into the ancestral ritual that was performed to begin the ceremonies of the new year each time a fifty-two-year cycle was completed and the festival of the New Fire was celebrated, as well as any time a new ruler was installed or the founding events of the kingdom were commemorated. The story of the origin of the kingdom and the beginning of civilized life was the hymn most often sung in the ancient capitals of Mesoamerica.

Before an integrated story of the creation of the cosmos and the beginning of the kingdoms existed, there were many versions

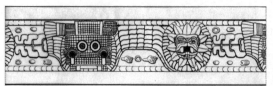

Teotihuacán
(150–200 B.C.)

Xochicalco (900)

Cacaxtla (800)

Tula-Xicocotitlán
(900-1000)

Fig. 18. The graphic evolution of the emblem of the Plumed Serpent as a symbol of royal power in Teotihuacán, Xochicalco, Cacaxtla, Tula-Xicocotitlán, Chichen-Itzá, and México-Tenochtitlán. As can be seen in these enlightening images, from the time the emblem of the Plumed Serpent appeared as the symbol of royal power in Teotihuacán in the second century until the fall of Tenochtitlán in 1521, it was always associated with the governor. (Drawings by Raúl Velázquez.)

Chichén Itzá (800–900)

Ce Ácatl Topiltzin en Tula,
grabado por los mexicas
(1450–1500)

Coixtlahuaca (1100)

Tilantongo
(1000)

Tenochtitlán (1500)

Table 1. The Palenque Myth of the Origin of the Cosmos and the Beginning of the Kingdom (A.D. 692)

I. First creation of the cosmos	II. Creation of the earth	III. Founding of the kingdom and chronicle of the dynasties
On December 7, 3121 B.C., when there was nothing in the world, the eight Lords of the Night ruled and the First Mother was born. On June 16, 3122 B.C., the First Father was born. On August 13, 3114 B.C., the thirteenth era ended and the new creation began. Later, the gods who protected Palenque were born. God I was born on October 21 of the year 2360 B.C. and is associated with Venus. God II was born on November 8, 2360 B.C.; he had one leg like a snake and was the god of lineages. On October 25, 2360 B.C., God III, the Jaguar god, also called Ahaw-Kin, or Lord Sun, was born.	One of the first actions of the First Father (whom other Mayan texts of the Classic Period identify with Jun Nal Ye, the god of maize) was to raise the sky and create a house on the north side, divided into eight parts. There he also raised a cosmic tree, the primordial tree (Wakah-Chan). In this manner the First Father divided the cosmos in eight directions and created three vertical levels: heaven, earth, and the underworld.	Next, the Palenque text said the ruling dynasty descended from the First Father and the First Mother. It stated that on March 11, 993 B.C., U-Kix-Cham was born, who was crowned king on March 28, 967 B.C., at the age of 36 years. Then the text jumped forward to the founder of the dynasty of Kam Balan, the king of Palenque, who ordered this text written in the year A.D. 692.

Source: Data from Linda Schele and David Freidel, *A Forest of Kings: The Untold Story of the Ancient Maya* (William Morrow and Co., 1990); 237–61; and David Freidel, Linda Schele, and Joy Parker, *Maya Cosmos: 3000 Years of the Shaman's Path* (William Morrow and Co., 1993), chap. 2.

of the various episodes, sung or performed in isolation. The rituals that celebrated the birth of the sun, marked the renewal of plants in the spring, and remembered the ancestors were all old cults, hundreds of years older than the story of the creation of the cosmos. And they were surely celebrated in isolation, according to the appropriate occasion and time. Archaeologists inform us that in the Neolithic period (10,000–9,000 B.C.), long before the invention of agriculture, the hunter-gatherers of Europe and the Near East had a spectacular revolution: the invention of symbols and visual images that made known the supernatural world, the gods, and creative powers. The function of these symbols, as described by Claude Lévi-Strauss, was to make the world around them intelligible to human beings as well as to establish their proper place in that world.[29] In Mesoamerica, many years before the invention of agriculture and the appearance of the first cities and states, stones were carved with the figure of a woman representing fertility and images alluding to supernatural powers.[30] But those cults and gods were not integrated into a political organization dedicated to reproducing and disseminating them throughout the social unit.

What distinguished the cosmogonic myth from previous cults was the integration of the different episodes in the creation of the world into a single story that imparted unity of both content and form. I maintain that the story of the creation of the cosmos was written when the first kingdoms were founded, because earlier than that there were no records of it in any of its versions, and because only the power of the State could have integrated those different versions and transmitted them uniformly by means of the codices, songs, myths, visual representations, and calendar. I suggest that the codex that was born with the kingdom was the text that united the different episodes of creation into one linear story, ordered by the events that culminated in the appearance of the surface of the earth and the origin of human beings, cultivated plants, the sun, and the founding of the kingdoms.[31]

Out of these founding events, the theme that dominated was the history of the kingdom. The stelae, monuments, pictures, and hieroglyphic texts of the kingdoms of the Classic Period emphasized the narration of history starring the ruling lineage. The cosmogonic myth engraved on the Palenque temples was the oldest example of this kind of story. This text began with the creation and division of the cosmos, then celebrated the emergence of the land, and concluded with the founding of the kingdom and the listing of the rulers whose deeds gave prestige to the Kingdom of Palenque. The text underscored the continuity between the origins of creation and the history of the kingdoms that grew out of that fundamental genesis. In this sense the history of the earth was a gift directly attributable to divine creation.

The historical narration of the kingdom that appeared in the last part of the cosmogonic myths became the central theme of the stories, which adopted the form of annals. The succession of the creations and of the rulers was recorded in the form of annals in Palenque, and the historical narrations of the Classic Period followed that same model. The description of the actions of the sovereign at a precise time and place determined the ordering of the historical Maya and Zapotecan records of the Classic Period. Among the Mayas, painting, sculpture, the abundant hieroglyphic texts, and the monuments dedicated to the recording of historical deeds emphasized the acts of the sovereign. Maya history of the Classic Period was completely focused on the personality of the *ahaw,* the supreme ruler. The origins of the kingdom, its expansion and conquests, its wars and alliances, the founding of new cities, the building of temples dedicated to the gods, the monuments that commemorated the passage of time and the rituals that celebrated the sowing of the crops, the arrival of the rainy season and the harvest, all these events were represented in the figure or name of the ruler.[32] Even the design of the city, which attempted to reproduce the configuration of the cosmos, was a great stage of power, a deployment of symbols intended to legitimize and exalt the ruler.[33]

All these were literally a history of the power concentrated in the sovereign. In the stories there was no room for the farmers nor the artesans who built the grandeur and prestige of the realm.

By suppressing the collective actors and starring the persona of the ruler, the records showed the compulsion to legitimize the inequality that was the basis for the creation of the hereditary kingdom. The disappearance of the social actors and the attribution to the sovereign of all memorable historical events was an inverted image of reality. One can thus conclude that the principal ideological function of the myth of the creation of the cosmos and the beginning of the kingdoms was to disseminate the idea that the rulers descended from the gods and were born to exercise power, while the obligation of the farmers and artesans was to sustain the rulers.[34]

This conception of the origin of the cosmos, human beings, and the history of the kingdoms is the same one found in the historical records of the kingdom of Monte Albán.[35] The story told by its palaces and temples, stelae, paintings, tombs, and ceramics was organized around the rulers. In the case of the Mayas, this canon began to be diluted when the number and strength of the noble lineages increased, a phenomenon that was accentuated from the sixth to the ninth centuries. During that time, at the side of the figure of the supreme ruler, there appeared figures of the personages and lineages that governed subordinate cities in the kingdom, and representations of other members of the royal family such as war captains, administrators, priests, and scribes began to proliferate. That is to say, the *ahaw* lost his absolute power and now shared it with members of the royal family and individuals who represented other noble lineages. Nonetheless, the historical story continued to be a record of the actions of the ruler, an exaltation of his power, and a celebration of the ancestral lineage that was the proof of his legitimacy.

II. THE CANON OF THE POST-CLASSIC PERIOD, 1100–1521

The real and mythological collapse of Tollan-Teotihuacán sowed chaos throughout the political system of Mesoamerica and gave origin to one of the darkest of enigmas: What were the causes that precipitated the catastrophe? On the one hand, a period of instability and political earthquakes took place that finally destroyed the ancient kingdoms based on the absolute power of the divine *ahaw*. This general disaster, which archaeologists place between 650 and 900 A.D., was followed by an unprecedented diaspora and a period of extreme changes and violence. One after another, the old territorial, ethnic, linguistic, cultural, and political borders forged throughout many centuries collapsed. Then began a time of endless migrations, assaults, and depredations, which in turn encouraged the formation of armed bands and mercenary armies that added to the instability and uncertainty. Wars pitting everyone against everyone else characterized that turbulent epoch.

No corner of Mesoamerica escaped the effects produced by the dissolution of the political order. The old lineages were expelled from the kingdoms, were uprooted and persecuted. In some regions an effort was made to contain the debacle by forming new states. To the south of the Valley of Mexico, in the hot country of Morelos, the city of Xochicalco was built, protected by high terraces and barricades. On the border between Puebla and Veracruz, Cantona grew up on the edge of the mountains, surrounded by walls. The city of Tajín, on the northern coast of Veracruz, was another enclave surrounded by fortifications. In the highlands of Guatemala, the

K'iche' and Kakchiquel built the cities of Utatlán and Iximché, protected by thick bulwarks and deep pits. And in the same manner many other cities put up steep walls, impassable moats, and tall ramparts to protect themselves from destructive onslaughts.

That time of anxiety encouraged the creation of new political organizations. Perhaps because, among the surviving chiefs, there were none with the force necessary to check disorder, unusual alliances were forged. The chiefs of the ancient lineages allied with the leaders of the invading clans, the warrior groups made accords with the sedentary peoples, and there came to be intense interaction between different ethnicities, languages, and cultures like never before.

From this fusion new states developed, such as the one that had as its capital the well-known city of Chichén Itzá and the famous kingdom of Tula, founded by Chichimec and Nonoalca peoples in the present-day state of Hidalgo.[1] These two were the first states that gained their own impetus after the fall of the ancient kingdoms. Both were born of the association of two or three cities that joined together to establish political order in their region. Tula, a city founded by northern Chichimec tribes associated with the old people of Teotihuacán, joined with Otumba, an Otomí city, and these two joined with Culhuacán, the prestigious home of the ancient Toltecs in the Valley of Mexico. Chichén Itzá was founded by the Itzas, Mayas from the southern region of the Petén, and ancient peoples of the peninsula of Yucatán, who had lived with people from the center of Mexico for a long time. When Chichén Itzá and Tula later declined, a series of small kingdoms developed in the Oaxacan Mixtec, and in the south of Puebla a Toltec-Chichimec group settled and founded new political organizations.

Interestingly, these new states reconstructed their past following the canon of the Classic Period. It was not surprising that each one of them would make an effort to relate the history of their origins and rhetorically celebrate their ascent to power. But amazingly, as we will see, they told that history faithfully following the canon established by the legendary Tollan-Teotihuacán.

The K'iche' Canon Recorded in the Popol Vuh

The *Popol Vuh,* the cultural treasure left by the Mayas of the Post-Classic Period (1200–1521 A.D.), was the book in which the most highly esteemed traditions of those peoples were stored. It preserved the ancient myths that told of the origin of the cosmos, interspersed with newer ones that legitimized the invasion of the K'iche' and transformed the occupation of the highlands of Guatemala into an epic. Its pages contained a generous catalog of popular rituals and feasts, a summary of the values most appreciated by the K'iche' people, and various conceptions of the cosmos, the gods, and the ethnic groups the people lived among and competed with. With ample justification Adrián Recinos has called it "the most notable book of American antiquity."[2] Others have nicknamed it the *American Bible* because, like the sacred book of Christianity, the Mayan volume narrated the history of mankind from the beginning of the world, emphasizing the incarnations of the K'iche' people.

Its five sections constituted a harmonious whole, its contents summarizing the canon developed by the Mayas of the Post-Classic Period to tell the story of the world from the primordial creation to the appearance of the K'iche', when history became a recounting of deeds in which the K'iche' took the lead.[3] In the following pages I will present the characteristics of the canon, which told of divine and human happenings over a broad area of the Maya territory.

In the 1970s, when the decoding of Mayan glyphs was just beginning and archaeologists were groping forward without the aid of epigraphy, astronomy, or newer studies of myths and religion, the first part of the *Popol Vuh,* which told of the fantastic struggle between the heavenly powers and those of the underworld, seemed impenetrable. There was no reasonable explanation of the battle between the celestial and terrestrial gods, the theme dominating the first part of the book. Nonetheless, new studies reveal that One Junajpú and Seven Junajpú, the first heavenly couple, who

Fig. 19. Junajpú and Xbalanqué (left) confronting the lord of the underworld, Itzamná (right). Painting on a Maya vase of the Classic Period. (Drawing based on *Schatten uit de Nieuwe Wereld*, 1992: 243.)

descended to the underworld to confront the lords of Xibalbá, were led by One Junajpú, who in Mayan texts of the Classic Period was the god of maize, Jun Nal Ye (One Kernel of Maize). Thus, when the *Popol Vuh* said that the gods of Xibalbá defeated the heavenly emissaries and decapitated One Junajpú, then burying his head at the side of the ball court, it was a symbolic narration of the first efforts to sow maize seed in the underworld and the denial of the gods of the underworld to allow it to produce on the surface of the land.[4]

The end of the third part of the *Popol Vuh* told of another great battle, which pitted the lords of Xibalbá against Junajpú and Xbalanqué, the sons of One Junajpú, who descended to the icy regions of the underworld to rescue the remains of One Junajpú, the First Father. In this case One Junajpú symbolized the first maize kernel and the human seed (the bones) resting in the depths of the earth, the underworld, the place of fertility and unending rebirth. The third part of the *Popul Vuh*, one of the most dramatic, was depicted on the beautiful painted pots of the Classic Period (fig. 19).[5] In the book and on the pots, Junajpú and Xbalanqué appeared as the Divine Twins, who thought of several false arguments to avoid the snares set for them by the lords of Xibalbá and were finally able to confuse, humiliate, and sacrifice them (fig. 20).[6]

The climax of that episode was the resurrection of the First Father, the first kernel of maize, changed now to the resplendent

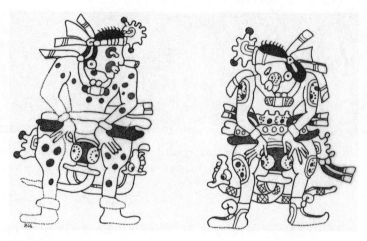

Fig. 20. Representation of the Divine Twins in the earthenware vessels of the Classic Period. On the left is Junajpú (who bears the name of Uno Ahaw on the earthenware), recognizable by the black body painting. On the right is Xbalanqué, the Yax Balam of the Classic Period, who is distinguished by body decorations of jaguar skin. (Drawing based on Hellmuth, 1987: figs. 426 and 427.)

young maize god (Jun Nal Ye), reborn from the underworld. Many testimonials celebrated that exultant passage, which became the symbol of the victory of creative forces over destructive ones, in the allegory of the annual rebirth of nature and the metaphor of the ceaseless regeneration of life (figs. 21 and 22).

The uplifting of fertile land and the birth of the maize god ended the first battle of celestial forces against the underworld. From that time on, those formidable protagonists, instead of fighting, united their powers of fecundity and germination to reproduce life on earth. In turn, that ordering event led to the two last sections of the *Popol Vuh*. The fourth part of the book narrated how the creator gods discovered the place of the storage mountain, from which they extracted the precious kernels of yellow maize and white maize. Then Xmukame, the divine midwife, ground the kernels nine times, and from that dough the gods fashioned the bodies of the first four human beings: Jaguar Quitzé, Jaguar Noche, Mahucutah, and

Fig. 21. Maya funerary vase showing three episodes in the journey of Jun Nal Ye through the underworld. In the lower part the maize god appears lying down, as if newly born, and at the upper right he is seen in the midst of the rowing gods, bearing a bag of the kernels of maize that he has rescued from the mountain of sustenance in his lap. On the left two nude women help him to dress himself at the moment before his rebirth. (Drawing based on Freidel, Schele, and Parker, 1993: fig. 2:27.)

Jaguar Oscuro, heads of the lineage of the K'iche' and founders of the K'iche' people.

As I have indicated, in the *Popol Vuh* the foundation of the cosmos, the birth of human beings, and the beginning of sedentary life were associated with the origin of maize. The identification of the origin of maize with the beginning of civilized life demonstrated the importance the people of Mesoamerica attributed to the domestication of this plant. Jun Nal Ye, the maize god of the Classic Period and the *Popol Vuh*, was the first American deity whose very body, the ear of maize, became both the creation and the food of the new human beings. According to that conception, the creator god and his creatures had the same origin and were made of the same substance.[7]

After the creation of the K'iche' founders' lineage, the story described their travels to the fabulous Tulán Zuyuá, a late reincarnation of the legendary Tollan-Teotihuacán. As the reader will remember, in the Teotihuacán tradition Tollan was the capital of

Fig. 22. The rebirth of Jun Nal Ye, painted on a Maya vase. His children Xbalanqué, on the right, and Junajpú, on the left, help him come out of the interior of the earth, symbolized by a turtle shell. (Drawing based on Robicsek and Hales, 1981: 155.)

the kingdom, where the rulers were invested and legitimized. The *Popol Vuh* told the story of the journey of the founders of the K'iche' lineage to Tulán Zuyuá (which may be the present-day Chichén Itzá) and said that in that place their patron gods were given the gift of fire and the insignias of power. That is to say, the founding of the kingdoms, the establishment of the dynasties, and the symbols of power in the Post-Classic Period repeat the model of the Classic Period forged in Tollan-Teotihuacán.

The *Popol Vuh* described Tulán Zuyuá as the capital of a conquering power that had subdued both great tribes and small. Tulán was a cosmopolitan city, inhabited by people of different ethnicities and languages and ornamented with marvelous buildings. It was likewise a religious center that attracted pilgrims from remote regions. Nevertheless, the chiefs of the K'iche' lineages, instructed by Tojil, their guiding god, decided to abandon this prodigious city and begin a migration to the lands where they would settle and be powerful. From that moment, the migration became a heroic saga of the K'iche' people in search of the promised land. Impelled by that mandate, they were dazzled by the contemplation of the appearance of the sun that initiated the present era, began their pilgrimage, and arrived in the highlands of Guatemala, where they faced the original tribes of that region, inflicted crushing defeats on them, and began their climb to eminence.

In the fifth and final part of the book there was a simultaneous diminishing of the role of the gods and increasing importance of military chiefs, rulers, and the ethnic group as central characters of the story. Three episodes stand out in that section: the second trip to Tulán Zuyuá; the increase of the lineages and disputes over power; and the founding of a new capital (Q'umarkah), which symbolized the strengthening and expansion of the K'iche' kingdom.

The second trip to Tulán Zuyuá confirmed the legitimizing role that the political capital of Tollan-Teotihuacán had exercised in the history of Mesoamerica ever since its founding. That time, those who traveled to the legendary capital were the chiefs of the K'iche' lineages who had succeeded the founders, and their trip had as its object the idea of sanctioning recent victories over the original tribes and legitimizing their ascent to the level of leaders of the K'iche' people. Both objectives were fulfilled when they came before Nacxit (a Nahua name that means Four Feet), the supreme ruler of Tulán Zuyuá. In a ceremony that the K'iche' kept forever in their collective memory, Nacxit granted them the insignias of power, a complete set of the symbols of royalty, and the writings of Tulán—the book in which the true traditions had been entered.

Later in the book, the *Popol Vuh* described the consolidation of the K'iche' power structure in the conquered lands. It told of the establishment of new towns, the deeds of its captains, the founding of Q'umarkah (Utatlán in Náhuatl), and the glories of its rulers. The last pages of the book were an apology for the expansion of the kingdoms, the tributes, the military power, the growth of the noble lineages, the ceremonies that celebrated their gods, and the creation of the songs and books that ennobled the history of the K'iche' people.

As the reader will have noticed, the *Popol Vuh* repeated the narrative structure of the cosmogonic myths of Teotihuacán and Palenque in the Classic Period. It began with the creation and ordering of the cosmos; continued with the emergence of land and the origin of human beings, maize, and the sun; and ended with the story in the form of annals of the kingdom's founding and the deeds of the K'iche' people. Just as in the stories of Tollan-Teotihuacán and Palenque, the mission of the *Popol Vuh* was to narrate the history of the K'iche' people, exalt their values, and transmit that memory to their descendents.[8]

The Mixtec Canon

The fall of Monte Albán as the center of the Oaxacan isthmus caused changes throughout the towns of the Upper Mixtec north of Monte Albán. According to recent studies, the happenings that the Mixtec codices recorded under the name War of the Heavens referred symbolically to the confrontation between the ancient residents of that region called Ñuhu, Men of Stone, and the Mixtec invaders between the years 900 and 1000 A.D. The codices described a prolonged, five-hundred-year period of that history, telling how the Mixtecs defeated the Zapotec enclaves dependent on Monte Albán and founded the new dominions of Suchixtlán, Jaltepec, Coixtlahuaca, and Tilantongo. According to Bruce Byland and John Pohl, the painted books told the story of the political ascent that allowed the Mixtecs to dominate this region and contained a new interpretation of the past.[9]

The Mixtec obsession with carefully recording their origins and the historical events that affected their development confirmed that the people of the Oaxacan high country adopted the universal Mesoamerican canon but imposed their own touches on its content and narrative form. In their historical records we do not find the maize god as the founding father of the cosmos and civilization. That role was attributed to Ehécatl, the god of

Fig. 23. Painting from the *Códice de Viena* that shows the moment in which 9 Wind was born from flint, the day 9 Wind from the year 10 House. (Drawing based on Furst, 1978: plate 49.)

the wind, who was called 9 Wind in the codices. That god intervened in the creation of the Mixtecan lands and was the progenitor of the new humanity and the founder of the noble lineages, dynasties, arts, and sciences.[10] The Mixtecan creation myths, like those of the Maya, emphasized the history of the kingdom, or *altépetl*, itself. But beyond praising the kingdom, the myths exalted the lineage of the founder of the dynasty and sang songs in praise of his descendents. The Mixtec story remembered the ancestors as the source of power, wisdom, tradition, and political legitimacy.[11]

Like other cosmogonic myths, the paintings in the *Códice de Viena* began with a preamble in heaven. Two primordial couples who prepared the creation appeared. Later, according to the text, from a great flint stone born of one of those couples, 9 Viento (Nine Wind, fig. 23) was born. That god possessed extraordinary powers, as indicated by the titles that accompanied him: Lord of

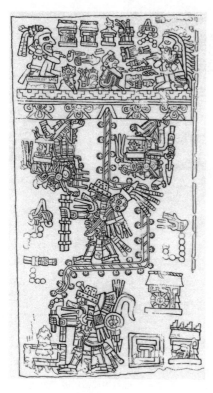

Fig. 24. In this plate from the *Códice de Viena*, 9 Wind, in the night sky, receives the attire that will identify him as Ehécatl, the god of the wind, and then shows himself on the earth, dressed in all his ornaments and symbols. (Drawing based on Kingsborough, 1967: plate V.)

Jade, Lord Sacrificer, Lord Conquerer, Lord of Beautiful Words, Lord from Whose Breast Songs Are Born, Lord Who Writes with Red and Black Ink, Lord who Carries the Ñuhu (the Deity) in His Breast.

Another page of the *Códice de Viena*, perhaps the best known, showed the image of 9 Wind on the top level of the heavens speaking with the creator-god couple, who were giving him instructions and their adornments (fig. 24). In the lower part of that same sheet, 9 Wind could be seen descending in majesty from heaven to earth through an opening in the ceiling of the celestial arch. A cord hanging from that opening served as a stairway, which 9 Wind descended, dressed in his magnificent adornments.

Those adornments and the symbols that accompanied them were the same ones that years later would distinguish Ehécatl of the Mexicas. The codex then described the characteristics of the Mixtec lands, naming the different regions and praising their properties.

The second part of the *Códice de Viena* described the origin of Mixtec humanity. In a scene dominated by a great tree with an opening in the top, the first women and men of the Mixtecs could be seen coming out of the tree (fig. 25). The codex named fifty-one personages who were born from the tree. The central part of this section emphasized a description of the noble persons who founded the lineages and dynasties of the Mixtecs. Later, the text enumerated other events presided over by 9 Wind: the celebration of the first ceremony of the New Fire; the ritual of piercing the ears and septum of those individuals who rose to noble ranks; the rituals of the rain and the harvesting of the maize; the ceremonies of pulque and hallucinatory mushrooms.

The third and final section told of the appearance of the sun and the beginning of the kingdoms and dynasties. The thirteen pages painted on the reverse of the codex described the history of the dynasty of Tilantongo, which was also recorded in other Mixtec documents, such as the *Códice Bodley* and *Códice Nuttall* and the *Mapa de Teozacoalco*. With the information from those texts, Alfonso Caso built his famous reconstruction of the *Reyes y reinos de la Mixteca*.[12] Like the text inscribed on the temples of Palenque, the *Códice de Viena* began its story with the creation and organization of the cosmos and concluded it with praise of the terrestrial kingdoms. The intent of those books was to record that the kingdoms were the work of the gods and that the ruling lineages descended directly from the charismatic 9 Wind, the god whose symbolism represented the most admired values of the Mixtec people. Like no other testimony of the Post-Classic Period, the *Códice de Viena* described in images the origin of the Mixtec people, their relationship to the gods and the nearby kingdoms, and the values that distinguished the Mixtec nation.[13]

Fig. 25. Plate from the *Códice de Viena* showing a tree with a split in it from which the noble Mixtec lineages sprout. (Drawing based on Furst, 1978: 155, fig. 11.)

The Canon of the Lords of Cholula, Cuauhtinchan, and Coixtlahuaca

Much like the collapse of the powerful Kingdom of Teotihuacán around 750, the destruction of Tula-Xicocotitlán around 1170 A.D. caused a dispersion of people that was dramatized in a famous episode of the migration and founding of new states. Various testimonials suggested that this second dispersion of people took place in the so-called Mixcóatl cycle.

Several texts indicated that at the end of the ninth century a Chichimec chief called Mixcóatl or Camaxtle burst upon the scene in central Mexico with his followers, beginning a series of conquests that culminated in the founding of the kingdom of Tula-Xicocotitlán.

Since Tula was the first political organization that slowed the disintegration of states caused by the crumbling of Tollan-Teotihuacán, the exploits of Mixcóatl acquired the brilliance of memorable deeds, becoming a canon that would later serve to narrate other migrations in the central and southern parts of Mesoamerica.[14] To legitimize the founding of this new kingdom, its capital Tula-Xicocotitlán was given the prestigious name of the first Tollan.

In those texts Mixcóatl (Cloud Serpent) was a formidable warrior who, after penetrating into central Mexico, achieved one victory after another and made conquests in the four corners of the world. During his travels, he met an aboriginal woman, Chimalman, whom he fought and vanquished. From the relationship between the warlike Chichimec and the native woman related to the ancient Toltecs, Ce Ácatl Topiltzin Quetzalcóatl was born. In the saga Mixcóatl was an accelerator of new realities, since he founded a kingdom in Culhuacán peopled by Chichimecs and ancient descendants of Tollan-Teotihuacán. Soon his son, Ce Ácatl Topiltzin Quetzalcóatl, was established in Tula, which became the capital of a powerful confederation formed by Culhuacán and the Otomí dominion of Otumba. When that confederation was destroyed by internal conflict, another migration cycle began, following the diaspora model that had shaken Mesoamerica when the first Tollan collapsed.

This second cycle narrated the vast dispersion of the Toltecs who left Tula-Xicotitlán at the end of the twelfth century. The stories said that one group, led by Mixtécatl, a descendent of Mixcóatl-Camaxtle, settled in the lower Mixtec area between Acatlán and Tututepec, between the highlands of Oaxaca and the southern coast of the Pacific. According to some documents, the name of this conqueror was the source of the tribal name that distinguished the Mixtec people and their language.[15]

Another group, called Nonoalcans, left Tula under the leadership of Xelhua and settled in Cholula, which became the political capital of this region and the most important sanctuary in central Mesoamerica, known for its dedication to Ehécatl-Quetzalcóatl,

Fig. 26. Representation of the Chichimecs as hunters, dressed in rough hides, wandering through the Valley of Mexico as though this region was without population. (Drawing based on the *Mapa de Quinatzin*, Boone, 2000: 193.)

god of the wind and the supreme arbiter of religious cults. The most notable building of Tollan-Cholula was the pyramid dedicated to Quetzalcóatl. One chronicler said that it was built to honor "a captain who brought people to this city long ago to settle here from very distant places to the west . . . and this captain was named *Quetzalcóatl,* and when he died, they built him this temple." In the temple lived the highest rulers and the priests dedicated to the cult of "the image of Quetzalcóatl that was . . . in the great temple, made in the round and with a long beard." To that image of the god "they prayed that he would give them good weather, health and the tranquillity of peace in their republic."[16] In those stories Quetzalcóatl was the founder of the kingdom of Cholula, the creator of the lineage of the Plumed Serpent, the archetype of the wise ruler, and the protecting god of the city.

Another variant of the Chichimec migration was told in the *Historia tolteca-chichimeca* (Toltec-Chichimec History). This book, following the model of the annals or "story of the years," told of the conquests and foundings accomplished by the Toltec-Chichimecs in the southern part of the contemporary state of Puebla. Fortunately for historians, a series of four maps accompanied that *Historia,* the so-called *Mapa de Cuauhtinchan,* which described in detail the route followed by the Toltec-Chichimecs from their place of origin to their final settlements in the regions of Tlaxcala, Puebla, Tehuacán, and Coixtlahuaca in northern Oaxaca.[17]

The *Historia tolteca-chichimeca* and the *Mapa de Cuauhtinchan* drew an idealized picture of the Chichimec ancestors and their relations with the people who lived in the lands that they invaded, who were surely descended from the people of Teotihuacán and Tula. The book told of the Chichimec migration from far-off Chicomoztoc to their settlement in the lands of Puebla and Tlaxcala, where they founded the dominion of Cuauhtinchan. It described their ancestors as true hunter-gatherers, dressed in rough skins and armed with bows and arrows, wandering around a territory that we know to have been densely inhabited by traditional farmers who lived in sedentary communities in solidly built houses and built temples dedicated to their founders and protecting gods (fig. 26). The *Historia tolteca-chichimeca* described how the Chichimecs, who came out of the Seven Caves of Chicomoztoc, settled in the lands of the people, mixed with Toltec women, founded cities that they called Tollan in memory of the ancient Toltec capital, and established the dominion of Cuauhtinchan (fig. 27). The chronicle gave precise information on each group, its chiefs, its social organization, and its arguments over land. And it made very clear that between the twelfth and fifteenth centuries the people of Cuauhtinchan lived under the kingdom of Cholula, to which they paid tribute and in which capital their chiefs received their royal investiture (fig. 28). The people of Cuauhtinchan proclaimed that in Cholula their ancesters

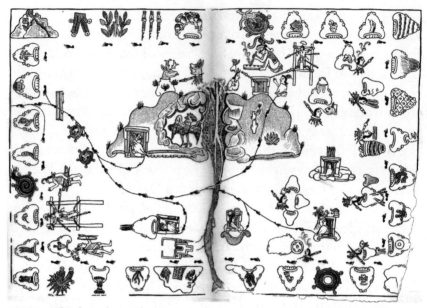

Fig. 27. The founding of Cuauhtinchan, according to the *Historia Tolteca-Chichimeca*. (Photo from Kirchoff, Odena Gúemes, and Reyes, 1976.)

had received the emblems of power and the historical traditions of Tollan.[18]

Another important series of linens, maps, and codices described the migration of the Chichimecs through the Upper Mixtec and the founding of the dominion of Coixtlahuaca. The *Lienzo de Tlapiltepec* (fig. 29) and other documents described in pictures the pilgrimage from the caves of Chicomoztoc to the glorious founding of their dominion in the lands of the contemporary state of Oaxaca. Other scenes represented the ceremony of the New Fire, which symbolized the establishment of the Toltec-Chichimec government in the area of Coixtlahuaca. The *Lienzo de Tlapiltepec* featured the figure of Atonal, founder of the kingdom, and described his long dynasty, which continued for nineteen generations, as well as the alliance between Coixtlahuaca, in the Upper Mixtec, and the royal house of Cuauhtinchan, in the south of Puebla.[19] Those maps and the stories of Cholula and Cuauhtinchan

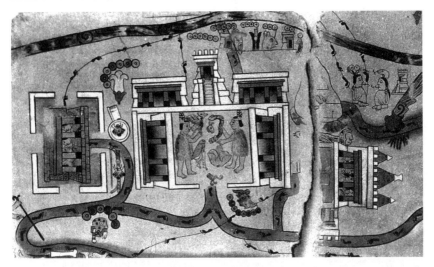

Fig. 28. The ceremonial center of Cholula, painted on the *Mapa de Cuauhtinchan 2*. (Photo from Boone, 2000: 175.)

clearly celebrated the migration of the Toltec-Chichimecs, their conquests in foreign lands, and the founding of new towns, which they claimed to be descended from ancient Tollan, the first kingdom. The hero of those stories was always the leader of the migration: Mixcóatl, Mixtécatl, Xelhua, Quetzalcóatl, or Atonal.

The Migration of the Chichimecs of Xólotl and the Founding of the Kingdom of Texcoco

The dispersion of the Toltecs was accompanied by migrations of hunter-gatherers from the north who transformed the population of Mesoamerica. An extraordinary testimony, the *Códice Xolotl*, related the migration of a group of Chichimecs led by Xólotl through central Mexico and described their settlement in the eastern and southern part of the valley, where they founded the kingdom of Texcoco. It was an important document, giving detailed information on the settling of that region and describing the material, social, political, and cultural changes that the group

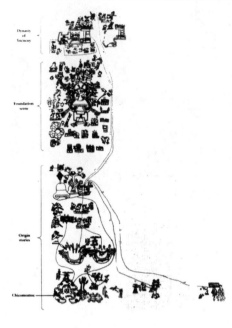

Fig. 29. Founding of the dominion of Coixtlahuaca according to the Tlapiltepec Canvas. This canvas is read from bottom to top. The lower portion tells of the exit from the cave of Chicomoztoc, in the interior of which the head of Nine Wind can be seen. It then follows a pilgrimage to several places until it ends in the founding. (Photo from Boone, 2000: 148.)

underwent from their entrance into the valley until the ascent of Netzahualcóyotl as king of Texcoco, the dominion described in the codex. Some authors have pointed out that the purpose of the *Códice Xolotl* was to legitimize the claim of Netzahualcóyotl to the throne of Texcoco after the defeat of the Tepanecas in 1427. The codex stated that the Chichimecs of Xólotl originally dominated the valley and supported the settlement of other Chichimec groups that came later.[20]

The first page, bottom left, of the codex described the entrance of the Chichimecs, dressed in rough skins and carrying bows and arrows, led by Xólotl. In one scene Xólotl was shown on the top of a hill, looking at the breadth of the valley and speaking with his son Nopaltzín about the best way to settle there. Foot tracks showed the journey that father and son made around the valley, marking the area where they would settle (fig. 30).[21] Fernando de Alva Ixtlilxóchitl, the Mestizo chronicler who used this and other documents, described the area as unpopulated and the ancient

Fig. 30. Plate I from the *Códice Xolotl.* The lower left side, on the top of a hill, shows Xólotl speaking with his son Nopaltzín. Then both travel through the region of the lakes and found the city of Texcoco, the capital of their kingdom. (Photo from Dibble, 1980.)

Toltec cities as in ruins and abandoned. Ixtlilxóchitl affirmed that Xólotl settled in the vast area in a peaceful manner, "not taking anything from anybody, . . . since all the Toltecs were already gone." And he added that to settle in that territory, Xólotl and his son went up to a high hill and carried out possession ceremonies.[22]

Although the codex described the Chichimec invasion as a peaceful entrance into an unpopulated territory, other evidence suggested that it was a region inhabited by the ancient Toltecs, whose presence and deeply rooted civilization explained the rapid Chichimec transformation. The codex showed Toltec places and personages, represented with a glyph formed on top by a handful of reeds and on the bottom by a jawbone, which together—*tul* and *teca*—formed the patronymic Toltec (fig. 31). The information provided by the codex indicated that the Náhuatl language, together with the culture and traditions of the Toltecs, served to transform the Chichimec hunters into a sedentary agricultural people. It was contact with the ancient Toltec culture, then, that led the Chichimecs to create complex political organizations such as the kingdom of Texcoco. The capital of the kingdom, the city of Texcoco, because of that symbiosis with the ancient culture, became the heir to the famous Toltec legacy, the best known in Mesoamerica and a precious repositary of the Toltec tradition.[23] Through this civilizing process, the aggressive Chichimecs became

Fig. 31. Toltec characters represented in the *Códice Xolotl.* They are identified by the glyph in the upper part, composed of the reed (*tul*) plant and the human jaw (*teca*), which together make up the word *Toltec.* The Toltecs are represented in this codex with their ancient cities (Tula, Culhuacán) and are distinguished by their cotton clothing and their Náhuatl speech, both cultural characteristics foreign to the Chichimec invaders. (Drawing based on Dibble, 1980.)

heirs to the Toltec culture. Their historical stories were a celebration of the founder of Toltec civilization, Ce Ácatl Topiltzin Quetzalcóatl, and his capital, Tula-Xicocotitlán.

The migration stories that ended in the founding of the dominions of Cholula, Cuauhtinchan, Coixtlahuaca, and Texcoco showed common traits that are worth mentioning. First, the origin of the movement was brought on by the collapse of the powerful kingdom of Tula, whose fall sowed disorder and caused the dismemberment of numberless peoples. In turn, that destruction became a diaspora that resulted in the founding of new states.

Furthermore, the Chichimec warriors acquired the rank of civilized people through marriage to native women and the adoption of Toltec institutions, which those testimonies tied to Teotihuacán and to the kingdom of Tula in Hidalgo, the continuation of the primitive Toltec tradition. The text described how the Chichimecs adopted the political and cultural institutions of the Toltecs. Thus, for example, the manner in which the Chichimecs ascended to the ranks of nobility was a ceremony whose origin dated to the political traditions of Tollan-Teotihuacán. Luis Reyes states that the ceremony "involved the ritual eating of maize so as to be able to speak the Nahua language; fasting for four days and four nights . . . , having the septum perforated with eagle and jaguar bones, receiving the seat and the matting that were the symbols of the power being acquired."[24]

The kingdoms founded by those migrants were multiethnic states including groups from different cultural traditions who spoke different languages, so that as they came together they gave rise to new political organizations and lineages. Reyes indicates that the political rise of the Toltec-Chichimecs was the result of their deeds in war. As a reward for those skills, the rulers of Cholula with whom they allied themselves raised them to the category of lords and gave them lands and peasants to cultivate them. This was the origin of the *tecalli*, or great manors, that proliferated in the region of Puebla and Tlaxcala in the fourteenth and fifteenth centuries, until that political development was interrupted by the ascendent power of Mexico-Tenochtitlán.[25]

The Mexica Canon

The stories in which the history of the peoples of the Post-Classic Period was collected culminated in the Mexica canon, a summation that gathered ancient traditions and at the same time expressed a peculiarly Mexica worldview. The Mexicas formed part of the Chichimec tribes that abandoned the hostile lands of the north in the twelfth and thirteenth centuries and settled in the Central Highlands. This was a massive migration, since Mexica sources said that the Matlatzinca, Chichimec, Malinalca, Cuitlahuaca, Xochimilca, Chalca, and Huexotzinca people migrated with them.

That great population movement left an indelible impression on the memory of the Chichimec people. All began their histories with the story of the migration and established their place of origin in Chicomoztoc (Seven Caves), which they described as a desert site, full of cactus (fig. 32). In contrast to the Teotihuacán, Maya, and Mixtec peoples, who identified their place of origin as a fertile

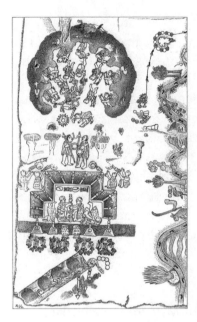

Fig. 32. The exit of the Chichimec groups from the seven caves of Chicomoztoc, according to the *Mapa de Cuauhtinchan 2.* (Drawing based on Boone, 2000: fig. 114.)

Fig. 33. Representation of the well-known mythical caves of Chicomoztoc, birthplace of the Chichimec tribes that later settled in the basin of Mexico. This drawing shows a hill covered with plants suitable to the north of Mexico (cactus), in which there are seven caves inhabited by different tribes. (Drawing based on Kirchhoff, Güemes, and Reyes García, 1989.)

cave located in their own area, the Chichimecs described their site of origin as a far-off desert country, and instead of one cave, they showed seven, to indicate that many peoples came from there (fig. 33). Those identity features of the northern tribes mixed with the symbols elaborated by the older peoples of Mesoamerica, and from that seedbed of old and new traditions the Mexica canon was forged to explain the course of humanity.

Following the ancient tradition of Tollan-Teotihuacán and the *Popol Vuh,* the Mexicas began the story of their origin with the tremendous battle of the heavenly forces against those of the underworld before the creation of the cosmos. In the *Leyenda de los soles* and in monuments such as the *Piedra del Sol,* the Mexicas told the well-known cycle of the creation and destruction of the first four suns, probably based on the Teotihuacán model of the creation of the current era of the world (fig. 34).[26] Just as in earlier myths, the cycle of birth and destruction of the four suns was governed by battles between earthly and celestial gods, by the opposition between the suns linked with the underworld (the Earth Sun and the Fire Sun) and those associated with the heavenly regions (the Wind Sun and the Water Sun). As has been discussed, that conflict began to be resolved when the creator gods met in Teotihuacán and by common accord decided to found the Fifth Sun.

Once the sun and the moon were created, the gods turned to the task of forming human beings. Here again the Mexica story followed the ancient traditions to explain the emergence of the human race. But instead of continuing with the Teotihuacán tradition, the Mexica story inserted Ehécatl, the Mixtec cultural hero who in the *Códice de Viena* was the civilizing god, the hero who brought all the benefits of civilization to earth. In written testimonies, in codexes, and on Mexica monuments, Ehécatl, the Mixtec god, seemed to be confused with Quetzalcóatl, a Mexica deity of probable Teotihuacán origin who intervened in the creation of the Fifth Sun and was a civilizing god. According to the Mexica stories, Ehécatl-Quetzalcóatl descended to the underworld, where the bones of the ancient humans (the primordial seeds) were

Fig. 34. The Fifth Sun. This drawing is based on the so-called Piedra del Sol, a Mexica monument in the National Museum of Anthropology. In the rectangles surrounding the central face of this monument, from right to left, are the four suns or previous eras of the world, with the dates of their creation: the Sun of the Earth; the Sun of the Wind; the Sun of the Fire; and the Sun of the Water. Solar rays emerge from the central disc, marking the four directions of the cosmos and the intercardinal directions. In the top part of the monument is the date 13 Reed, which corresponds to the year 1011, the year of the birth of the Fifth Sun. The royal diadem and the glyph One Tecpatl, located on both sides of the sun's ray that designates the east, where the sun comes up, refer respectively to the seat of royal power in Mexico-Tenochtitlán and the calendar date of the birth of Huitzilopochtli, the protector god of the Mexicas. In the center of the disc, where the four earlier suns and the four directions of the cosmos come together, emerges the fearful effigy of the Fifth Sun, the Sun of Movement, whose creative rhythm must be fed with the sacrifice of human hearts. (Drawing and description based on Townsend, 1992: 118.)

buried; fought for them against the gods of that region; won the battle; and took his precious burden to Tamoanchan.

The gods met again in Tamoanchan and did penance and made sacrifices. They finely ground the bones of the past generations, mixed that powder with maize dough, and moistened it with their own blood, and from that substance were born the beings who populated the Fifth Sun.

After the creation of the cosmos and human beings, the Mexica texts emphasized three episodes dense with symbols of identity: the story of their migration from far-off Aztlán to their arrival in the Valley of Mexico; the encarnation of their protector god, Huitzilopochtli; and the founding and exaltation of Mexico-Tenochtitlán, the capital of the kingdom.

La Leyenda de los soles, La historia de los mexicanos por sus pinturas, the *Códice Boturini,* and the *Mapa Sigüenza*[27] showed that those episodes were told following the annals established by the Palenque texts and probably by the first Teotihuacán story of the creation of the Fifth Sun. While the other Chichimec groups stated that they had come from Chicomoztoc, the Mexicas affirmed that they were from Aztlán, a place in the same region but, as an island surrounded by fertile fields, distinguished from the dry lands of Chicomoztoc. The trip to the central valley was interrupted by various adventures and obstacles that the Mexicas overcame one by one. It was a tour that tested their perseverence, strength, and faith in the guiding god Huitzilopochtli, since the ruses that disturbed them on their pilgrimage were not sufficient to change their minds about reaching their intended goal.

After their nostalgic departure from Aztlán, the second event worth recording was the encarnation of Huitzilopochtli on the hill at Coatepec. According to the story, while the goddess Coatlique was sweeping a temple on top of the hill, she found a ball of feathers, which she picked up and put away at her breast. The contact of those feathers with the body of the goddess produced the marvelous gestation of Huitzilopochtli. When they noticed the pregnancy of their mother, the daughter of the goddess, Coyolxauhqui, and her brothers, the four hundred Huitznaua, became enraged and plotted the deaths of her and her child. But just as the plotters were hastening to carry out their plan, Huitzilopochtli sprang from the body of his mother, fully armed, and immediately decapitated Coyolxauhqui, dismembered her body, threw it from the heights of the hill, and did away with the four hundred Huitznaua. That was the way Huitzilopochtli came to life—a lightning-like demonstration of his strength and his determination to exterminate the enemies of the Mexica peoples (fig. 34).

At last, the story of the pilgrimage paused to celebrate the founding of Mexico-Tenochtitlán in the place selected by the clairvoyance of Huitzilopochtli: the island in the lake where a prickly pear grew, with an eagle sitting on it, flapping its wings (fig. 35). This final act of the pilgrimage involved a conjunction of political symbols and ideological messages related to the Mexica people. The founding of the city in the center of the lake, in the midst of powerful kingdoms, acquired a triple meaning: the ending of the dangerous pilgrimage; the beginning of the greatness of Mexico-Tenochtitlán; and the establishment of the symbol of the Mexica State.[28] Countless songs, monuments, and paintings transformed the foundation myth into an image that corroborated the providential destiny of the Mexica people. The image of a prickly pear growing out of a rocky hillock, with an eagle on top of it, singing a war hymn or battling with a serpent, became the nation emblem of the Mexica.[29]

The story of the origins of the Mexica peoples ends in the same way as the other creation myths already considered: with the story of the first rulers, who laid the foundations of the kingdom, and the praises of the conquering chiefs, who continued the work of the founders. As in the Palenque text, the *Códice de Viena*, and the *Popol Vuh*, the creator gods and patron gods of the Mexica gave up the starring roles to men of flesh and blood, to the chiefs who enlarged the territory and established lengthy dynasties, and to the ethnic group itself, whose development and history became central to the story.[30]

Fig. 35. The priests who led the Mexica pilgrimage discover the signs that indicate the site where they must found Tenochtitlán. (Drawing based on Durán, 1995: plate 13.)

Characteristics of the Post-Classic Canon

It is perplexing to realize that the essential features of the Classic Period (250–900 A.D.) continued into the canon of the Post-Classic Period (1000–1521). Perhaps since an earlier time, since the birth of the Olmec states (1150–500 B.C.) and the Teotihuacán state (100 A.D.), Mesoamerican kingdoms had adopted a basic pattern to tell of their origins and the crucial episodes of their development. Clearly, those stories shared a common narrative structure that aimed to tell the origin of three founding events: (1) the creation of the cosmos and the birth of the surface of the earth; (2) the origin of cultivated plants, the sun, and human beings; and (3) the founding of the kingdoms and the chronicle of the people.

Even though each people told that story from their own ethnic and political perspective, all agreed on the tripartite division of the story and on the narration of the central episodes. Both the Classic and the Post-Classic canons maintained an unbreakable tie between supernatural creations (the founding of the cosmos, the earth, the sun) and human events (the origin of human beings, cultivated plants, and kingdoms). That is to say, rather than separating the divine from the terrestrial, the cosmogonic story made the earthly world derive directly from the genesis of the cosmos as ordered by the gods. For that reason, the gods were always present in human affairs. The link that united the stories of the Classic Period with those of the Post-Classic was that both described the origin of the kingdom and exalted the identifying values of the group. In both cases political history was absorbed into the construction of the kingdom and the forging of community identities.

The biggest change between the canon of the Classic and that of the Post-Classic Period was the reduction of the figure of the supreme ruler. While in the Classic Period he presided over public acts and his person was the required reference point of historical relations, in the Post-Classic Period the protagonist of historical relations was the State, the capital of the kingdom, or the ethnic group. The limitless praise of Tollan-Teotihuacán in that period was an idealization of the State. In the founding of kingdoms in the Post-Classic Period, references to Tollan-Teotihuacán or Tula de Hidalgo were obligatory, since both were the prototypes of the political capital. Tollan, to those pilgrimage people, would always be a copy of the first one, and the legitimacy of its ruler would depend on his ability to reproduce the political traditions of the first Tollan.

Clearly, the myths of the creation of the cosmos, of Quetzalcóatl, and of Tollan were the paradigms that dominated Mesoamerican thought. The story of the creation of the cosmos tirelessly repeated the same story of the ordering of the world, the origin of human beings, and the establishment of the kingdoms. Likewise, the archetype of the first Tollan was the model from which all later capitals would be built, just as Quetzalcóatl would always occupy the position of chief of the peoples and wise ruler. In those societies human events seemed to lack reality if they did not imitate the archetype established at the moment of the creation of the cosmos. This was a mentality that rejected the deed, the individual act, and temporality. Its obsession was the repetition of the first archetype and the negation of time and history by resorting to the beatitude of the origin, when everything was created new and imbued with absolute vitality.

Consequently, the attachment to the archetype of the first kingdom provided the energy that drove the resurrection of the states that had disappeared in the debacle of the end of the eighth century and were reborn from the ashes in the Post-Classic Period in the tenth to fifteenth centuries. That is to say, at the end of the greatest crisis ever suffered by the peoples of Mesoamerica, the State rose again with a political plan whose legitimizing myth claimed to be the heir of the original Tollan, the marvelous kingdom in the center of the cosmos and protected by the creator gods.[31]

Another noticeable change in the Post-Classic Period was the new importance ascribed to the recording of migrations, a theme that became the inescapable episode of the historical story in that period. As seen earlier, the *Popol Vuh;* the chronicles of the founding of Cholula, Cuauhtinchan, and Coixtlahuaca; as well as the *Códice Xolotl* and the Mexica texts dedicated extensive stories to that journey and considered the occupation of the invaded lands to be the legitimizing act of their new political situation. Perhaps the migration of the people and their settlement into foreign lands inhabited by ancient rural populations was the diagnostic event of that period, an episode that could not be left out of their chronicles. In her excellent book on the forms of written history developed by the Mexicas and Mixtecs, Elizabeth Boone observed that the Mexica stories of migration, although numerous, followed a stable model that assumed the existence of a unifying canon.[32] According to my interpretation, which is supported by the ideas of Rudolf Von Zantwijk, the canon that standardized the migration stories of the Chichimec, Toltec, K'iche', Kakchiquel, and Mexica cultures had the following characteristics:

- The place of origin was always a far-off land.
- The departure from that origin site was in obedience to an order of the gods.

- The people who abandoned the place of origin were accompanied by other adjacent tribes.
- During the migration, one or several groups separated off, and those divisions gave place to other "myths of dispersion."
- The departure from the native land occurred on a date marking the beginning of a new era. (According to Mexica tradition, 1 Técpatl was the date when the pilgrimage began, new foundings were celebrated, first rulers were named, and so forth.)
- The route of the migration was indicated by the patron god, a divine messenger, or leaders gifted with supernatural powers.
- The final place of settlement was anticipated by supernatural signs.[33]

Another characteristic that distinguished Post-Classic historical texts was the diversity of forms for reconstructing the past derived from the canon of the Classic Period. As has been seen, the oldest historical testimony came from texts engraved on the temples of Palenque in 692 A.D., emphasizing the story of the origin of the cosmos, the birth of human beings, and the succession of its rulers. One characteristic of the story that would continue in later chronicles was the recording of deeds at a precise time, along with a description of the most important events that occurred in the kingdom (res gestae, or deeds accomplished).

Perhaps the most distinctive characteristic of the stories was that the deeds recorded were associated with the *altépetl*, the territory of the kingdom. The stories, developed from the viewpoint of the kingdom, included the main occurrences in the kingdom according to its rulers and from an ethnocentric perspective. The history narrated was always the history of the territory itself, which was located in the center of the universe, at the navel of the world.

In Mesoamerican memory one legend attributed to the founders of the kingdom of Tollan the creation of a book of books that summarized the traditions of the Toltec people—a sort of encyclopedia containing the stories tied to the creation of the world and the history of the kingdom. That legend said that one of the first rulers

> gathered all the histories that the Toltecs had had, from the creation of the world until that present time, and had them painted in a very large book, where their persecutions and efforts were included, their prosperity and good examples, temples, idols, sacrifices, rituals and ceremonies they used; astrology, philosophy, architecture and other arts . . . and a review of all things of science and wisdom, successful and unsuccessful battles, and many other things, and entitled this book . . . Teomoxtli, which carefully interpreted means . . . Divine Book.[34]

Without achieving the dimensions of this comprehensive encyclopedia, suitable for powerful states such as Tollan, the information accumulated here shows that the Mesoamerican kingdoms had a fundamental book or codex that synthesized their origins, their history, their vision of the world, and their identity. From those primordial stories, today we have only the cosmogonic myth engraved on the temples of Palenque; the magnificent *Códice de Viena*, which conserved in images the history of the Mixtec kingdom of Tilantongo; the *Popol Vuh*, the most complete and detailed of all, which told of the formation of the K'iche' kingdom in the highlands of Guatemala; the *Historia de los mexicanos por sus pinturas* and the *Leyenda de los soles*, which reconstructed the history of the Mexicas; the *Historia Tolteca-Chichimeca*, which told the history of the domination of Cuauhtinchan; and the *Relación de Michoacán*, which told the history of the Tarascan kingdom.[35]

The thesis I propose is that the story the history told since the beginnings of the world and the founding of the kingdom was born with the first Olmec State and acquired canonical rank with the powerful Teotihuacán State. From that founding canon came the other forms of relating, reconstructing, and transmitting the past.

After the general chronicle of the kingdom, perhaps the most common form of historical story was the biography of the ruler and the relation of the noble lineages.³⁶ This reconstruction emphasized aspects of the sovereign's personal power: his birth and line of descent, his weddings, his political alliances, the achievements of his government, and his war deeds. In that sense the stelae of the Olmec, Zapotec, and Maya rulers scattered around the plazas, accompanied by the pictographs, ideograms, and glyphs that described the rulers' names, political acts, and conquests, were the first examples of that form of historical recording. Another variant was the famous painted books of the Mixtecs, grounded in the chronicle of lineage and commemoration of the founding ancestors. It was not by chance that the first biography of a ruler of the American continent was one of a Mixtec chief, Eight Deer.³⁷ Nonetheless, even though we have this enormous accumulation of testimonies about the rulers, we still lack a biography of the power in Mesoamerica. The generalized presence of those records in the cities and kingdoms of Mesoamerica indicates that the dominant story was the political construction of the kingdom and the history of its rulers.

Another genre of historical stories derived from earlier forms was that of the annals. In contrast to the biographies of the rulers and chronicles of the lineages, which were focused on the personal achievements of the sovereigns and the exaltation of the ancestors, the annals had as their subject the *altépetl,* the territory of the State. Their theme was those matters relative to the community that inhabited a delineated territory and was presided over by a *tlatoani,* or supreme ruler. It could be said that the annals descended from the canon established by the cosmogonic myth that described the creation of the world and the founding of the kingdoms. As will be remembered, the last part of that story told of the succession of the rulers, the political deeds worth recording, and the events that held the ethnic group together, ascribing to each of those events a precise date.

What we might call the orthodox model for the annals or "story of the years" was the *Codex Mexicanus* (fig. 36). As can be seen, in that text each year was represented by a series of squares

Fig. 36. Fragment of the *Codex Mexicanus* telling, in the form of annals, the events that took place in Mexico-Tenochtitlán between the years Four House (left) and Nine Cane (right). Below is the story of the years and above is the event occurring in that year.

reading from left to right. Above the year the events that occurred were recorded in simple ideographs. In the year 4 Reed a funerary bundle indicated the death of the *tlatoani* (supreme ruler) Axayácetl, the ascent of Tízoc, and the renovation of the Main Temple. The year 6 House recorded the defeat of the Mexica by the Huexotzinca. In the year 7 Rabbit, the death of Tízoc and the ascent of Ahuitzol to the throne were noted, and so forth in succession. That is to say, history was structured in the annals around time: every event was expressed through a precise date.[38]

Somewhere between the great stories formed around the founding events (chronicles of the creation of the cosmos and the beginning of the kingdoms) and the annals were the cartographic testimonials. Those documents were based on a map, and the history that was told therein was that of the movement of people in space. It was a story that united space and time with the actions of personages and was preferred to represent the migrations that occurred in central Mexico from the eleventh century onward.

Perhaps the best example of that genre was the *Códice Xolotl,* which told of the invasion by the Chichimecs in the Central Highlands under their leader, Xólotl (fig. 30).[39] Maps and drawings were often used to tell local and regional history, as in the case of Oaxaca and Cuauhtinchan.[40]

Those examples and many others that might be cited show that before the European invasion the Mesoamerican peoples, like no other culture on the American continent, had developed a great variety of historical records and methods of transmitting the past, derived from one fundamental canon. By the period in which the Spaniards invaded the Mesoamerican territory, that canon had already generated a number of forms of recording the past, as attested to by Fernando de Alva Ixtlilxóchitl. That Mestizo historian, who wrote his chronicles in the seventeenth century, summarized the historical knowledge amassed by his ancestors:

They had writers for each genre, some that dealt with the annals, ordering those things that happened in each year by the day, month, and hour. Others were charged with the genealogies and descendencies of the Kings and Lords and personages of the lineage. . . . Others with the books of the laws, rituals and ceremonies which they used in their unbelief and the priests of the temples in their idolatry . . . and of the festivals of their . . . gods and calendars. And finally the philosophers and wise men that they had among them had as their responsibility to paint all the science that they knew and had achieved, and teach by heart all the songs that preserved their science and history.[41]

III. The Western Canon versus the Mesoamerican Canon

Immediately after the conquest, the inevitable clash between the European and the Mesoamerican concepts of history began. The conquest of Mexico, like the earlier discovery of America, was first described using European ideas, making use of the written alphabets of the Romance languages (Spanish and Italian) and under the Christian and Renaissance canons of history. That is to say, American geography, human beings, and history began to be defined by European mental and written codes at the same time that the native ways that had earlier served to interpret and name American reality were challenged as incomprehensible and discredited, using criteria that denied them the condition of being civilized. The distortion of the history of the Mesoamerican people began with the denial of the tools that they had created to record their own history.

People Without Writing, Unlettered

Pedro de Gante, one of the first Franciscans to come to Mexico, informed Spanish King Philip II in 1558 that the natives were "people without writing, unlettered, without characters and totally without the light of reason."[1] The argument that the aborigines lacked writing was added to those that described them as barbarians, at the margins of civilization. Juan Ginés de Sepúlveda, the Spanish humanist who argued with Bartolomé de las Casas in the well-known meeting in Valladolid (1550–51) in which the justice of the procedures used in the conquest of America were discussed, maintained that the aborigines not only lacked culture, but that they did not know how to write. Sepúlveda read the works of the first chroniclers on the novelty of America from the viewpoint of European humanists and on that basis argued that the natives lacked a written language and were incapable of constituting civilized societies.[2]

The great revolution that substituted a written for an oral culture in Europe during the eleventh and twelfth centuries introduced an essential presupposition of negative consequences for non-Western people: the thesis that a written alphabet was synonymous with rationality (fig. 37). That idea spread during the Renaissance and imposed the belief that the written culture was the highest achievement of humanity and the standard whereby disciplines such as history, literature, law, philosophy, theology, and science must be measured. Therefore, in the Renaissance that which was "rational" and prestigious was equivalent to classical antiquity, and that model became the ideal of the civilized world.[3] A man of letters versed in the cultures of antiquity, such as Erasmus of Rotterdam, came to be looked on as the archetype of the humanist (fig. 38).

The invention and dispersion of printing accentuated the dominion of writing over oral discourse. As Elizabeth Eisenstein has indicated, printing was the instrument that made it possible to put before the reader the "original of a text, map, letter, or diagram, free of the copyist's errors." Printing contributed to the development of "a tradition of accumulative research" that revolutionized scientific knowledge. The changes driven by printing transformed the bases that sustained knowledge and culture: "confidence passed from divine revelation to mathematical reasoning and to maps made by man."[4] The book, according to Jack Goody, became a formidable instrument of power, to such an extent that in the sixteenth century an English poet maintained that the pen was mightier than the sword.[5]

This conception of civilization and the prestige applied to literacy were transferred by Spain to its American possessions.

Fig. 37. Representation of a medieval scribe. (Photo from Goody, 1992: cover.)

Fig. 38. Humanist Erasmus of Rotterdam, writing in his office, in an engraving by Albert Dürer.

Juan Bautista Pomar, son of a Spaniard and a noblewoman from Texcoco, assumed these ideas when, in his *Relación de Texcoco* in 1582, he described the cultural level achieved in antiquity by the natives of that kingdom:

> The noblemen and even the commoners made an effort [to] compose songs in which they introduced as history many successful and unsuccessful events and notable deeds of the kings and of illustrious persons of valor; and he who reached the top of that ability was held in very high esteem, because the memory and importance of things was virtually immortalized by those songs . . .
>
> *And it was understood that if they had been able to write, many natural secrets would have been available; but because paintings are not very successful at holding the memory of the things which are painted, they are not handed forward, because when even*

the most talented of those who practice that art dies, his science dies with him.[6]

The first people to accept the superiority of written over oral culture were men of letters and the Spanish kings, who promoted a policy of Castilianization of their American possessions that paralleled their settlement in those territories. In 1492, the same year in which Columbus had his unexpected meeting with the lands of America, Antonio de Nebrija published his *Castilian Grammar*. Nebrija dedicated his book to Queen Isabella with the intention that it might serve the linguistic unification of Spain and better control the populations that she might eventually conquer. The aphorism that language should be the "companion of empire," as Nebrija recommended, became an effective policy in the territories that Spain conquered in America.[7] The union of arms with the diffusion of the alphabet and Western culture was one of the most persistent policies of the Spanish Crown. For Nebrija, as well as for the Catholic kings, teaching the "things of the nation" in the language of the nation was the equivalent of a policy of national integration (fig. 39).[8]

Nevertheless, the subordination of the innumerable American languages to the domination of the Spanish language raised the objections of the friars responsible for the unusual project of evangelizing the vast American territory. The concept of imposing Spanish on the indigenous languages was rejected by the friars, who argued that the best way to Christianize the infidels was to learn their languages and translate the precepts of the faith of Christ into them.[9] Driven by their monastic ideals, the friars saw in American humanity the ideal means for transferring the apostolic principles of Christianity to the New World and founding a true church there, one similar to that of the first apostles. Inspired by those ideals, they hastened to investigate the origin of the native people, and that curiosity caused them to recognize the people's diverse forms of recording the past.

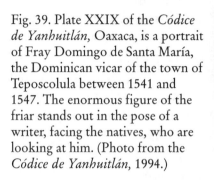

Fig. 39. Plate XXIX of the *Códice de Yanhuitlán*, Oaxaca, is a portrait of Fray Domingo de Santa María, the Dominican vicar of the town of Teposcolula between 1541 and 1547. The enormous figure of the friar stands out in the pose of a writer, facing the natives, who are looking at him. (Photo from the *Códice de Yanhuitlán*, 1994.)

Historical Mesoamerican Records

Since the first days of the European invasion, the soldiers and friars recognized the presence of books in the native towns. When he entered the region of Cempoala on the coast of Veracruz, Bernal Díaz del Castillo wrote: "We found the houses of idols and sacrifices . . . *and many books of their paper, gathered in folds* like lengths of duffle."[10] For his part, Franciscan friar Toribio de Benavente (Motolinía) advised that the natives of New Spain had books "of characters and figures, for thus was their writing, since they did not have letters, only characters." And later he noted that they had five kinds of books: "The first speaks of years and times. The second of the days and festivals they had throughout the year. The third of the dreams . . . and omens they believed in. The fourth for baptisms and the names they gave their children. The fifth for rituals and ceremonies. . . . Among these, one, which is the first one, is creditable because it speaks the truth, *for although they were barbarians and unlettered,* they kept a very orderly count of time, days, weeks, months and years."[11]

Walter Mignolo claims that the affirmation that the American aborigines were savages rested on the argument that they lacked a written alphabet (which was the symbol of culture for the men of the Renaissance) and therefore lacked valid historical records, for which the models were the Greek stories of Herodotus and Thucydides and the Roman histories of Tacitus. For European humanists, alphabetic writing was the greatest achievement of civilized people and historical records one of their most exalted expressions.[12] The Jesuit José de Acosta, a conspicuous representative of that tradition, based on those criteria his evaluation of the historical traditions of the people of Mexico and Peru, whom he had come to know during a fruitful stay that later led him to write his famous *Historia natural y moral de las Indias.*[13] Like all intellectuals of that time, Acosta communicated with his equals through letters, by which means he came in contact with the Mexican Jesuit Juan de Tovar, who was then living in New Spain and with whom he maintained an interesting correspondence between 1586 and 1587.

At that time Juan de Tovar was one of the priests who best understood the ancient historical traditions of Mexico, since he had completed a collection of them, unfortunately lost to us today. Knowing Acosta's interest in this topic, he sent him a manuscript that summarized the collection. Acosta was extremely grateful for the courtesy and took advantage of their written exchange to bring up some doubts that worried him: What authority did those histories have? How could the Indians, without writing, maintain the memory of so many and such diverse things for so long?

Tovar answered the first question by saying that he had at hand, in order to write his history, the "libraries" accumulated by the wisest natives of Mexico, Texcoco, and Tula, who had been brought together for that purpose by the viceroy Martín Enríquez. That same viceroy had charged Father Juan de Tovar with composing all those resources into a story in Spanish. Tovar commented to Acosta that he then saw "all this history in characters and hieroglyphs which I did not understand, so it was necessary for the wise men of Mexico, Tezcoco and Tulla to deal with me" to translate and explain them. Thus, with the help of that "library" and of experts in the ancient Toltec traditions, Tovar composed "a very complete history" that was lost when it was sent to Spain. He added that he had also used "a book done by a Dominican friar [the notable *Historia de las Indias* of Fray Diego Durán] which best followed the ancient library that I have seen." Based on this work and the information that he remembered, Tovar wrote the story that he sent to Acosta, arguing that the authority his history had was that it was based on the "characters and hieroglyphics" maintained by the wisest natives of New Spain.

Tovar's response to the second question—How could the Indians, without writing, remember so many things?—was as follows:

> I say, as has been proven, that they had their figures and hiero- glyphics with which they painted things in this manner: the things that did not have their own image had other characters that stood for them and with those things they could represent whatever they wanted. And as to the time at which each thing happened [they had a cycle of time every fifty-two years] which was like a century, and with those calendar wheels they could memorialize the times at which important things hap- pened, painting them around the sides of the wheels with the characters as earlier described.

Father Tovar admitted that "those figures and characters with which they described things were not as complete as our writing." That is to say, he accepted that there was not an exact correspon- dence between the paintings and the interpretation made of them by whoever read or translated them. He said that the readers of those images and characters "concentrated only on the concepts." He added that to keep the memory of those images and characters faithful, there were orators and poets, experts in their conservation by means of "the continuous repetition" of the songs. In that manner, he said, everything "was maintained in their memory, without any disagreement over words."[14]

Like Tovar, other friars, captivated by the ancient Mesoamerican cultures, approached the testimonials that referred to the past and described in detail the ideographic and oral methods that the Indians had developed to preserve their traditions. Francisco de Burgoa, a friar familiar with the notable school of painted books in Oaxaca, wrote:

Along with the barbarity of these nations, there were many books which they did in their way, on sheets or cloths of special tree bark . . . which they cured and dressed like parchment, . . . where they wrote their complete history with characters so abbreviated that [on] only one flat sheet they could express the place, site, province, year, month and day . . . and for this purpose they showed and taught the sons of the men whom they had chosen for the priesthood from childhood, having them decorate those characters and learn by heart their histories, and I have had these same instruments in my hands and have heard them explained by some of the old men with considerable admiration, and they used to put up these papers like cosmography charts, fastened the length of the receiving rooms of the lords, who because of their magnitude and vanity boasted of dealing with them in their meetings and visits.[15]

In other regions the Europeans did not find painted books or pictographic records of past things, but they were aware of the presence of special procedures for recording historical events. For example, Fray Bartolomé de las Casas observed the following:

In some places they did not use this way of writing [the codices;] rather, the information on the ancient things was passed from one person to the next, from hand to hand. They were so well organized not to forget . . . that they instructed four or five [people] or perhaps more in the antiquities, *whom they used as historians,* referring to them all kinds of things that were a part of their history, and those people remembered them and recited them, and if one did not remember something, the others corrected him and all agreed.[16]

Antonio de Herrera, the official Chronicler of the Indies, referred to that form of oral recording of the past, saying that since pictograms were "not as sufficient as our writing," they had the custom of "learning in chorus the Speeches, Discourses, and Songs. They took great care that their children learn them from memory, and therefore had many schools where the old men taught the boys these things, which through their tradition they have always maintained in a very complete fashion."[17] These and other testimonials show that the European soldiers and religious leaders recognized the painted books and the oral forms (songs) as ways of remembering the past and the schools where that knowledge was taught and transmitted as specialized indigenous techniques for the collection of historical memory. Nonetheless, they considered them to be tools of a ranking inferior to that of alphabetic writing and placed those nations on the rung reserved for "peoples without writing."

Writing as a Symbol of Wisdom among the Mesoamerican Peoples

Mesoamerican peoples not only developed their own written form of history; they considered that art as one of the most elevated, synonymous with wisdom, and attributed to it the nobility of an ancient art. The peoples of central Mexico related the invention of writing to the Toltecs, the founders of Teotihuacán, which for them represented the beginning of civilized life. Sahagún said: "As concerns the antiquity of these people, it has been ascertained that they have lived for more than two thousand years in this land which is now called New Spain, because in their ancient pictures there is information on that famous city which was called Tulla, which was destroyed a thousand years ago or very close to it."[18] Fernando de Alva Ixtlilxóchitl, the chronicler of the kingdom of Texcoco, also identified the Toltecs with the beginning of the painted books.[19]

The Mayas, who developed computational systems of extraordinary precision, put the origin of the cosmos in the year 3114 B.C. and used that date as the beginning of all things, so they started to date their historical narrations from that mythic time. They maintained a virtual worship of deeds that had occurred in remote times and placed the origin of writing at the moment in which the kingdoms were founded and civilization was born. Writing was something so exact that it had the aura of the primordial foundations. The Mayas' obsession with past deeds and their mania for situating them at a precise time made them a people of memories. They may well have recorded, with the greatest exactitude, the historical events that occurred in their kingdoms. We owe to this love of memory and the measurement of time the most detailed and extensive historical chronology of the American continent: a record that extends without interruption from the third to the ninth centuries. "This means," as Michael Coe states, "that the ancient Maya are the only truly historic civilization in the New World."[20]

The esteem in which the Mesoamerican peoples held history can be seen in the fact that they put that art under the patronage of their most revered gods. The Toltecs and their descendants considered the god Quetzalcóatl to have been the first historian and protector of the scribes and of the Calmécac, the institution where they taught writing and the memorization of the songs of past events. According to Alva Ixtlilxóchitl, the Mexicas had recorded that among "the most serious authors and historians that ever were . . . Quetzalcóatl was found to have been the first, and in modern times Nezahualcoyotzin, the king of Tetzcuco."[21] The predecessors of the Aztecs also attributed a high value to the

Fig. 40. Here 9 Wind, the Mixtec cultural hero, sings and plays a drum in the shape of a skull with his right hand. (Drawing based on Furst, 1978, plates 18 and 24.)

writing of history. The Mixtecs painted many images of the god 9 Wind, their cultural hero, and attributed the creation of writing and singing to him (fig. 40).

The research of Michael Coe has established that during the Maya splendor of the Classic Period (250–600 A.D.), the patrons of the painted books were Itzamná, the chief god; Pawahtún, the old god (fig. 41); the maize god; the monkey god; and the Divine Twins, Junajpú and Xbalanqué. Other testimonials mentioned Itzamná, the "first priest" and "first scribe," as the inventor of writing (fig. 42). The polychrome jars of the Classic Period show the youthful figure of the maize god, the creater of the cosmos and civilized life, painting codices (fig. 43). The Divine Twins, Junajpú and Xbalanqué, archetypes of Maya genius, can also be seen on those jars, handling the brush of a painter of codices (fig. 44).[22] The best analysis of Mayan writing can be seen in the handsome work of Michael Coe and Justin Kerr, which includes an expressive series of representations of the scribe. The collection

Fig. 41. The old god of the Mayas, Pauahtún, teaches mathematics with a paintbrush in his hand. From his mouth issue the numeric signs of the bar and the point. (From Coe and Kerr, 1997: 104.)

Fig. 42. A hand with a paintbrush comes out of the mouth of the god Itzamná, represented as the mouth of a dragon. (Drawing based on Coe and Kerr, 1997: 102.)

of pictures of scribes and their instruments of work shows the high value that Mayas attributed to the art of writing.

The Destruction of the Painted Books

Contemporary research indicates that very few of the works the Mesoamerican people created to conserve and transmit the past were respected by Spanish evangelizing zeal. The friars branded those traditions as "creations of the devil," and later ethnocentric Europeans saw in them a fabric of superstitions transcribed in

Fig. 43. Maya vase with the dignified figure of the maize god painting a codex. (Photo from J. Kerr, 1980–92.)

Fig. 44. The Divine Twins, Junajpú (left) and Xbalanqué (right), shown as painters, with the paintbrush and the shell that held the colors in their hands. (Photo from Coe and Kerr, 1997.)

"unintelligible characters." The chronicles of the conquest of Mexico record the destruction of the famous library at Texcoco, the repository that stored all the codices, lienzos, and maps that had gathered the traditions of the Toltecs and Chichimecs. Alva Ixtlilxóchitl stated that the great majority of that legacy was burned "without forethought and rashly at the orders of the first priests, one of the great damages done to this New Spain" (fig. 45). Regarding the importance of that library, he wrote:

Fig. 45. Destruction of the idols by fire, according to the *Descripción de la ciudad y provincia de Tlaxcala* by Diego Muñoz Camargo.

because in the city of Texcuco were the royal archives of all those things described, since it had been the metropolitan center of all sciences, uses, and good practices, since the kings of that place esteemed this and they were the legislators of this new world; and what escaped the fires and calamities mentioned, which my superiors kept, came into my hands, and from them I have extracted and translated the history that I have promised [to write].[23]

In the Maya area, the bloodcurdling auto-da-fé that took place in the town of Maní on July 12, 1562, caused by the persecutorial zeal of Bishop Diego de Landa, resulted in the burning of dozens of codices and painted lienzos in which the Mayas of Yucatán had stored up the treasured ancient traditions of their people. In 1633 Bernardo Lizana, remembering this literary holocaust that in an overwhelming moment had focused the intolerance, superiority,

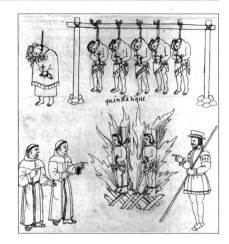

Fig. 46. Repression of the idolaters by hanging and burning, according to the *Descripción de la ciudad y provincia de Tlaxcala* by Diego Muñoz Camargo.

and contempt the Spaniards had built up against the natives, noted that on that occasion many valuable books on the origins of ancient Yucatán were burned.[24] We do not know the number of codices that were incinerated in that infamous ceremony, but doubtless there were many, and their loss was irreparable. The most devastating effects of those actions were felt in later years, for from then on the mere possession of books and ancient traditions became anathema and a justification for atrocious persecutions of those who could not or did not want to break their ties to the culture that had nourished them (fig. 46).

In the Oaxaca region, historian Manuel Martínez Gracida collected this impressive testimonial on the destruction of the ancient indigenous memory:

An old man . . . from the town [of Tilantongo] stated that his great-grandfather told his grandfather in 1600 that he had seen the Royal Palace [of Tilantongo] uncovered, after the Indians there in around 1580 to 1590 had buried it, not without rough encounters with the Spaniards when they moved into it, since the Spaniards began to destroy it. Afterwards, the friars, supported by the Spaniards, continued their work of destruction, not only to erase from the face of the earth the prestige of the Mixtec sovereigns, their good taste and wealth, but also to take from the Indians their memory of their ancestors and suppress idolatry, which they believed occurred in the presence of the statues, inscriptions, hieroglyphics, small idols, etc., that were on the columns, walls and niches, and which perished, reduced to dust by religious imprudence.[25]

The destruction of the codices and testimonials of ancient indigenous memory was implacable. It lasted for three centuries during the Colonial Period, taking on a variety of forms of repression. In the decades that followed the conquest, the persecution of idolatry began, culminating in complicated inquisitorial trials such as that instituted against the chief of Texcoco, Carlos Mendoza Ometochtli, or Chichimecatecutli, as he called himself. It was stated that upon making a search of his house, "undeniable indications of his pagan cult" were found, among them *an Indian book or picture,* altars and a number of idols."[26]

One of the most dramatic episodes in the war against ancient indigenous memory took place in the Oaxacan Mixtec. It is known that as of 1558, when the first Dominican evangelizers reached Villa Alta, they began the persecution of the testimonials that recorded ancient Zapotec and Mixtec memory. Around 1560, Fray Pedro Guerrero began the first campaign for the eradication of idolatry in that region. Guerrero demanded that the natives turn over their idols, and when he got no response he employed the whip and torture. This punishment provoked suicides and great fear in the towns and was the motive for a reproof from the Crown and the High Court of Mexico in 1562.[27]

In the second half of the seventeenth century, the persecution of idolatry and the destruction of books worsened. Between 1686 and 1690, Bishop Isidro Sariñana, following the example of the Holy Office of Mexico, built a "perpetual prison for idolaters" in the city of Oaxaca. In celebration of this deed, Sariñana had twenty-six Indians imprisoned, accused of being specialists in the ancient rites, and condemned in the first auto-da-fé ever carried out in that region.

Later, in 1700, something happened that revived the persecution of idolatry. On September 14 of that year, Fray Gaspar de los Reyes and another Dominican father surprised the majority of the populace of Francisco Cajonos as they were sacrificing birds and a deer and saying sacrilegious prayers in Zapotec. The residents of Cajonos learned that two treasury officers, Juan Bautista and Jacinto de los Ángeles, had denounced them to the priests. On the next day a furious mob of Indians demanded that the Dominicans turn the offenders over to them. Juan Bautista and Jacinto de los Ángeles were savagely beaten and executed by the enraged town. When he found out about it, the mayor of Villa Alta started a trial that lasted until 1702, with the result that fifteen of the leaders of the riot were condemned to be hanged and a new wave of terror was unleashed.[28]

Also in 1702, when Fray Ángel Maldonado occupied the seat of the bishopric of Oaxaca, he made two visits to the region of Villa Alta. He was thus able to discover that its residents were recalcitrant idolaters, expert in the use of sacrilegious texts, rituals, and calendars that celebrated their ancient gods and traditions. Instead of carrying out another auto-da-fé, Maldonado sent inspectors to the town offering clemency to anyone who would denounce and inform on the rituals and "books of the devil." Thanks to those arrangements, Maldonado was able to gather ninety-nine versions of the Zapotec ritual calendar of 260 days as well as the transcriptions of some thirty Zapotec songs.[29] This information shows that at the beginning of the eighteenth century the ancient memory and the ancestral calendars remained in force in the towns of the Oaxacan Mixtec and that its transmitters were the "teachers" or "men of letters" among the Indians who had learned the Spanish alphabet.[30] Years later in this same region, Fray Benito Fernández, a persecuter of idolatry, received the news that in the cave of Chacaltongo the Mixtecs paid homage to their ancestors and kept relics and representations of their gods. Fray Benito hastened to visit this isolated spot, accompanied by a number of terrified Indians. As related by the chronicler Francisco de Burgoa, what Fray Benito saw there caused an uncontrollable anger in him, which heightened his destructive fury:

After the servant of God found the place, he discovered . . . some stone urns, and on them a great number of bodies . . . in rows, shrouded in rich garments of their clothing, and a variety of jewels of high-quality stones, strings and medals of gold, and drawing closer he recognized some bodies of chiefs who had recently died . . . and whom he had taken as good Christians, [and] burning with zeal at the divine honor, he attacked the bodies and throwing them on the ground stepped on them and dragged them around like the spoils of Satan . . . [then he saw] farther along, like a bedchamber, another station and entering found it to have small altars like niches, in which they had an immense number of idols, of a diversity of figures and a variety of materials such as gold, metals, stone, wood, and *lienzos de pinturas*, [and] here his holy fury went wild and he broke whatever he could with blows and threw the rest at their feet, cursing them as spirits of the shadows. The Indians, seeing how long he was, were certain that he was now dead and the gods had taken vengeance for that lack of respect, when they saw him come out, tired and sweaty, bringing in the skirts of his habits the most venerated idols, which he threw down in front of them and stamped on them and scoffed at them . . . and beginning to pray to that numerous concourse [of Indians,] so great was the efficacy of his reasoning, so ardent his spirit, that he softened those hard hearts as if they were of wax, reduced them to the point of making there a great bonfire [and obliging them to throw into it] all the idols and the bodies of their dead lords . . . and with this frightful triumph he left them so confused and ashamed at considering the deceitful fear in which they had lived, that a great number of conversions followed.[31]

The Western Concept of History versus
Other Memories of the Past

If it is true, as indicated by cited texts, that Europeans recognized the strange forms of collecting and transmitting the past in use among the American peoples, they never granted them the same value as that of alphabetic writing. Forms that differed from that canon were considered barbaric and challenged as lacking in literacy. This early disqualification was followed by the devaluing of Mesoamerican techniques of representing the past; since these did not imitate the canon established by Thucydides or Polibius, they were classified as incapable of transmitting past events. Thus, as stated by Walter Mignolo, the complicity between alphabetic writing and the Greco-Roman model of historical discourse conspired to decree that American records of the past did not fulfill the requirements of real history.[32]

Edouard Glissant maintains that history and literature were the instruments that Western imperialism used to suppress or reject the forms of recording the past that were native to other cultures. His argument is summarized in the following text, where he says that for the West, history was a functional instrument

> which was born at the precise time when the latter seemed to "make" the history of the world by itself. . . . In this phase, History was written with a capital H. It was a totality which excluded other histories which were now joined with western history. . . . [At the same time,] writing . . . became an all-powerful sacred sign which allowed those peoples who possessed it to use it to govern and impose itself on peoples of an oral civilization.[33]

In the famous *Monarquía indiana,* written by Franciscan friar Juan de Torquemada in the seventeenth century, there is a passage about the methods used by the natives of New Spain for collecting the past that adopts the criteria of Western ethnocentrism to disqualify them. Torquemada stated:

> One of the things which causes the greatest confusion in a republic and which most exasperates men who wish to deal with their causes is the limited accuracy one finds when considering their histories; *because if history is a narration of true things which happened and those who saw them and knew them did not leave a memory of them,* it is like forcing those who after the events wish to write about them to proceed like blind men in dealing with them, . . . This (or almost this) is what has happened in this history of New Spain; *because since the ancient dwellers therein were unlettered, and could not write, neither could they make histories.* It is true that they used a kind of writing (which was pictures) through which they could make themselves understood; . . . [but] each one of them meant one thing and at times it happened that a single figure contained the majority or all of what had happened . . . *so that it was easy to vary the way of history and often distance it from truth and even separate it completely.*[34]

As can be seen, Torquemada's disqualification was founded on the claim that the Americans had no writing (letters written in an alphabetic form), but rather pictures. And pictures, according to the friar, did not lend themselves to being translated or deciphered, so "it was easy to vary the way of history and often distance it from truth." Stated in another way, American representations of the past were not trustworthy, because they did not resemble their European counterparts.

The lowering of American cultural values reached one of its climaxes during the Enlightenment. Since the middle of the eighteenth century, some of the most influential authors of that movement—among them the Count of Buffon, Father Raynal, Cornelius de Paw, and the well-known Scottish historian William Robertson—agreed in affirming that the American continent had a climate that diminished human creatures and stifled the intellect. According to this interpretation, the native dwellers had not crossed the portals of the Stone Age and, despite the abundance of talent that the European invasion brought with it, letters and science continued at a rudimentary level.[35]

During the nineteenth and twentieth centuries, Western ethnocentrism battled non-European cultures with the armament of alphabetic writing. Linguists considered the alphabet to be the highest expression of civilized life and measured American, Asian, and African cultures against that yardstick. The students of the written word conceived of the alphabet as the final step in a long march that began with drawings and more elementary pictographs, continued with different types of syllabic writing, and culminated in the alphabet. One of the leaders of this evolutionary school, I. J. Gelb, wrote that none of the cultures of the New World, including the Mayas, had had the intellectual capacity to reach the level of phonetic writing.[36] To Gelb, "the so-called Mayan and Aztec writings" did not correspond "properly to writing but rather to its antecedents." These pejorative qualifications placed the American peoples on the lowest threshold of civilization and contributed to raising the formidable barrier that for a long time delayed the deciphering of writings like those of the Mayas.

The Obsession with Writing and the Neglect of the Main Transmitters of Indigenous Memory

The obsession with comparing American historical records with alphabetic writing not only slowed the understanding of their true nature, it also restricted the analysis of historical recovery to its written forms. This fixation on writing produced one of the major distortions in the understanding of the native systems of recording, storing, and transmitting the past, since in Mesoamerica this was and continues to be done mainly through oral and visual means, rituals and calendars. Nonetheless, for almost five centuries students of the American past, formed in the Western canon, concentrated their attention on the written testimonials, leaving the immense continent of nonwritten traditions virtually unexplored.

In contrast to the memory of contemporary historians, who are fixed on the written word and dependent upon it, native memory imagined many ways to rescue the past and transmit it as a legacy for future generations. Among that variety of devices, five methods of transmission of messages stand out that have come down to us without losing their evocatory force.[37]

Rituals and ceremonies. One of the principal distributors of social symbols and values was the body of rituals and religious ceremonies carried out at precise times of the year. In those ceremonies the singing, dancing, speeches, music, and decorations displayed in the temples and plazas united individuals with the group. By taking part in those many acts, each person received the messages that emanated from the ceremonies and became, in turn, a transmitter of the collective memory. As the language and symbolism of the ceremony were repeated on specific dates, the ritual came to be one of the most reliable conservators of the ancient traditions among new generations. Because of these virtues, the Jewish historian Josef Yerushalmi maintains that collective memory is transmitted more vigorously through rituals than in written form.[38]

Visual images. The language of image was another bearer of durable messages among the peoples of Mesoamerica. Since the founding of the first chiefdom, the rulers had produced powerful molded images to transmit messages to the gathered populace and create a unified system of values and social behaviors. Perhaps in the most remote times the preferred methods were the use of rituals and myths, which were transmitted orally. Later, when the first cities grew up, architecture, sculpture, painting, and other arts were the vehicles chosen to capture new symbols and transmit them to diverse sectors of the population.

At La Venta, one of the first population centers constructed by the Olmecs, a great pyramid was built in the shape of a mountain, in imitation of the hill that in their myths emerged from the primordial waters on the first day of creation. Those myths said that within the mountain there was a cave, which was the place where humanity had developed and where the basic food was kept. The geometric design of the pyramid reproduced the three levels of the cosmos (underworld, land surface, and heavens) and the four cosmic directions. Its architecture was a representation of the movement of the sun in its annual journey. That initial function as a spatial representation of the cosmos was maintained through time. Ever since the creation of the first kingdoms, the pyramid was combined with the stelae, sculpture, painting, and urban design to transmit visual messages of great power (fig. 47).[39]

Visual messages spread by the pyramid, the stela, and the temples built in the ceremonial center communicated a summary notion of the origin of the cosmos, the meaning of human life, and the ultimate finality of the kingdoms. If we gather together the different visual objects that the Olmec, Maya, and Teotihuacán peoples engraved on the hearts of their cities, we will see appear, in succession, the dazzling images of the primordial mountain, where the nutritious seeds and fertilizing waters were stored; the cosmic tree, which reproduced the three vertical spaces of the universe; the ball court, which commemorated the victory of the Divine Twins over the destructive powers of the underworld; the temples dedicated to the creator gods and to the patrons of the city; and the statues of the ruler in his triple role as captain of the armies, supreme priest of the cults, and first farmer and dispenser of crops.

This visual representation was a didactic lesson that described to the population of the city and its dazzled visitors the crucial moments that gave form to the new era of the world, the order that had come out of that genesis, and the values that set the norm for the lives of the inhabitants of the kingdom. It could be said that the inhabitants of the cities of Mesoamerica, just like those in the ancient Greek cities, lived in a kind of city museum, literally filled with monuments and symbols that alluded to the

Fig. 47. Ceremonial center of Copán. To the right is the acropolis, with the most sacred enclosures and temples. To the left is the great courtyard, with the stairway of the glyphs, the ball court, the ceremonial courtyard, and the stelae with the portraits of the governors. (Reconstruction by Tatiana Proskouriakof, 1946.)

founding events of the kingdom. This was an image that the rulers imprinted on each city they built and whose lesson they repeated again and again in the ceremonies that year after year celebrated the origin of the gods, human beings, cultivated plants, and the grandeur of the kingdom. The repetition of these images identified the populace with the proper features of their ethnicity and unfolded their singular historical tradition, which was different from that of the towns with which they competed and coexisted.[40]

The calendars. Among the best conduits to native memory was the calendar. Rituals recorded on the Mesoamerican calendar emphasize two kinds of mnemonic devices. The first is a detailed record of the agricultural tasks that rural people needed to carry out through the course of the year to assure a good crop. This was the agricultural memory of the rural community condensed into a ritual calendar managed by the rulers. According to the calendar, the phases of the sowing and cultivation of plants were dominated by different divinities to whom homage should be paid and offerings made to obtain their favors. In turn, the rituals that good crops required were accompanied by a great number of festivals in which the participants sought the favor of the gods and offered them sacrifices and offerings.[41]

As time passed, the ancient calendars that prescribed agricultural tasks and celebrated the gods of fertility were linked with the political memory of the kingdom. Ever since their origins, the creators of the calendar had tied the tasks that assured the survival of the group with the remembrance of the origin of the kingdom and the establishment of the ruling lineage. It was likewise clear that the origin of the calendar was inseparable from the founding of the kingdom—the power that made the ancient rural calendar an institution of the State, whose standardization was instituted in the general population. The events and astronomical almanacs that those calendars celebrated indicated that the agricultural rituals had become political celebrations.

Myth. As indicated earlier, myth was one of the most effective cultural devices for gathering human experience and transmitting it to other groups by means of an efficient and attractive language. A prime quality of myth was its emphasis on events relating to the origin of the cosmos and the first human creations. Myth revealed in the marvelous language of simplicity the mysteries of the supernatural world and the meaning of human actions.

By making fables of the original creation, myths also established the key for later creations, since to be true they had to follow the original model. Therefore, the story of the first creation of the cosmos contained the narrative structure, language, and symbols that would serve to validate later creations and foundings. As we know, myths do not explain anything. But through a simple story they inform us that the cosmos or human beings have been created; they manifest the ordering of the far-off regions of the universe;

they show how the ancestors or supernatural powers made themselves present in the earthly world; they reveal the appearance of the gods and the exact scope of their influence.

The myth shared with history the obsession for origins. But unlike history, it had no interest in events that followed the primordial moment of creation and developed in time. It rejected the idea that the present and future could change the meaning of the first creation. The task of myth was to see that the present and future remained faithful to the past, to the original moment in which the true sense of things was manifested for the first time.[42]

Jan Vansina observed that myths that narrated the creation of the cosmos, rituals that dramatized the beginning of the agricultural year, or songs that described the origin of the people or the founding of the kingdom were oral traditions that stressed the transmission of important messages to the whole population.[43] The ultimate purpose of those messages, constantly repeated and recreated by each generation, was to strengthen the identity of the ethnic group and the foundations of the kingdom.

The codex. Western tradition, in its European as well as its American version, favored the study of the codices, or *amoxtli*, which were more similar to books. As has been indicated, in Mesoamerica all kinds of books were created, with images and glyphs within which memories could be maintained of those deeds that it was desirable to transmit to future generations. The accumulated knowledge about the gods, religious ceremonies, calendars and astronomical computations, plants and animals, the geographic dimensions of the territory, the inventory of the wealth of the kingdom, the story of subordinate provinces and the tribute they paid, the genealogy of the kings and noble families, and the stories that were told of the ups and downs of the ethnic group were all collected in the painted books. As Dominican Fray Diego Durán stated, using characters and figures, they recorded in their codices the combined knowledge that they wished to remember:

These figures . . . served in place of letters. And they generally always made use of these letter paintings to write with pictures and effigies their histories and antiquities, their memorable deeds, their wars and victories; their hunger and pestilence, their prosperity and adversity: they had it all written and painted in books and long papers, with an account of the years, months and days when they had occurred. They had in these paintings their laws and ordinances, their patrons, etc. Everything was done with great order and harmony. There were very fine historians who composed ample histories of their ancestors using these pictures. They would have given us considerable insight, if ignorant zeal had not destroyed them for us.[44]

After the Classic Period, the painted book had become the preferred instrument for recording and ordering the memory of the past. The remains of that tradition that have endured indicate that the Mayas and the people of the region of Puebla and the Oaxacan Mixtec region stood out in the manufacture of codices. At that time the codex was the ideal tool for storing the largest amount of information about the past, an instrument able to systematize specialized information on any area of the supernatural or natural environment. It included the qualities that we now appreciate in books: an economy of resources for gathering and ordering different information, facility of updating and revising accumulated information, variety of sizes and forms, and availability for reference and reading.[45]

Lorenzo Boturini Benaduci: A Response to the Western Canon

In the now limitless library of Western studies of American history, I have found only one author who saw clearly the richness of the oral, visual, calendrical, and ritualistic testimonies of Mesoamerican cultures. This was Lorenzo Boturini Benaduci, the unfortunate

Italian traveler who lived in New Spain from 1736 until 1743. Boturini was a rare example of receptiveness to the strange writing and of sympathy for historical languages different from his own. During those seven years, perhaps the happiest of his life, Boturini was captivated by the fervor the criollos [Creoles, Spaniards born in the New World] professed for the Virgin of Guadalupe and by the codices, maps, linens, monuments, and oral traditions that were part of the ancient Mesoamerican civilization.

Fascinated by the appearances of the Virgin to the Indian Juan Diego, he took on the double task of gaining the approval of the Roman Pontiff for the crowning of the Virgin of Guadalupe as Queen of New Spain and gathering the resources to assure that her crown was of heavy gold. His main interest, nonetheless, was to gather testimonials about the origin of the miraculous Virgin. This initial curiosity put him in contact with American antiquities, an encounter that became an uncontrollable passion, driving him to form his extraordinary "Historical Indian Museum."

Boturini's "museum" consisted of an impressive collection of ancient historical documents that he acquired or had copied from the valuable library put together by the wise Carlos de Sigüenza y Góngora in the seventeenth century and from the archives of the Chapter House of the Cathedral of Mexico, the Royal Tribunal, the library of the University of Mexico, and other repositories, both public and private. The curiosity awakened in Boturini by his acquaintance with those treasures led him to travel through many parts of central Mexico seeking ancient documents. He traveled, according to his own statement, through many places, submitting himself to "such heavy labor that I cannot even stand to think of them," and finally reached Metztitlán, where he discovered traces of the Apostle St. Thomas. He later visited Huejotzingo, Cholula, Tlaxcala, Toluca, the land of the Matlatzincas, and several places in the "Kingdom of Michoacán." In this manner, copying, buying, and trading, he was able to put together the greatest collection of codices and documents on ancient Mexico ever assembled by an individual or an institution.[46]

In addition to constituting the patrimony that later became the base for all serious study of ancient Mexico, Boturini was the first to propose a new interpretation of the documents and to undertake a reevaluation of the American past. More than any other researcher, Boturini recognized the value of the different ways used by the ancient Americans to maintain the memory of their past. He said that in his search for documents he found in the towns of New Spain "materials that other historians did not find and *with so many excellent or sublime things that I dare to state that this history not only can compete with the most celebrated histories in the world, but can surpass them.*"[47] This unusual praise of native historical records was not limited to written documents; it is significant that he extended it to the

four manners of entrusting to public memory their important things. The first, in figures, symbols, characters, and hieroglyphics, which in themselves include an abundance of erudition, as will be seen later. The second, in knots of various colors, which in the language of Peruvians are called *quipus* and in that of our Indians, *nepohualtzitzin.* The third, in songs of exquisite metaphors and elevated concepts. The fourth and last, after the Spanish Conquest, in manuscripts in both languages, Indian and Spanish . . . by which one can understand the peculiarities of their civil life.[48]

That is to say, Boturini was the first European to elevate hieroglyphics, *quipus,* and songs to the level of written testimonials and to consider them fully valid. Another feature that attracted Boturini's admiration was the form of recording time that he noticed in those pages. He stated that they were decorated with "a chronology so exact that it exceeds in skill that of the Egyptians and Chaldeans, since it explains their years based on . . . a high level of astronomical scholarship."[49]

The quality that made the books of Boturini on the ancient history of Mexico a modern work was the method he used to interpret the past. Instead of adopting the Christian concept of history that was then in fashion or turning to Greco-Roman models, Boturini was inspired by the *Sciencia nuova* of Gianbattista Vico, whose first edition was published in 1725 and the second in 1730. In that revolutionary work, which would not be appreciated for its true value until many years later, Vico divided the history of humanity into three periods: the age of the gods, the age of the heroes, and the age of human beings.[50] Boturini adopted that innovative scheme in his two works: *Idea de una nueva historia general de la América Septentrional* and *Historia general de la América Septentrional* (figs. 48 and 49). Instead of imposing a foreign historiographic model on American history, which would certainly have detracted from it, he made use of the ideas of Vico, who recommended an inside approach to the past obtained from the people themselves or from the subject of the history.

Vico introduced a new interpretation of history by considering that human deeds that occurred in the past, no matter how distant and strange they might seem, were susceptible to being understood and explained in the present. According to Isaiah Berlin, Vico's greatness lies in having discovered the principle that "man can understand himself because in the process he understands his past; because he is capable of reconstructing in his imagination what he did and what he suffered . . . , his actions and works, his as well as those of his neighbors."[51] Vico rejected the Cartesian proposition that affirmed that the only knowledge was based on precise observations of the object examined, as occurs in mathematics. He accepted the superiority of mathematics as scientific knowledge but said that mathematical truth did not lie in the objective understanding of its axioms. By doing mathematics, he said, we do not discover the unchanging characteristics of an objective world, but we are *inventing* a logical system for understanding it. That is to say, we can understand that system completely because *we made it.* He therefore concluded that the only understanding that can

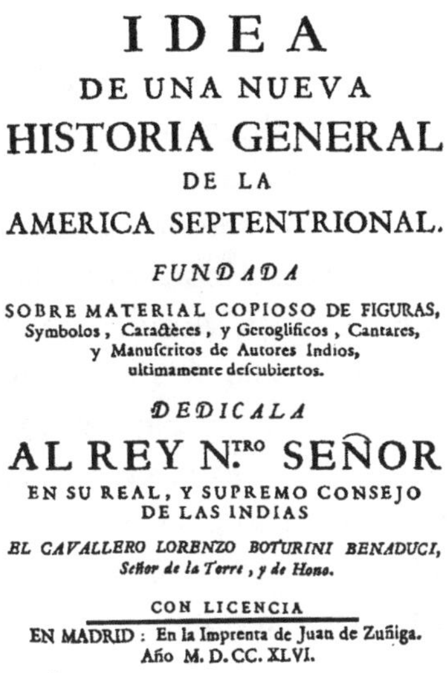

I D E A
DE UNA NUEVA
HISTORIA GENERAL
DE LA
AMERICA SEPTENTRIONAL.

FUNDADA

SOBRE MATERIAL COPIOSO DE FIGURAS,
Symbolos , Caractères , y Geroglificos , Cantares,
y Manufcritos de Autores Indios,
ultimamente defcubiertos.

DEDICALA

AL REY N.ᵀᴿᵒ SEÑOR
EN SU REAL, Y SUPREMO CONSEJO
DE LAS INDIAS

EL CAVALLERO LORENZO BOTURINI BENADUCI,
Señor de la Torre , y de Hono.

CON LICENCIA
EN MADRID : En la Imprenta de Juan de Zuñiga.
Año M. D. CC. XLVI.

Fig. 48. Portrait of Lorenzo
Boturini Benaduci. (From *Idea de
una historia general de la América
Septentrional*, 1974.)

Fig. 49. Cover of the book
published by Lorenzo Boturini
Benaduci in 1746.

totally understand a thing is the understanding that created it.[52]
With those ideas, Vico presented a new interpretation of primitive peoples and of classical antiquity, renewing the theory of
decadence and rebirth of peoples (*corso e ricorso*), reevaluating
myth as a source of historical understanding, and offering a
new idea of human evolution.[53]

Boturini incorporated those ideas into his two Mexican works
but was not able to develop them fully because of the loss of his
valuable "Historical Museum." Unfortunately, he did not have
immediate successors, which without doubt was influenced by
the disastrous fate of his museum. The magnificent collection that
he had made such an effort to amass was confiscated when he was
accused of claiming authority to which he was not entitled in an
effort to promote the coronation of the Virgin of Guadalupe in

Rome. Later, he was expelled from the country and definitively lost his beloved "Museum," which he never saw again and which he considered his most loved possession.

Despite the work of Boturini and other precursors, the great obstacle to valuing Mesoamerican techniques of gathering and transmitting the past continued to be the persistent adhesion to the Western canon. Most historians, particularly those who dealt with the native world, evaluated American communication systems in terms of the Western canon. For linguists, writing researchers, and historians of the West, writing was invented to record spoken speech. Therefore, signs that were not phonetic could not be classified as writing; at most they were considered to be a precursor of real writing. Even experts in Mayan hieroglyphic writing, the only truly phonetic American writing system, excluded Aztec and Mixtec glyphs from the ranks of authentic writing.[54]

Perhaps the most alarming thing to realize is that the Western canon continues to abound at the present time, for which Elizabeth Boone gives strong evidence with two examples. On one side, she cites the often discussed book of Tzvetan Todorov, *La conquête de l'Amerique* (The conquest of America, 1982), whose purpose is to make an analysis of the communication systems in order to establish how otherness manifested itself in the discovery and conquest of America. Nonetheless, if his objective is to reveal the European concept of otherness—or rather, of the native American—he indulged in surpising contradictions. As Boone observes, when Todorov tries to record and represent the Mexica point of view, he does not base it on the pictographic or written works of the Mexica, but rather on European sources. "One sees the Aztecs beaten by signs, dominated by rhetoric and the superior symbolic systems of their conquerors." Consequently, according to Boone's judgment, this book was another conquest, a "discursive conquest" of the ancient Mexicans.[55]

On the other side is the book of Hugh Thomas, *Conquest: Montezuma, Cortés, and the Fall of Old México* (1933), which proposes a new interpretation of the conquest of Mexico. But even when Thomas refers to Nahuatl texts, he bases his argument primarily on Spanish sources. Consequently, Boone concludes, "by favoring European texts and perspectives, these works place themselves on the slippery slope of historical literature dominated by modern (and post-modern) occidental discourse above the others."[56]

IV. THE CONQUEST AND THE IMPOSITION OF THE CHRISTIAN CANON ON HISTORY

The Spanish Conquest and colonization forever changed the future of the indigenous people and within a few decades led to the formation of a hitherto unknown social structure made up of populations with diverse and contrasting cultural roots. The European invasion decapitated the autonomous design of American civilization and imposed upon the native people a new language and the religious, social, and political values of the Western world.

Simultaneous with that vast transformation, a new form of recording and explaining the past began, followed by the intrusion of a new protagonist of the historical narration: the conquistador. The conquest ejected the native from the historical forefront, installing in his place a new topic of discourse on almost all levels.

The Language of the Conquistador

After arms, language was the primary instrument of domination in the Americas. The Spanish language began to control American reality when it became the narrator of Spanish discoveries, conquests, and settlements in the New World. The *Diary* of Christopher Columbus, the *Letters* of Hernán Cortés (fig. 50), the *General History* of Gonzalo Fernández de Oviedo, and the *True History* of Bernal Díaz del Castillo, all are testimonies to the new writing that the conqueror imposed for narrating his expansion in the American territories (fig. 51). The Spanish language

HISTORIA
DE NUEVA-ESPAÑA,
ESCRITA POR SU ESCLARECIDO CONQUISTADOR,
HERNAN CORTES,
AUMENTADA
CON OTROS DOCUMENTOS, Y NOTAS,
POR EL ILUSTRISSIMO SEÑOR
DON FRANCISCO ANTONIO
LORENZANA,
ARZOBISPO DE MEXICO.

CON LAS LICENCIAS NECESARIAS
En México en la Imprenta del Superior Gobierno, del Br. D. Joseph Antonio de Hogal
en la Calle de Tiburcio. Año de 1770.

Fig. 50. Cover of the edition of the letters of Hernán Cortés produced by the Archbishop of Mexico, Antonio Lorenzana, in 1770.

Fig. 51. Cover of the book by Francisco López de Gómara, *Historia de las Indias y conquista de México,* published in 1552.

kept pace with the Spanish invasion, naming and giving new meaning to nature, men, and native cultures.

The American continent began to lose its indigenous connotations as soon as the conquerors started to classify it with geographic and cartographic concepts of their own. Indigenous cosmological ideas that ordered the territory were scoffed at when that space became the territory of the conquistador (fig. 52). By describing, naming, and classifying nature with the Spanish language, the chronicler became a translator and owner of that strange reality. The new language that now described the American reality, at the same time that it allowed the conquistador to make his own a natural environment that had until then been foreign, created an estrangement between nature and the native population, who

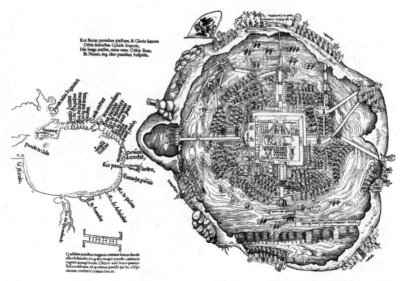

Fig. 52. First plan of the city of Mexico-Tenochtitlán, published in Nurem-
burg in 1524. This map, engraved on wood by an unknown author,
attempted to represent the Aztec capital when the Spaniards led by Hernán
Cortés entered. Although the map included information given by the first
Europeans who visited the city, it followed the conventions established for
urban maps. The map accompanied the second letter from Hernán Cortés,
published in 1524.

from then on found incomprehensible the language that named
it, the system that classified it, and the exploitation to which it
now fell victim.[1]

From the navigators who first saw and named the Caribbean
Islands to the discoverers of the northern lands of New Spain in
the eighteenth century, no explorer failed to make a geographic
recording of the territories he crossed. The natural inventory was
also an instrument that revealed Spanish exploits to the world.
Spain was the country that showed the Old World a New World.
And that privileged mission became a historiographic and cosmo-
graphic mission, a task emphasizing the description of a humanity
until then unknown and the detailed recording of an unknown land
(figs. 53 and 54). The King of Spain in 1532 created the position of

Chronicler of the Indies and later, in 1571, that of First Chronicler and Cosmographer of the Indies, so that he might know the exact dimensions and possibilities for exploitation of the newly discovered world.[2] Naming, describing, and classifying the physical world of the Americas was one way of owning it. By naming the territory in the Spanish language, the conquistador began to order the knowledge that would allow its strategic exploitation, and later, in possession of that knowledge, he could take on the task of transmitting the epic and transforming character of Spanish action. As Michel de Certeau has said, the history that from that time forward was written by Western man was written with Western ideas about the physical body of America.[3]

The first official chroniclers of the American reality gave over large parts of their work to collecting geographic novelties and naming and classifying seas, coasts, islands, peninsulas, mountain ranges, rivers, plants, and animals. Gonzalo Fernández de Oviedo, in addition to writing his *Sumario de la natural historia de las Indias* (Summary of the natural history of the Indies), dedicated many books of his *Historia general y natural de las Indias* (General and natural history of the Indies) to descriptions of nature. Francisco López de Gómara did the same thing; before dealing with themes of the conquest of Peru and Mexico, he inserted a description of geographic discoveries into his *Historia general de las Indias* (General history of the Indies). Juan López de Velasco, the first official cosmographer-chronicler, systematized that interest in American geography with a meticulous questionnaire requesting strategic information about the territory and its resources. From the responses obtained he amassed an arsenal of data on geography, natural resources, history, and ethnography of the New World.[4] Later chroniclers such as Antonio de Herrera (*Historia general . . . de las Indias Occidentales* [General history . . . of the West Indies], 1596–1615) took advantage of that information in works that included numerous volumes dedicated exclusively to American geography and nature. This double attention to the recording of the natural world and the human beings who inhabited it reached its

Fig. 53. This illustration of the scene of the discovery of America appears in the Latin edition of the *Letter* of Christopher Colombus, printed in 1493 in Basel.

Fig. 54. Columbus reached the Caribbean Islands and "discovered" the native population under the supervision of the king of Spain, who appears as the main witness to the event. This illustration from the discovery of America is in the Latin edition of the *Letter* of Christopher Columbus, printed in 1493 in Basel.

height in the *Historia natural y moral de las Indias* (Natural and moral history of the Indies, 1590) by Jesuit José de Acosta.[5]

New Historical Discourse

The language that had covered the American territory with new meanings also both governed the telling of contemporary reality and rewrote the memory of the past. Few things reflected so strongly the relationship that existed between the taking of power by one group and the elaboration of a new historical discourse as the dramatic experience that Mesoamerican people began to live through as a result of the conquest. Military defeat was immediately followed by the suppression of their historical memory. The ancient memory that told of the origins and greatness of native civilization was destroyed, persecuted, and declared invalid for the telling of a true story. In the chronicles that the conquistadors began to write, Indians disappeared as actors and protagonists of history or only appeared in them as reflections, mirrors, or testimonies to the actions of their conquerors. The real protagonists of history as written by the conquistador were that nation that won over a new world and a vast pagan humanity and the agents of that great saga: the conquistadors, the evangelizing friars, and the new settlers (fig. 55).

At the same time as the conquest, which established a new subject for history, the conquistador introduced the European tradition of interpreting historical happenings to the New World. The conquistador transferred to the American scene the ancient Judeo-Christian concepts of history, mixed with eschatological, millenarian, and providentialist ideas that were proliferating in medieval Europe (fig. 56). It did not bring with it one single image of the past or one unique concept of historical development; rather, it brought to American soil the accumulated weight of multiple pasts (those of pagan antiquity, primitive Christianity, medieval heritage, and the new horizons opened by the Renaissance) and

Fig. 55. This fragment of the *Códice de Tlatelolco* shows the principal authorities of the government of New Spain appearing in the middle of the sixteenth century. From left to right, the first figure is Doctor Alonso de Zorita, judge and president of the Royal Court. Beside him are Viceroy Luis de Velasco, followed by the Archbishop of Mexico, Fray Alonso de Montúfar. Last is Doctor Diego López de Montealegre. (Photo from the *Códice de Tlatelolco*, 1994.)

distributed diverse interpretations of history and different ways of understanding and recording time.[6]

Hebrew and Christian Concepts of Historical Development

In Hebrew tradition, historical development was a revelation to those designated by God—a manifestation of the divine plan. The past and historical events had a teleology, a final sense or purpose that for Jews resided in the fulfilling of God's promises to the cho-

Fig. 56. Cover of the *Doctrina Christiana en lengua mexicana* by Fray Pedro de Gante, printed in 1553. It is probably the first book in Náhuatl printed in Europe. These books and the direct sermons of the mendicant brothers were the first diffusors of Christianity in New Spain.

sen people, which was later interpreted as universal salvation, no longer limited to the Jewish people. Human history was conceived as the scene on which the will of God was majestically displayed, leading to its ultimate design of eternal redemption. Arnaldo Momigliano has stated that "the idea of a historical continuum begun in creation came to dominate, and all other interests were sacrificed to it, including curiosity for non-Hebraic history. A privileged succession of events represented and signified the continuing intervention of God in the world which He himself had created."[7]

According to the oral and written tradition of the Jewish people, the salvation of humankind would come through the intervention of a divine redeemer, a messiah who would be made man on earth to destroy nonbelievers and establish an earthly paradise in which the chosen people would live in abundant peace and joy. The fulfilling of the divine will acquired a messianic character, with final salvation depending on the arrival of a providential and eschato-logical man, since salvation would be preceded by a catastrophic destruction of the world.[8]

Christians of the first century believed that human salvation would occur soon, when Christ in all His power and glory would return to earth for the second time to fulfill His eschato-logical and purifying mission. But as His return was delayed and the Church became a temporal power, other explanations of the end of the world, the mission of the Church, and the historical process began to appear.

The end of the world and the day of eternal salvation were no longer imminent events because, as Mark had said, before that could occur, the bearers of the word of Christ had to preach the Gospel to all nations. This idea conferred on the Church a terres-trial mission of singular importance: now it had to guide and console believers that were born and died in the hopes of final judgment. The Church thus became the mystical body of Christ, a divine entity founded on earth to fulfill God's plan for salvation there. Thus, in the future the care of the faithful, the preaching of the Gospel, and the conversion of innumerable pagans became tasks that had to be accomplished year after year and century after century, until such time as God should determine to end the world.

The acceptance of these ideas changed the historical perspec-tives of Christianity. Just as the time of the earthly mission of the Church was expanding, so were the lives of believers expanding into the future, which was divided into two parts. In the first, of an unknown but brief time, the believer had to suffer through his earthly life for the venal sins he had committed. But in the second, which would begin at the time of final judgment, the believer would receive eternal blessing, unless the gravity of his sins resulted in the condemnation of his soul.[9] These new interpretations pro-moted a concept of temporal development also divided into two parts: the first began with the creation of the world and of human beings and ended with the birth of Christ. The second began with the birth of the Lord and would end at an unknown time in the future with the final judgment. The nexus that united those two parts was the birth and death of Christ, the earthly life of Him sent by God, who had revealed to mortals the purposes of the divine plan. Christians were thus the first to unite past and future into a single process that began with the origin of the world and extended into the future, including the history of all nations and races, without excluding—as did the Hebrews—the pagan peoples.

One overwhelming event, the sacking of Rome by Alaric's Goths in 410 A.D., which threatened to pull down the foundations of Western Europe, cast doubt on the idea that the passage of time favored divine purposes. St. Augustine wrote *The City of God* with the precise intent of combating the claims of pagans who attributed the destruction of Rome to Christianity (which had taken over the Empire), and of showing that however catastrophic the ruination of the State, the City of God—that is to say, the Church—would survive triumphant until the inexorable end of time. *The City of God* also fought against apocalyptic and messianic ideas proclaiming the imminent arrival of a messiah and the establishment of a kingdom of the saints on earth.[10]

St. Augustine interpreted the history of mankind as a battle between the Civitas Dei and the Civitas terrena (the City of God and the Earthly City). He saw in the history of Egypt, Assyria, Greece, and Rome the inevitable ruin of the earthly city. On the other hand, the city that would endure and grow with the passage of time was the City of God, the Church.

From that time on, the "Age of the Church" was seen by Christians as the second part of the divine plan. The first, which had concerned the relationship of God with the people of Israel, was the "evangelical preparation," ending with the birth of Christ. The second, that of the Church, had as its commission to increase the community of the faithful and to carry the true word to all the nations. Thus, the Church came to be the expression in history of the divine purpose.[11] In this way the missionary duty of the Church, the preaching of the Gospel, was granted its meaning in the history of salvation for the period between the resurrection and the second coming of Christ. If the historical existence of Christ created the possibility of salvation, the founding of His church imposed on each of its members the obligation of fulfilling that possibility.[12]

The New Concept of the Past

As these ideas were consolidated, Europe began to be

> dominated by a notion of the past which was very different from that held by earlier civilizations and even by the contemporary civiliations of China and India. The past was, it might be said, a story with a precise and limited beginning . . . , an array of events which made clear the intentions of God and the destiny of man and culminated in the dramatic episode of the life and death of Christ, followed by the pilgrimages of mankind toward final judgment, which also would occur at a precise moment in time. This narrative aspect of human destiny was clear; it could be seen in the painted murals of churches, in the rituals and in the representations of miracles. The notion of history as an inexorable unfolding narration put out deep roots in the European conscience and contributed not only to the acceptance of the changes but also to the very idea of an orderly process of development. . . . The past took on a dynamism—one might even say an impetus—that it had not had until that time.[13]

As the reader will have noticed, the time of the Bible and of primitive Christianity was a theological time. It began with God and was dominated by Him (figs. 57 and 58). The unfolding of time was the necessary condition for every divine action. Since then and through the Middle Ages, Christian time was linear time, given a sensitivity that turned toward God.[14] The inner and external lives of Christians, their entire mentality, all were dominated by the continuing perception of this divine time. The time of God—His incarnation, crucifixion, and resurrection and the day of final justice—were merged into the everyday lives of human beings, with their mission here on earth, and with their hopes of the time after their death.

Time acquired a central meaning in every moment of daily life; its passing was observed with fear and recorded in a solemn manner. The liturgical calendar of the Church marked the succession of days, not only reminding men and women of the passing of the months and seasons, but also reminding them of each one of the acts of God and of the road to salvation. The daily passage of time was introduced into the lives of human beings in a manner that was earlier unknown. In the country and in the city, the passage of time was indicated, more than by the movement of the sun, by the tolling of the bells, which after the seventh century rang the canonical hours seven times a day, their peals calling the faithful to celebrate happy events or informing them of the death of a Christian soul, reminding everyone of the nearness of their own demise.[15]

Nevertheless, if for the orthodox Church the date that had changed the history of humanity was the date of the incarnation of Christ, for the poor and for dissident Christians the most attractive date came to be that when the apocalyptic prophesies were to be fulfilled: the arrival of the Messiah, who would destroy the power of the devil, instituting the kingdom of the saints in its place. That moment would be the high point of history, because the kingdom of the saints would bypass all the former kingdoms in glory and would have no end. That ancient Jewish tradition, taken over by some Christians even though it was opposed by the Church, supported multiple messianic movements during the Middle Ages among the oppressed, the dissident, and the unbalanced.[16] And after the twelfth century it took on new resonance when it was joined by the restless ascetic and mystic movements, which rejected the corruption of the secular Church and proposed living in apostolic poverty to form a great Christian community like that described in the book of Acts: "And all those who believed were together and had all things in common . . . and no one had any possession of his own."[17]

Fig. 57. Representation of Jesus Christ as Pantocrátor (the All Powerful) in the Byzantine cathedral of Monreale, Sicily, in the twelfth century. The Savior was represented seated and blessing, framed in a circle. In this image the right hand offers the blessing in the Greek manner. In the left hand He holds open the Gospel, which reads, in Greek and Latin, "I am the light of the world, he who follows me will not walk in the shadows."

The criticism of the increasingly profane orientation of the Church, the ascetic inclinations of monks and dissidents who sought to restore the ideals of the early Church, and the persistence of messianic and eschatological ideas among groups were summarized in the thoughts of Joaquín de Fiore, a surprising catalyst of these aspirations who disseminated a new kind of eschatological prophesy throughout the world.[18] These prophecies must have had the greatest influence in Europe and in the Spanish

Fig. 58. Representation of Christ as the Pantocrátor in a native image made of feathers. National Museum of the Viceroyalty.

colonies of America, where they were reborn in new forms in the sixteenth, seventeenth, and eighteenth centuries and even later.

Three centuries afterward, when the first twelve Franciscans who came to preach the Gospel disembarked on the coast of Veracruz in 1524, the redemptorist and salvationist ideas coming from the centers of Christianity were reborn in strength and fed the hopes of many missionaries (fig. 59). No small number of those who disembarked in America believed that it was the promised land, where they could bring about the monastic ideal. In addition to this eschatological concept, the Spaniards brought to New Spain Hebrew and Christian religious traditions, the ideals of the orthodox Church, and other providential ideas about the mission of Spain in the world. Thus, the founding of Colonial society was powerfully influenced by the medieval Judeo-Christian religious tradition, which was the source of the concepts that developed in America regarding the meaning of history and temporal events.

Fig. 59. Mural painting from the convent of Huejotzingo depicting the twelve Franciscans who, imitating the twelve Apostles, came to New Spain to preach the Gospel.

Conquest and Evangelization as a Providential Mission of the State-Church

Spain inherited the universal and providential concept of history that Christianity had elaborated and with it faced the surprising discovery of new lands and the even less anticipated meeting with civilizations hitherto unknown. The confusion brought on by the meeting with American aborigines could be absorbed and explained with the Christian idea of a humanity created in the image of God and called, without distinction as to race, to eternal salvation. A creature of God, the aboriginal American was one more member of the extensive human family. His rationality, therefore, could not be in question. As shown by Bartolomé de las Casas, the Christian idea of human beings discredited those who denied the human condition and rational capability of the American natives, so from then on the debate centered on a consideration of their historical and cultural development, not their rationality.[19]

The Christian idea of history also supported the expansion of Spanish imperial power, infusing it with a providential and messianic feeling. The medieval Christian Church was considered universal, but before the era of discovery Christianity was confined to a very limited area of the world. Surprisingly, the discoveries of the fifteenth and sixteenth centuries for the first time opened up the possibility of expanding Christianity throughout vast regions and complying with the universal aspirations of the Church. And among all the nations of Christendom, few felt as strongly as Spain the privilege of being predestined to realize those ideals that Christians saw as enunciated in Holy Scripture. The discovery of unknown lands and the conversion of the pagan people seemed to the Spaniards a clear sign of the providential mission that God had given to his chosen people (fig. 60).

After the conquest historical discourse evolved within the margins of the Christian idea of history, with its apostolic, messianic, and providentialist aspects, and was nourished in the powerful current of Spanish imperialism, which it defended and legitimized. We know that some protagonists of American history, such as Columbus and a number of soldiers and missionaries, acted in the firm belief that they were agents of Providence. Also, the historians, among them Pedro Mártir de Anglería and especially Gonzalo Fernández de Oviedo and Francisco López de Gómara, transmitted in their work the certainty that the successive discoveries and conquests were part of a providential plan designed to unify all peoples and races of the world beneath the mantle of Christianity and the Crown of the Catholic kings.[20] And for mystic temperaments like those of the first missionaries who preached the Gospel in America, "this possibility seemed to them a vision so blindingly radiant that its execution foretold the proximity of the end of the world. They believed that after all the races of humanity were converted, nothing more could happen in this world."[21]

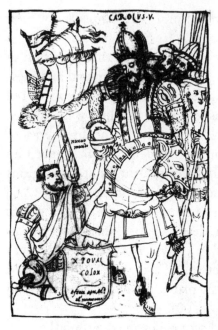

Fig. 60. Christopher Columbus offers the New World to the Spanish King Carlos V in a drawing by the Mestizo chronicler Diego Muñoz Camargo, reproduced in his *Descripción de la ciudad y provincia de Tlaxcala*.

The Teaching of Christian Doctrine to the Indigenous People

The first friars to reach New Spain saw in the natives the qualities most esteemed by the Christian flock: they were poor, tame, docile, humble, obedient, pliant as children, and suitable, "like tabula rasa and very soft wax," to have imprinted on them anything that might be desired (fig. 61). Based on this interpretation was the belief that the Indians would achieve Christian perfection if they remained under the exclusive tutelage of the friars, since in that way they would come to be "the best and healthiest in Christendom and the model of good order for the universe/world."[22]

The teaching of Christian doctrine emphasized the sacraments: baptism, matrimony, extreme unction, and penance. In the missions and parishes the mendicant brothers themselves, in the local language and through images, taught the natives the rudiments of Christian doctrine and established schools to teach the catechumens.

Fig. 61. The arrival of the Franciscans in New Spain in 1525. In this drawing, found in Mestizo Diego Muñoz Camargo's *Descripción de la ciudad y provincia de Tlaxcala,* the monks begin by elevating the Cross. The raising of the Cross causes the flight of the local demons, who are represented by the symbols of pre-Hispanic gods.

The cloisters of the seminaries became great classrooms, where collective instruction was combined with singing, theater, and festivals (fig. 62). The business of teaching the Indians the precepts of the faith of Christ led the friars to use ancient traditions and to put innovative methods into service. As Robert Ricard has pointed out, "inspired by the native manuscripts, some friars adopted the custom of helping themselves with pictures, with 'paintings,' for the teaching of Christian doctrine." Ricard states that Bernardino de Sahagún, Jerónimo de Mendieta, and Pedro de Gante put this method into practice.[23] Constantino Reyes Valerio has suggested that the first Franciscans used ancient Indian techniques of transmitting knowledge through images and cites as proof a testimony of Mendieta. Mendieta said that some friars

used a manner of preaching that was very successful with the Indians, *since it conformed to the custom that they had of dealing with all their things through paintings.* And it was in that manner that they had painted on one linen the Articles of Faith, on another the Ten Commandments, on another the seven sacraments, and the rest of the Christian doctrine. And when the preacher wanted to preach on the Commandments, he hung up that linen . . . beside him, so that with one of the sticks that the Indian governors carried he could point out the part that he wanted.[24]

As Ricard has stated, the use of native techniques to transmit the Christian faith through images was a widely used procedure in the first decades of evangelization. Fray Diego Valadés, the Mestizo son of a conquistador and a woman from Tlaxcala who entered the Franciscan order in 1550 and later published a work on the methods of evangelization (*Retórica cristiana,* Perugia, 1579), drew an engraving that explained in detail the characteristics of this method (fig. 62). The famous engraving of Valadés, reproduced later in the works of Jerónimo de Mendieta and Fray Juan de Torquemada, was commented upon thus by Franciscan Esteban Palomera:

A. Here is the preacher of the word of God . . . preaching in their own language. B. Since the Indians were unlettered, it was necessary to teach them with illustrations; therefore the preacher is showing them with a pointer the mysteries of our redemption so that, meditating on it later, it might be fixed in their memory. C. Those who are seated in this part, who have sticks in their hands, are those who carry out the duties of judges among our natives.[25]

According to Valadés himself, the procedure for using images to teach the natives Christian doctrine was started by the Franciscans, for he stated: "For this purpose they have linens on which have been painted the main points of the Christian religion . . . *which invention is otherwise very attractive and notable . . . which honor, with all rightness, we claim as ours . . . [since] we were the first to* work diligently to adapt *this new method of instruction.*"[26]

Thus a good part of religious instruction was transmitted through images, just as it had been done in ancient Mesoamerica. Reyes Valerio has observed that the thousands of square yards of paintings that covered the walls of the seminaries, churches, and

Fig. 62. The famous engraving of Fray Diego Valadés, showing the atrium of the church where the main work of evangelizing was carried out. In the middle, toward the right (A), a friar reads Christian doctrine to the natives. Immediately above, to the right (N), another friar shows them a painting that represents the creation of the world. To the left (O), Fray Pedro de Gante shows the doctrine to other natives.

chapels served the function of spreading the basic principles of Christianity through the native population. He has also indicated the role that the painted religious scenes played in churches and seminaries, saying that they "were not distributed by chance, but rather, to the contrary, the missionaries distributed them with the intention that they serve to teach the basics of the doctrine." Predominant in these scenes were the Annunciation, the birth of Christ, the Adoration of the Magi, the Passion of Christ, the Last Supper, some episodes of the Old Testament, and so forth.[27]

As Serge Gruzinski has observed, Christianity multiplied its images everywhere, both in big cities such as Mexico City and Puebla and in small towns and the countryside, where many seminaries and monasteries were built. This form of diffusion of Christianity was so popular that the Dominican Bartolomé de las Casas was able to write around 1555 that he had seen "a good part of Christian doctrine represented in figures and images, thanks to which the natives could read it as well as I can read it written with our letters on a page."[28]

The diffusion of Christian images throughout the Indian world makes one think, Gruzinski says, that that period went through a war of images.

> Ever since Christopher Columbus trod the beaches of the New World, the question of images was discussed. Without delay, the newly arrived were questioning the nature of those that the natives possessed. Very soon, the image came to constitute an instrument of reference, and after that of acculturation and domination when the Church resolved to Christianize the Indians from Florida to Tierra del Fuego. European colonization captured the continent in a snare of images which continued to grow, spread, and modify in step with the styles, politics, and reactions and oppositions encountered.[29]

In spite of their all-encompassing appearance, the training by the friars was selective and strategic. The mendicant brothers knew

Fig. 63. An Indian school of the sixteenth century, according to the *Códice de San Juan Teotihuacán*. The chronicler of the Franciscans said the following: In all the churches "there are schools, which are in the courtyard of the church, where children are taught to help with mass, to read, and always in the courtyards of the church; because it needs to be so general for everyone, it is good that the place be public. There they divide . . . the boys in one group and the girls in the other. . . . And with this care all are very well instructed." (From Gamio, 1922, vol. 2: 473.)

the difficulty of converting adults and concentrated their efforts on children, who did not put up any resistance and were more susceptible to the seduction of the gifts that they were offered (fig. 63).[30] Education concentrating on children and youths produced results that the friars celebrated as miracles of evangelization, but which cannot but cause discomfort and even repugnance because of the insidious practice of turning children against their parents and deliberately promoting the destruction of the family.

The schools of the mendicant brothers soon became the centers of distribution of reading, writing, music, singing, theater, arts, and Western culture. There the children and youths learned the catechism, Christian hymns and psalms, European techniques and practices, dance, theater, and the use of Western musical instruments, which they also learned to make and combine with the music and traditions of the native population (fig. 64). The religious center became the place where Western traditions were acclimated, in an environment of interchange between European and native traditions, and where new cultural relations were forged that transformed the face of New Spain. In those spaces

Fig. 64. The model of the preacher surrounded by Indians, teaching them the precepts of the faith of Christ, according to an engraving by Diego Valadés.

the cloister was the perfect public area; "its principal use was as a training site: there the boys and girls practiced among themselves that manner of instruction taught by the missionaries. The cloister was the chapter house of the faithful . . . as it was the precinct of processions, of open-air festivals, of sacred dances, and in total, of all manifestations of the collective religious life"[31] (fig. 65).

Just as the first Western books, written in Latin, Greek, Spanish, Italian, French, and other Romance languages, came to the monasteries and churches, so also did the facades of these monuments reproduce the plateresque, mudéjar, churrigueresque, and baroque archicture then stylish in Europe. The scenes, characters, and symbols of Western painting appeared on the walls of the seminaries and churches of New Spain and told, for the instruction of the Indian multitudes, the episodes of the creation of the world according to the Old Testament, the birth of humanity according

Fig. 65. Preaching to the natives inside the church, according to an engraving by Fray Diego Valadés. With his pointer, the friar shows the Indians scenes of the Passion of Christ.

to the Bible, the forming of heaven and of hell, the sermons of the first Apostles, the dramatic events of the passion and death of Jesus Christ, the discovery of America under the initiative of the Catholic kings, the distribution of Christianity through the New World, and the marvelous arrival of the mendicant orders and the Catholic Church in New Spain (fig. 66).[32]

Sculpture, another method chosen to transmit visual messages, became an instrument of catechizing and a promoter of devotions to the founders of Christianity, the religious orders, the numberless images of the Virgin, the saints, and the Christian symbols.[33]

Likewise, if one consults the studies dedicated to the theater at the time of evangelization, it is easy to see that the dramatized arrangement of the ancient *mitotes* (Aztec dances) and *areitos* (Central American and Antillean songs and dances) and the performance of the first pieces of Western theater "did not have literary purposes, but rather the preaching of the Gospel."[34] The specific purpose of

Fig. 66. The religious instruction of the friars, by Jacobo de Testera. (Photo taken by Cline, 1975: fig. 94.)

the auto or religious theater "was to inculcate into the Indians a highly ideological vision of the conquest, forging at the same time in their minds a historical consciousness of their own defeat and subordination as the Spanish wished them to remember it."[35]

Perhaps the most important ideological change that the evangelizers brought about was the suppression of the ancient calendar of Indian rituals and its replacement with saints' days and Christian festivals. When they suppressed the old cult days, the priests broke the continuity of memory that celebrated the founding events of Indian life. And by substituting Christian worship and ceremonies for those dates, they gradually imposed Christian commemorations, rituals, festivals, and sanctoral calendars, creating a calendar that only remembered the memorable acts of the conquistador.

On the day after the taking of Tenochtitlán, the zeal of the conquistadors for making the ancient gods, temples and cults disappear became clear. The Franciscans adopted the strategy of burning native temples, knocking them down, and building the first hermitages and Christian churches on their foundations. Bernardino de Sahagún mentioned that the Franciscans chose three ancient Indian temples on which to build Christian churches: the hill of Tepeyac, where homage was paid to Tonantzin; the hill of Tlaxcala, where Toci was venerated; and a place near Popocatépetl, where Tezcatlipoca was celebrated. This policy spread throughout the territory.

Franciscans planted the Cross three times on the highest part of the pyramid of Quetzalcóatl and in 1595 built the hermitage of Nuestra Señora de los Remedios there. In Tlaxcala, the place where the temple of Xochiquetzalli had been, they built Nuestra Señora de Ocotlán, to whom the beautiful baroque church that now holds the image of the Virgin was dedicated. The policy of razing Indian churches and building Christian temples on their ruins was repeated in many places, such as the seminary of Izamal in Yucatán and the church of Teotitlán del Valle in Oaxaca, both constructed on the foundations of ancient Indian churches. In these and other cases the intention of substitution is clear. As is stated in the *Códice Franciscano*, "it seemed reasonable that where there was a particular memory and adoration of demons there should now be veneration of Jesus Christ our Redeemer and His saints."[36]

One of the most subtle instruments for erasing native memory and replacing it with Christianity was the manipulation of the calendar. Little by little the Indian festivals that celebrated the end of the dry season and the arrival of rain, the festivals of planting and harvesting of grain, the ceremonies of hunting and the gathering of fruit were all replaced with Christian celebrations. The festival dedicated to the god who protected the town was replaced by the festival of the Christian patron saint. In this manner the recollection of the ancient pre-Hispanic founding was transfigured into a remembrance of Christian evangelization.

The birth and epiphany of Christ (December 25 and January 6) replaced the ceremonies that in the Indian calendar celebrated the first movement of the sun, the beginning of the year, and the start of agricultural tasks. The great festivities of Holy Week began to replace the important Indian date that announced the arrival of rain and the beginning of the planting season. After the middle of the sixteenth century, the rituals commemorating the passion and death of Jesus Christ became the most celebrated Indian festivals. And the ceremony of Easter Sunday came to be the apotheosis of that long celebration and the most impressive group event, since most of the people in town participated.

One after another, ancient festivals were replaced by Christian ceremonies or were joined and synchronized with Catholic worship in a symbiosis that has not yet been studied with the attention that it deserves. What is certain is that by these substitutions the ancient political calendar of the indigenous people was erased and their agricultural calendar became a calendar of Christian festivals and rituals whose purpose was to make the Indians into fervent Catholics and vassals devoted to the forms of Western life.[37]

V. The First European Versions of the American World and the Origin of the Mestizo Chronicle

The clash between European invaders and indigenous peoples produced a cascade of consequences that altered the course of the following centuries. Perhaps the greatest effect of the discovery of unknown lands and the coming together of continents that had until then been separated was the birth of a society formed from divergent cultural roots. But for a long time few were interested in inquiring into the nature of this mixture and even less interested in understanding the different concepts of the past that were born and coexisted then. In intellectual circles very little attention was paid to the peculiar idea of the world of the American people, which was literally erased by the vision imposed by the conquistadors.

It is only recently that the idea has been gaining ground that the reconstruction of history by our ancestors was, in its point of view and its sources, a Western rather than an American interpretation. It was a lens that, when focused on the native reality, superimposed European values rather than listening to the original voices and recognising their way of recounting history. It was an interpretation that did not admit the existence of historical records that differed from the Western canon.

The arrival on the American coast of European arms, writing, religion, and culture involved the unusual proposition of westernizing a civilization that for centuries had been nourished by its own roots. That unbounded venture, the first that attempted the large-scale homogenization of the plural American reality, caused cultural cataclysms and successive movements of rejection, submission, acculturation, and defense against world concepts based on foreign historical traditions. Probing those confrontations and explaining the rupture of identity that occurred requires a return to the time when European concepts of the past clashed with those born in the American territory.

European Visions of the American World

In Europe the discovery of America unloosed political ambitions of continental dimensions and unleashed utopians who dreamed of building societies governed by harmony and fraternity. At the same time it encouraged projects dedicated to the rebirth of the church of the first Apostles and mystical enterprises that aspired to recreate human beings. The propagation of these ideas created an illusion of adventure through the search for new horizons that captured the imagination of the residents of the Old World. These ideas, rather than issuing from American reality, were an extension of the imaginary, born of European mentalities. They were investigations driven by circumstances that the epoch of great discoveries had inaugurated. The most widely circulated interpretations of the American world then in vogue included those that follow.

The Renaissance Idea of the New World

Even in 1492, when Christopher Columbus published a brief report on the journey that changed the dimensions of the world, he was not the messenger who made known the configuration of a continent heretofore unimagined. It was the text of a Florentine adventurer, Amérigo Vespucci, fortunately entitled *Novus mundus,* which—by clothing itself in the trappings of "a Renaissance fable, a relatively brief and simply written story"— divulged the existence of the new lands and achieved worldwide resonance. The *Novus mundus* was first published in 1507, while a new edition of Vespucci's letters was being prepared, at which time a German cartographer commissioned to illustrate them had the daring idea of baptizing the lands the Florentine described with his name: America.

Vespucci presented a glowing description of the nature of the New World and declared "that if earthly paradise is to be discovered in any part of the world, it will not be far from these lands." This image of fortunate shores was accompanied by exalted praise of its people, whom he described as living in joyous freedom, without the shackles of individual property, law, or religion. According to Vespucci, these aborigines were unaware of individual ownership of goods, since they held "everything in common. They live together without kings, without authorities, and each one is lord of himself."[1]

Pedro Mártir de Anglería (1457–1526), another Italian humanist then living in the Spanish court, helped to strengthen this paradisical image of the new lands. In 1514 Anglería published a collection of letters that gave fresh news of the New World, which he entitled *De orbe novo*. In these letters he made known information provided by Christopher Columbus and other discoverers, embellished with elegant Latin and with images taken from classical antiquity. He wrote that the natives "are nude, know neither weights nor measures, nor that source of all misfortunes, money." Anglería stated that they practiced a primitive communism, "since among them the land belongs to everyone, just as the sun and the water. They acknowledge no difference between *meun* and *tuun*, that source of evil."[2] Thus, both Vespucci and Anglería circulated an idyllic image of the land and the men and women of America, scarcely diminished by the recording of their fierce internal conflicts, their practice of cannibalism, and the atrocities committed by the invading Spaniards.[3] These and other accounts contributed to the creation of an image of America that—as brilliantly shown by Edmundo O'Gorman—was a European invention.[4]

The Vision of the First Narrators of the Conquest of Mexico

The idea of the New World as Eden was dramatically transformed by the accounts of Hernán Cortés, Bernal Díaz del Castillo, and other explorers who discovered the existence of great Indian kingdoms in the interior of the continent. These first reporters on the lands of Mexico were not men of letters, but they transmitted to the chronicles their astonishment at the splendor of the landscape, their encounters with the numerous indigenous peoples who came out to meet them, the mountainous amphitheater that surrounded the Valley of Mexico, and the resplendent city built in the middle of the lake. And above all, the writings of Hernán Cortés and Bernal Díaz del Castillo transformed the vulgar search for gold and power into an epic tale in which a handful of intrepid Europeans, beset by enormous armies, took over kingdoms until then considered invincible.

Cortés and Díaz del Castillo described their encounters with the American lands in brief, direct pictures, illuminated with clarity and simplicity. In this way the "burning of the ships" in Veracruz, the fortunate addition of Malintzin (Doña Marina) to the forces of Cortés, the entrance into the dominion of the chief Gordo at Cempoala, the battles against the Tlaxcalans and the fortuitous alliance with them, the frightful killings at Cholula, and the daring ascent to the highlands—passing between high volcanoes—were episodes that revealed the magnitude of the discovered lands and the strength of its kingdoms. With a style far removed from rhetoric, they told of the unusual meeting between Cortés and Motecuzoma (Montezuma), the amazing route of the Spaniards through the city crossed by canals, the overwhelming spectacle of the Indians' bloody temples, the tragic defeat of the "Noche triste," the saving shelter in Tlaxcala, the reorganizing of Spanish forces and the support of their Indian allies, the siege and final assault on Tenochtitlán, the terrible destruction of the city, and the imprisonment of Cuauhtémoc. As we know, these deeds came to be considered stellar moments in the conquest of Mexico,[5] episodes that the European imagination rewrote and described again and again. The deeds of Hernán Cortés, who was crowned later for the conquest of a territory larger than the known Europe, became a most famous chapter in the story of Spain's eminence.

Cortés was an amazing and careful observer of the new reality he was discovering. He was also surprised at the variety of his new surroundings and tried to record their nature precisely. Some authors saw his *Cartas de relación* as an imitation of the *Comentarios a la guerra de las Galias* of Julius Caesar. But the attitudes of the two were inspired by different purposes and styles. While Julius Caesar forever saw Gaul as a foreign land, Cortés described the Indians, their customs, and their cities with admiration and satisfaction, to such an extent that the reader can perceive how the land gradually took over the heart of the conquistador.[6]

José Luis Martínez has pointed out that "Bernal Díaz, as narrator, is somewhat more sensitive than Cortés, and some of his descriptions are memorable. He appreciates what surrounds him, especially if it is a question of obstacles or adversity . . . and he has a special delicacy, which Cortés lacks, to report environments and circumstances, as when he points out the drizzle and the fireflies on the night of Narváez' attack, or when he remembers the terrible silence after the defeat at Tenochtitlán."[7]

Cortés and Díaz del Castillo began the story of what was really lived in American literature; they made of writing a means of bringing the reader close to extraordinary moments of history, so that he might see people like himself reacting to extraordinary circumstances. In his chronicles Díaz del Castillo combined everyday deeds and timely anecdotes with dazzling events that changed the sense of history. It has been complained that his style, compared to Gómara's, was rough and unpolished. But he knew how to tell well a story that he had lived through, and he had the gift of imbuing his report with the freshness of real life.[8] Cortés's *Cartas de relación* and Díaz del Castillo's *Historia verdadera* continue to be the works that best describe the astonishment of the Europeans when they saw the native cities, and they continue to be unsurpassable stories of the conquest of Tenochtitlán.

The Version of the Official Chroniclers of the Spanish Crown

With the establishment of the post of Chronicler of the Indies (1532) and later that of Chief Chronicler and Cosmographer of the Indies (1571), the writing of the history of the American world became an exclusively Spanish function and a task reserved for the learned. Spaniards had struggled for centuries against infidels and by the beginning of the sixteenth century, by their own free will, had become the champions of the Counter-Reformation. Therefore, as would seem natural, in the discovery of the vast lands of the New World and the conquest of so many people they saw the signs of a providential venture appointed by God to His chosen people.

Almost the entire history of the discovery and conquest of the American territory is imbued with this concept, which in turn rests on the idea that the ultimate purpose of those grandiose events was the salvation of humankind under the unified control of Christianity and the Spanish monarchy. In the unexpected scenario of the sixteenth century, marked by unanticipated events, the Spanish people became the instrument of divine intentions. They were designated, through the mediation of their kings, conquistadors, and missionaries, to implant the universal Catholic monarchy in all the land until the time of the final judgment and eternal salvation. The task of historians, then, was to make known the meaning and importance of that great providential mission, which must end in the religious and political unification of the world under the Spanish Crown.

The official chroniclers of the Crown were the first to disseminate these ideas. Pedro Mártir de Anglería, official chronicler of Castile and the first narrator of the discovery of the New World, wrote in his *Décadas*: "Great praise does Spain deserve in our time, for she has made known to our people so many millions of people hidden at the far side of the world." In his turn, Gonzalo Fernández de Oviedo, author of the *Historia general y natural de las Indias* (1535–49), who wrote of American deeds in world history, interpreted the discovery and conquest of the new lands as stellar episodes in the providential plan. The fact that Spaniards were chosen to be the agents who accomplished this plan was proof for him of their alliance with God and of the inevitable advent of the world monarchy under Castile. "Just as the earth is only one," he said, "pray to Jesus Christ that likewise there be only one religion and faith and belief among all men under the brotherhood and obedience of the Apostolic Roman Church and the Supreme Pontiff and vicar and successor of the Apostle St. Paul and under the monarchy of the Emperor King Charles, our lord, under whose will and merit we may see it quickly effected."[9]

Other Spanish chroniclers announced this messianic and evangelical imperialism, but it was Francisco López de Gómara who elevated it to the level of ideology. In memorable words he stated:

The greatest thing since the creation of the world, excepting the incarnation and death of Him who created it, is the discovery of the Indies; and so they call it the New World. . . . God wished—he said to King Charles—to discover the Indies in your time to your vassals, so that you might convert them to your holy law, as many wise Christian men say. The conquests of the Indies began right after the defeat of the Moors, because Spaniards have always fought against infidels. . . . And because Spaniards found them, the Pope of his own free will and intent, with the agreement of the Cardinals, made a donation and grant to the Kings of Castile and León of all the islands and *terra firma* that they might discover in the west, provided that as they conquered them they should send preachers there to convert the Indians, who were idolaters. . . . As much land as I have spoken of our Spaniards have discovered, traveling and conquering for sixty years. *Never at any time have king or people traveled through and subjugated so much in so short a time as ours have, nor have they done or deserved as much as they have, in arms and navigation as well as in the preaching of the Holy Gospel and the conversion of idolators. Therefore are the Spanish most worthy of praise throughout the world. Blessed be God who gave them so much grace and power!*[10]

When it acquired institutional rank, the post of Chief Chronicler and Cosmographer of the Indies established a canon for narrating events in the New World that the successive reporters of American history perpetuated. Supported by the power of the monarch and by the institutional character of their position, the Chroniclers of the Indies established the bases for the orderly accumulation of historical knowledge. Royal decree stipulated that all reports and descriptions of the Spanish possessions in America should be gathered in the department and archives of the Council of the Indies. The chroniclers enjoyed the benefits of this privileged information and, following the model of Greek and Roman historians, established the obligation of documenting the deeds that they reported. After the creation of the position of chronicler, historical narration became an exercise for the educated, monopolized by literary professionals and subject to the rules of their guild.[11]

The Chroniclers of the Indies introduced models from classical antiquity and the Renaissance into the American narrations and elevated historical work to the level of the educated man. They instituted the fashion of inserting erudite citings, composing voluminous books, and writing in an affected style. Between the end of the sixteenth century and the beginning of the nineteenth, the Chroniclers of the Indies were almost always men of letters who wrote American history from Spain, using European concepts. As shown in table 2, their work emphasized the exalting of the actions of Spaniards in America. In their pages the native Americans were almost never considered the subjects of history. This was a historiography whose purpose was to immortalize the deeds of the Spanish people.

Table 2. Principal Official Chroniclers of the Indies, 16th–18th Centuries

Name	Nationality	Title of Work
Alonso de Santa Cruz (1505–67)	Spanish	*Libro de las longitudes y manera que hasta ahora se ha tenido en el arte de navegar: con sus demonstraciones y ejemplos/dirigido al muy alto y muy poderoso Señor Don Philipe II de este nombre rey de España por Alonso de Santa Cruz, su cosmógrafo mayor*
Juan López de Velasco (1530–1603)	Spanish	*Geografía y descripción universal de las indias, 1574*
Antonio de Herrera y Tordesillas (1549–1625)	Spanish	*Historia general de los hechos de los castellanos en las islas y tierra firme del mar océano, 1601–15*
Luis Tribaldos de Toledo (1558–1634)	Spanish	*Vista general de las continuadas guerras y difícil conquista del gran reino y provincia de Chile, 1635*
Tomás Tamayo de Vargas (1588–1641)	Spanish	*Restauración de la ciudad del Salvador, Bahía de todos los Santos, Madrid, 1628*
Gil González Dávila (1570–1658)	Spanish	*Teatro eclesiástico de la primitiva iglesia de las Indias, 1649*
Antonio de León Pinelo (1596–1660)	Spanish	*Epítome de la Biblioteca Oriental y Occidental, Náutica y Geográfica, Madrid, 1629*
Antonio de Solís y Rivadeneyra (1610–86)	Spanish	*Historia de la conquista de Méjico, población y progreso de la América Septentrional conocida con el nombre de Nueva España, 1684*
Pedro Fernández del Pulgar (1621–98)	Spanish	*Historia verdadera de la conquista de la Nueva España por Don Fernando Cortés, ca. 1690*
Luis de Salazar y Castro (?–1734)	Spanish	No publication
Miguel Herrero Ezpeleta (?–1750)	Spanish	No publication
Juan Bautista Muñoz (1745–?)	Spanish	*Historia del Nuevo Mundo, 1793*

Source: Data from Rómulo D. Carbia, *La crónica oficial de las Indias Occidentales* (Ediciones Buenos Aires, 1940); and Francisco Esteve Barba, *Historiografía indiana* (Ed. Gredos, 1992).

Later on, the Chronicler of the Indies came to be the only author entitled to write the general histories of the Spanish domains in America and the only one to receive American reports solicited by the Crown or submitted by overseas officials. Still later, the viceroys, the religious orders, and the capitals of the kingdoms had their own official chroniclers, so that the writing of history became more a function of political and administrative management of the leadership levels of colonial society. History was written not to provide information about an unknown world but to define territories and possessions, legitimize rights, and affirm the boasts of those in charge.

The submission of the chroniclers to these political demands affected the quality and plurality of historical discourse. Nothing expressed that submission better than the writing of history itself. While the chronicles of the sixteenth century excelled because of their vitality and inventiveness, those of the seventeenth and eighteenth were drowning in rhetoric and dedicated to compilation rather than creation. The only one of the numerous chronicles of that time which stands out is that of Antonio de Solís, *Historia de la conquista de México,* whose elegant style demonstrated its superiority over the pompous and bombastic writing of other chroniclers.[12]

The Interpretation of the Evangelizing Friars

In contrast to the contemporary news of the first narrators (Christopher Columbus, Pedro Mártir de Anglería), the stories on the merits of the conquistadors (Hernán Cortés, Bernal Díaz del Castillo), or the weighty compilations of the official chroniclers, we owe to friars the careful rescue of the ancient history of the native people and the effort to join that original process to the Christian concept of history.

The perspective of the past centuries permits us to say that it was to the credit of the friars that they designed an innovative method, one that we would now call historical-ethnographic, for recovering the past and investigating the customs and traditions of the American people. Driven by their evangelizing mission, they decided to go back in time and study the pagan traditions in order to better eradicate them and sow in their place the Christian faith. Bernardino de Sahagún, the eminent compiler of the Indian past, explains this plainly in the following text:

> A doctor cannot correctly apply medicine to the patient without first knowing from what . . . source the illness comes, so that a good doctor must know both medicines and sicknesses, so as to be able to apply to each sickness the medicine indicated. Preachers and confessors are the doctors of the soul; to cure spiritual illnesses one must have . . . [knowledge] of spiritual medicines and sicknesses . . . the sins of idolatry . . . and idolatrous superstitions and auguries and deceits and idolatrous ceremonies . . . [of the natives of New Spain]. In order to preach against these things, and even to know if they exist, it is necessary to know how they used them in the time of their idolatry, since if we do now know this they can do a number of idolatrous things without our understanding them. . . . So that the ministers of the Gospel who follow those who first came to cultivate this vineyard of the Lord may have no occasion to complain of the first for having left in the dark the things of these natives of New Spain, I, Fray Bernardino de Sahagún . . . have written twelve books on the divine, or better said, idolatrous things, as well as human and natural things of this New Spain.[13]

Guided by these principles, the Franciscans began an enormous recovery of Indian traditions based on the information given them by the natives themselves. Toribio de Benavente, who took the Indian nickname Motolinía (the Poor Man), was one of the first to trust the wisdom of the natives in writing his chronicles. He learned to read the ancient codices and systems for recording time, bringing together the oldest and wisest men to help him decipher that writing and to hear from their lips the songs that had been transmitted orally from time immemorial. In this manner he wrote a first historical description of the indigenous past, a considerable portion of which has fortunately survived.[14]

The idea of making use of the painted books and the Mesoamerican oral tradition to guide the actions of the conquistadors was a method imposed since the first days of the European invasion. Hernán Cortés began to use it when he noted that in the painted books there were maps that clearly indicated the regions rich in gold and pearls, the towns where tribute was collected, and the best routes for reaching those places. And when he was fortunate enough to meet Malintzin, he was able to fully appreciate her knowledge, accumulated and passed on by members of the Indian nobility. But it was the mendicant friars who converted those rudimentary forms of information into refined artifacts for penetrating the depths of the native culture.

The distinguished *Historia de la literatura náhuatl* was the first modern work that made known the richness of the literary, linguistic, and historical treasures of the native world, which were spread among a great number of texts, archives, and libraries. In this work Father Angel María Garibay recognized—in the writings of Andrés de Olmos, Juan de Tovar, and Motolinía—the embryo of the ethnographic and historical method that allowed the friars to recognize the foundations and the breadth of Mesoamerican culture.[15] To praise the antiquity and virtues of that method, Garibay cited the testimony of Fray Jerónimo de Mendieta, which stated:

> It is known that in the year 1533, while D. Sebastián Ramírez de Fuenleal was president of the Royal High Court of Mexico . . . Fr. Andrés de Olmos was charged with publishing in a book the antiquities of these native Indians, especially those of Mexico, Texcuco and Tlaxcala, so that there might be some memory of them. . . . And the aforementioned father did so *after having seen all the paintings that the chiefs and principals of these provinces had among their relics, and having gotten from the oldest among*

them answers to all the questions that he put to them, he made of all that a very ample book, and of it they made three or four copies which were sent to Spain. . . . And I, who write this, having some desire to know about these relics, many years ago met with Fr. Andrés as the spring from which all the streams of information on this material have flowed.[16]

Fray Diego Durán, a Dominican who lived in Texcoco from the age of five, faithfully followed the method developed by his Franciscan predecessors Andrés de Olmos, Juan de Tovar, and Motolinía. Durán wrote a book that is essential to an understanding of ancient Mexico, the *Historia de las Indias de Nueva España,* which is based on pictographic codices and oral tradition.[17] On many pages of his book he mentioned a painted "history," a "Mexican history," a "Narration of Cuyuacan," and a narration of Atzcapotzalco as his principal sources. At other times, when he had doubts about what one of those sources said, he compared it with another, seeking new evidence and making fun of the historian who was obsessed with "reliable" versions. He combined this information with interviews with elderly Indians and members of the ancient nobility who maintained the memory of their lineages and with Spaniards who had taken part in the conquest of the land.[18]

In another region, very different from the Mexican highlands, Fray Diego de Landa, author of the famous *Relación de las cosas de Yucatán,* likewise based his report on the ancient Mayan codices and on information given him by the Indian priests and descendents of the native nobility. Landa was the archetypal friar solidly brought up in the medieval scholastic tradition who, when faced with the deeply rooted idolatrous practices of the natives, became an implacable persecutor of those traditions. But at the same time, just like Motolinía and Sahagún, when he delved deeper into the native culture he ended up admiring that foreign world. His work, as recognized by J. Eric Thompson, is the most important source on ancient Maya civilization:

It is a mine of information about the customs, religious beliefs and history, which also contains a detailed explanation of the Mayan calendar, illustrated with drawings of the glyphs. This book was the irreplaceable foundation from which Mayan hiero-glyphic writing has been reconstructed [fig. 67]. It has thus come to be the closest thing to a Rosetta stone for that culture. . . . And certainly, without this book it is doubtful that we would have been able to take any steps in the deciphering of the glyphs, and we would know much less about the Mayas. . . . Landa, like any modern ethnologist, got his material from native informants.[19]

Sahagún and the Birth of the Mestizo Chronicle

There were other friars in different regions of New Spain who used codices and oral traditions to reconstruct the indigenous past (table 3). But it was the Franciscan Bernardino de Sahagún (1499–1590) who made of the collection of ancient pictographs and the interrogation of the native wise men a refined art and an indispensable instrument for historical investigation. A prime difference between Sahagún's procedure and the method adopted by his predecessors was the elaboration of a questionnaire that included specific questions to be answered by Indian respondents. He called this catalog of questions "a remembrance of all the materials that needed to be dealt with." With this questionnaire he began his ambitious inquiry, aimed at collecting information on the history, languages, customs, and religion of the ancient Mexicans. This investigation, which later took on inordinate pro-portions, began in a simple manner in the town of Tepepulco in 1559 and lasted until 1561. The Franciscan reported that when he reached this town he proceeded in the following manner:

In this town I called together all of the principal people along with the head man of the town, who was named don Diego de Mendoza. . . . When they were all there I told them what I was wanting to do and asked them to give me able and experienced

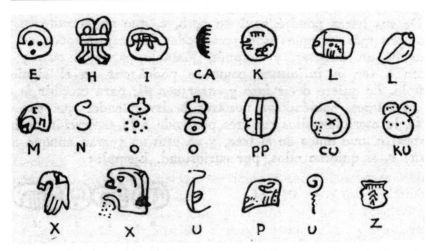

Fig. 67. The Mayan "alphabet" according to the interpretation of Diego de Lando in the *Relación de las cosas de Yucatán*. (Photo from Landa, 1959: 106.)

people with whom I might speak and who would know how to give me information on what I would ask them. . . . Another day the head man came to me with his principal people, and after a very solemn speech, as they were accustomed to giving, he pointed out to me ten to twelve of the elder principal men and told me that I might talk with them and they would give me information on whatever I might ask them. There were among them four Latin speakers to whom I a few years earlier had taught grammar at the Santa Cruz school in Tlatelolco.[20]

As is indicated, Sahagún's first precaution was to reach the informants who were best aware of the ancient traditions. In Tepepulco he also received the support of four Latin speakers, his old Indian students who had learned Latin in school at Tlatelolco. Later he was commissioned to the seminary of Santiago de Tlatelolco, and there he took his papers and continued his survey, assisted now by eight to ten wise men, "very capable in their language and in the things of their relics, with them and with four or five colleagues, all trilingual, for the space of a year

Table 3. Principal Religious Chroniclers of the Ancient History of New Spain

Name	Order	Area Covered	Title of Work
Diego Basalenque (1577?–1651)	Augustinian	Michoacán (1535–1644)	*Historia de la Provincia de San Nicolás Tolentino de Michoacán del orden de N.P.S. Augstín,* 1673
Pablo de la Purísima Concepción Beaumont (1710–80)	Franciscan	Western and northern Mexico and Michoacán (18th century)	*Crónica de la Provincia por Antonomasia Apostólica de los gloriosos apóstoles San Pedro y San Pablo de Michoacán,* ca. 1775
Toribio de Benavente (1482/91–1568)	Franciscan	New Spain, central México (1523–40)	*Historia de los indios de la Nueva España,* 1540. *Memoriales*
Francisco de Burgoa (1605–81)	Dominican	Oaxaca (1526–1650)	*Palestra historial de virtudes y exemplares apostólicos fundada del zelo de insignes héroes de la Sagrada Orden de Predicadores en este Nuevo Mundo de la América en las Indias Occidentales,* 1670. *Geográfica descripción de la parte septentrional del Polo Artico . . . y sitio de esta Provincia de Predicadores de Antequera, Valle de Oaxaca,* 1674
Francisco Javier Clavijero (1731–87)	Jesuit	New Spain, Baja California	*Historia antigua de México,* 1780–81. *Storia antica della California,* 1789
Diego López de Cogolludo (1610–86)	Franciscan	Yucatán (1640–56)	*Historia de Yucatán,* 1688
Agustín Dávila Padilla (1562-1604)	Dominican	Central México, New Spain (1526–92)	*Historia de la fundaceón y discurso de la Provincia de Santiago de México de la Orden de Predicadores por las vidas de sus varones insignes y casos notables de Nueva España,* 1596
Francisco Jiménez (1666–1729)	Dominican	Guatemala and Chiapas (from the time before Cortés to 1719)	*Historia de la Provincia de San Vicente de Chiapa y Guatemala de la Orden de Predicadores,* ca. 1721
Diego de Landa (1524–79)	Franciscan	Yucatán (from the time before Cortés to 1560)	*Relación de las Cosas de Yucatán,* 1566
Bernardo de Lizana (1581–1631)	Franciscan	Yucatán (from the time before Cortés to 1630)	*Historia de Yucatán,* 1633
Jerónimo de Mendieta (1528–1604)	Franciscan	New Spain, central Mexico (1510–96)	*Historia eclesiástica indiana,* ca. 1596
Alonso de la Rea (1610–16?)	Franciscan	Michoacán, Jalisco (from the time before Cortés to 1640)	*Crónica de la Orden de N. Seráfico P.S. San Francisco, Provincia de San Pedro y San Pablo de Michoacán en la Nueva España,* 1639
Bernardino de Sahagún (1499–1590)	Franciscan	Central Mexico (Aztec ethnography and Náhuatl language)	*Historia General de las Cosas de Nueva España,* 1547–70
Juan de Torquemada (1564–1624)	Franciscan	New Spain	*Monarquía indiana,* 1615
Agustín de Vetancurt (1620–ca. 1700)	Franciscan	Central Mexico, New Spain	*Teatro mexicano. Descripción breve de los sucesos ejemplares, históricos, políticos, militares y religiosos del Nuevo Mundo de las Indias,* 1698

Source: Data from Ernest J. Burrus SJ. "Religious Chroniclers and Historians. A Summary with Annotated Bibliography," in *Handbook of Middle American Indians (Guide to Ethnohistorical Sources,* vol. 12 (University of Texas Press, 1973), 138–85.

and somewhat more, closed up at the school, we amended, restated, and added to all that I had brought in writing from Tepepulco, and the whole thing was written again, in very poor penmanship because it was written in great haste."[21]

The information gathered in Tepepulco and Tlatelolco (1561–65) was compiled in the so-called *Primeros memoriales* (fig. 68) and in the collected documents known by the name of *Códice matritense de la Real Academia de la Historia* and *Códice matritense del Real Palacio*.[22] Sahagún was later transferred to the San Francisco seminary in the city of Mexico (1565–68), and there he revised and finished a third reordering and correction of his materials, which he himself described:

> For the space of three years I reviewed my writings again and again by myself, and I edited them again and divided them into books, into twelve books, and each book into chapters, and some books in chapter and paragraphs . . . and the Mexicans added and edited many things in the twelve books . . . so that the first sieve through which my works were sifted were those of Tepepulco; the second, those of Tlatilulco; the third, those of Mexico, and taking part in all of these scrutinies were collegial grammarians.[23]

This task lasted for more then twenty years, from 1559 until 1580, and took up most of Sahagún's energy. As can be seen, his effort was doubled. First, he worked hard to define the items in his questionnaire and to order the responses that the Indian wise men gave him. Next, he dedicated himself to revising, correcting, and occasionally soliciting new material in Náhuatl, until he had a text that satisfied him. He later added a partial translation of those materials from Náhuatl to Spanish, an effort that culminated in the best known of his works, *Historia general de las cosas de Nueva España*, whose first edition, suppressed and censored on a number of occasions, did not appear until 1829–30. Researchers of this monumental encyclopedia of Náhuatl culture observed

Fig. 68. Folio 252v of the *Códice matritense del Real Palacio de Madrid.* In these *Primeros memoriales* Sahagún ordered the text written in Náhuatl on the left, with the paintings to the right. (Photo from Sahagún, 1993.)

that in its composition there was "present a scholastic and medieval hierarchy, adapted, of course, to the religion and customs of the ancient inhabitants of New Spain."[24] In accordance with this medieval ordering, Sahagún began first with the gods, continued with heaven and hell, then with the terrestrial reign, and ended with a narration of human and natural matters. Nevertheless, Sahagún's work did not fit into the rigid classical or medieval pattern, for in the *Historia general* he included a story of the conquest of Mexico told by his collaborators from Tlatelolco as well as something that was completely new: the extraordinary collection of pictographs reproducing the ancient Indian forms of recording the past.

The *Historia general de las cosas de Nueva España* is composed of three parts, which suffered a variety of fortunes in their later printings and appreciation. The part called the *Códice florentino,* considered by critics to be the most complete original manuscript,

Fig. 69. The god Quetzalcóatl on a page of the *Códice florentino*.

included the Náhuatl text, a Spanish version of that text, and a collection of more than 1,850 illustrations (fig. 69). The first version of the Náhuatl text was written in 1559–61 and was the object of later revisions and modifications until 1569, the year in which Sahagún made a clean copy divided into twelve books. The Spanish translation of this text, finished in 1579–80, was the most widely circulated in the nineteenth and twentieth centuries. Alfredo López Austin and Josefina García Quintana have recently published the best paleographic version of that text.[25] The entire set of the *Códice florentino* was not published until 1979, in a magnificent facsimile edition.[26] This edition made available for the first time the color photographs of the extraordinary collection of illustrations that Sahagún insisted should accompany the bilingual text, which are a demonstration of the traditional way in which the Náhuatl-speaking people recorded and recounted their history.

We can see then that the *Códice florentino* is a type of palimpsest, an ancient manuscript that holds traces of three different versions of the Nahua past. The first version was the work of Sahagún and was in Spanish. As Father Garibay has stated, if only this version "had remained, we would still have an enduring monument of a beauty and scientific value unlike anything in the history of American culture." But as we have seen, the Franciscan was ahead of his time, and like an *avant la lettre* ethnographer, asked the natives to write their own version of history. "He arranged," as Father Garibay has said, "for the old Indians to dictate and communicate information; he had young Indians, already trained up in the western manner, to write information in their original languages and to collect from the lips of the old ones the dying ancient wisdom. And zealous about his data, he had it copied and recopied."[27] And to all this he added the formidable collection of illustrations, which prolonged the ancient pictographic tradition of Mesoamerica in the Colonial Period.

The originality of the history conserved in the *Códice florentino* lies in the three interpretations of the past that coexist within it. On one side is the Spanish text, which—along with the encyclopedic design of the book—is entirely the work of Sahagún, a product of his intellectual training and of his singular manner of seeing the native American. Sahagún had studied at the University of Salamanca and around 1516 had joined the Order of St. Francis. He had a solid religious education and had been raised in the medieval culture, a tradition that combined readings by the church fathers with readings by Greek and Roman authors. From this upbringing and from his unexpected encounter with the Nahua culture came the unusual project of collecting within a book a complete picture of the Indian world being threatened with destruction. In 1558 the Provincial of the order, Fray Francisco Toral, asked Sahagún, who was already recognized as an expert in the Náhuatl language, to write in that language whatever he considered useful "for the certain increase of Christianity among the natives and to help the ministers who are charged with their teaching." Sahagún himself wrote: "I was required by holy obedience to my lead prelate to write something in the Mexican language which seemed to me would be useful for the doctrine, culture, and the maintenance of Christianity of these natives of New Spain and to help the workers and ministers who are teaching them."[28]

But during the time that he was preparing this work, Sahagún changed its objectives. Books I to III are the most complete treatise that we have on the religion and gods of the Mexican pantheon, including a rich description of their calendars of festivals and a sample of their ritual hymns as well as the famous saga of the rise and fall of Ce Ácatl Topiltzin Quetzalcóatl in the legendary city of Tula (fig. 69). Books IV and V are concerned with astrology and auguries (fig. 70). Book VI, one of the most innovative, which Sahagún considered a summation of the rhetorical and moral philosophy of the Mexicans, is a collection of prayers, exhortations, and metaphors that demonstrate the excellence of the Náhuatl language. This book contains a selection of songs of praise to the gods and speeches that were made on solemn occasions, such as the election of a new lord or the admonishment of sons and daughters (figs. 71 and 72). Book VII records the myth of the Fifth Sun and the festivals that celebrated the fifty-two-year cycle. Book VIII is a story that reconstructs the history of the kingdoms and governors of Tenochtitlán, Tlatelolco, Texcoco, and Huexutla (fig. 73). Book IX extensively treats the customs and businesses of the merchants (fig. 74). Book X contains a detailed descripion of the men and women of Mexico, their social differences and variety of occupations, and their vices and virtues and expands on the classification of their sicknesses and remedies (figs. 75–76). In Book XI Sahagún includes a surprising treatise on natural history, which he entitled "Forests, Gardens, Orchards in the Mexican Tongue." Here there is a detailed description of the fauna of the Valley of Mexico as well as the flora, minerals, waters, and quality of land (figs. 77–78). Finally, Book XII contains the extraordinary story of the conquest of Mexico elaborated by informants from Tlatelolco, which synthesized the vision of the conquered in dramatic form. At last, as Sahagún himself declares in his expressive language:

This work is like a trawling net, bringing to light all the words of this language with their personal and metaphorical meanings and all their manners of speech, and most of their good and bad relics. It is to redeem a thousand grey hairs, because with considerably less effort than this has cost me, those who wish to can learn in a short time much about the relics and language of these Mexican people. This work will take advantage of the opportunity to know the value of these Mexican people, which is not yet known because on them has fallen that curse that Jeremiah . . . called down on Judea and Jerusalem when he said in Chapter 5: "I am going to bring upon you . . . a nation from far away. It is an enduring nation, it is an ancient nation, a nation whose language you do not know, nor can you understand what they say, all of them are mighty warriors. They shall destroy your sons and daughters and all you possess, and destroy your fortified cities and buildings." This to the letter has happened to these Indians because of the Spaniards.[29]

The second version of this history, the one to which the natives made a direct contribution, is written in Náhuatl using the Latin alphabet. In order to evaluate its true value, it is necessary to have a complete translation of it into Spanish, which Sahagún did not provide and which no expert in the Náhuatl language has undertaken so far. But even without that translation, this part is a treasure of the language and traditions of the Nahua world, the greatest repository of the language of that time and an invaluable testimony to the transformation that native societies were living through in the second half of the sixteenth century. It is above all a valuable testimony to the native mentality, its unusual ways of recording and transmitting the past, and its reactions and accommodations to the European invasions, as it must be remembered that it was written when scarcely three decades had passed since the fall of Tenochtitlán. That is to say, the text written in Náhuatl is a direct expression of the culture and mentality of the Mexicans and not of Sahagún.

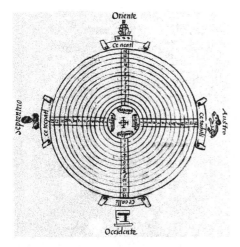

Fig. 70. The Aztec calendar wheel, *Códice florentino.*

Fig. 71. Speech of Tlatoani at the time he assumed the throne, *Códice florentino.*

Fig. 72. Warning from parents to their children, *Códice florentino.*

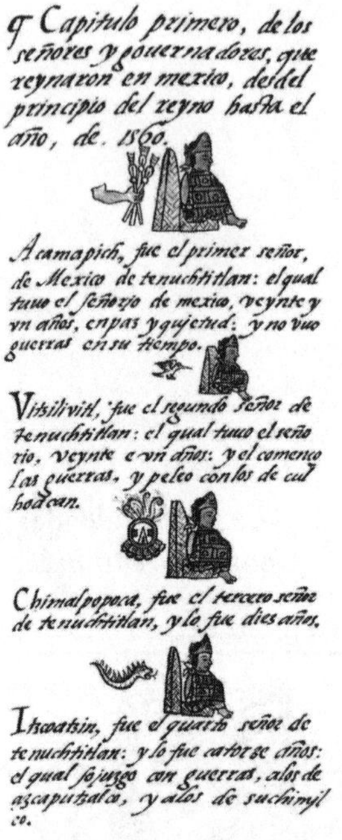

¶ Capitulo primero, de los
señores y gouernadores, que
reynaron en mexico, desdel
principio del reyno hasta el
año, de. 1560.

Acamapich, fue el primer señor,
de Mexico de tenuchtitlan: el qual
tuuo el señorio de mexia, veynte y
vn años, en paz y quietud: y no vuo
guerras en su tiempo.

Vitsilivitl, fue el segundo señor de
tenuchtitlan: el qual tuuo el seño
rio, veynte e vn años: y el començo
las guerras, y peleo con los de cul
hoacan.

Chimalpopoca, fue el tercero señor
de tenuchtitlan, y lo fue dies años.

Itzcoatzin, fue el quarto señor de
tenuchtitlan: y lo fue catorse años:
el qual se junto con guerra, alos de
azcaputzalco, y alos de suchimyl
co.

Fig. 73. Page from the *Códice
florentino* that describes the series of
governors of México-Tenochtitlán.

Fig. 74. Description of the
activities of merchants,
Códice florentino.

Fig. 75. The role of healers, *Códice florentino.*

Fig. 76. The Chichimecs, *Códice florentino.*

Fig. 77. Different kinds of hummingbirds in the *Códice florentino.*

Fig. 78. One type of plumed serpent in the *Códice florentino.*

One of the most important attributes of the *Códice florentino* is its gathering of the most intimate traditions of the Nahua people regarding their origins, concept of the world, and moral values. These texts, as Sahagún himself emphasizes when he refers to the Indian paternity of the *huehuetlatolli* [discourses of the elders], are the work of Nahua people, "because what is written in this book would not fit into the understanding of humankind to make up, nor could any living man make up the language in which it appears. And all informed Indians, if they were asked, would affirm that this language is the language of their ancestors, and these are the works that they made."[30]

They are texts that transmitted an interpretation of the past suitable to Mesoamerican thought, as can be appreciated in Book XII of the *Códice florentino,* which tells the dramatic episode of the conquest of Tenochtitlán. Just as the moral philosophy expressed in the songs and discourses included in Book VI establishes a tension with Western values, so the story of the conquest as told by the wise men of Tlatelolco creates an inevitable tension with the Spanish versions of that same event. This is one of the notable features of the *Códice florentino*: the inclusion of two or more interpretations of the same event; the coexistence of the native concept of the past alongside the Western interpretation. In the story of the conquest of Mexico contained in this work, the reader can live the drama of the defeated as they tell of their vanquishment and also feel the tension of the Indian writer when he tries to explain that ill-fated event within the ancient categories that had served to report the astounding dislocation of the historic passage of time.

The authors of the story of the conquest began the narration of that never-imagined event with omens, a typical native artifice for dealing with the unexpected.[31] Just as they had recorded in their ancient annals that the destruction of the legendary Tollan-Teotihuacán was preceded by a series of evil signs and the destruction of Tula and of Ce Ácatl Topiltzin Quetzalcóatl had been foretold by baneful auguries, so also the tragic loss of Tenochtitlán

Fig. 79. The landing of the Spaniards on the coast of Veracruz, *Códice florentino.*

was anticipated by malign omens. Further on, the text emphasizes a description of the astonishment caused among the native people by the arrival of foreign people in floating houses (fig. 79) and a narration of the comings and goings of the runners who carried news to the distressed lord of Mexico.

The Indian story of the conquest did not follow the ancient mold of the annals, for it adopted the European form of the chronicles of events (res gestae). The story is centered on the *altépetl,* the city, from the point of view of the leaders of Tlatelolco. In contrast to the European chronicle, which lauds the heroic acts of individuals and particularly those of Hernán Cortés, the indigenous story praises the defenders of the city. When it extols individual actions, it is because they constituted a defense of the community represented by the city. And it maintains an unmistakable native flavor. Thus, Hernán Cortés is transfigured as Ce Ácatl Topiltzin Quetzalcóatl, the mythic founder of the native dynasties, the dethroned governor who promised to return and regain his kingdom. That same theme impregnates the story recounting the terror that the arrival of the Europeans on the coast awoke in Motecuzoma (figs. 80 and 81), the dispatch of gifts to placate the

Fig. 80. Motecuzona is informed of the arrival of the Spaniards on the coast of Veracruz, *Códice florentino.*

Fig. 81. The deployment of the forces of Hernán Cortés, *Códice florentino.*

supposed gods, and the description of their physiognomies: "how they had white faces and blue eyes, and red hair and long beards, and how some black men were among them who had curly, dark hair." Or the story of how they came together for war: "they came in great numbers, in squadrons with great noise and great dust clouds, and from afar their arms shone and caused great fear among those who looked upon them. They were also very much afraid of the war dogs they brought with them, which were very large. They had their mouths open, their tongues out, and they were panting. This caused great terror among all who saw them" (figs. 82 and 83).[32]

This story, then, offers the native vision of the conquest. It describes the anguish that overcame Motecuzoma's spirit, his

Fig. 82. Battle preparations of Hernán Cortés for the conquest of México. Here he heads the expedition, accompanied by Malintzin and a black man. (Photo from the *Códice Azcatitlán,* 1995.)

Fig. 83. The passage of the army of Cortés between the volcanoes, with the smoking Popocatépetl on the right, *Códice florentino.*

dramatic encounter with Hernán Cortés (fig. 84), the massacre of the Mexican nobles on the grounds of the Main Temple, the Indian uprising, and the chronicle of the Spanish defeat, when Cortés and his army fled the city on the Tlacopan roadway (fig. 85). An extraordinary series of images illustrates the imprisonment, death, and cremation of Motecuzoma (figs. 86 and 87). The narration of the *tlacuilos,* or scribes, is a unique document that

155

Fig. 84. The meeting between Cortés (left) and Motecuzoma, with Malinche translating for both, *Códice florentino.*

integrates the Indian quality of detailed recording of events with European narrative techniques. Its high points are the description of the siege of Tenochtitlán by the forces of Cortés and his Indian allies (figs. 88–90), the building of the brigantines that decided the battle on the lake, and the dramatic episodes that ended with the imprisonment of Cuauhtémoc and the loss of the city (fig. 91) in a passage of overwhelming desolation and psychic devastation.[33]

Perhaps it is the third version of history in the *Códice florentino* that has been the most widely ignored and the least understood. This is the rich collection of illustrations that Sahagún particularly charged the native scribes with producing. The limited interest it has merited can perhaps be explained by the fact that the first editions of the *Historia general de las cosas de Nueva España* did not include the iconographic material and the later ones gave only a partial idea of their richness. So only with the 1979 facsimile edition of the *Códice florentino* did anyone have an idea of the volume and importance of the graphic material amassed in that work. The earliest studies based on that edition revealed the sur-

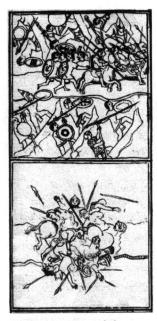

Fig. 85. Scenes of the defeat of the Spaniards in the battle of the "Sad Night," *Códice florentino.*

Fig. 86. Capture of Motecuzoma, *Códice florentino.*

prising abundance of graphic material that it included. Eloise Quiñones Keber has found that the *Primeros memoriales* included 544 illustrations and the *Códice florentino* the astonishing total of 1,852. Quiñones has observed that those images were perfectly integrated into the text and for that reason it could be concluded that the elaboration of that material was of special importance to Sahagún.[34] He himself stated that the reports he received from the native wise men were given in the form of paintings: "All the things that we conferred about they gave me as paintings, for that was the writing that they once used."[35]

We know that even before Sahagún, Olmos, Tovar, and Motolinía had recognized the importance of the native pictographs and collected them, made an effort to conserve them, and used them in the composition of their works. But among Europeans interested

Fig. 88. The Spaniards and their Indian allies prepare to attack Tenochtitlán, *Códice florentino.*

Fig. 87. Transfer and burning of the body of Motecuzoma, *Códice florentino.*

Fig. 89. The Spanish army and their allies attack the defenses of Tenochtitlán by land, *Códice florentino.*

Fig. 90. Scenes of the land attack on Tenochtitlán, *Códice florentino.*

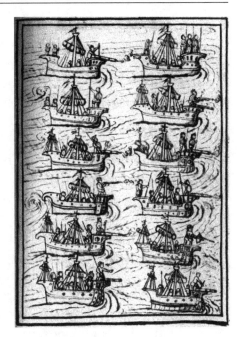

Fig. 91. The well-known twelve brigantines take up their positions on the lake to attack Tenochtitlán, *Códice florentino.*

in investigating the history of Indians, Sahagún was the first to assign special significance to the pictographs and to include them in his own work on a large scale. As Quiñones has observed, the corpus of images collected by Sahagún is unrivaled among the pictographic works produced in the sixteenth century.[36]

The images that fill the *Códice florentino* tell in plastic form a story different from those told in the Náhuatl and Spanish texts. It is true that they follow the model of the ancient pictographs, whose objective was to represent with a figure the central event that needed to be fixed in memory, which was then explained orally to a larger listening audience. Nonetheless, in the Colonial environment in which the *Códice florentino* was written, images no longer had that primitive force and appeared more like illustrations of the text. We even know that the text was written first and then the images were painted, an unthinkable procedure in pre-Hispanic antiquity.[37] It can also be seen that these paintings are of lower quality than those printed on the ancient codices.

According to the experts, this is due to the images' already having been contaminated by European iconographic traditions such as shading and perspective. The native scribes used European pens, inks, and papers to compose their images and the text.[38] In several images the scribes betrayed a high level of Westernization, as when they painted landscapes or urban scenes that seem to have been copied from European engravings.

In addition to incorporating European techniques, the *Códice florentino* introduced themes foreign to the native tradition. As will be remembered, the central events of pre-Hispanic codices were the creation of the cosmos, the origin of human beings, the founding of the kingdom, and the chronicles of the deeds accomplished by the leaders. On the other hand, in the pictures requested by Sahagún, the images that predominate are dedicated to the representation of daily life: ordinary women and men (*maceuales*), children, and artesans as well as the simple tasks of farmers and work of all kinds, from the most refined to the most humble (figs. 92 and 93).[39]

Therefore, on noting that a history narrated by the natives in the Náhuatl language, a version by Bernardino de Sahagún written in Spanish, and a story told in images by Indian scribes with their own techniques mixed with those of Europeans coexist in the same work, we realize that the *Códice florentino* is a hybrid text, the most magnificent Mestizo chronicle written in New Spain and one of the most original books human ingenuity has ever produced.

The *Códice florentino* is the discovery of a strange civilization by a particularly understanding mind. So strange and attractive did that culture seem to the European observer that little by little it seduced him and led him to construct an image driven by his interest in capturing its substantive legacy. From its beginnings, this project was a mixture of two cultures, shot through with the tension of the two opposite poles that nourished it. Sahagún learned the Náhuatl language and in this particular way came to know one of the most ancient indigenous cultures of Mesoamerica. And to hold the riches of that civilization, he was not able to find

Fig. 92. Women talking, *Códice florentino.*

Fig. 93. Bathing the children, *Códice florentino.*

a better vessel than the encyclopedic format designed by Pliny and by the medieval compilers of ancient knowledge. The questionnaire that he distributed in the hope of penetrating into Nahua thought was also a Western artifact, as were his categories of classifying things as divine, human, and natural and the entire theoretical and technical skeleton that supported his investigation.

The *Códice florentino* was born for the purpose of showing the preaching friars the nature of indigenous cultures. But the excitement that an understanding of the values that sustained that culture produced in Sahagún soon caused him to leave that goal behind. The admiration that Indian cultures awakened in him inspired him to collect so much new information about their origins, forms of government, education, philosophy, and moral principles, his project took on such dimensions, that there is not a similar example in Western history.

Thus, the compulsion to propagate the Christian faith forced the friars to investigate native traditions, and in turn the understanding of that legacy sharpened the fathers' interest in it and led them to fall in love with it. This contradiction is true of the works of Sahagún. But unlike Andrés de Olmos, Juan de Tovar, Motolinía, or Diego Durán, who also felt compelled to study the intimate substrata of the native culture, Sahagún recognized that he was not capable of interpreting that strange world by himself. Since his arrival in the country, he had been trained by Indians expert in the ancient traditions, so that in contrast to the chroniclers who had preceded him, he came to the conclusion that the Indians themselves should tell their own history, since no one could know it better.

In Tepepulco, in Tlatelolco, in the city of Mexico, and wherever he went to work, Sahagún brought together the Indians who possessed the ancient wisdom, established a dialogue with them, explained the things he wanted to learn, and gave them paper, paints, and the techniques with which to capture their responses, both in Náhuatl written with the Latin alphabet and in their ancient pictographs. And he listened. He received new information about matters of which he was ignorant, he was astonished at the metaphoric richness of the Náhuatl language, and he was surprised to see how the natives unfolded their codices and made clear to him events that he had not known of or had not been able to understand.

The concurrence of two divergent cultures was the force animating this work. Based on information given to him by his informants, Sahagún wrote his great encyclopedia of the ancient native culture in Spanish, from his Western perspective. But he did not superimpose his voice on that of the native storytellers, since they expressed their own interpretations in Náhuatl and through their pictures. As Tzvetan Todorov has indicated, Sahagún respected the Náhuatl version of his informants and abstained from rendering judgments on their value in his translation of even the most difficult parts of the text, such as those that referred to religion and human sacrifices.[40] These characteristics of the *Códice florentino*'s construction indicate that there is no basis for maintaining that the authors of the work were exclusively Sahagún's native collaborators or, on the other hand, that it was a book written by only one author, Bernardino de Sahagún.[41]

Perhaps the most unusual characteristics of the *Códice florentino* are the extensive presence of the Náhuatl language transcribed in the Latin alphabet and the authenticity that runs throughout the Indian discourse. In an unprecedented action, a religious figure from the conquering group asked the cultural elite of the vanquished to write a complete treatise on the origins, traditions, and religion of their nation in their own language. The elders of Tepepulco, Tlatelolco, and Tenochtitlán doubtless resented the tension naturally suffered by those faced with the unexpected challenge of explaining their own traditions to their conquerors, but they accepted the challenge and wrote invaluable pages on their origins and identities. Sahagún was not in accord with all the interpretations written down by his Indian collaborators, but as far as is known, he neither censored nor suppressed them. But he did not ignore them. In the Spanish version of the native text, he refuted, one by one, the references to gods and religion that he considered contrary to the Christian faith.

For example, in the appendix to the first book, which described the old gods, Sahagún presented his most incisive arguments against idolatry. He began his rejection of demons in the following manner: "You, the inhabitants of this New Spain . . . know that you have all lived in the great shadows of infidelity and idolatry in which your ancestors left you, as is clear from your writings and paintings and idolatrous rituals with which you have until the present time lived." And later on he stated sharply:

It is clear that Huitzilopuchtli is not a god, nor is Tláloc, nor Quetzalcóatl. Cihuacóatl is not a goddess; Chicomecóatl is not a goddess . . . Chalchiuhtliicue is not a goddess . . . Xuchipilli is not a god . . . Xipe Tótec is not a god . . . ; neither the sun, nor the moon, nor the earth, nor the sea, nor any of all the others that you once worshiped is a god; they are all demons. Thus does the Holy Scripture testify, saying: *Omnis dii gentium demonia.* Which means: "All the gods of the pagans are demons."[42]

And in another place, when referring to the calendar and the ancient forms of computing time and celebrating festivals, he attacked Motolinía and his native informants. He specifically refuted Motolinía, who affirmed that the calendar was based on natural science and had no traces of idolatry. Sahagún, on the other hand, replied that all of that "was completely false, because that count is not based on any natural order, because it was the invention of the Devil and the art of divination. . . . As to what was said [by Father Motolinía] about these calendars not having idolatrous content, that is the falsest of lies; they have many idolatrous things and many superstitions and many invocations of the demons, both tacit and express, as can be seen throughout this fourth book."[43] So wherever Sahagún saw signs of the old idolatry, he did not hesitate to refute them. The surprising thing is that he respected the free expression of his informants.

No other work, written either at that time or later, so liberally included in its pages the surprising confluence of two such opposing cultural traditions, nor collected with such vigor the drama of the first coming together of the ancient Indian culture and Western civilization. The *Códice florentino* has the rare quality of holding two strange and contradictory concepts of the world in the same receptacle and at the same time being the mortar with which the two began to mix and to forge a new reality—Mestizo history.

VI. The Canon of Memory Wrought by the *Títulos primordiales*

In historical literature one group of documents relating to the lands held by the native populations is referred to as the *Títulos primordiales*. Some of these papers were published in the nineteenth century, but a careful analysis of their content did not begin until the 1970s and 1980s.[1] The *Títulos* that were first known in central Mexico were written in Náhuatl and dated to the first years of the Spanish Conquest. They were presumed to be ancient papers that legitimized the ownership of lands by the indigenous people since time immemorial.

The discovery of another notable group of documents called the *Códices Techialoyan,* written in Náhuatl and accompanied by pictures that alluded to the possession of lands by the native people, awakened suspicions that they were false because those documents changed dates and the names of individuals and because they were developed following an archetype that served as a model for numerous *Títulos.*[2] Due to those traits, some historians labeled them as false.

Later, when a large number of similar documents were discovered, the *Títulos primordiales* and the *Códices Techialoyan* provided an attractive field of study for historians. Some stated that they reflected the collective interests of the natives.[3] Others, in addition to recognizing their value as expressions of the group mentality of the people, perceived that they held worthwhile historical information.[4]

In this chapter I propose to review the interpretations of the *Títulos* that have been offered, clarifying the antiquity of their origins and pointing out their presence in different regions, not only in the Náhuatl-speaking areas. To maintain consistency, I shall start by summarizing the characteristics present in the Nahua, P'urhépecha, Mixtec, and Maya environment. Finally, I will undertake an interpretation of them as a group and will consider their importance as new seedbeds and channels of indigenous memory.

The Títulos primordiales *of the Nahuas, the P'urhépecha* Títulos, *and the* Códices Techialoyan

In 1972 Joaquín Galarza published an innovative book, *Lienzos de Chiepetlan*,[5] which reviewed the content and style of a group of Nahua documents from the state of Guerrero. These papers contained the substantive nucleus of indigenous memory and the means that made them flow and be reborn down through the centuries. In the town of Chiepetlan, high on the mountain ridges of Guerrero, the local notables showed some astonished ethnologists several boxes in which they had kept a treasure that they had kept hidden from the eyes of outsiders for over two hundred years. It was a collection of painted cotton canvases that described the migration of a group of Nahua people from the center of Mexico and their settlement in the region of Tlapa, where they were given the lands painted on the maps. These canvases and a *Libro de títulos de tierras de San Miguel Chiepetlan,* found in the Archives of the Department of Agrarian Affairs, offered Galarza a solid basis for advancing the analysis of the *Títulos primordiales,* which had just begun.

As I shall propose, the map showing the boundaries and the texts in which the chiefs of the town maintained their historic rights of possession are the cornerstone that supports the structure of indigenous memory. Canvas I, done at the beginning of the sixteenth century, and Canvas II, painted a century later, represent the ancient pictographic tradition of Mesoamerica. The history they relate is painted in images, and the scribes who drew them show—especially in Canvas I—a masterful control of space. The description of the geographic features of the site, the characters in movement in that space, the glyphs and buildings that appear there—each of them has its own meaning, but they are organized to transmit a message: the emigration of the Nahua groups, their arrival in the Tlapanecan lands, their settlement in that region, the organization of their city, and the establishment of their borders. The second part of this history, the defense of territorial possessions against outside threats, is told in other later canvases and through the written declarations deposited in different courts to defend the lands that belonged to the town. Suits over land began in the Tlapa region around 1696 and continued throughout the eighteenth and into the nineteenth century. That is to say, because of their origin, content, and style, the Chiepetlan canvases are a synthesis of the *Títulos primordiales* that proliferated in different regions of New Spain and Guatemala in the seventeenth and eighteenth centuries.

Years earlier, Luis Reyes had discovered a *Título* from the town of Santo Tomás Ajusco (now Ajusco, D.F.) whose purpose was also the defense of land.[6] But in contrast to other *Títulos,* the one from Santo Tomás used violent language to describe the Spanish invasion. It was dated February 4, 1531, but its content indicates that it was made after the congregation of the populations in the middle of the sixteenth or beginning of the seventeenth century. This *Título* was addressed to the citizens of the city, reminding them of the avarice of the Spaniards, the unbridled abuses against native women, and the massacres, such as the execution of noblemen ordered by Pedro de Alvarado in the courtyard of the Main Temple. It said: "So much blood was shed! The blood of our fathers! And why? . . . Know this: it was because they alone wanted to rule. Because they are hungry for the precious metals and wealth of others. And because they want to have us under their heels. And because they want to mock our women and even our young maidens; and because they want to take over our lands and all the riches we possess." Then he warned the people against the congregation of native people as ordered by the Spanish government and the effects that this could have on their lands:

There, *By the Water,* Mexico, it is already common knowledge that the man [Hernán] Cortés from Castile, was authorized there in Castile to come divide up the land. . . . So it is said, they talk of this Marquis who will come to take our land; and he will also show us new lands where we will form new towns. Now, as for us, where will we be cast off to? Where will they put us? Sadness is too close around us. What are we to do, my children? But despite everything, I take heart and agree to form a town here, at the foot of this hill of Axochco Xatipac [today the town of Ajusco, D.F.] only because from down below to here is . . . the settlement of the Axochtepecanos. The land is ours from down below, our grandfathers left it to us. It was theirs, from down below, since ancient times. And I agree to build a temple for worship where we must place the new God that the Spaniards have brought us. They want us to worship Him. What are we to do, my children? It is advisable for us to be baptized, it is advisable for us to turn ourselves over to the men from Castile, in the hope that they don't kill us. It is advisable that we limit our boundaries; and what remains, it is advisable that our fathers defend it, those who rule in Tlalpan, Topilco, Totoltepec, Azicpac, Tepeticpac and Xalaatlaco [the town of Ajusco was subject to Tlalpan, which belonged to the regional capital of Coyoacán]. So now I shall cut back and reduce our lands as must be, and my will is that our borders begin on the side where the sun rises [what follows is a statement of the new borders being established by the chief who is speaking]. I calculate that for this little piece of land perhaps they won't kill us. What does it matter that what we once had was larger! But this is not done by my will, but only because I don't want my children to be killed that we will have only this little bit of land and on it we will live and also our children after us. And we will only work this piece of land, in the hope that they don't kill us.

Years later James Lockhart reevaluated the *Títulos primordiales* written in Náhuatl, formulated a synthesis of their characteristics, and highlighted their interest as expressions of the identity of the indigenous peoples.[7] Even though the *Títulos* vary from one town to another, the feature that unifies them is their detailed description of the territory belonging to the city. They are documents that sought to legitimize the ownership of land through an inventory of its extension, the definition of its borders, and the demonstration that the town, since long before, had enjoyed the ownership of those territories. The demarcation of the property almost always predated the Spanish founding of the town, which happened some years after the conquest, or when the people had been gathered into formal towns (1551–58 and 1593–1605). The delineation of the land was an event parallel to the building of the church, the baptism of the nobility, the giving of a Christian name to the town, and the designation of a patron saint. Land, church, Christian name, and patron saint were all attributes that gave individuality to the town and conferred identity on it. These acts were always presided over by Spanish authorities: the Nahua *Títulos* mentioned the King of Spain, Hernán Cortés, the viceroy or mayor, and the religious leaders of the province as executors of the adjudication of lands, even when in fact those individuals were never present in that place.[8]

Mesoamerican features joined with the Western characteristics surrounding the foundation of towns. The demarcation of borders, before they were noted in documents, was a ritual in which the members of the community participated. A committee of representatives, accompanied by outside authorities, walked the territory and performed acts of possession there, such as collecting herbs and sprinkling them toward the four directions of the cosmos or gathering stones and trees for the construction of the temple (fig. 94).[9] These rituals mixed ancient Mesoamerican traditions with those of Spain. The festival that followed the rituals of founding also came from the indigenous past. Several *Títulos* from the region of Chalco placed last the meal that the authorities of the town offered after the rituals of founding, which was attended by the members of the town and the leaders of nearby villages. The main dish was mole and tortillas, and it was common for a band to play ancient wind instruments such as the conch. The musicians served to animate the festival, and their names were noted on the pages describing this ceremony.[10]

In many *Títulos* the founding acts were followed by a solemn speech, with one of the elders in charge. It was an admonitory speech, directed at the community but especially at its younger members, which reminded them of the collective task of protecting the land. The speech represented the words of the founding fathers and had as its purpose keeping alive in everyone's memory the fact that the survival of the town depended on the conservation of communal lands (fig. 95). As Lockhart has observed, it is difficult to determine whether this voice came from the present or the past. In contrast to the ancient indigenous annals, where every action was recorded at a precise time, the writing of the *Títulos* was not set at a precise time, and events from the past were mixed with contemporary deeds, with an effort made to present the town as an entity that could resist threats from without and changes in history.[11]

The memory that was conserved in the *Títulos,* even though it seemed a mixture of disjointed recollections to Western eyes, brought together the important events that had originated the *altépetl* and tied them to the founding acts of the period of the Spanish Conquest. In several *Títulos* indigenous characters of mythic proportions appeared, linked to pre-Hispanic ancestors. In others, these characters had indigenous names but wore European clothing. They were almost always the ones who received the gifts of land from the authorities and served as defenders of the communal property against threats from outside and as conservators of ancient traditions.[12]

Fig. 94. Painting that accompanies the first *Título primordial* of the town of San Pedro Atlapulco (municipality of Ocoyoacac in the state of Mexico). In the center is the figure of a representative of the government of Spain at a table on which lie the documents that show the legal limits of the town's lands. Beside him are the headmen of the town, accompanied by their wives, who are seated below them. Around them are the members of the community, carrying materials to build the village church or posed in attitudes that imply ownership of the territory. (Photo from Fane, 1996: 83.)

There was no negative vision of the Spanish Conquest or of European settlement in the *Títulos*. There were no references to defeat or allusions to the catastrophic end of an epoch. In some cases the arrival of the Spaniards was presented as a peaceful agreement between both parties, whereby the indigenous people consented willingly to the settling in of the invaders. Neither was there any opposition to Christianity. On the contrary, Spanish

Fig. 95. Two Indian characters in the *Códice de San Antonio Techialoyan.* (Photo from Béligand, 1993.)

friars, authorities, and institutions appeared as new forms of legitimacy for the traditions of the people. The Spanish Conquest is scarcely mentioned, nor are opinions against it recorded. Those events seemed rather to have the quality of cosmic events that did not need to be explained; they were seen as new arrangements of the world that were self-justifying:

When the Marquis brought the Catholic faith, the friars of the order of our father Saint Francis came, bringing the Holy Spirit to the fore, and the Spaniards, those with the white skin and with the buckets on their heads, wore their swords at their sides; they said they were called Spaniards, and that they had given permission to them [the Indians] to establish themselves formally in towns and that they [the Indians] should think which saint they would like for their patron since the Catholic faith was already established in the city of Mexico [fig. 96].[13]

Fig. 96. The entrance of the patron saint into the town of San Simón Calpulalpan. (Photo from Cline, 1975: vol. 15, fig. 86.)

Nevertheless, there was a continuing warning in the *Títulos* against the danger that foreigners represented. In different passages the people were advised to show these documents to no one, especially not to Europeans. "The *Título* of Zoyatzingo warns the people to mistrust the Spaniards who might come in the future, since they will make friends with your descendants, eat with them, and be their friends, and then will force them to sell or give them their land on the basis of friendship."[14]

The *Títulos* were the bearers of an ethnocentric vision. They considered the town as the center of the world. The main subjects of their story were the communal lands and the residents of the town, to such an extent that the outside was only perceived when a relationship was formed with another town. The image that emanated from those documents was one of a community that had begun its existence in remote times and since then had maintained its own lands and uniqueness. Its residents felt united to that land and did not want that situation to change in the future. They wished to maintain their ancient traditions, which by this time were a mixture of indigenous and Spanish legacies. They were considered vassals of the King of Spain, who gave them their lands. They claimed to be devoted to their patron saint and guardians of their temple and its relics. Even when some of the documents were presented in the courts of the time to defend the rights of the people, they were addressed to members of the town. They sought to unite the people around their community rights and create a collective spirit to defend them.[15] The style of the *Títulos* indicates that they were prepared by the elders of the town for the benefit of generations to come. The rhetoric and declamatory style that pervaded them was reminiscent of the *huehuetlatolli,* or discourses of the elders, who in earlier times had transmitted to the young the values that had regulated the lives of their ancestors.

The P'urhépecha *Títulos* also joined ancient pictographic images with documents written with Spanish letters to offer a recording of the origins of the city and a demonstration of its continuity under the Colonial government. Recent studies by Hans Roskamp show that the *Títulos* and canvases were the most powerful arguments for legitimizing the ownership of land and the record that gave identity to the people of the lake regions and canyons of Michoacán.[16] Thus, the *Códice Plancarte* records the ghostly presence of a King Harame and a King Carapu. According to this story, in the earliest times both kings had marked out the territory of Carapan, affirmed themselves to be its legitimate owners, and arranged for this possession to be left to their descendents (fig. 97). The chiefs of Carapan claimed in other documents to be descended from the powerful Uacúsecha lineage, the founders of Tzintzuntzan, which was the capital of the P'urhépecha kingdom.

The *Códice Plancarte* stated that the chieftain Zuangua ordered Sirundame, one of his most courageous captains, to bring together the people of the canyon and the uplands of Michoacán to repopulate Carapan. According to this codex, Sirundame brought the people to Carapan, gave them possession of it, and made them "absolute owners of all the places of Carapan, springs, canyons,

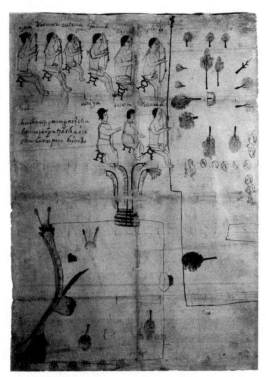

Fig. 97. *Códice de Carapan.* In the upper left part are the leaders of Carapan, identified by glosses in the P'urhépecha language written in Spanish. To their right is a bordered field, and below on the left is another territory with its borders. (Photo based on Roskamp, 1998.)

forests, hills, and plains, and later went to advise his King, to tell him all he had done in his name."[17]

The *Lienzo de Pátzcuaro* showed Sirundame entering the region and taking possession of the lands of Carapan (fig. 98). The figures of the kings of the dynasties of Tzintzuntzan, Harame, and Uacus Thicatame, were prominent on the canvases. For example, on the *Lienzo de Pátzcuaro* those characters stood out at the side of the coat of arms, which was dominated by an eagle with its wings outstretched. Harame occupied the left side of the shield and Uacus Thicatame, founder of the governing lineage of the eagles (Uacúsecha), the right. Therefore, as explained by Roskamp, in that scene the founding of Carapan was doubly protected: on one side by the lineage of the eagles, the founders of Tzintzuntzan,

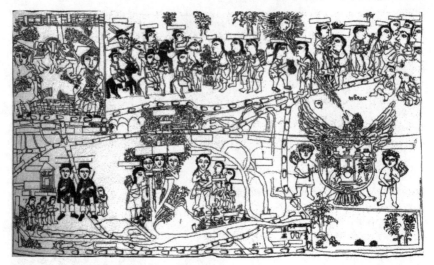

Fig. 98. *Lienzo de Pátzcuaro,* showing the native settlement in the region of the lakes. The upper central part (right) describes the arrival of Hernán Cortés and the missionaries. Below (right) is the new settlement of the city, supported by the presence of the mythic native kings and by the Indian leaders of the Colonial Period (left) and the emblem of the eagle. Drawing by Martijn van de Bel. (Photo taken from Roskamp, 2003.)

and on the other by the arrival of Hernán Cortés (appearing in the central scene at the top part of the canvas). As can be seen, the eagle that protected the eagle lineage was unified on the shield with the Hapsburg eagle (fig. 99).[18]

The ownership of the lands of Carapan in the Colonial Period was ratified by multiple legitimacies. On the *Lienzo de Pátzcuaro* and the *Lienzo de Carapan* (fig. 100), the scene of the pre-Hispanic founding was illustrated, followed by the arrival of Hernán Cortés (not Christopher of Olid, the captain who actually entered this region); the baptism of the chiefs by Friar Ángel de Valencia and Friar Martín de Jesús; the confirmation of those events signed in 1589 by don Antonio Huitzimengari, descendent of pre-Hispanic chiefs; and finally, the Spanish Crown, represented in the *Lienzo de Pátzcuaro* at the upper left by Philip III and Margaret of Austria. It can also be seen that oral, pictographic,

Fig. 99. The coat of arms of Tzintzuntzan, with the figures of King Harame to the left and Uacus Thicatame, founder of the dynasty, to the right. The coat of arms imitates Spanish symbols, combining Hispanic heraldry (the design of the shield, the castle in the center, and so forth), with that of the P'urhépecha. Tzintzuntzan means "place of the hummingbirds." (Photo from Roskamp, 1998.)

documentary, and symbolic sources were used in the preparation of these *Títulos,* united for the purpose of legitimizing the land-holdings of the city of Carapan and ratifying the territorial rights of the ancient indigenous nobility. Even though the authors presented them as wills and testimonies that originated in the fifteenth and sixteenth centuries, Roskamp shows that the *Títulos* and the canvases were made at the end of the seventeenth century and into the eighteenth.[19]

Similar purposes drove the creation of the famous *Códices Techialoyan.* These documents made an unusual impact on historical literature because of their stated intent of restoring the Mesoamerican pictorial tradition (fig. 101), their number (the current inventory surpasses fifty), the frequency with which dates and characters cited are inauthentic, and the uniformity of style and format. In general these documents seem to be divided into two parts, one section written in Náhuatl, the other composed of pictures.[20]

The first part is richer and more substantive. To explain its nature I here follow the story of the *Códice de San Antonio Techialoyan,*

Fig. 100. *Lienzo de Carapan.* It shows (as does the *Lienzo de Pátzcuaro*) the refounding of the city under the Colonial regime and the extent and limits of the territory. (Photo from Roskamp, 1998.)

the copy that gave its name to the collection and for which we have a good edition.[21] The narration begins with the entrance of the Viceroy Antonio de Mendoza to this lake area, where Lerma Lake once stood. The arrival of the Viceroy caused the founding of the towns and the adjudication of their lands. The representative of the native community who participated in these ceremonies was don Miguel de Santa María Axayácatl, descended from Tezozómoc, the ancient lord of the Tepanecas of Azcapotzalco. Don Miguel recorded this founding in his hand in the *altepetlamatl,* the paper on the city lands, in the presence of members of the community. The founding of the town was simultaneous with "the arrival of the faith," the building of the temple, the giving of a Christian name to the community, and the adjudication of lands following a rigorous land-registry process.

The above was included "in the writing with black ink so that it may always be told" to their children and descendants of their children, and they in turn would preserve and care for "this paper of the people." A detailed route through the land and the adjudication of plots to the subject towns followed, giving the

Fig. 101. The so-called Círculo del Tepanecáyotl from the *Códice Techialoyan García Granados*. This drawing is apparently a copy of a mural painting that existed in the indigenous palace of Azcapotzalco. The hills that surround the central shield are the place-names of the towns that make up the Tepanecas kingdom. Here the place-names and the native leaders share space with Hispanic emblems. (Photo from the *Códice Techialoyan García Granados*, 1992.)

specific description of the size of each plot, the quality of the land, the beneficiaries (those assigned for tribute, those for the leaders, and those held in common), and the different crops on the plots.[22]

Then came the pictures. Even though these were proposed in order to revive the ancient Mesoamerican tradition, they had a plasticity and movement that distanced them from those origins and tied them to European tradition. The paintings of the *Códices Techialoyan* made use of perspective and shading, incorporated designs from the old continent, and depicted natives with moustaches and beards. They included coats of arms, shields, and extraordinary family trees, such as the one that described the

179

indigenous ancestors in the *Códice Techialoyan García Granados* with symbols, emblems, and drawings that contrasted with Nahua traditions (figs. 102, 103).

The similarity of format, pictorial style, and attitudes of the characters in these documents leads one to believe there were individuals expert in their preparation or perhaps actual forgery studios. This is what Stephanie Wood encountered in the area of Toluca. While studying eighteenth-century documents, she uncovered the activities of Diego García Mendoza, a native chief from Atzcapotzalco who had a herd of pack mules and also fabricated genealogies, coats of arms, and land titles. Don Diego was accused of falsifying and selling a "map or title" on maguey paper to the community of San Pedro Totoltelpec in the Valley of Toluca. During the investigation into the proceedings against him, he confessed that those documents were written on paper that seemed old because he made it of maguey fiber, a technique that he had used to produce other titles and genealogies that he had sold to different towns.[23]

Pedro Villafranca, an Indian from the community of Jilotepec in the Valley of Toluca, offers another example of the falsification of *Títulos*. Pedro learned Spanish writing in the sixteenth century, along with common legal forms for land grants and the drawing of ancient maps. He soon made these talents into a lucrative business, selling false land titles and supposedly ancient documents to the towns of Santa Ana Tlapaltitlán, Metepec, Calixtlahuaca, Cuajimalpa, and probably many more towns. His business included the falsification of documents that imitated Spanish legal forms, smoking them with flaming pitch pine to give them an ancient look.[24]

With these examples and other isolated proofs of falsification, the authenticity of the *Códices Techialoyan* has been made suspect. But as comparative analysis of the set of codices and individual study of several of them have shown, these are authentic documents. They were made by the headmen of the town or representatives of the community at the repeated demands of the authorities, who

Fig. 102. Family tree of the governing lineage of Tenochtitlán and Tlatelolco. (Photo from the *Códice Techialoyan García Granados*.)

Fig. 103. *Códice Techialoyan* of the town of San Antonio Huixquilucan, from the state of Mexico. Representation of two Indian men with ancient clothing and arms. (Photo from Cline, 1975.)

asked that written documents be presented based on the legal standards in use. Except for dates and the names of some characters who figured as witnesses to the founding of the town, the information provided by the *Códices Techialoyan* matched the geography and the historical circumstances of the place to which they referred. We now know that those documents were not made in the sixteenth century, since they began after the land arbitration started in 1643 and 1647.[25] In additional to providing true, abundant, and exceptional information on the origins and organization of several towns, the *Códices Techialoyan* and the *Títulos primordiales* offer invaluable documentation of the forms in which identity was articulated and strengthened in these towns and their particular methods of recreating the past.

Their writing in colloquial Náhuatl and their use of pictographs indicate that they were addressed to the population of the *altépetl,* the town leaders—to a public that could read the images easily. The decision to write these affidavits in Náhuatl, even though the towns for which they were written spoke Otomí or Mixtec, revealed the intent that their contents be read by speakers of the lingua franca of those times, which was also the common language of legal proceedings.[26] And as Joaquín Galarza argues so well, the *Códices Techialoyan* formed a new type of document, a hybrid affidavit, based both on the indigenous tradition of defending the town and on the legal proceedings of the European tradition. They were not a falsification but rather a creation, a new manner of expression. "In these *Códices,*" says Galarza, "European art and techniques serve to transmit events which correspond to indigenous thought. They are mixed, hybridized, Mestizo documents, halfway between the paintings of the seventeenth century and traditional indigenous writing."[27]

Historians, accustomed to the chronological precision of the ancient annals and the narrative unfolding of the codices as they told of the glories of the Mesoamerican kingdoms, believed—when they did not find indications of that kind of memory in the towns in the sixteenth century—that it had disappeared and been exhausted. But an examination of the *Títulos* shows that the memory of the people had become concentrated in the preservation of territorial rights, the magnet that gave social cohesion to its residents, and in the recollection of those deeds that gave life to the town. The daily events and happenings that celebrated the origins and changes of the town were the required themes of this story. In this great effort to reconstruct their past, the people included the ancient oral memory, the old pictographic techniques, and the new procedures that legitimized their rights to the land in the *Títulos.* The result was the creation of a new historical memory, the history of the people, centered on their ancestral rights to the land.[28]

The Oaxacan Canvases, Maps, and Títulos

The early study of the *Títulos* written in Náhuatl and perhaps the splendor and number of the *Códices Techialoyan* overshadowed the presence of this genre of documents in other latitudes, where they were equally abundant and significant, as was the case in Oaxaca. In that region, as much in the mountainous Mixtec land as in the Zapotec areas, a notable series of documents (canvases, strips, and maps) was produced which—in a manner similar to that of the ancient Mesoamerican codices—told the story of the *altépetl* and the genealogy of its governors and documented the ownership of land from time immemorial.

In contrast to the making of the ancient codices, which were done on amate leaves or on strips of deerhide that were doubled to form a kind of folding screen that had to be displayed leaf by leaf to know its content, the canvases and maps joined the characters and topics of the story in the same space, so that the reader could know the history told on them at a single glance (figs. 104 and 105). Franciscan Juan de Torquemada affirmed in the seventeenth century that the painting of canvases was a pre-Hispanic tradition. He said that for the best understanding of the ownership and distribution of lands, "they had them painted on large canvasses so that the lands of the *calpules* or citizens were painted light yellow, those of the leaders a pinkish color, and the property of the king a very bright red; and thus with these colors, *upon opening any picture one could see the entire town, its terms and its limits,* and could understand whose they were and where they were located."[29]

In the sixteenth century the purpose of the canvases and maps of the Mixtec region was to relate the origins of the ancient kingdoms and to advise their continuation into the Colonial Period. The canvases of Zacatepec, Ihuitlán, Tlapiltepec, and Tequiztepec

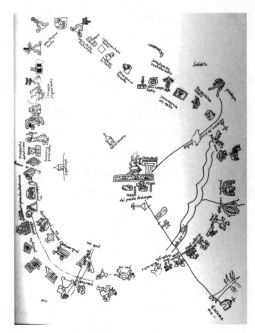

Fig. 104. The *Lienzo de Jicayán,* completed around 1550, is made of three lengths of woven cotton that were later painted in a vigorous pre-Hispanic style. The town of Jicayán is in the center, and the circle that surrounds it shows the neighboring towns. (Photo from Marcus, 1992.)

(figs. 106–108), done in the middle of the sixteenth century, told the story of those towns, brought together the succession of the lineages that governed them, and described the territory of the *altépetl* and the changes it underwent through time. That is to say, in contrast with the Nahua and P'urhépecha *Títulos,* the Mixtec canvases and *Títulos* had an unusual historical depth that in some cases covered three centuries or more.

The canvases, for example, support the history of the *altépetl* with the wills and testaments that corroborate the ownership of the land since time immemorial. As Mary Elizabeth Smith has observed, the specific function of those documents was "to protect the lands of the community and the properties of the local nobility."[30] They told of three decisive aspects of the formation of the city: the moment in which the city was founded, the origin and succession of the governing lineage, and the borders of its territory. Even though some maps adopted the round format of the European plan (fig. 104), the majority of the canvases had a

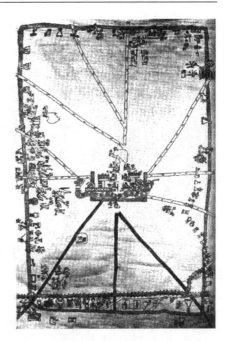

Fig. 105. *Lienzo de Coixtlahuaca number 1 (Códice Ixtlán)*. In the center of the canvas is the palace of the governor, encircled by a plumed serpent. On the edges are the towns near Coixtlahuaca. (Photo from Cline, 1975: fig. 30.)

rectangular form (figs. 106–108). The canvases linked the narrative part of the ancient codices with the graphic description of the territory. But as Elizabeth Boone indicates, time seemed frozen in the maps that described the territory of the city. The territorial features, even when they corresponded with a precise date, seemed to extend through time without change. "The map which dominates most of the canvasses describes the territory as a spacial entity which existed at some moment in the past, but also carries this entity into [the reader's present and toward the] future, and in this manner confers on it a lasting quality."[31] As will be seen, this feature of the map drawn on the canvases allowed for the future conversion of the canvas into a *Título*, a legal document used by the towns to prove their ownership of their lands from time immemorial.

The founding of the town was an event that was painted very forcefully on the Oaxaca canvases. The *Lienzo de Ihuitlán*, for example, marked the moment in which Ihuitlán, Tlapiltepec, and

Fig. 106. *Lienzo de Zacatepec I.* The center represents the founding of Zacatepec, which is surrounded by various neighboring towns that limit its territory. (Photo from Boone, 2000: fig. 44.)

Coixtlahuaca were founded with the mythic features of pre-Hispanic codices such as the *Códice de Viena*. The *Lienzo de Ihuitlán* was made around 1550, but in its lower section the place symbols of Tlapiltepec and Coixtlahuaca were drawn with images of the gods and sacred forms that in ancient Mesoamerica sanctified the founding of the *altépetl* (fig. 107). Inside the place symbol of Coixtlahuaca was the figure of 9 Wind, the founding hero of the Mixtec kingdoms in the *Códice de Viena,* consecrating that event (fig. 109). In the upper section, seated on a throne covered with a jaguar skin, were the founders of the lineage of Coixtlahuaca.[32]

The *Lienzo de Tlapiltepec,* painted on cotton cloth in the middle of the sixteenth century, presented a similar foundation scene (fig. 108). The bottom section featured a representation of the legendary cave of Chicomóztoc, where, according to central

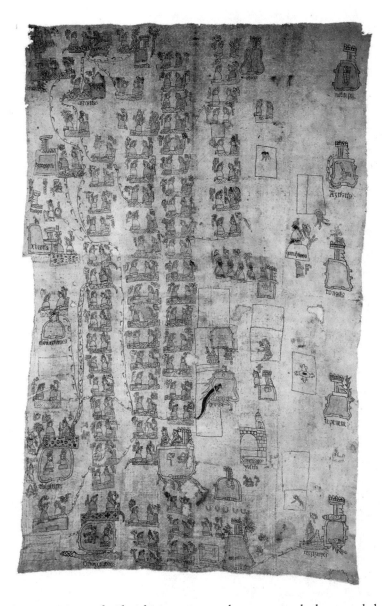

Fig. 107. *Lienzo de Ihuitlán,* constructed on cotton cloth around the middle of the sixteenth century. It shows the founding of the towns of Ihuitlán, Tlapiltepec, and Coixtlahuaca, with the governing lineages sprouting from their symbols. (Photo from Fane, 1996: 76.)

Fig. 108. *Lienzo de Tlapiltepec,* painted on lengths of cotton around the middle of the sixteenth century. It shows the founding of the town (left side), first depicting the birth of the new humanity in the cave of Chicomoztoc (lower left side) and then the scene of the founding and formation of the lineages. (Photo from Boone, 2000: 148.)

Fig. 109. The place sign of Coixtlahuaca in the *Lienzo de Ihuitlán*. Within this symbol, on the right, is the figure of Nine Wind, the protector god of the Mixtec kingdoms, with his calendar name. (Photo from Boone, 2000: 139.)

Mexican traditions, the present humanity was born. Inside this cave were the faces of the founding deities of the ancient Mixtec kingdoms, identified by their calendaric names: 9 Wind and 1 Reed (fig. 110). Above Chicomóztoc was an ancestral couple that emerged from a river, bore children, and founded a city, which was the main scene of the canvas on the left side. This founding was celebrated with the ritual of lighting the New Fire, which signified the beginning of a new era. The first and second canvases of Tequixtepec reproduced these founding scenes, which were distinguished by the presence of the creation gods.[33] Alfonso Caso's studies on the Mixtec canvases and the *Códice Selden* offered abundant evidence to prove that the founding scene was one of the most important events in the canvases and codices, equivalent to the origin myths of the Mesoamerican cosmogonic records.[34]

In the *Códice Selden II*, painted in the middle of the sixteenth century, the cultural hero 9 Wind appeared in one scene speaking in the heights of the heavens with the creator gods of Mixtec tradition, Lord 1 Deer and Lady 1 Deer (fig. 111). Then he descended to earth, and four priests hastened to bear offerings to

Fig. 110. On the left side of this figure is the cave of Chicomoztoc, and within it the calendar names of the patron god of the Mixtec kingdoms, Nine Wind One Cane. (Photo from Boone, 2000: 154.)

the sacred form that represented him (fig. 112). In another migration scene, the four priests were seen carrying the bundle that contained the relics of 9 Wind (fig. 113). Finally, in the central scene, the priests arrived at the predestined site to found a new city, depositing there the bundle that held the sacred force of 9 Wind and then lighting the New Fire (fig. 114).

It is interesting that these pre-Hispanic foundation cults were kept alive in the foundings recorded in the Oaxaca canvases of the sixteenth century (fig. 115).[35] As can be seen in the *Lienzo de Tlapiltepec* (fig. 108), after the scenes that described the founding acts came the list of the governors. The canvases were particularly rich in this series of governors who succeeded, one after another, after the founding of the city, projecting an image of duration over time.

On some canvases these lists were painted horizontally and read from left to right, as in the *Lienzo de Tequixtepec I* (fig. 116). Mary Elizabeth Smith suggests that this form of representing the

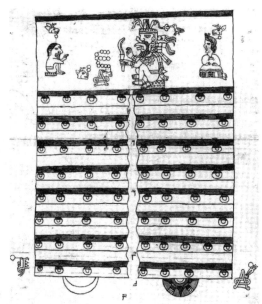

Fig. 111. A view of 9 Wind speaking in the sky with the creator gods, Lord 1 Deer (left) and Lady 1 Deer (right). *Códice Selden.* (Photo from Kingsborough, 1964: vol. II, 100.)

governors was Mesoamerican. On the other hand, the vertical list of lineages, the most common on the Oaxaca canvases—as seen on the *Lienzo de Tlapiltepec* (fig. 108), the *Lienzo de Ihuitlán* (fig. 109), and the *Mapa de Teozacoalco* (fig. 117)—was an adaptation to the Colonial mandate that demanded the governors be listed in a "straight line."[36]

Clearly, the intent of these canvases was to unite the record of the city and its subject people with the list of governors, since the latter seemed to emanate from the place signs of the towns. The integration of the map with the genealogy of the governors suggested that it was the governors who ordered the canvases to be made, since they were the owners of the best lands and the heirs of the canvases and the ancient pictures.

After the founding of the town and genealogy of the governors, the third subject of the Oaxacan canvases was the map of the town. The map outlined the territory owned by the town and pointed out the physical existence of the principal town and the

Fig. 112. Four priests come to a temple where the sacred bundle of 9 Wind is kept. *Códice Selden.* (Photo from Kingsborough, 1964: vol. II, 1ll.)

Fig. 113. The four priests from figure 112 take the sacred bundle of 9 Wind and begin a pilgrimage. The priest who leads the march carries the wrapped bundle of the god. *Códice Selden.* (Photo from Kingsborough, 1964: vol. II, 112.)

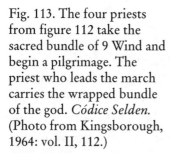

Fig. 114. The four priests reach the predestined spot, deposit the sacred bundle of 9 Wind, and proceed to light the New Fire, ritual acts that accompany the founding of the town, as symbolized by the intertwined serpents. *Códice Selden.* (Photo from Kingsborough, 1964: vol. II, 113.)

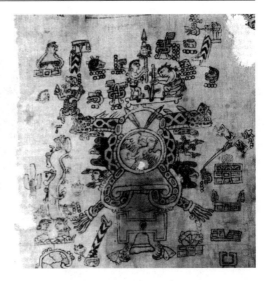

Fig. 115. A replica of the founding ceremony of the previous figure from the *Códice Selden* in the *Lienzo de Tlapiltepec.* Here the founding at the place of the intertwined serpents is accompanied by the lighting of the New Fire, the rite of the ball game, and other founding rites of pre-Hispanic origin. (Photo based on Boone, 2000: 156.)

towns subject to it, described geographically where they were located, and indicated their borders with neighboring villages. In reality the most significant character on the canvases was the *altépetl,* the territorial unit on which the political entity called the town and its governors were located.

Thus the canvases, in describing the origins of the town, the succession of its governors, and the features of the territory, became the memory nucleus of the community. They stored on simple painted cotton cloths the bases on which the historical existence of the town rested, and for that reason the towns carefully kept the cloths during the three centuries of the Viceroys. In Oaxaca the canvases were the principal instrument for defending first the lands of the chiefs and later the communal lands of the towns.[37]

Mary Elizabeth Smith was perhaps the first to point out the shift of the canvas as a memorial of the governing lineages to a legal testimony managed by the chiefs to defend their properties in the viceregal courts. In her indispensable book on the pictorial language of the Mixtecs, she has recorded the testimony of the chief of the town of Amusgos, Juan Rafael de Ávila, written in 1629. In this document Ávila alleged as a proof of his rights "a

Fig. 116. *Lienzo de Tequixtepec I.* The series of governors who followed the founding of the town is shown here. (Photo from Parmenter, 1982: 55.)

painting of my descendence and fortune" and, basing his claim on them, stated: "these lands, hills, and canyons are legitimately mine." The old people of the town who testified in favor of Ávila also mentioned "the picture which he has on ancient cloth of his descendence." Later, during the legal process that followed this testimony, Ávila declared: "I have a picture on cloth that, since I could not include it in the acts, I do not present, telling how it was based on the ownership by my ancestors of those mentioned towns and lands, which I am disposed to show if necessary in this court or in other supreme courts."[38]

Other testimonies confirm that the canvases and maps were presented as legal proofs to defend the lands of the towns in the seventeenth and eighteenth centuries as well as later. Therefore, in August of 1676, the administrator of some lands situated on the Mixtec coast, the attorney Pedro Martín, asked the Royal High Court to require Indians to present only "legitimate titles" and not maps to defend their property claims. Martín argued that the maps were easily created by the Indians, "since by making a picture they could institute litigation. And in this case, not only I but Your Majesty would be damaged by the Indians with reference to the lands that are composed and belong to the Royal

Fig. 117. The list of governors of Tilantongo (left) and Teozacoalco (right) painted on the *Mapa de Teozacoalco*. (Photo from Boone, 2000: 132.)

Crown, since by making a map drawn for their purposes they could claim to be owners and be usurpers of what does not belong to them." As can be seen, he here referred to the process of *composition* of lands initiated by the Crown in 1643. The Royal High Court replied in September of the same year that the Indians had the right to present their maps as legal testimony, *"since they were instruments of their usage and style, and it is the responsibility of this Royal High Court to admit them as titles;* if they should desire . . . to falsify them (which is not a legal presumption) with new ones and added ones; the remedy remains to repudiate them as false."[39]

The recognition by the Royal High Court of the maps and *Títulos* as legitimate instruments for proving the territorial rights of the towns provided perhaps the strongest motivation for communities of this region to hold on to their ancient cloths as sacred objects, similar to the bundles that once represented the "heart of the town," and to continue to present them in the courts in defense of their territorial rights. The Ramo de Tierras [Land Branch] of the Archivo General de la Nación [General Archives of the Nation] and the archives of the Agrarian Reform have numerous maps and canvases that the people took before the judges, confident in the belief that those documents would be sufficient proof to defend their lands.

Ancient agrarian disputes multiplied as the towns were consolidated in the middle of the sixteenth century and were rekindled in 1643 and 1667, when the Spanish Crown stipulated that all lands without clear title would be legalized through a proceeding known as *composition* (the payment of a sum of money to legalize irregular possessions and "bad titles"). Shortly thereafter, in 1687, a royal warrant defined the *fundo legal,* or community property of the towns.[40] That is to say, the challenge of adjusting the indigenous forms of landholding to the legal procedures established by the Spanish obliged the towns to use their paintings and maps as the basis of their legal claims and introduced important changes into the old paintings. Those changes caused a transformation in the forms of recording the past: the ancient memory, earlier fixed in images and songs, little by little became a written memory, with justifications sustained using the letters of the Spanish alphabet.

Thus, the canvases and maps originally drawn with pictographs began to be changed when the so-called glosses or commentaries written in Mixtec, Náhuatl, P'urhépecha, and Spanish were added. For example, a land dispute in the region of Tututepec transformed an ancient pre-Hispanic codex (the *Códice Colombino*) into a written document that described the lands of Tututepec and its borders with neighboring towns. In 1717 that ancient codex was taken before the courts with numerous added glosses that had

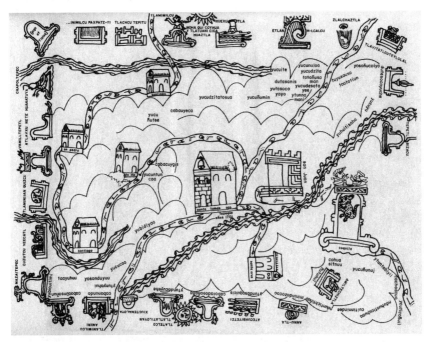

Fig. 118. *Lienzo de Ocotepec.* Drawing by Mary Elizabeth Smith, showing the addition of glosses in Náhuatl (capital letters) and Mixtec (cursive) to the original canvas. (Photo from Smith, 1973: 337.)

nothing to do with the original document, since they were limited to identifying the lands that belonged to Tututepec. This also occurred in the *Lienzo de Jicayán,* painted around 1550 (fig. 104), which later had three additions of glosses and pictures describing the borders of the town on three different dates, because in the seventeenth and eighteenth centuries the borders of Jicayán no longer matched the map painted in the middle of the sixteenth century.[41] The *Lienzo de Ocotepec* is another example of the constant reuse of the old pictorial testimonies, with its original outline altered by the addition of later glosses in Mixtec and Náhuatl (fig. 118).[42]

Similarly, the Zapotec and Mixtec *Títulos* done in the seventeenth and eighteenth centuries are an updated translation of the ancient canvases.[43] An analysis of the *Lienzo de Tabáa* showed

Fig. 119. *Lienzo de Tabáa.* This Zapotec canvas shows several generations of leaders prior to the European invasion as well as the entrance of the Spaniards and gives a listing of Colonial leaders. (Photo based on Glass, 1964: plate 125.)

that this cloth was composed of two parts: a genealogy of the governors and a map that described the lands of the community. One item in the cartographic section mentioned that Juan de Salinas, the mayor of Villa Alta, who had held that position between 1556 and 1560, "established the borders with the neighboring towns and properties of 'the district capital of San Juan Tabáa'" (fig. 119).

Michel Oudijk, the author of this analysis, then compared the information contained in the canvas with the land *Títulos* of the nearby towns of Solaga, Tetze, and La Olla, arriving at the conclusion that the *Títulos* were translations of the canvas. Both testimonies tell of the arrival of the Spaniards; describe the founding of the town and the construction of its church, the baptism of the chiefs, and the raising of the crosses at the borders of the village; and give the location of the lands of Tabáa. The canvas and the *Títulos* agreed on the limits of the Tabáa lands. According to Oudijk, the repeated references to sites located on a map or cartographic document, such as "here in this place" or "there in that place," suggest the existence of an earlier map or canvas. As I have tried to demonstrate here, this earlier canvas must have been a codex similar to the *Códice de Viena.*

A search of the Mixtec canvases, maps, and *Títulos* sheds light on the way historic memory was reconstructed. Of primary importance is the prolongation of memory that was maintained in the ancient codices on the canvases, maps, and *Títulos* constructed in the sixteenth and seventeenth centuries. As will be remembered, the *Códice de Viena* told in pictures of the founding of the *altépetl,* or city, the origin of the lineages, and the borders established for the kingdom. It is surprising that this millennial design still governed the contents of the canvases and *Títulos* of the sixteenth and seventeenth centuries. There is an astonishing continuity of ancient memory manifested in its basic contents (the original founding, genealogy of the rulers, and description of territory) and its forms of transmission: pictography. The ancient paintings continued in the canvases and maps until the seventeenth century, when *Títulos* written in the Latin alphabet began to replace them.

The Oaxaca canvases, maps, and *Títulos* were also a testament to the creativity of the indigenous people. They demonstrated the people's capacity to face the changes unleashed by the Colonial regime with new devices and their inventiveness in transforming the ancient pictographic memory to a canvas that condensed their tradition or to a written memory adapted to the legal procedures of the Spaniards. María de los Ángeles Romero Frizzi points out the continuity of the oral traditions in the canvases of the Colonial Period.[44] As in the case of the Nahua and P'urhépecha *Títulos,* the Oaxaca canvases and *Títulos* recreated the ancient oral, visual, and pictorial procedures for transmitting memories to their descendents. Like the Nahua *Títulos,* the Mixtec and Zapotec examples were dedicated to the service of the community itself: those who enunciated them were the authorities and principal officers of the local town and its residents, as they were written in Mixtec and in Zapotec.

Kevin Terraciano and Lisa Sousa observed the presence of several styles and traditions in the Oaxacan *Títulos.* They found traces in them of the legal proceedings used in the land hearings, the florid tone of pre-Hispanic oral discourse, cadences of the ancient songs, a pictorial similarity to the codices, the dramatic action of theatrical performances, the tendency of the annals to focus the story on significant happenings, as well as myth and propaganda.[45]

The texts in question mixed indigenous traditions with the legal requirements imposed by the conquistadors. Their adhesion to pre-Hispanic traditions was matched by their adoption of Western political, legal, and cultural legacies. God, the King, and Spanish authorities presided over the ceremonies described in the canvases. The chiefs of the towns, followed by the community members, adopted baptism and their Christian names. The founding of the *cabildo,* or town council, an event that gave the town a personality and political legitimacy, appeared to be an internal decision on the part of the members of the *altépetl,* not something imposed from without.[46]

The Maya Títulos primordiales

The works of contemporary anthropologists, ethnohistorians, and historians have demonstrated the unfortunate tendency of those who study the Nahua people to completely ignore the Mayas, Mixtecs, and Huichols, and vice versa, to such an extent that today it is almost impossible to find comparative studies of different ethnic groups, in spite of the fact that some authors, starting with Eduard Seler at the beginning of the twentieth century, argue that Mesoamerican peoples shared similar ideas about the origin of the cosmos, the gods, human beings, and historical memory.[47] This academic distortion is attributable to the fact that there have been no comparative analyses of Nahua *Títulos* and those of the Mixtec or Maya in spite of the facts that they share similar structures and that one clarifies the other, as I shall endeavor to prove in this chapter.

An awareness of the Maya *Títulos* began early, in 1885, when the Count of Charencey published a document in Spanish and

French that had been found by Brasseur de Bourbourg in Guatemala in 1860. In 1950 Adrián Recinos brought the same document to light in Mexico under the title *Título de los señores de Totonicapán,* in an 1834 translation from K'iche' to Spanish by the parish priest Dionisio José Chonay.[48] The study of the contents and characteristics of these documents took on a new urgency in the decade of the 1980s with the critical editions that Robert Carmack and James Mondloch made of the *Título de Totonicapán* and the *Título de Yax.*[49] I shall begin my analysis with these two texts and then compare them with other less-known *Títulos.*

The Títulos de Totonicapán *and* Yax *and the Tradition of the* Popol Vuh

In 1973 the search for sources of ethnological studies led Robert Carmack to Totonicapán, Guatemala, where he found a veritable treasure trove of ancient K'iche' documents. Among them were the *Título de Totonicapán,* the *Título de Yax,* the *Título de Pedro Velázquez,* and the *Título de Cristóbal Ramírez.* Their publication threw unexpected light on the ancient history of the K'iche' people and opened a window onto understanding the formation of K'iche' memory through several centuries. Perhaps the discovery that most astonished Carmack was the verification of the fact that these papers, originally written in the middle of the sixteenth century, were based on the *Popol Vuh,* the great book that summarized the cultural legacy of the K'iche' people.

According to Carmack, one of the scribes of the version of the *Popol Vuh* that we know, Diego Reynoso, also participated in the making of the *Título de Totonicapán.* Carmack proved that the genealogy of the K'iche' governors of both texts was similar, even though it was more complete in the *Título.* And he established that except for the mythological section of the *Popol Vuh,* the themes that followed were treated in a similar fashion in the two documents.[50] A comparison of the narrative and thematic structure of the *Popol Vuh* and the *Título de Totonicapán* and *Título de*

Yax (tables 4, 5, and 6) shows that the influence of the first on the other two was decisive.[51]

As indicated in these tables, the structure that organized the story of the *Popol Vuh,* the *Título de Totonicapán,* and the *Título de Yax* was similar. All three divided their story into a triad: first, they told of the original creation of the cosmos; then they described the creation of human beings, the sun, and the first settlements of the people; and last, they praised the founding of the kingdom, the genealogy of the governing lineage, the broadening of the borders of the territory, and the power achieved by the K'iche' kingdom.

Except for the intrusion in the *Título de Totonicapán* of the Biblical story of the creation of the world, the content of these texts came from Mesoamerican traditions, where it was the dominant and most profound theme. These traditions predated the epoch of splendor of the K'iche' people in the fifteenth century, when the episodes told in the *Popol Vuh* were probably composed in paintings and songs. Carmack maintains that those texts reflected the Mexica tradition that flourished in the Classic Period (A.D. 300 to 900) in Teotihuacán. That is to say, they allude to "the Toltec cultural tradition which was inherited by several ethnic groups in Mesoamerica after the fall . . . of Tula."[52] According to Carmack, this was a tradition that expanded through different regions of Mesoamerica. One of its regions, that of the Gulf Coast, had a decisive influence on K'iche' history, since "its manifestation in the highlands of Guatemala began in the early years of the thirteenth century," when the construction of that kingdom was begun.[53]

Carmack affirms that the main influence on the *Título de Totonicapán* came from the Toltecs. He says that "Nahua words from the *Título* with few exceptions came from Náhuat, the language of the Gulf Coast. In the second place, its historical tradition located the origin of the K'iche' founders in Tulán, a place associated with sites on the Gulf Coast. Third, the 'Mexica' institutions in the

Table 4. Principal Deeds Narrated in the *Popol Vuh* (1554)

I. First creations of the cosmos	II. Creation of human beings, the sun, and the first settlements	III. Founding of the kingdom and the governing lineages, chronicle of the ethnic group, and the limits of the territory
The gods arranged for the appearance of the land, created the plants and animals, and tried three times to create human beings, but without success. Before the fourth effort, the text tells of the adventures of the Divine Twins in the underworld when by vanquishing the lords of Xibalbá they established conditions whereby the earth and the sky would receive human beings favorably. After the lords of Xibalbá were defeated, the gods undertook a fourth creation of human beings, who were made of maize. Thus were born the four first men, Jaguar Quitzé, Jaguar Noche, Mahucutah, and Jaguar Oscuro, who, when they received their respective wives, formed the first K'iche' lineages.	Each lineage decided on its patron gods and agreed to go to Tulán, where they received their respective gods. Tojíl, the guide god of the K'iche', created fire. They agreed to leave Tulán and find a place to settle. Their pilgrimage reached its high point when they assisted with the first sunrise. The first chiefs of the four lineages died and left their remains to their descendents in the form of sacred bundles, which their heirs promised to honor.	The chiefs of the group decided to return to the east, to Tulán, to receive their emblems of power, which were given them by Nácxit-Quetazalcóatl. They continued their journey, founded towns, built K'umarcaah, the capital, and became a powerful kingdom. The text described the successive deeds of the chiefs which made them great, the expansion and demarcation of their territory, and praised the power achieved by the K'iche' kingdom.

Source: Data from *Popol Vuh: Las antiguas historias del Quiché,* trans. Adreán Recinos (Fondo de Cultura Económica, 1950).

Table 5. Principal Deeds Related in the *Título de Totonicapan* (1554)

I. First cosmogonic creations	II. Creation of human beings and the sun and the beginnings of permanent settlements	III. Founding of the kingdom and of the governing lineages, chronicle of the ethnic group, and the limits of the territory
Biblical story of the creation of the world based on the *Theología Indorum*, written by Dominican friar Domingo de Vico. This text occupied the first eight pages of the *Título*.	The appearance of the first K'iche', Balam Q'uitsé, Balam Ak'ab, Majucotaj, and Iqui Balam. It is said that these four chiefs of the lineages came from the east, from Tulán Sewán. In Tulán Nacxit they were given the sacred bundle (*Pisom c'ac'al*). Next came a pilgrimage, which took them to Jak'awits, in the territory of Totonicapán. Their settlement in this place caused wars with the original tribes. Then the four chiefs of the lineages decided to go toward the east to visit Nacxit to receive their "seigniory" (lordly rights and privileges), which symbols were described. The celebration of the great daybreak was described, celebrating the appearance of the sun. The four founders of the lineages died and left their successors the sacred bundle. New generations were born. The chief undertook a journey from Jak'awits to Chiismachí, traveling through 21 towns.	They established themselves in Chiismachí, where they made sturdy buildings and founded their political offices. In Chiismachí they deposited their symbols of authority, which they had received from the east (Tulán). Each clan was given its charges and symbols of power and their functions were defined. There was a war against the Ts'utujiles of the lake region. The dominion of the K'iche' was extended throughout several regions. The genealogy of the kings K'ucumats and Q'uikab was described. A new capital of K'umarcaaj was founded, there was a meeting of all the chiefs, and the houses of the principal clans were built. Military groups were sent to found colonies in different areas of Totonicapán. A warrior group conquered the southern coast. "The great power and glory" of the lineage of the Cawek was proclaimed, "who went around the limits of the lands of the K'iche'." They divided Lake Atitlán in two and established new landmarks. They finally received the news of the arrival of Pedro de Alvarado, "Tonatiu."

Source: Robert M. Carmack and James Mondloch, eds., *Título de los Señores de Totonicapán—Titre généalogique des Seigneurs de Totonicapán*, 1983.

Table 6. Principal Events Related in the *Título de Yax* (ca. 1560)

I. First creation of the cosmos	II. Creation of human beings and the sun, and the beginning of permanent settlements	III. Founding of the kingdom and the governing lineages, chronicle of the ethnic group, and the limits of the territory
	Description of the chiefs of the lineage who first settled in the Yax territory. Conflicts between them and the native tribes and a description of the false arguments used by the K'iche' to vanquish the tribes. Settlement of the invaders in the territory. Disappearance of the chiefs who had founded the lineages and the ascent of their descendents to the governing roles. How they received the *Pisom c'ac'al*, or sacred bundle, which contained the relics of their ancestors. Their pilgrimage to the east, the place from which "our ancestors came." There Nacxit gave them their symbols of power and "the writing of Tulán, the writing which they chose to put into their tradition." The different clans met at K'ak'awits and then abandoned this place. They founded the town of Chicayix, and there they stayed for a long time. They abandoned that site and came to Chiismachí, where they built sturdy houses and created their first political positions.	Later, they founded K'umarcaaj, where several clans met and made "a new territorial division of the town." The principal theme of this part was the development of the K'iche' kingdom. It was said that they "increased their subjects," and with their help built the temples and homes of the city. They established "the ranks of the lords. Their birthdays were celebrated by their subjects." They described the deeds accomplished by the governors. Nevertheless, the surrounding tribes did not accept their domination by the lords of K'umarcaaj peacefully, and there were wars. Warrior groups were sent to oversee the political divisions of the kingdom. A list was given of the regions that provided warriors for the conquests and colonization. Subjects who distinguished themselves in war were given rewards. The *Título* praised the capital of the kingdom, the temple dedicated to Tojíl and the increased tributes that the subjects paid the governors of K'umarcaaj. It praised the governors, attributing to them clairvoyant powers: "They knew if there would be death, hunger, or war," because it was said that to know all this they had "a book, the *Popol Wuj*, as it was called." Finally, it gave the genealogy of all the lords, "our first grandfathers and fathers." It ended with the invasions and wars with the Spaniards. The so-called *Fragmento de un Título de Yax* contained a detailed description of the territory of Yax, which Carmack supposed once formed a part of the *Título de Yax*.

Source: Robert M. Carmack and James Mondloch, eds., *El Título de Yax y otros documentos Quichés de Totonicapán, Guatemala,* 1989.

Título—marriage, rituals, settlement of towns, militarism, etc.—
were more similar to Toltec than to Aztec or Pipil."

Carmack adds that the best proofs of the Mexica influence on
the *Título* were the abundant Nahua names, especially those that
referred to the migration from Tulán, war, religious ceremonies,
and the symbols of power.[54] I share his opinion. Elsewhere I
have maintained that the so-called Toltec culture originated in
Teotihuacán and that this city was the model for later political
capitals, the cradle of the songs and of the painted codices that
narrated the origins of the cosmos and the chronicles of the
kingdom, and that it was the primitive Tollan, from which were
derived the later incarnations: Tollan-Cholula, Tula de Hidalgo,
Tulán Zuyuá (Chichen Itzá), and Tollan-Tenochtitlán.[55] Not
long ago Karl Taube supported this thesis. In a study of the language of Teotihuacán, he proposed that this was Náhuat, an
ancient variant of Náhuatl.[56] The old Teotihuacán tradition is
present in the *Popol Vuh* and in the majority of the *Títulos* from
Chichén Itzá, the Yucatan metropolis that flourished in the ninth
to eleventh centuries, which in my opinion is the legendary
Tulán Zuyuá of the K'iche' and Kakchiquel texts. Verifying
that the *Título de Totonicapán* and the *Título de Yax* of the
K'iche' repeated the content, thematic division, and essential
purpose of the *Popol Vuh* provides key information in explaining
their origins. The similarity and parallelism of the three texts
show, without the shadow of a doubt, that the two *Títulos* were
different versions of the *Popol Vuh* or were texts derived from
the same source that nourished the book that immortalized the
history of the K'iche' people. I wish to state that the texts of
Totonicapán and *Yax* are not land titles as their names proclaim,
but rather variants of the ancestral stories that the people of
Mesoamerica constructed in order to remember their origins
and preserve their identities. That was the understanding of
Adrián Recinos when he mentioned that his first editor, Charles
Etienne Brasseur de Bourbourg,

who was not always correct in naming indigenous documents, called this the *Título de los señores de Totonicapán*; but in reality, although at the end it speaks of land measures and marks the sites that King Quikab recognized and the markers that indicated the towns on the Pacific Coast, most of the document is a narration of the origin of the three K'iche' nations or factions and their journeys through the territory of the current Republic of Guatemala to the kingdom of that conquering chief whose arms brought to submission almost all of the people of this region of Central America.[57]

If this is the case, then one must ask why it was that the ancient chronicles of the K'iche' kingdom were changed into legal titles for claiming the ownership of land.

The Transformation of the Chronicle of the Kingdom into a Legal Document

The richness of the Maya texts, transferred early into the Spanish alphabet, allowed for the steps that were to change the ancient chronicle of the kingdoms into a legal file. The first step, as is shown in the *Título de Yax,* included adding a few paragraphs to the chronicle that described the places and markers that delineated the territory. Robert Carmack also published the *Fragmento de un Título de Yax,* dated 1562, which was a description of the extension and limits of the town of San Miguel Totonicapán preserved by the descendents of the Yax lineage. Carmack assumed that this text, entirely dedicated to a description of territorial possessions, was perhaps a part of the *Título de Yax.* The complete text would then include the chronicle narrating the founding of the kingdom as the first part and the description of the territorial limits from the *Fragmento* as the second part.[58]

Another example that shows the accommodation of the ancient memory of the town to the legal record demanded by Spanish authorities is the *Historia quiché de don Juan Torres,* dated 1580. This *Historia,* written in K'iche' by a descendant of the Tamub lineage, contained a type of summary of the *Popol Vuh* in its first part and at the end incorporated a description of the lands associated with that lineage.[59]

As is apparent in these last documents, the second step in the transformation of the ancient chronicles was their conversion to *Títulos* that legitimized the traditional possessions of the chiefs. Most of the K'iche' *Títulos* of the sixteenth century were written at the request of the chiefs of the lineage, who demanded the preparation of new documents to which they gave the name of *Títulos* and whose responsibility it was to present them as a verification of their property rights. *La historia de los Xpantzay de Tecpan Guatemala* (sixteenth century) and the *Título de los indios de Santa Clara de la Laguna* (1583) showed that the chiefs had new titles made, bringing together and receiving the testamentary support of the main people of the place, then argued their ownership from time immemorial and demanded that their lands be protected by those documents.[60]

The third step that hastened the transition of the ancient genealogies of the chiefs into legal documents was the testament or will. In the K'iche' tradition a variety of terms and legal procedures were used to assure that territorial properties remained in the hands of the descendents of the ancient lineages. Carmack states that the K'iche' *Títulos* of the sixteenth century were also identified by legal terms such as *testamento* (will), *libro* (record), *auto* (warrant), *probanza* (verification), and *poder* (proxy), words that came from the European judicial tradition.[61] In their struggle to keep their lands, the chiefs made use of this legal terminology and accepted the yoke of Spanish writing as well as the Spanish courts, in whose archives were filed the innumerable documents that defended their owners' right to the lands.

Among the ancient Kakchiquel papers written in the Spanish alphabet were some that bore the name *Testamento.* Nevertheless, they did not in any way conform to the Roman or Spanish judicial tradition, which set forth rigid procedures for writing out the last will and testament of individuals and for handing down their property. Thus, the *Testamento de los Xpantzay,* dated 1554, did not express the individual will of one person as was customary under Western norms, instead stating: "This is the will and testament of our fathers and grandfathers, the head men of Xpantzay." And later, instead of referring to the property to be inherited, the *Testamento* recorded the genealogy of their ancestors since they had left Tulán Zuyuá, concluding: "I make this my will and title, which contains the truth before God. And I write this story which should not be erased. I, Alonso Pérez, for you my children and for my grandchildren, from now until the end of the world, let this story not be lost."[62] We can see here that the Western will and testament had been changed by Alonso Pérez into a kind of ethnic memory that collected the deeds of the ancestors and also an admonition to his children and grandchildren that they not forget that ancestral memory.

It is clear then that the Maya *Títulos,* like those of the Mixtecs, were based on the pre-Hispanic model conceived to maintain the memory of the kingdom, whose preeminent expression in this region was the *Popol Vuh.* This was the memory that gave ethnic and cultural legitimacy to the Maya *Títulos.* But in contrast to the Nahuas, Zapotecs, and Mixtecs, the Mayas lost their pictographic tradition and were only able to maintain their written language through the Spanish alphabet (fig. 120). The rare illustrations included in these texts show the degradation that had affected the ancient languages of imagery in the Colonial Maya culture (fig. 121). The oral and written media dominated the *Títulos,* verifications, and wills and testaments. It is clear that the diffusion of writing with Spanish characters was the most important cultural process of that period, a process that had an early beginning in the Maya area.

The use of the alphabet first resulted in the transcription into Spanish of the ancient codices and songs (*Popol Vuh, Título de Totonicapán, Título de Yax*), then led to the description in Spanish

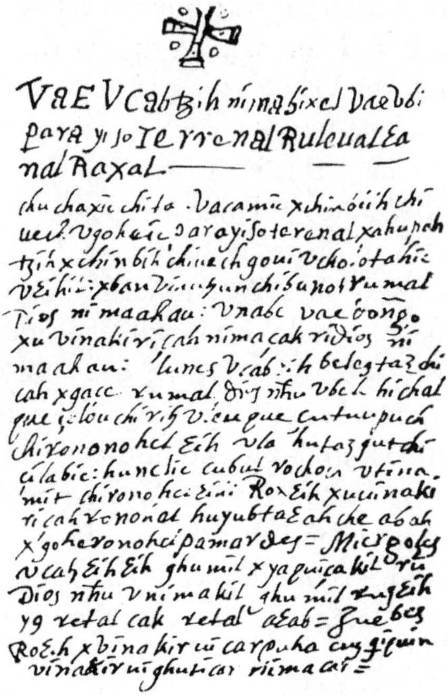

Fig. 120. First page, in the K'iché language transcribed in Latin characters, from the *Título de Totonicapán.* (Photo from Carmack and Mondloch, 1983: 42.)

of the first territorial limits of the towns, and later expanded into the *Títulos,* verifications, wills, and legal documents used to defend the properties of the chiefs, alleging that they were ancestral properties owned since time immemorial. The demands of proving the ancient ownership of property also explains the proliferation of family trees of the chiefs that were so frequent on the canvases and documents of the Colonial Period.

The process that transformed the ancient chronicle of the kingdoms into a text that legitimized territorial properties, ending with the *Título,* which linked that tradition with Western legal proceedings, was the work of the chiefs and the towns. The testimentary literature produced by both shows the transformations that the conservation and transmission of the Maya memory underwent. Most important, by the end of the sixteenth century the Mayas as well as the Nahuas, P'urhépechas, Zapotecs, and Mixtecs had constructed efficient mnemonic devices to transmit their past,

Fig. 121. Drawing of a native with a bow, arrows, and a quiver, which appears in the *Título de Yax*. (Photo from Carmack and Mondloch, 1989: 72.)

based on the pre-Hispanic as well as the Western legacy. Those instruments, even when they were produced and manipulated by the chiefs, strengthened the defense and the identity of the towns. As Matthew Restall states, their scope was summed up in the population of the city, and their intent was to support the political and territorial interests of the community.[63]

The New Canon Constructed by the Títulos primordiales

The existence of the so-called *Títulos* in the Nahua and P'urhépecha environment as well as among the Mixtecs and Mayas proved that it was a universal phenomenon, a cultural expression with common roots, content, and format. The revision of the *Títulos* in different cultural traditions allows us to sustain the argument that we are faced with a device specially created to conserve and transmit collective memory, a product of the interaction between the Mesoamerican and Western cultures. The Spanish administration, by imposing a new form of settling and legitimizing the possession of lands on the native people, obliged them to develop a wide range of devices for satisfying that demand. They first turned to their own traditions, to the vessels where they had stored the memory that explained their origins and the settling of their towns. The songs that told of the origin of human beings, the founding of the kingdom, the lineage of the governors, and the avatars of the ethnic group—to those the people turned to sustain their identity and affirm the antiquity of their territorial possessions (table 6).

The canvases, maps, and *Títulos* of Oaxaca took their historical information and identifying substance from the *Códice de Viena*, that great encyclopedia wherein their ancestors had stored the founding of the kingdom and the nation. The Mayas so used the *Popol Vuh*—the seedbed that nourished the *Títulos* and verifications that sustained the antiquity of their people and territorial possessions—as did the Mexicas and the Nahua people, the heirs of Teotihuacán, the womb of Mesoamerican civilization.

This ancient support was threatened with extinction after the introduction of the Colonial regime. Before the conflict over lands took place, the old political and identity foundations were put at risk by the program for the congregation of peoples promoted during the decade of the 1540s. Several royal warrants in 1546, 1551, and 1568 declared that "the natives of that land who are spread out should be put together into towns." The King ordered that new towns be founded, called the Indian Republics, and that lands be marked as woodlands, *ejidos* (community lands), and fields, which would henceforth be entered in the rolls of community properties. This gigantic project included the central area of New Spain south as far as Guatemala. It resulted in the uprooting of millions of individuals and thousands of villages forced to leave their thousand-year-old settlements and found new towns. And it became a policy of uprooting on a scale never seen before. In the new towns, laid out in the Spanish style, an extensive program of hispanization of the individual, family, and collective lives of native people was carried out. Thus, religion, forms of government, language, fashions of dress, and other customs of Western culture became the traditions of the so-called Indian Republics.[64]

However, mass deaths in the form of devastating epidemics threatened the very existence of the original populations. The violent epidemics of 1531–32, 1538, 1543–48, 1563–64, and 1576–81 left behind a dreadful remnant. Of 25 million inhabitants in 1521, only a third remained by the end of the century. Thousands of villages were left virtually unpopulated, others disappeared, and in some only old people and sick families survived. In the countryside fields were not cultivated or were worked at an intensity far below that of thirty years earlier. And to all of that was added the scourge of famine, which struck the population with unprecedented violence in 1538, 1543–44, 1550–52, and 1563–64.[65] This devastation meant that the rebuilding of indigenous memory occurred in the midst of a radical breakup of the old order. In those years the gods, governors, institutions, traditions, and material life of the people themselves were moved off their foundations and suspended due to the changes unleashed by the Spanish government and by natural catastrophes. That dark backdrop must not be forgotten when we try to explain something so intertwined with life itself as the recovery of historical memory. As if the native peoples had challenged themselves to avert the collapse that was inexorably destroying their world through the art of recollection, between 1530 and 1560 they transcribed into the Spanish alphabet the master works of indigenous memory, the great summations of their historic tradition: the *Relación de Michoacán* (fig. 122) of the P'urhépechas (ca. 1541), the *Popol Vuh* of the Mayas (1554–58), the *Códice Selden II* of the Mixtecs (sixteenth century), the *Códice Xolotl* of the Texcocans (mid-sixteenth century), the *Historia tolteca-chichimeca* of the founders of Cholula and Quauhtinchan (1547–60), and the *Historia de los mexicanos por sus pinturas* (1531) and the *Leyenda de los soles* (1558) of the Nahuas (table 7).

Fig. 122. The moment when Fray Jerónimo de Alcalá turns over the manuscript of the *Relación de Michoacán,* translated into Spanish, to Viceroy Mendoza. (Photo from Alcalá, 2000.)

In this process of destruction and transformation, new works were also born that tried to recover the past of the people by weaving native forms of recording history with those from Europe. The *Títulos,* maps, and canvases discussed earlier are not—as some recalcitrant Indianists maintain—native works, but rather hybrid products, unpublished mixtures that linked American traditions with those of the Western world. At the critical moment that joined the decline of the great aboriginal culture with the progressive encroachment of the West, canvases and maps were painted and written that brought ancient traditions up to the Colonial present: *Lienzo de Jicayán, Lienzo de Zacatepec I, Lienzo de Tlapiltepec, Lienzo de Ihuitlán,* the *Códice Selden II,* and other works created in the middle of the sixteenth century.

From a continuing symbiosis between indigenous and Western traditions, a new identity of the people was born. Perhaps the most significant contribution of the canvases, maps, and *Títulos* from the different regions of New Spain was their capacity to clarify for us the process whereby native groups built their new Mestizo identity. It was a process through which they rewrote

Table 7. Genealogical Reconstruction of the Basic Texts of Indigenous Memory

Period	Maya Tradition	Mixtec Tradition	Mexica Tradition
Prehispanic Period	Palencan myth of the origin of the cosmos and the beginnings of the kingdoms (A.D. 692) *Popol Vuh*, first pictographic edition, probably 13th–14th centuries	*Códice de Viena* *Códice Nuttall* *Códice Colombino* *Códice Bodley* *Códice Selden* *Códice Becker I and II* *Códice Sánchez Solís*, 14th–15th centuries	The Toltec book of books, where, according to Alva Ixtlilxóchitl, "all of their persecutions and travails, prosperities and good fortune, kings and lords, laws and good government of their past, . . . and a summary of all their things of science and wisdom . . . and they entitled this book . . . *Teoamoxtli*, which when well interpreted meant . . . divine book."
Colonial Period	*Popol Vuh*, 1554 version, K'iche' written with Spanish characters *Título de Totonicapán*, 1554 *Título de Yax*, ca. 1560 *Título de Pedro Velasco*, 1592 *Memorial de Sololá. Annals of the Cakchiqueles*, beginning of the 17th century	*Códice Selden II*, 16th century *Lienzo de Jicayán*, ca. 1550 *Lienzo de Tlapiltepec*, ca. 1550 *Lienzo de Ihuitlán*, ca. 1550 *Lienzo de Coixtlahuaca*, 16th century *Lienzo de Zacatepec I*, 16th century *Lienzo de Tequixtepec I*, 16th century *Mapa de Teozacoalco*, 1580	*Historia de los mexicanos por sus pinturas*, 1531 *Leyenda de los Soles*, 1558 *Códice Azcatitlán*, 16th century *Códice Xólotl*, 16th century *Mapas de Cuauhtinchan* I and II, 16th century *Historia Tolteca-Chichimeca*, 16th century *Anales de Tula*, 16th century *Códice Mendoza*, 16th century *Historia general de las cosas de la Nueva España*, 16th century *Relaciones históricas*, Fernando de Alva Ixtlixóchitl, 17th century

Source: Robert M. Carmack and James Mondloch, eds., *El Título de Yax y otros documentos Quichés de Totonicapán, Guatemala,* 1989.

their past, creating historic wills and testaments based on both legacies, but at the same time they were bearers of a new identity. The memory that burned in the Oaxacan and Mayan canvases, maps, and *Títulos* was, as has been seen, a memory with a very profound historical background, supported by the most remote archetypes of Mesoamerican consciousness but transformed by the disruptions of the Spanish invasion—by conquest, congregation of peoples, introduction of Christianity, creation of the Fundo legal (imposition of Spanish legislation on native lands), expansion of a language written in the Latin alphabet, and the constitution of new towns as axes of the material and cultural life of the community. The canvases, maps, and *Títulos,* as they incorporated those diverse processes, became invaluable historical testimonials to their time, relating and transmitting the past in new forms. They were stories that transmitted the collective memory of the members of each of the towns.

The Maya, Zapotec, Mixtec, P'urhépecha, and Nahua *Títulos* shared the intent of setting down the forms of population imposed by the Colonial regime on the bases of their ancient traditions. They were instruments dedicated to the strengthening of the town and the protection of its lands. But to the surprise of either the historian dominated by the Western vision or the anthropologist addicted to Indianist dogma, the founding of the Colonial towns was a mixture of both traditions. Their creation brought together the paraphernalia that surrounded the ancient foundings: the New Fire, the protecting gods, the patronage of the ancient ones, the participation of the entire community, the celebratory festival . . . but within the framework of European institutions and symbols: the Spanish writing used to legalize the founding documents; the presence of Viceregal authorities; the building of the church and the erection of crosses on the four sides of the town; the baptism of the headmen or chiefs. Such was the hybrid nature of the canon that now sanctified the constitution of the towns.

The deepest substratum of the *Títulos,* maps, and canvases was indigenous, but their creation was hybrid (table 7). Their origin went back to pre-Hispanic times, but their elaboration throughout the sixteenth century was contaminated with legacies that came from the Western tradition, while in their content we find an intrinsic mixture of oral, pictographic, and written traditions whose ancestry it is difficult to trace. These wills and testaments often included in their new format songs paired with *huehuetlatolli* (discourses of the elders); "glosses" in the Spanish alphabet added to paintings or canvases; ancient pictographs accompanying written documents; legal and religious formulas from the European tradition; traces of the ancient annals expressed in Latin characters; and various kinds of interactions between those different traditions.[66] Their construction likewise steered between flexibility and change. In contrast to the ancient chronicle of the kingdom, which froze form and content into a codex that survived almost without change for more than fifteen hundred years from its birth in Teotihuacán until the Spanish invasion, the *Títulos* were born under the sign of change. From chronicles of the kingdom they became canvases and maps, then the painted canvases became hybrid texts, and these later abandoned the pictographs and became documents in which letters ruled. Since they were a Mestizo product, they had the quality of mutation and a permanent facility for adapting themselves to new historical circumstances. The process was dominated by the imposition of the written word and positive rights, which unavoidably displaced images and the ancient usages and customs.[67]

A revealing example of that willingness to change was the conversion of the relics of the founders of the city, the sacred bundles that represented the heart of the people (*altepetlyolotl*) in the *Títulos primordiales*. As the reader will recall, in ancient times the territorial state was represented by the glyph of the hill, in whose interior there was a cave where the waters of fertility and the seeds of the maize rested. This was a representation of the first mountain that emerged from the primordial waters on the day of creation, a symbol of the growth of fertile land, and the deepest expression of the tie of people to the earth.

Fig. 123. Plate II of the *Códice de Yauhuitlán,* which describes a meeting in the palace of Yauhuitlán presided over by the two men at the upper right. In the foreground is a group of nobles and princes, meeting to deliberate the affairs of the town. (Photo from the *Códice de Yauhuitlán,* 1994.)

All the Mesoamerican states reproduced that primordial mountain at the heart of their ceremonial centers, and in the interior of that pyramid they put the relics of the founder of the kingdom and the dynasty. The bundle in which they kept those relics thus became the sacred deposit of the origin of the kingdom, the symbol of the power of the governors, and the emblem of the State. That ancient symbolism was transferred to the church, the town council, and the *Títulos* of the Colonial town, which symbolized the "heart of the city," the thing most sacred, beloved, and protected by the members of the community. The *Títulos primordiales,* the heart of the town of the Indian Republics, came to be the talisman that held the strength of the ancestors, the chest where the relics of the patron saint were kept, the storehouse of collective memory, and the shield of the people in the context of the new legal order (fig. 99).[68]

The keeping of the community lands thus became the collective business that unified the members of the town (fig. 123), and the *Títulos primordiales* became the strong box where the life memory of the populace was kept safe. The *Títulos primordiales,* in their content and form, constituted a new way of representing and relating the past, a canon that the dominating tradition in historical studies tried to separate into two opposing aspects: the indigenous on one side and the Western on the other. This was an arbitrary division that made the penetration of the mystery of its origin and the recognition of the nature of its changing development difficult for more than five hundred years.

VII. From the Creole Homeland to the History of the Nation

During the first two centuries of Spanish government, different interpretations of the past proliferated, though they were limited by a narrow vision of the totality of the nation. The mendicant orders promoted a story that spoke of their settlements in the foreign country, praised their evangelizing work, and lauded the religious ardor of their members. The cities, beginning with the capital of the kingdom, spoiled their distinguished men of letters, who wrote chronicles in praise of the territory, the monuments, and the will of the settlers. The ethnic groups, shut up within the limits of the Indian Republics, wrote stories of their towns dedicated to the protection of the community lands and the local identity. As can be seen, these were self-absorbed discourses that ignored the memory of others and reflected the profound division that separated the settlers of New Spain into mutually antagonistic classes, groups, and ethnicities. During those years there was no way to imagine a history that could include the entirety of the Viceroyalty.

Creole Patriotism

As the enlightening studies of Francisco de la Maza, Edmundo O'Gorman, Luis Villoro, Luis González, and David Brading show, the Creoles, descendants of Spaniards born in the New World, were the first to affirm their identities by turning to introspection based on their remote origins. From that river, born as a trickle in the sixteenth century with the first generations of Creole people but overflowing by the eighteenth century, there were three identifiable streams: the establishment of identity links with the land in which they lived; the rescue of the ancient indigenous past in order to establish in it the legitimacy of the homeland that was being built; and the creation of symbols for the values of the homeland.

Taking over the foreign land both physically and culturally was one of the first goals established by the Creole people. By the end of the seventeenth century, the Creoles found in the exuberant American landscape and the exotic Indian past two elements that separated them from the Spaniards and affirmed their identity with the land of their birth. Imperceptibly, the task of discovering and reconnoitering the territory—a commitment that had earlier fallen to European explorers—became the responsibility of the residents of the country. The Creoles became experts on the territory by personal experience, by taking possession of it and reconnoitering it, and later they became surveyors in the endless land suits brought on by the new settling of the rural people into towns laid out in the Spanish style. Then the first urban plans, freight roads, and regional charts were laid out, many of them by Creoles.[1]

In the *Relaciones geográficas,* which Philip II had collected around 1580, many Creoles cooperated with the old Indians and the Viceregal authorities in order to put together the records and maps of the villages of New Spain.[2] In the eighteenth century the preparation of the *Relaciones topográficas* increased their knowledge of the geography of the country.[3] The Age of Enlightenment was also the century of expanding the borders of the Viceroyalty. To limit the spread of the Russians along the Pacific Coast and the English and French on the Atlantic, a defensive advance party scattered military presidios, religious missions, mining camps, and new towns throughout the far-flung Spanish territories.

The extension of the northern border coincided with scientific exploration and with the custom of inventorying the territory and classifying the flora and fauna. New settlements, scientific expeditions, and defensive strategies brought an avalanche of fresh

Fig. 124. General map of the Viceroyalty of New Spain by José Antonio de Alzate, 1772. (Photo from *El territorio mexicano*, 1982: 30.)

information, which created a new image of the country. The map, a means of communication that gained importance during those years, added a graphic dimension to that image. In 1748 the legendary map of the territory that don Carlos de Sigüenza y Góngora had been working on since the turn of the century was published for the first time in Mexico. Later, José Antonio Alzate added new information to it, and in 1768 he dedicated it to the Royal Academy of Sciences in Paris (fig. 124).[4]

In 1779 engineer Miguel Constanzó designed a plan for marking the political divisions of the Viceroyalty and the new borders of the northern lands, called the Internal Provinces. These plans and charts for the first time showed the Creoles the great extension that the territory of their homeland now embraced (fig. 125). It was not by chance that the first authors of the general map of New Spain were Creoles such as Carlos de Sigüenza y Góngora

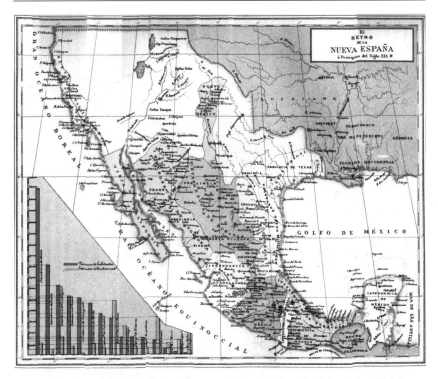

Fig. 125. Map of the kingdom of New Spain with its administrative divisions.

and José Antonio Alzate. It was also Creoles who provided Alejandro de Humboldt with the most up-to-date information for his *Atlas* of New Spain. According to Manuel Orozco y Berra, this map "came to be something akin to a summary of the geographic progress of the colony, the ultimate expression of what the government and the residents of New Spain had accomplished in order to understand the topography of their country" (fig. 126).[5]

With uncommon visual force, the map transmitted to the Creoles the diversity of a vast territory; the agricultural, mining, industrial, and commercial abundance contained within its borders; and the sensation that a providential fate was protecting the Creole homeland. As Orozco y Berra has observed, the settlers of New Spain were convinced that the eighteenth century had been the epoch of their splendor:

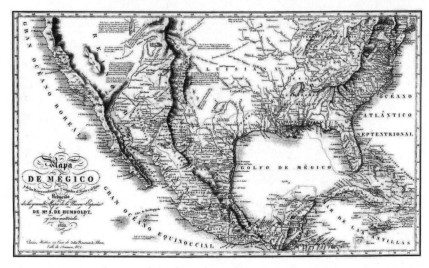

Fig. 126. General map of the kingdom of New Spain drawn by Alejandro de Humboldt.

The brilliant signature of the colony was the eighteenth. The administration was very much improved, with erudite authorities who well understood the advantages which could accrue from broadening scientific knowledge, and did not object to its expansion as far as the exceptional circumstances of New Spain permitted. Teaching methods changed; public establishments improved; there was special emphasis on physical sciences and mathematics; and the School of Mines was a great monument to the demands of the luminaries of the century. The government undertook naval exploration to reconnoiter the northwestern coast of the continent, resulting in a series of scientific expeditions which have not yet been well understood or appreciated. The Gulf coasts were resurveyed, their hydrography updated and improved to a level that had been virtually unknown before. The country was crisscrossed and traveled in every direction, now by experts who located sites with exact methods using state-of-the-art instruments, now by individuals with less training, but who nonetheless revealed the configuration of the terrain. Delicate and clever astronomical observations were taken . . . topography took unaccustomed flight, and besides the private maps of the provinces and intendencies, erudite Viceroys like Bucareli and Revillagigedo had general charts constructed with either the old or new political divisions included. On their own part, private sources made up a large contingent, and geography developed more rapidly in the last third of the century than it had in all earlier times.[6]

The Rescue of the Indigenous Past

Identification with the land complemented ties to the past. During the seventeenth century, Carlos de Sigüenza y Góngora, Juan de Torquemada, and Agustín de Vetancurt made collections of indigenous antiquities, rescued oral traditions, and praised the qualities of nature in America. In the *Monarquía indiana* of Franciscan friar Juan de Torquemada, published in 1615, the Mesoamerican past was raised to the level of classic antiquity. In this work Torquemada recognized the wisdom accumulated by his predecessors (Andrés de Olmos, Motolinía, Diego Durán, Bernardino de Sahagún, and Jerónimo de Mendieta), and with that information he composed a summation of the past and the traditions of the natives of the country that enjoyed fame in his time and had great influence in later years. Nonetheless, Torquemada maintained the disparaging idea that until then had impeded the recovery of that past: the idea that the religion and works which that culture expressed were the product of the devil.

Surprisingly, the satanic image began to change in the middle of the eighteenth century. One revealing sign of the appreciation that the Mesoamerican past now gained was the extraordinary collection of Mexican antiquities brought together by Lorenzo Boturini between 1736 and 1743. Rather than collecting potsherds or carved stone, the Italian traveler's obsession was the collection of pictographs and codices in which the past of the aboriginal people was summarized. To Boturini those documents contained "such excellence of sublime things that I dare to say that this history can not only compete with the most celebrated in the world, but outshine them."[7]

One outside circumstance renewed interest in the identities of the Creole homeland. Between 1749 and 1789, some of the most influential authors of the Enlightenment (the Count of Buffon, Abbot Reynal, Cornelius de Pauw, and the Scots historian William Robertson) wrote disparagingly of the American culture and indicated a natural incapacity of natives of America to create works of science and culture.[8] First to respond to those attacks were the friars and the educated Creoles who had distinguished themselves by supporting a positive interpretation of the Meso-american past and affirming the creative virtues of those born in America. Thus, Juan José Eguiara y Eguren answered those invectives with his *Bibliotheca mexicana* (1775), a monumental work dedicated to showing the merits of scientific and literary production by Mexicans from the earliest times until the first decades of the eighteenth century.[9]

Francisco Javier Clavijero was the leader of the new erudite Hispanic humanists who flourished in the second half of the eighteenth century. Outstanding among his numerous contributions was his proposal that the past of his country should be looked at from another perspective, an idea that he developed in his *Storia antica del Messico* [Historia antigua de México], published in 1780 in Cesena, Italy, during a bitter exile that he underwent along with his Jesuit companions.

Contrary to the Christian interpretation of history canonized by the religious chroniclers who preceded him, the *Historia antigua de México* was a record of human deeds explained by their geographic, political, and social conditions. As Luis Villoro has stated: "We open Clavijero's book, and from its first pages we find ourselves with a history in which every supernatural dimension seems to have disappeared."[10] Clavijero made use of the models and techniques of Western historians to write a unified, coherent, reasoned, and elegant description of the history of an indigenous nation. It was a story of the Mexican people devoid of the satanic and providential stigmas disseminated by religious chroniclers. Instead of seeing natives as inferior beings, Clavijero viewed them as equal to any other human beings. He said that "in the make-up of the character of the Mexicans, just as in the character of other nations, bad as well as good participate."[11] In contrast to his religious predecessors, who evaluated the American people in the light of the Bible or by following the European concept of history, Clavijero emphasized the analysis of human deeds and the natural environment in which they occurred.

Clavijero chose the historic development of the Mexicans from their origins until the Spanish invasion as the focus of his story. It was an epic history that traced the shadowy beginnings of a people who in less than one century became the most powerful nation in Mesoamerica. As stated by Luis Villoro, it was "a story which told of the life of an historic people," a story that reminded one of "the young Rome, as sung by the ancients."[12] And it was also a tragic story, since the last chapters—the best in the book—told of the dramatic events of the siege and conquest of Tenochtitlán.

Clavijero masterfully combined "the history of the man of flesh and blood"[13] with an analysis of the political, social, and educational systems that forged the culture of the Mexicans. The *Historia,* in addition to collecting and explaining deeds, was a history of the culture. The analysis Clavijero made of the laws, religion, customs, politics, economics, and arts and sciences of the Mexicans strove to explain the high level of civilization they had achieved.[14] The most diverse characters moved through the *Historia*'s pages: brave warriors such as the Tlaxcalan Tlahuicole, beside that prototype of fidelity, Tochnantzin; the Wise Kings (Netzahualcóyotl); the treacherous tyrants (Maxtlaton); the astute and valiant chiefs (Xólotl and his son Nopaltzin, the great Tlacaélel); together with the deeds of common men and women whose lives were also "eternal sources of teachings on morality. They show us of the vanity of human glory."[15] Clavijero was also the first American author to recognize the essential contribution of the indigenous population to the construction of Colonial society, as revealed in this page, which is unique in Mexican historiography:

The Americans are the ones who work the land, the ones who plow, sow, hoe, and reap the wheat, maize, rice, broad beans, beans and other grains and vegetables; as well as the cacao, vanilla, cotton, indigo, and all the plants useful for sustenance, clothing and business from those provinces, and without them nothing is done . . .

But this is the least of it: they are the ones who cut and haul out of the forests all the wood which is needed; the ones who cut, haul and work the stones, and those who make the lime, gypsum, and bricks. They are the ones who build all the buildings. . . . They are the ones who make and maintain the roads, the ones who build the canals and dikes, and the ones who clean the cities. They work in many gold, silver, and copper mines. They are the shepherds, cowboys, weavers, pottery makers, bakers, cooks, couriers, stevedores, etc. In a word, they are the ones who bear all the burden of public works, as is clearly seen in all the provinces of that great kingdom.[16]

José Emilio Pacheco has stated that Clavijero's book "is of basic importance to our culture," because "it is the first one that in the century of the Enlightenment suggests that the European is no longer the center, a first effort to show that there are other cultures and other human groups who are different from the Greco-Latin paradigms. . . . In this area the *Historia antigua de México* is the equivalent of an intellectual declaration of independence."[17]

Concurrent with this vindication of American history, Clavijero deployed the most subtle arguments to combat Western prejudices that denigrated the American land and culture. His famous *Disertaciones,* which accompanied the *Historia antigua de México,* were a refutation of the ideas expressed by the Count of Buffon, the naturalist Cornelius de Pauw, Abbot Reynal, and the historian

William Robertson on the inferiority of American nature and its people. Combining a masterful handling of reasoned argument with an educated understanding of the ancient chronicles and the most up-to-date information on contributions to scientific understanding, Clavijero made a sort of "Mexican encyclopedia" of the *Historia antigua de México,* as José Emilio Pacheco has stated.[18]

Gathering in its pages the most advanced historical and scientific information of his times and embellishing his text with elegant dialectics in a polished and well-turned Spanish, Clavijero made the *Historia antigua de México* a manifest of Creole consciousness, the most accomplished expression of the European Enlightenment in America. His work, as it took on the defense of Mexican antiquity, provided erudite friars and Creole intellectuals with the instruments for taking over that past from the natives and presenting it as their own to the Spanish government. As David Brading has observed, "The American Spaniards found in history and in religion [the Virgin of Guadalupe] the symbolic means that would permit them to reject Colonial status." The *Historia antigua de México,* by proudly rescuing the indigenous past, became a symbol of Creole patriotism and a historic argument with which to demand the independence of the nation.[19]

In recent years students of Clavijero's work have pointed out his importance as the cornerstone of Creole patriotism. Nonetheless, we must not forget that above and beyond its ideological nature, the enduring value of the *Historia antigua de México* resides in its historiographic merits. Clavijero carefully studied the ancient indigenous codices and texts and made extensive use of the Colonial chronicles, particularly the works of Fray Juan de Torquemada and Diego Durán. He thought to unite this disperse collection of data and images into a single book—the work that gave us the first shining image of a past that until then had been fuzzy and hard to grasp. He also used dialectical argumentation to give order, harmony, and persuasive force to those arguments in such a way that the sentences, paragraphs, and conclusions overlapped until they struck the reader with the clarity of noonday.

Clavijero centered his work on the narration of the origins of the nation, the most ancient lure of the art of historical story-telling. In the dedication he wrote that his book was "a history of Mexico written by a Mexican," which he offered as a proof of his "most sincere love of country." Thus, by rescuing the depth and originality of that past, Clavijero projected the ancient Mexican nation into the future, and his book took on the shape of foundation, memory, and future of the nation.

With these same motivations, the rescue of the indigenous past accelerated in the last decades of the eighteenth century. At the same time that Clavijero was writing his *Historia,* Mariano Veytia, a Creole who admired Boturini, wrote a *Historia antigua de México* that was later published. José Antonio Alzate, the famous editor of the *Gazetas de literatura,* also became interested in ancient monuments. He believed that "a building shows the character and culture of the people" and dared to state that it could throw light on the "origin of the Indians." With that outlook, he published an article in which the archaeological monuments of Tajín were described for the first time, and he later issued his *Antigüedades de Xochicalco* (1791), the first publication illustrated with engravings of an ancient city. Studies of historic monuments bore fruit in the work of Antonio de León y Gama, whose *Descripción histórica y cronológica de las dos piedras* (1792) was an innovative analysis of the Coatlicue and the Piedra del Sol, monoliths found in the main plaza of the city of Mexico in 1790. In his study of the Piedra del Sol, León y Gama made his mark on archaeological investigations. For the first time, an archaeological monument served to support the explanation of an entire system of ideas. And working against the currents then in fashion, he made clear that the indigenous calendar was governed by its own unique ideas and could not be explained in terms of the European calendar.[20]

Interest in ancient American civilizations extended into a field that had been ignored until that time: the exploration of archaeological cities and monuments. In 1773 an expedition to Palenque was organized, and in 1784 the first information and drawings were released on an area of ancient monuments. Charles III later ordered new explorations in the region, and Charles IV continued that policy, supporting an expedition led by Guillermo Dupaix and the Mexican draftsman Luciano Castañeda, who traveled through the center and southeast of the Viceroyalty between 1805 and 1807, amassing an important collection of archaeological pieces and spurring interest in the understanding of antiquities.[21]

In 1803 Alejandro de Humboldt visited a New Spain in the process of transformation. In that intense year, full of reconnoitering, surprises, and discoveries, the wise German traveled through the northern mining country, visited the main regions and monuments of the nation, and climbed the highest peaks, and wherever he went made scientific measurements with modern instruments; studied the geography, flora, and antiquities; and collected an astonishing amount of information on the physical environment, population, mineral riches, economic activities, and administrative and political organization of the Viceroyalty. In his *Ensayo político sobre el reino de la Nueva España* and his *Vistas de las cordilleras y monumentos de los pueblos indígenas de América,* he presented the image of an enormous country, until then lacking a study eloquent enough to show its real dimensions. The great vision that appeared in those books was in large part the optimistic image that the Creoles had created of their country and had transmitted to the wise German.[22]

Symbols of the Creole Homeland

By the middle of the eighteenth century, the image of a powerful country had merged with the image of an ancient land protected by the divinity. Since the travels of Columbus, it had been the custom to distinguish each of the four continents with the figure of a woman decorated with the attributes of her region. But unlike the beautiful figures of Europe, Africa, and Asia, America was represented by a naked woman bearing arrows and wearing

Fig. 127. Amerigo Vespucci "discovered" America, which is personified here as a nude Indian woman with a feather headdress. (Photo from Honour, 1975: 88.)

primitive attire (fig. 127). The Creoles of the Spanish possessions in America rejected that savage image and after the seventeenth and eighteenth centuries depicted America and its nations with the image of a beautiful and richly dressed native woman. The Creoles added to that image the coat of arms of ancient Tenochtitlán, the symbol that located the beautiful woman in Mexican territory (fig. 128).

In this war of images, the coat of arms of the ancient Mexican kingdom was persistently rejected by Viceregal authorities and replaced by other emblems (fig. 129). Nevertheless, in the struggle to find symbols representative of the new identities being forged in America, the Creoles and Mestizos adopted the emblem of the eagle standing on a prickly pear and fighting a serpent, and little by little they imprinted it on symbols of the most beloved representations of the homeland. On official documents the native emblem slowly usurped the place of the Spanish shield imposed by Charles V on the city of Mexico (fig. 130).

Fig. 128. Allegory of New Spain in an engraving by Joseph Sebastian and Johann Baptist Klauber, eighteenth century. (Photo from Cuadriello, 1994: 109.)

The chronicles that the Creoles wrote to celebrate the city and recall their ancient history were distinguished by bearing the insignias of the ancient Aztec kingdom on their covers or on the pages themselves. In the second half of the eighteenth century this insignia invaded maps and plans that depicted the city or the kingdom (fig. 131) and were added to the monuments that showed what was characteristic of the country. This irresistible advance reached the very heart of the church, the institution that had first rejected it as a pagan symbol.[23] In the book dedicated to the first Mexican saint (*Vida de San Felipe de Jesús,* 1802), the emblem of the eagle appeared as the symbol that confirmed the saint's Mexican nature (fig. 132).

Perhaps the most surprising part of the extraordinary process of forming and purifying the identity symbols of this period was the union of the ancient Mexican symbol with the image of the Virgin of Guadalupe. This link became unexpectedly strong when in 1737 the Virgin of Guadalupe was declared the patron saint of the city of Mexico and then elevated to the rank of Protectress of New Spain (1746). Pope Benedict XIV consecrated this choice of

Muy Noble e Insigne Muy Leal e Imperial
Ciudad de Mexico

Fig. 129. Coat of arms of the
city of Mexico, dominated by
Spanish heraldry, as granted
by the Emperor Charles V.
(Photo from Benítez, 1982.)

Fig. 130. (A) Emblem of the city of Mexico, printed on the new *Ordenanzas de la muy noble y leal Ciudad de México,* 1663; (B) seal of the town council of the city of Mexico, which was used to stamp the license of a master mason. (Photo from Florescano, 1998: 51.)

Fig. 131. Map of North America dedicated to the Marques de las Amarillas, 1755. The coat of arms of the Viceroy rests on the extended wings of an eagle standing on a prickly pear. (Photo from the National History Museum.)

the brown virgin in 1754, when he gave her the title of Protectress of the Kingdom and disposed that a liturgical feast day in the Christian calendar be dedicated to her. As demonstrated by Jaime Cuadriello, each of these events was celebrated with religious pomp and popular joy and with a splendid series of sculptural works that showed the intimate relationship established between the emblem of the eagle and prickly pear and the Virgin of Guadalupe (figs. 133 and 134).[24]

Thus, in a noteworthy painting by José Ribera y Argomanis (1737), the figure of Juan Diego can be seen at the left, offering the Virgin his blanket and some flowers so that she might produce the miracle of imprinting her image there. On the right side stands an Indian man who represents the kingdom of New Spain, stating the canonical words that were emblematic of the Virgin at that time: *Non fecit taliter omni nationi* (Such a thing was not done in

Fig. 132. Engraving showing the naming of San Felipe de Jesús as patron saint of the city of Mexico. To the left, a woman with a crown represents Spain; to the right, a native woman represents New Spain. (Photo from Cuadriello, 1994: 104.)

any other country). In the lower part, the eagle standing on the prickly pear supports the Virgin and the frames that describe the exultant moment of her appearance (fig. 134).

This series of paintings, engravings, altar backs, and sculptures, which we unfortunately cannot reproduce here, show that by the end of the eighteenth century the image of Guadalupe had become a many-faceted symbol whose diverse representations affirmed the identity of those born in New Spain. It was an expression of the kingdom of New Spain, the mother intercessor of the Indians, and the celestial protectress of the new Mestizo population. In the main scenes of these works, the Viceroyalty showed its individual nature in the presence of Spain, while the display of Mexican coats of arms expressed identification with the American territory.

The image of the Virgin of Guadalupe, accompanied by the ensigns of ancient Tenochtitlán, thus became the most genuine representation of the kingdom of New Spain: it was the symbol of what was purely Mexican, uniting the territory once occupied

Fig. 133. Eighteenth-century metal engraving by Miguel de Villavicencio, with the image of the Virgin of Guadalupe above the Mexican coat of arms. (Photo from Cuadriello, 1995: 19.)

Fig. 134. Painting by José Ribera y Argomanis (1737), celebrating the designation of the Virgin of Guadalupe as patron of the city of Mexico. (Photo from Cuadriello, 1995: 21.)

by the Mexicas with the site miraculously designated for the appearance of the Mother of God. In an original formula, the concepts of territoriality, political sovereignty, divine protection, and collective identity were united in a religious symbol that was the most widely venerated by the citizens of New Spain by the end of the eighteenth century.[25]

The War of Independence and the Beginnings of a New National Plan

Through armed insurgency, Miguel Hidalgo and José María Morelos proclaimed independence from Spain, recognized that the people were the original source of sovereignty, repudiated the government of the old regime, and established the bases for the political organization of the liberated nation. First in the decrees that Hidalgo and Morelos promulgated during the insurrection, later in the *Acta de Independencia* and the documents before the Congress of Chilpancingo, and finally in the *Sentimientos de la Nación* and the *Constitución de Apatzingán*, the constituent principles of the nation (autonomy, sovereignty, self-determination, will of the populace, equality) came to form a part of the collective memory.

Miguel Hidalgo (fig. 135) and José María Morelos were identified with the masses that constituted their armies and assumed the responsibility for acting in their name. They agreed to be leaders by popular demand. If the revolution, at the moment it began, transferred sovereignty to the armed masses, which from that point on acted on their own behalf and transformed reality, the decisions that Hidalgo made during the war were consistent with that new reality. As stated by Luis Villoro, the "decrees of Hidalgo did no more than express the effective sovereignty of the people." After Hidalgo's speech of September 16, 1810, the abolition of tribute payments symbolized the destruction of the existing rule: "For us, neither the king nor his taxes exist."[26]

The abrogation of taxes announced a profound modification of reality: the destruction of the old order. This is the sense of the other decisions adopted by Hidalgo as the representative of the masses. "Clothed in the authority that he exercised through the acclamation of the nation, Hidalgo abolished the distinctions of classes and slavery, signs of the infamy and oppression exercised by other classes against blacks and Mestizos."[27]

In the case of Morelos (fig. 136), his identification with the aspirations of the popular movement is even more genuine: "Morelos began his military career like so many leaders who moved up from the lower clerical ranks. He was no man of letters; he belonged, on the contrary, to the lowest classes . . . coming from the people,

Fig. 135. Anonymous portrait of Miguel Hidalgo. (Photo from *Los pinceles de la historia*, 2000.)

Fig. 136. Painting of Morelos by Claudio Linati. (Photo from Linati, 1956: plate 46.)

always sharing his life with them, he was the most authentic representative of the popular conscience."[28]

Under pressure from the educated and lettered Creoles, who demanded that he define the political purpose of the insurgent movement, Morelos, in emotional and simple words, stated a political purpose centered on popular sovereignty and the disappearance of the inequalities that divided the populace:

I want [the nation] to have a government which emanates from the people. . . . I want us to declare that there is no other nobility than that of virtue, of wisdom, of patriotism, and of charity; that we are all equal, since we are all of the same origin; that there is no privilege nor nobility; that it is not rational nor human . . . for there to be slaves, since the color of one's face does not change one's heart or thoughts; that the children of laborers and miners be educated just as are the children of the richest landholder; that anyone who complains with justice have a court which listens to him, shelters him, and defends him against the powerful and arbitrary.[29]

Morelos was also a leader who created new heroes and symbols. He was the first to elevate the indigenous leaders who defended their peoples against the troops of Hernán Cortés to the ranks of heroes of the homeland. He was also the first to attempt to blend the cult of the heroes of Indian antiquity with the cult of the heroes of the insurgent movement. In his speech at the opening of the Congress of Chilpancingo (1813), after referring to the country by its ancient name of Anáhuac, he invoked the "genius of Moctezuma, Cacama, Quautimozin, Xicoténcatl and Caltzontzin" to celebrate with them "the auspicious moment in which your illustrious children have gathered to revenge the outrages and abuses committed against you and free themselves from the grasp of the tyranny of the freemasons who would have drained them dry forever." With that same purpose, he called to participate in the Congress of Chilpancingo "those souls of the dead from Cruces, Aculco, Guanajuato, Calderón, Zitácuaro and Cuautla, along with those from Hidalgo and Allende!"[30]

Available information indicates that it was José María Morelos who first placed the ancient emblem of the eagle and the prickly pear in the middle of an insurgent flag (fig. 137). In July of 1815, in a decree issued in Puruarán, Morelos agreed that the national flag should have "a field of white and sky blue panels," the colors of the Virgin Mary, and "in the center the arms of the great seal of the nation: a Mexican eagle face on, with wings extended, looking toward the right, with a serpent in its beak, standing on a prickly pear which is growing out of a lake. All of this surrounded by a gold oval topped with a laurel wreath and a white ribbon which reads: National Independence."[31]

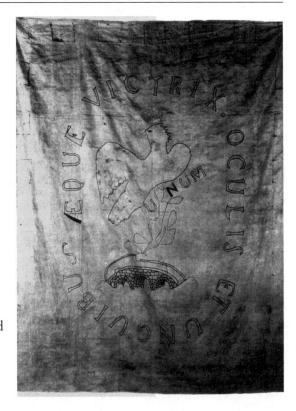

Fig. 137. Flag attributed to the troops of Morelos. (Photo from the National History Museum.)

As can be seen, the insurgent movement began a new historic plan and at the same time created its own political anchorage, its heroes and symbols, and the songs that praised those exploits. In the movement led by Hidalgo and Morelos, the mythic and religious traditions of native groups were stressed, along with the social demands of the most downtrodden sectors and the ideals of autonomy, patriotism, and fervor for the Virgin of Guadalupe of the Creoles. This pluralistic and powerful movement, which for the first time joined the pressure of the indigenous masses with the political aspirations of the Creole group, found its greatest expression and opportunity for success in Hidalgo and Morelos.[32]

The Founders of Historical Nationalism: Fray Servando Teresa de Mier and Carlos María de Bustamante

In 1813 Fray Servando Teresa de Mier wrote his *Historia de la Revolución de Nueva España* to refute the diatribes against the insurgency that the Spanish royalists were circulating and to present a declaration in favor of independence to Europe as well as to the Americans themselves.

The first part of the *Historia de la Revolución de Nueva España* told of the overthrow of Viceroy Iturrigaray. The second described in impassioned prose the insurrection of Father Hidalgo and the cruel repression unleashed against it by the royalist forces. Inspired by his hero, Bartolomé de las Casas, Teresa de Mier equated that repression to the savage episodes of the conquest. The last part, book fourteen, which took up a third of the work, was a formidable demonstration of the causes that, in Teresa de Mier's opinion, justified independence.

Teresa de Mier was not only the first chronicler of the insurgency and one of the actors in the revolutionary drama who took up the pen to defend the rebel cause. He was also the creator of an original historical and political argument in favor of independence. Teresa de Mier's central argument was that the tie that joined the people of America to the kings of Spain was founded in an ancient pact, written in the Laws of the Indies: "a solemn and explicit pact which the Americans made with the kings of Spain . . . and was authenticated by their legal code itself. *This is our magna carta.*"[33]

After proving the existence of that ancient constitution, Teresa de Mier developed another idea that was no less original, mentioned earlier by Francisco de Vitoria: the Americas, Teresa de Mier said, were not colonies but true kingdoms. Although they theoretically formed part of Castile, they had their own institutions: Viceroy, Council of the Indies, Royal High Court, University, Royal Treasury, and so forth. This meant that their political situation was comparable to that of the kingdoms of

Aragon, Portugal, and Flanders, "with a similar sovereign principality, and maintaining their laws, customs, and pacts."[34]

Nevertheless, Teresa de Mier argued that the ancient constitution that protected the liberty and development of the Americans was cancelled by the despotism of the monarchy. The Indians were virtually exterminated by the avarice of the Spaniards and then subjected to a supervision that reduced them to the condition of perpetual children; the Creoles lost their rights, and any possibility of social or political advance was denied them; the half-castes and Mestizos were declared low-class citizens; the Viceroys, High Courts, and institutions became tyrannical; the commercial monopoly absorbed American riches; the humanitarian Laws of the Indies became a dead letter. In a word, the ancient American kingdoms lost their character and became authentic colonies despoiled by despotism. Teresa de Mier concluded that the despotism of the Spanish kings had annulled the ancient social pact contracted with the Americans, so that they had the right to break the political tie that linked them to the Crown.

Teresa de Mier later set about destroying the supposed titles that Spain used as the basis of its right to dominate its overseas possessions. The discovery, conquest, and pacification of the land were intrinsically void titles, because the discovery became an exploitation, the conquest a massacre, and the pacification a depopulation. The missionaries who taught the Gospel in America did not exercise their missions at the behest of Spain but were requested to do so by the conquistadors and the Americans themselves, who paid with their own resources for the Christianization of the Indians and the establishment of religious institutions. The Papal See could not make any gift of American lands for the simple reason that it had no legal property title to them. America did not owe its civilization to Spain; on the contrary, it was Spain that benefited most from its contact with America, since from American soil came the plants, crops, fauna, precious metals, new understandings of geography, and commerce that transformed Spain into a world power. Instead of allowing those riches to drive the development of the Americas, Spain used them for its own exclusive benefit and converted its relationship with America into a servanthood that opposed the material and cultural progress of the Americans. Teresa de Mier argued that America needed nothing from Spain, but that it was Spain that needed American riches to survive. Based on those reasons, he affirmed: "We are the nation. You are the accessories of the monarchy and the Americans are the principals." He then concluded that to break the bonds that held back the development of its potential, the Americans had no alternative but to make themselves independent of Spain.[35]

After observing the dangers that beset new nations that opted for freedom, Teresa de Mier called for the unity of the American nations in order to defend their independence in a lasting form: "We shall be free," he said, "if we are united." Thus, in the way of political compromise, Servando Teresa de Mier moved from patriotic discourse that did not dare utter the word *independence* to discourse involved in the total liberation of his homeland. Like other priests and erudite Creoles, Teresa de Mier took part in the struggle for independence as an insurgent and a pamphleteer, but he was the first to translate those experiences into a discourse that showed the historical reasons for independence, helping his homeland free itself from Spanish subjugation. Unlike the Creole patriots preceding him, who limited themselves to rescuing the historic symbols that would not conflict with the Colonial legacy, Teresa de Mier wrote his *Historia* accepting the contradiction between the insurgents' goal of independence and the goal of saving New Spain as a subject of the mother country.

This was the political watershed that separated Teresa de Mier's *Historia* from the earlier reconstructions of the past made by the Creoles. From the moment when Teresa de Mier began his struggle to create an independent nation, his reading of the past acquired a meaning opposed to earlier interpretations. With this focus, the saga of the conquest and the celebrated history of peninsular institutions and government became a chronicle of the destruction of the Indies.

This unique interpretation of the past that Teresa de Mier circulated in his *Historia* had a double effect. On the one hand, his virulent criticism of the conquest and of Spanish dominion transformed the three centuries of the Viceroyalty into the dark ages of Mexican history. The *Historia de la Revolución de Nueva España* was the first work that put in check the images of the conquest elaborated by the Spanish chroniclers; it was the first chronicle of the Hidalgo insurrection and a provider of anti-Spanish arguments, metaphors, and images.

The interpretations that later critically revised the Colonial past were nurtured from the breeding ground established by Teresa de Mier. His work crowned the difficult process that, for Americans, signified a break with the political and mental bonds that tied them to Spain. As will be remembered, the abdication of Charles IV in favor of Joseph Bonaparte gave cause for the Creoles of the city council of the city of Mexico to declare that as long as the usurpation continued, New Spain would reassume its sovereignty and determine its own destiny, but without breaking ties to Ferdinand VII. Hidaldo and Morelos later headed the struggle for independence and channeled it toward the vindication of the popular masses, but without completely rejecting the Spanish monarch.

Teresa de Mier was the final rupture in that series of liberating breaks. His *Historia* is a *total rejection* of Spanish dominion. As pointed out long ago by Luis Villoro, this denial of the Colonial past began the second ideological period of the insurgency. The rejection of the tie that bound New Spain to its dominator and Hidalgo's Cry of Independence were key episodes of the first phase of the process. The second phase began with the judgment of the Colonial regime and the rejection of the Viceroyalty, which was the precise conclusion reached in the *Historia* of Servando Teresa de Mier.[36]

Teresa de Mier refuted the monarchical and imperial plans that were then appearing. He was a spokesman for republican values, convinced of the irrevocable exercise of citizens' rights, and a believer in the virtues of democratic life. As opposed to his liberal opponents, however, he believed that those values demanded sufficient time and proper institutional forms to become effective practices for the populace, which, according to him, was in large part made up of ignorant masses without the capacity to reflect on the grave problems that challenged the nation. The nation's enemies were despotism, militarism, and religious obscurantism. He wrapped his political doctrine in an emotional nationalism that brought together the historical traditions shared by a wide sector of the population. Thanks to Teresa de Mier's works, the Virgin of Guadalupe, the identification of Quetzalcóatl with Saint Thomas, the Black Legend of Spanish dominion, the heroic struggle of Hidalgo and the first insurgents, and the myth of the indigenous nation freed by the declaration of independence came to be the basis for the new memory of the nation.[37]

Carlos María de Bustamante, an educated Catholic and patriot, further diffused the nationalist sentiment that grew out of the insurgency, which Teresa de Mier had been one of the first to capture in print. Bustamante was born in Oaxaca in 1774 and in 1797 moved to the city of Mexico, where he came in contact with the erudite ideas and ideological changes that the Bourbon leaders had introduced. In 1799 he traveled to Guanajuato and met Miguel Hidalgo; later recollecting that meeting, he would anticipate Hidalgo's role as a revolutionary.

Bustamante came to be known in public life as a journalist, a vocation that he continued throughout his life. In 1805, with Jacobo de Villarrutia, he founded the *Diario de México*. In this activity, already clearly identified with the group of educated Creoles near the Viceroy Iturrigaray, he was surprised by the coup d'état directed against the Viceroy by businessmen. He was able to avoid the imprisonment that destroyed his friends, joined the clandestine group called "Los Guadalupes," and began to collaborate anonymously in the insurgent press promoted by the Junta of Zitácuaro.

In 1813 Bustamante went to Chilpancingo, met Morelos, and served as a deputy to the "Congreso de Anáhuac," to which he gave its name. After that he allied himself with the rebel movement, became a disciple of Morelos, embraced the popular movement party, and distanced himself from the educated elite, who put the sovereignty of the Congress above popular sovereignty. Bustamante tied his fortunes to those of Morelos from 1813 until the death of the southern leader.[38]

We are in debt to Bustamente for two works because of which his name will forever be entered in the book of the founders of national memory. The best known is his *Cuadro histórico de la Revolución mexicana,* which he began publishing in 1821 and finished in 1827.[39] It is a work written as a series of letters, which were published as the author turned them in for printing then were later collected into five volumes that totaled almost two thousand pages. The accumulation of documents is mixed with disjointed comments by Bustamante himself, which are difficult to understand because of the lack of structure in the topics covered and the interjection of anecdotes and trivial matters.[40]

Bustamante's second great work was the *Diario histórico de México,* a torrent of manuscript pages totaling forty-two volumes. The *Diario* exhibited the same deficiencies of which the *Cuadro histórico* was accused: that it was a disorderly mass of documents; lacked rigor in the selection and presentation of the texts; contained unnecessary comments; was a mixture of substantive events with trivial anecdotes, patriotic loquacity, and so forth. But despite those deficiencies, the *Cuadro* and the *Diario* comprised the first documentary body of the insurgency, the first written memory of the happening that changed the lives of Mexicans and defined a new direction for the nation.

The works of Bustamante contained a message that overcame the limitations of the author and made them lasting. In the first place, the *Cuadro histórico* and the *Diario* were narrations that extolled the popular insurrection headed by Hidalgo, Morelos, and the early patriots. The popular movement begun at dawn on September 16, 1810; its leaders were the heroes of Bustamante's narrations. The popular masses, the humble and anonymous men who became the revolutionary flame, and the leaders who led the popular cause were heroes who deserved the chronicler's most fervent praise.

With those heroes and the story of their battles, triumphs, and defeats, Bustamante built a patriotic pantheon, a heroic map, and an emotional chronicle of the independence movement. In opposition to the writing of Servando Teresa de Mier, Bustamante's works promoted indigenous ideas. They exalted Aztec antiquity and established the thesis of an indigenous nation enslaved by Spaniards and then freed by insurgents, who thus became the heirs of Cuauhtémoc. The image of historic continuity between the idealized empire of the Aztecs and the independent nation liberated by the insurgents shone from many of the pages of the *Cuadro* and the *Diario*. Bustamante was responsible for the neo-Aztecan sentiments that proliferated during the war and in the years after the declaration of independence. Because of Bustamante, the Congress of Chilpancingo received the name "Congreso de Anáhuac."

Moved by those forces, they requested that the Congress change the *bandera trigarante* [the flag of the three guarantees: independence from Spain, equal treatment for Spaniards and Creoles, and the supremacy of the Catholic religion] of the Plan of Iguala for one that bore the colors of the kingdom of Montezuma. In several of his works, Bustamante spoke of the ancient indigenous kings as *manes,* spirits of the dead, the shades who protected the heroes of independence. He composed galleries of the ancient Indian kings, offering them as images of the virtues of rulers, and through those idealizations transformed ancient Mexico into an illustrious age. His eagerness to give the liberated nation a prestigious image of its past led Bustamente to write his *Mañanas de la Alameda* (1835), a work animated by the desire to "*instruct the people in what it is most important for them to know, which is the ancient history of their country,* so that they might appreciate its worth and try to imitate the heroic actions of our ancestors, whose memory the Spanish government attempted to bury."[41]

These propagandists of the glories of ancient Mexico were also the founders of a new historical mythology, the creators of a pantheon of heroes, the initiators of a new civic cult, and the diffusors of a national rhetoric that was destined to endure. More than Teresa de Mier, Bustamante was a compulsive creator of nationalistic myths, heroes, ceremonies, and symbols inspired by his patriotism and his historical Indianism. He collected the old Creole myths and managed to include them in the civil rituals of the republican nation. As a good Creole, he was a fervent supporter of the Virgin of Guadalupe and on several occasions found time to publish writings on the appearance of the Virgin to those who defended the authenticy of the miracle and the identification of Quetzalcóatl with the Apostle St. Thomas.

It is almost certain that it was Bustamante who suggested to Morelos that December 12 be declared a national holiday, so that on that day the entire nation might celebrate the Patroness of Mexico. From Bustamante and Teresa de Mier came the proposal, later approved by the Congress, that September 16 be celebrated as the national Independence Day. The compulsion to commemorate led Bustamante to propose the first monument dedicated to honor the memory of the heroes of Independence: he planned the construction in the main plaza of the capital of four columns dedicated to Hidalgo, Morelos, Ignacio Allende, and Xavier Mina. He also proposed raising a column in Santo Domingo plaza to celebrate Independence and suggested that on one of its pedestals the memory of Agustín de Iturbide be honored. In the *Cuadro histórico,* the *Diario,* and his numerous books and newspaper publications, he established the model for panegyrics, celebrations, anniversaries, and monuments that would later recall the deeds of the heroes of the homeland and celebrate the founding events of the nation.[42]

From the first years of the insurgency, Bustamante foresaw the need to create symbols, heroes, and cults of the revolutionary movement, and he assigned the mission of becoming the first supplier of nationalistic images to himself. More than anyone else, he contributed to disseminating the patriotic profiles of the list of heroes of the insurgency (Morelos, Hidalgo, Allende, Aldama). To these he added the mythic names of Quetzalcóatl, Netzahualcóyotl, Montezuma, Cuauhtémoc, and many others, creating a mixed pantheon of indigenous and insurgent heroes that supported his thesis of continuity from the native nation to the republic. Bustamante was also one of the most effective propagators of the inflamed nationalist rhetoric that became common in the patriotic celebrations of the independent nation: a rhetoric that neglected to explain the deed being praised in order to concentrate on the purely emotional force of his declaration, the evocative intensity of his message, and the sentimental response that this provoked in his listeners.[43]

Bustamante was also a precursor in that task that later occupied the efforts of several generations of learned men: the rescue and publication of the works of missionaries and other lay authors not published by the Spanish government. The same books that he had read on ancient Mexico, along with his access to the archives, revealed to him the existence of a considerable number of unpublished texts, and from that time until his death he used his limited resources to publish them, to such an extent that he became the major publisher of historical works of his time.

During the years in which he was publishing the *Diario de México* (1805–12), he began the publication of the manuscripts of the native historian Chimalpahin. In 1821 he sent to press the *Galería de antiguos príncipes mexicanos dedicada a la suprema potestad nacional que les sucediera en el mando para su mejor gobierno,* which was followed by the *Crónica mexicana* of Alvarado Tezozómoc, the *Historia de la conquista de México* by Francisco López de Gómara, a monograph, *Tezcoco,* by Mariano

Veytia, and the first edition of the monumental *Historia general de las cosas de Nueva España* by Bernardino de Sahagún. In addition Bustamante published valuable works on the Viceroyalty, such as the chronicle of the three centuries of Spanish government by Fr. Andrés Cavo, the *Historia de la Compañía de Jesús* by Francisco Javier Alegre, and the *Enfermedades políticas* of Hipólito de Villaroel.[44]

An unscrupulous publisher, Bustamante changed the names of the works he published, mutilated or expurgated their contents, and added prologues, notes, extraneous documents, and laborious discourses of his own that affected the substance and form of the original texts. His publishing compulsion had little to do with the idea of circulating books valuable in and of themselves. When Bustamante published the works of Sahagún, Chimalpahin, Veytia, and Alvarado Tezozómoc, his purpose was to combat the anathemas that the Spanish had unleashed against the ancient native civilizations and to show, in the words of the friars and the erudite Creoles, the cultural development that those people had attained. In his mind the texts about the ancient Mexicans were a kind of authoritative argument against the Spanish concentration on devaluing that past. This also occurred with the chronicles on the Viceroyalty, which Bustamante published because they described the evils prevalent in the colonies or because they justified the civilizing work of the Jesuits, the order he most admired and wished to reestablish.

Through the process of publishing and commenting on texts prohibited by the Viceregal authorities, Bustamante began Mexicanizing the chronicles written by the conquistadors, introducing into them the viewpoint of the vanquished, who—when they looked with the eyes of men who had stopped being the passive subjects of history—discovered in them voices and contents that expressed a meaning far different from that given to them by Spanish publishers. Like Teresa de Mier's legacy, that of Bustamante was profoundly political work based on historical reasoning.

From this mix of the political demands of the insurgency and the compulsion to identify with the remote past came the singular historical nationalism of Mexico.

The Consummation and Celebration of Independence

September 27, 1821, the date of the triumphant entry of the Army of the Three Guarantees into the capital of the nation, and September 28 of the same year, the date of the installation of the Sovereign Provisional Governing Junta and Regency of the Empire, celebrated the arrival in the capital of the nation of the liberating hero, the installation of the governmental body of the independent nation, and the consummation of Independence.

After ten years of war, the entrance of Iturbide and the Army of the Three Guarantees came to be the first collective celebration and a popular festival (fig. 138). These acts and the formal proclamation of Independence established a model to which later commemorative celebrations would adhere. A form of historical recall and a popular civic calendar were born at that time that would be consolidated in the following years.

On September 28, the Army of the Three Guarantees paraded through the principal streets of the city, led by General Agustín de Iturbide (fig. 139). At the head of the column were "Indian representatives, the main Castilian nobles, and very large numbers of Mexicans." At different times during the march, authorities of the city and of the populace honored the liberators. Near the San Francisco seminary, the advance guard was received by the city council with a triumphal arch and the surrender to Iturbide of the keys to the city, copied in gold. The parade continued, accompanied by "the very energetic and expressive shouts of the immense crowd that filled the streets, balconies, and flat roofs, forming the most animated and sublime picture that Mexico could ever have seen in its historic past."[45]

"Throughout the immense distance from the Belén sentry box to the palace," said the *Gaceta imperial,* "nothing could be heard

Fig. 138. Triumphant parade of the Army of the Three Guarantees through the city of Mexico. (Photo from Benítez, 1982: vol. 2, 218–19.)

other than 'Long live the Father of the Country, the Liberator of New Spain . . . the guardian angel who brought us the best of good things.'. . . The second object of the admiration of the people was the Army of the Three Guarantees, composed of 8,000 infantrymen and 10,000 horsemen."[46]

Carlos María de Bustamante, the chronicler who narrated the heroic deeds of Independence, described the transfer to the cathedral of the leading officers of the army, the members of the city council, the native representatives of the tribes, and the Títulos de Castilla. In the church, he said, "The *Te deum* hymn was intoned by the Archbishop, which lasted until almost three in the afternoon, and the artillery volleys and the ringing of the bells were unceasing." When this event concluded, the committee returned to the palace, where the city council offered "food and drink, attended by the principal people of México, as they like-wise attended the afternoon excursion."[47]

Fig. 139. Victorious entrance of Agustín de Iturbide and the Army of the Three Guarantees into the city of Mexico. (Photo from Jiménez Codinach, 1997: 256–57.)

On the next day the Provisional Governing Junta was duly constituted and Independence was declared in the Treaty Salon of the National Palace. Then the members of the Junta "went to the cathedral, where each one, putting his hand on the Gospel, swore to faithfully comply with the Plan of Iguala and the Treaties of Córdoba." In the evening the Junta unveiled the Act of Independence, which basically declared:

The Mexican nation, which for three hundred years has not enjoyed self-determination, nor free speech, today rises above the oppression under which it has lived.

The heroic efforts of its sons and daughters have been crowned and this forever memorable undertaking . . . has been achieved, overcoming almost insuperable obstacles thanks to a Being beyond all admiration and praise.

This part of the north, restored to the exercise of such rights granted it by the Author of all nature . . . with the liberty to constitute itself in the manner which is most conducive to its felicity . . . solemnly declares, through the Supreme Junta of the Empire, *that it is a sovereign nation, independent of old Spain.*[48]

Those consecutive acts—the entrance of the Army of the Three Guarantees into the capital, the installation of the Governing Junta, the pronouncement of the Act of Independence, and the naming of the Regency of the Empire—gave legal status to the independent nation. The jubilant festivities made the political separation from Spain public, and its celebration in the towns and far corners of the country made the good news clear to the different social sectors.

Perhaps the most important feature of that celebration was that during the same year in which it was celebrated in the capital, it spread to the rest of the territory. In his study of the acts that greeted Independence, Javier Ocampo has indicated that the celebration included the entire country and everywhere assumed the same collective, festive, and optimistic character that characterized it in the capital.[49]

The New Rituals and Calendars of the Nation

The forerunner of the collective celebration in Mexico was religious commemorations. The first festivities of the independent nation assumed the forms and symbols of a religious celebration, but they added a new meaning and sought to define other actors, spaces, times, and symbols.

The actors in the new civic ceremony were the liberating hero, the Army of the Three Guarantees, and the independent nation itself. Iturbide and his army occupied center stage in the ceremonies; they were the focus of acclaim in the streets and public squares and were most often represented on the floats, triumphal arches, paintings, and scenes showing the liberation of the nation in realistic or symbolic form (figs. 138–139). In almost every scene, the nation was represented beneath the figure of a young native woman who was freed of her chains by Iturbide or was led by the hero to occupy the highest seat of honor.

The old sites, planned for the celebration of other ceremonies and heroes, were transformed and made fit for the new national cult. One example of such transformations was the main plaza of the capital, which had had the equestrian statue of Charles IV located in its center. This location underwent the following physical and symbolic modification for the ceremony of the Oath of Independence on October 27.

In the beautiful main plaza, within the ellipse which held the colossal bronze equestrian statue of Charles IV, they put up a round pavilion . . . on the top of the pavilion was an eagle standing on a prickly pear, symbolizing the liberty of the nation. The drapes which covered the pedestal represented, first and foremost, the elevation of North America to the rank of an independent and free nation. . . . America, represented with all its symbols and dressed in the mantle of sovereignty, climbs the stairs led by her worthy son the great Iturbide . . . on the other side are the strong generals of the Trigarantide Army with their crests and tricolor sashes . . . on the steps of the throne is a character armed with a quiver, bow, and war club, the ancient arms with which the Mexicans once fought.[50]

As can be seen, those acts showed the mixing of ancient traditions with modern political concepts. In the capital, the cities of the interior, and even the villages, plans multiplied for the erection of statues, columns, altars to the homeland, pyramids, obelisks, and other monuments to honor Independence and its heroes.[51]

As in other political movements, in the Mexican insurgency the management of time and the fixing of the revolutionary calendar were important; only those dates and commemorations dictated by the triumphant movement could be allowed.[52] For that reason, the date of the consummation of Independence by Iturbide was

Fig. 140. Celebrations in the main square on October 27, 1821. (Photo from the National History Museum.)

assumed as definitive in the insurgent process and as the founding moment of the nation.

The followers of the Independence movement of 1821 proclaimed September 27, 1821, to be the day on which the nation was born and erased September 16, 1810, as well as the important dates that the first insurgents had proclaimed to be glorious moments of revolutionary deeds. These last were characterized as negative phases: times when cruel wars, violence, anarchy, looting, destruction, and civil contests were the rule. Those destructive phases were in contrast to the kindness of the Iturbide movement, led by the principles of conciliation and unity, which culminated in a bloodless revolution.[53]

The triumphant revolution forgot its violent origins and remembered the moment of the bloodless, unifying revolution that was open to the future. It used the celebration to propagate its version of revolutionary events and to distribute it throughout the different sectors of the population. The new calendar proclaimed the end of revolution and the beginning of a fraternal and optimistic era.

Symbols of the Liberated Nation

The revolutionary festivities also produced new visual symbols and images. Hidalgo and Morelos were priests and gave their armies religious symbols as standards. On the other hand Iturbide, formed in the Royalist army that fought against the first insurgents, availed himself of military symbols to spread his libertarian programs. As has been seen, he made the military parade a focus of public admiration and a collective celebration. As first officer of the army and head of the empire, he made use of the paraphernalia of insignias, uniforms, decorations, ceremonials, pomp, and ostentation that would later characterize his person and the court of the military leader.

The institutionalization of one of the prime symbols of the nation, the flag, was also due to Iturbide. The Plan of Iguala, which he proclaimed in 1821, rested on three principles: "the conservation of the apostolic Roman Catholic religion, without tolerance for any other; independence under a moderate form of monarchic government; and union between Americans and Europeans. These were the three guarantees from which the army which sustained that plan took its name, and to them the three colors of the flag which were adopted allude" (fig. 141).[54] The color white symbolized the purity of religion, red the union of Americans and Spaniards, and green Independence.

When the Empire of Iturbide fell, the Congress adopted the federal republic as its form of government and transformed the ancient emblems of the homeland into the emblems of the nation. In the Federal Constitution of 1824 one can see the eagle fighting the serpent, without a crown, standing on the heraldic prickly pear, which grows out of a mound emerging from a lake (fig. 142). The Republic maintained the tricolor flag of the Army of the Three Guarantees, and that flag became the representative

Fig. 141. Flag of the Empire of Iturbide, 1822–23. As can be seen, it shows the colors of green, white, and red in vertical stripes, with the eagle crowned. (Photo from Jiménez Codinach, 1997: 247.)

symbol of the independent nation. It was the visual image that identified the liberated nation and expressed the sentiments of national unity and identity in all public events. This flag was the first nonreligious civic emblem to unite the ancient insignia of the Mexicas with the principles and the flags that came out of the war for national liberation.

Traditional patriotic sentiments (the idea of sharing a single territory, language, religion, and past) became part of the modern plan of constituting a sovereign nation dedicated to the pursuit of the common good. Thus, resting on armed insurgency and on modern political thought, the nation considered itself to be free and created a future to achieve its own historic plan, centered on the independent state and the sovereign nation. In turn, the radical transformation of the present and the creation of a horizon open to the future modified the concept that the nation held of its memory.

Political independence from Spain and the decision to carry out a national political plan created a new subject for historical

Fig. 142. Coat of arms of the
Federal Republic of Mexico in
1824. (Photo from Rodríguez,
1994: 141.)

narration: the national state. For the first time, instead of a fragmented territory governed by foreign powers, Mexicans considered
their country, the different parts that made it up, its population, and
its past as one single entity. From that time on, independent of
internal contradictions, the nation saw itself as a territorial, social,
and political unit that had a common origin, development through
time, and future. The emergence of a political entity that integrated
the different parts of the nation was the subject for the new history,
which was to unify the social and cultural diversity of the population in a search for national identity.[55]

VIII. Oblivion and Memory: From the Collapse of the Republic to the History of the Nation

The nineteenth century was one of the most promise-laden historical transits in the history of Mexico. Its trajectory began with the ascent of the nation to independent life, the building of the Republic, and the thrilling prospect of a model nation. And at the same time, it was an epoch afflicted by horrible events: the erosion of internal unity, struggles among different factions, ungovernability, foreign invasions, the loss of more than half of the national territory, civil war, political traumas, moral disasters. In the short lapse of fifty years, between 1821 and 1867, the country that had dreamed of becoming the most powerful nation on the American continent saw itself plunge into political ruin and economic bankruptcy, until it faced the sinister nightmare of threatened extinction.

It is not so strange, then, that those moments of humiliation and defeat should be the ones least recorded by historical memory. Nor is it surprising that shortly thereafter, the brief resuscitation of the economy and national unity during the government of Porfirio Díaz should evoke the first work that considered the nation as an integrated community, as a plan originating in the distant past that developed over time and gathered energy at the end of the century with the manifestations of the first signs of a promising future.

In the pages that follow I shall try to collect the episodes of that epoch that left lasting marks on the national consciousness. They are inescapable landmarks on the memory of the nation, even though one was covered with the mantle of tragedy and the other gleamed with the sheen of optimism.

Faded Memory: Political Disaster and Loss of Territory

> The in-depth study of the North American invasion should be a required course in the education of every Mexican to help us acquire a clear and complete awareness of our vices and defects, our failures and limitations, of our falterings and incompetences, of the disproportion between what we dream ourselves to be and the stature that reality imposes on us.
>
> ANTONIO CASTRO LEAL[1]

Between 1821 and 1846 Mexicans tried out the most varied forms of political organization: constitutional monarchy, federal republic, central republic, dictatorship. From none of those models came a political framework capable of containing the disorderly partisan contenders battling in the political arena, each model taken up with affirming its own principles without ever perceiving that the art of politics is a pluralistic construction, a game among different interests, which, to be managed wisely, must be accepted as such by the contending parties.

The fleeting Empire of Agustín de Iturbide (September of 1821 through March of 1823), basing itself on the old centralist plan, was overthrown by claims of autonomy and federalism that were expressed by the majority of the regions. Those demands, with the support of the provinces, in the Constituent Congress of 1823 shaped the founding forces of the Federal Republic of 1824.[2] The Constitution of 1824 indicated that the new nation was to be composed of free and sovereign states, guaranteeing a republican, representative, and popular form of government for each of them. As Timothy Anna has claimed, Mexican federalism was not simply a copy of the North American model.[3] Far from it, it was born of aspirations founded in deeply rooted regional and local interests, later supported by the administrative divisions (Intendencias) promoted by the Bourbons and based on the vigorous participation of the provinces in the struggle for Independence and the defense of regional interests.

An ominous shadow, the shadow of the caudillos [bosses or leaders], led the 1824 constituents to create a weak executive branch, a legislative branch with broad rights, and a national government dependent on the states and secondary to them in two vital areas: the collection of taxes and the recruitment of troops. The lack of proper resources or an effective force to require compliance with the rulings of the federal government were two deficiencies that soon began to undermine its authority.

Guadalupe Victoria, the first president elected by the majority of the population, predicted a happy future for the nation in his inaugural address. Nevertheless, one year later, when the citizenry came together to renew the Congress, the nation was divided into two opposing bands. The so-called Scottish [Masonic lodge] faction included the old Colonial elite (clerics, businessmen, miners, and large landholders) and supported class structure and political centralism. Against them were the York [a different Masonic lodge] followers, who supported federalism and the autonomy of the states, equality under the law, freedom of opinion, and a democratic government that guaranteed individual above corporative liberty. The conflict of interests between these groups produced a disruption in the political classes that later extended to social classes through the new media sources (newspapers) and political participation (elections).

Independence brought with it freedom of the press, and the political struggle changed newspapers into decisive factors in the formation of public opinion. Each group had its own newspaper and was a distributor of thousands of flyers and brochures dedicated to the defense of its interests. "In every city, daily, twice-weekly, and weekly newspapers started up, and the best of them circulated throughout the nation," and these were the ones that formed public opinion. As one foreign observer stated, "the principal topics for conversation were supplied by . . . periodical publications."[4]

The Yorkists triumphed in the city of Mexico and in the states in the elections of 1826, and the feigned political harmony proclaimed by President Victoria collapsed. The discovery on January 18, 1827, of a conspiracy led by a Spanish monk to restore Colonial power started an endless cycle of pronouncements and exacerbated political divisions. That incident was the basis for a growing campaign to exile Spaniards, a decision that would divide the country even more and would provoke a further outflow of capital. The confrontation between Scottish and York supporters gave way to a "war of words in which lies, attacks on reputations and all forms of verbal injury were common. . . . As newspapers degenerated into mere instruments for propaganda for the contending parties, the pamphleteers similarly gave up all pretense of honor or truthfulness and were not backward in publishing inflamatory and terribly inexact information. . . . Soon open political and periodical war reigned."[5]

The law of December 20, 1827, requiring the expulsion of Spaniards was the excuse for the so-called Rebellion of Tulancingo, which, among other demands, required the resignation of Victoria's cabinet. Even though it lacked military strength and was soon controlled, it had political repercussions because its most visible leader was none other than Nicolás Bravo, Vice President of the Republic and known head of the Scottish faction. The conflict between the two groups came to a head with the presidential elections of 1828. Vicente Guerrero, the hero of Independence and a faithful soldier of the Republic, was the strong candidate of the York faction and the popular sectors and seemed to be on his way to an easy victory, despite the fact that he was a mulatto and the product of a rural environment.

But surprisingly, Guerrero's social origin caused the alliance of the Scottish, monarchic, Spanish, Creole, military, and aristocratic groups against his candidacy. The individual who put together this singular amalgam was Manuel Gómez Pedraza, who—in contrast to Guerrero—was a rich, cultivated white Creole and Minister of War; that is to say, close to the military, an organization of increasing power in political contests. Thus, supported by centralists and the economic and social hierarchy, Gómez Pedraza turned out to be the winner.[6]

The political panorama was obscured when General Antonio López de Santa Anna, then governor of the state of Veracruz, rose up against the results of the constitutional election, asked that Gómez Pedraza's election be set aside, and proposed that Vicente Guerrero be declared president. This rebellion was followed by that of several colonels who, on November 30, 1828, took the Acordada building in the capital because of the inexplicable passivity of governmental forces. At that moment of indecision, for reasons no one has been able to explain, Gómez Pedraza decided to abandon the struggle. On December 27 he renounced the presidency, and the following year he went into exile.

The disappearance of constitutional authorities from the capital and the exacerbation of political antagonisms resulted in turmoil. The popular classes who supported Guerrero invaded Parián, the commercial center of the capital, and after several hours of looting destroyed the stores and sowed terror. The city was a prisoner of anarchy. By the time the government was at last able to restore order, the political damage was fatal: the constitutionally elected president had been deposed. Even worse, a commission of the Chamber of Deputies declared the election of Gómez Pedraza void and designated Vicente Guerrero President and Anastasio Bustamante Vice President.[7]

Guerrero took office on April 1, 1829, but his time as President was brief and unfortunate. When he applied the law that ordered a second expulsion of Spaniards, he did it with so much flexibility that it actually strengthened the group that supported the Spanish reconquest. The feared invasion took place on July 27 under General Isidro Barradas, who disembarked with 3,500 men on the coast of Tampico. But instead of the expected supporters, they faced the superior forces of Antonio de Santa Anna and Manuel Mier y Terán, who defeated them and for a short time restored the diminished prestige of the military.

The happiness produced by that victory was the most felicitous success of Guerrero's administration. When he tried to clean up the corruption that had invaded the army, he gained the animosity of those officials who used it as a special way of meddling in politics. At that time the army absorbed more than half of the national budget. The deficit in the public treasury in turn caused foreign indebtedness and brought the government to its knees before national speculators, who amassed fantastic fortunes making unfair loans. The government's loss of prestige reached the point that newspapers publicly denounced Vice President Anastasio Bustamante for conspiring with Santa Anna to impose a centralist government. At last, in a movement hatched in Jalapa with the support of the military, the leading clerics and business owners pronounced against Guerrero, and on December 31, 1829, Bustamante captured the capital and took over the executive position. Once again, a small sector of the military had deposed the established government.[8]

Bustamante's government meant a political shift in favor of the centralists and conservatives. The full cabinet, headed by Lucas Alamán, supported that tendency. An immediate campaign began against the federalists and the members of the York faction; the latter were virtually suppressed as a political party, and their newspapers were closed. Vicente Guerrero and Juan Álvarez, who continued as rebels in the south, were hunted down until the unfortunate assassination of Guerrero.[9]

Later, when Bustamante's government began to impose its conservative politics, another military rebellion appeared, this one headed by Santa Anna. This ambitious man, his vision clouded by an irrepressible passion for personal power and glory, designed a plan to defeat Bustamante, delay the elections, and create conditions whereby he could run for the presidency himself. On the night of January 2, 1832, the so-called Plan of Veracruz was published, with a main article proposing the resignation of Bustamante's cabinet.

Fig. 143. Anonymous historical painting, showing the main deeds of General Santa Anna. (Photo from the *Segundo calendario de Pedro de Urdinales para el año bisieto 1858.*)

One year later, Bustamante was driven to resign by force of arms and his place was occupied by the earlier deposed Gómez Pedraza, who at the direction of Santa Anna called for elections in March of 1833 (fig. 143). On March 30 the official review announced the election of Santa Anna as President and Valentín Gómez Farías as Vice President. Santa Anna then proceeded to unfold the bizarre procedures for which he was famous and requested permission to seclude himself in his legendary Manga de Clavo hacienda, leaving Gómez Farías in charge of the executive branch. Under the latter's leadership, the political pendulum swung another 180 degrees, this time favoring the liberals.

The confusing presence in the political arena of the Masonic lodges and of groups and bands without programs or articulated purposes began to sort itself out when those forces grouped themselves under the names of centralists and federalists. As Michael Costeloe has stated, the leaders of both parties were slowly evolving. Instead of continuing to be absorbed in the fetishes of constitutions and abstract ideas, they began to see that the root of the nation's problems lay in its economic structure and social organization. One of these groups took the name of liberals and the other of conservatives.[10] The influence of Lucas Alamán in the government of Bustamante defined the profile of the conservative plan, while the program of the liberal party was made public by Valentín Gómez Farías as of 1833, when in the absence of Santa Anna he took up the reins of government.

The administration of Gómez Farías distinguished itself by imposing the federal republican system, redefining the relation between church and state, reforming education, and converting the army into an institutional body. Those were the basic principles of the liberal creed, the first and last objectives requiring a full century to become reality. Educational reform and the separation of church and state were concepts that became governmental policy under the administration of Gómez Farías.

From his inaugural address on, Gómez Farías pointed out the necessity of reforming education. He started that program with changes in the area of early education and then concentrated on advanced learning. On October 21, 1833, he closed the university, which was then dominated by traditional ecclesiastical groups, and established an Office of Public Instruction, which from that point forward would control the politics of the schools and preparatory schools of the state. He decreed that for their support the latter would be given the properties of old ecclesiastical institutions and closed several religious prep schools.

A more delicate matter was the discussion of whether the state or the church was responsible for naming ecclesiastical personnel, which for the liberals was undoubtedly a civil right. The liberal group maintained that the state was in charge of the administration and supervision of public matters and tried to end the participation of the church in those areas. The adoption of these ideas by the Congress, as well as actions taken by several state government officials against church property, together with proposals to reform the army, brought about a unified reaction against the administration of Gómez Farías. Conservative forces supported by Santa Anna violated the Constitution once again, dissolving the Congress and overthrowing the legally constituted government. Finally, on December 29, 1836, the Federal Constitution of 1824 was replaced by the Seven Constitutional Laws, on which a centralist Republican government was based.[11]

These legal instruments were an attempt to "reconstitute the nation" based on principles dear to the conservative party: the preeminence of the Apostolic Roman Catholic faith; absolute respect for property rights; and the establishment of a strong government under a centralist Republican format sustained by "men of property"—that is to say, by those citizens who, because of accumulated properties, social influence, and tradition would be the natural conservatives of the Republic.[12]

That was the plan implemented between 1835 and 1846, one of the most catastrophic periods of the epoch. Ten men (eight military men and two civilians) occupied the presidential seat, and with the exception of one, all were removed from their position by armed rebellions. According to a number of observers, the old values were weakened during that period, and there was talk of "social dissolution" and the disappearance of the old values. "As concerns the Church, and even faith, the decline continues, in the opinion of the bishops." "The administration of justice was universally considered to be inefficient and corrupt," and the army, instead of maintaining peace and respect for institutions, became one of the great evils that were then overwhelming the nation—a body that had lost prestige because of its venality and inefficiency. To all of this was added a deep social malaise, since most of the population was living in poverty. Banditry and insecurity had become generalized plagues. "Thus, nothing seemed to have been achieved in a decade of centralism."[13]

What was true was that neither York nor Scottish lodges, federalists nor centralists, liberals nor conservatives—none of the administrations that governed between 1821 and 1846—could curb the unstoppable bankrupting of the public treasury, put an end to the mad struggle between factions that overpowered the news media without their looking beyond their own interest, or control the ill-fated military leaders who used the army to satisfy their personal appetites. Even worse, the opposition between the federal government and the states, along with the struggle between factions, not only destroyed internal unity but also made it difficult to face threats of territorial dismemberment, first shown in the independence efforts of the province of Texas and later by North American expansionism.

Ever since the Independence declaration of 1821, it was clear that the northern border was in the sights of U.S. expansionists. During that time the population of the United States tripled, it acquired Louisiana in 1803, and it bought Florida from Spain in 1819. Texas was the most distant province of Mexico toward the east, and it was populated largely by North American settlers, who totaled some twenty thousand. Because of their ethnic origin and political mentality (the majority were Protestants and favored slavery), this population shared the idea of annexing itself to the United States. Mexican policies and the lack of stability of the nation supported that tendency.

The Constitution of 1824 put settlement policies into the hands of the states, and Texas was joined to Coahuila, denying its autonomy. Then Texans were required to pay taxes at the federal customs houses, and the entrance of North American settlers to that area was forbidden. The Texans rebelled and sought annexation to the United States. The centralist government of 1835 decided to fight that threat and sent Santa Anna to subdue the rebels. After several victories, the Mexican forces were surprised during their afternoon siesta by the army of Sam Houston, and Santa Anna, beaten and humiliated, was taken prisoner. The Texans declared their independence on March 2, 1836, protected by the scarcely hidden support of the North American government.[14]

Faced with the military debacle of Santa Anna and the threats of U.S. expansion into New Mexico and California, the sensible thing for Mexico to have done would have been to accept the advice of Great Britain. Charles Eliot, the British commercial representative, had suggested that if Mexico recognized the independence of Texas, the Texans would agree not to join any other country, and England, in turn, would guarantee the border between Mexico and the United States. The Mexican government did not accept that sensible offer and inevitably became a defenseless witness to later developments: the annexation of Texas to the United States and a U.S. invasion.[15] As of that date the military parties and the press gave accounts of the inexorable advance of the North American army into national territory and the successive Mexican defeats.

Zachary Taylor, an experienced and energetic general, was the point of the lance of the North American military offensive. At the beginning of June 1845, he moved with a force of two thousand men to the Texas-Mexico border. This was not, as had been said, an army charged with protecting Texas from probable aggression by the Mexican government. It was clearly an army of occupation, the advanced troop of the North American invasion of Mexican territory, as confirmed by the formal declaration of war by North America on May 11, 1846. A short time earlier, on May 5, Taylor's forces had clashed with Mexican troops for the first time at Fort Texas. Three days later, Taylor encountered the troops of General Mariano Arista blocking the road to Matamoros. In the pond at Palo Alto the two armies made contact, and they fought again on May 9 at Resaca de la Palma, where the invaders achieved an impressive victory.[16]

From that point on the professionalism and superior artillery of the U.S. troops strung together one victory after another. In August more troops joined Taylor's forces, until he had an army

Fig. 144. Defense of the city of Monterrey, according to a painting of F. Bastin. (Photo from Garciadiego, 1997: 94.)

of eleven thousand men. His objective was to extend the occupation and take the city of Monterrey. On September 12 Taylor ordered the assault on Monterrey, and that was probably one of the worst days of his life, for the Mexicans killed nearly four hundred of his soldiers. On the 22nd and 23rd, the North Americans reorganized, and on the 24th they entered as victors into the city, which, after a heroic defense, gave the appearance of an "enormous cemetery. Unburied bodies, dead and rotting mules, silent streets, everything gave the city an appearance of utter devastation" (fig. 144).[17]

Between 1846 and 1847 the war against Mexico took a new turn in the offices of the White House. Against the war of limited occupation recommended by Zachary Taylor, President James Polk decided on a general siege that would end with the taking of the capital and the surrender of the Mexican army. Thus, the positions already established by Taylor in the northeast were followed by the occupation of the west (New Mexico and California) and the great offensive that departed the port of Veracruz for the city of Mexico, commanded by General Winfield Scott. The New Mexico territory was annexed in 1846, practically without the firing of a single shot, under the command of General Stephen W. Kearny. In 1947, Kearny also took possession of Alta California.[18]

At the beginning of 1847 Santa Anna undertook an action that affected the outcome of the war: he recruited an army of more than twenty thousand men and decided to attack Taylor, who had set himself up in Saltillo. But Santa Anna committed the error of marching that army from San Luis Potosí to Saltillo, three hundred miles across inhospitable mountains and deserts, causing the desertion and death of hundreds of his men. In the battle of La Angostura on February 23, the Mexicans began the battle well, but the next day Taylor received reinforcements and his artillery devastated the ranks of the Mexican army. The defeat demoralized the national forces, since they had had larger military forces and some of their best-known generals in that battle.[19]

The final course of the war was decided by the army commanded by Winfield Scott, which followed the same route as Hernán Cortés. Scott began his expedition with unusual maneuvers. He disembarked eight thousand men at one time on the coast of Veracruz on March 12, 1847, the largest amphibian invasion ever seen in military annals up to that time (fig. 145). Then, instead of attacking the city, he laid siege to it and caused its surrender with a regular firestorm of shell fire (fig. 146). Later, on April 17, he faced the twelve thousand men that Santa Anna had brought together in Cerro Gordo, near Plan del Río. On the next day Scott took Cerro Gordo after a massacre that decimated the Mexican army and caused the shameful flight of Santa Anna. Scott's victorious march continued through Jalapa and Puebla, which were taken without resistance. Thus, one month after his landing on the coast of Veracruz, Scott was one day's march from his main objective, the capital of the invaded country.

Scott had to remain in Puebla for three months, waiting for replacement troops for his reduced army. In June and August the

Fig. 145. Disembarkation of North American troops in the port of Veracruz on March 12, 1847. (Photo from Christensen et al., 1998: 162.)

replacements arrived, and he had a full force of nearly fourteen thousand men, some three thousand of whom were sick. On August 7 Scott's divisions began the march to the Valley of Mexico, where Santa Anna had gathered a force of some twenty thousand. The reconnoitering of the terrain that Scott's engineers had done led him to concentrate his attack on Padierna and Contreras in the south and later toward the east, in the direction of the Churubusco River. On August 19 the North American troops were in danger of being crushed by the fortuitous coming together of Santa Anna's army with that of General Gabriel Valencia, but quarreling between the two frustrated that opportunity. On the following day, the North Americans put the defenders to flight. The war then concentrated on Contreras and Churubusco (fig. 147). The combined action of the artillery and the final charge with fixed bayonets shattered the Mexican forces in Churubusco. That day Santa Anna lost four thousand men

Fig. 146. From March 22 to March 26, 1847, Veracruz faced the attack of U.S. forces, which the town heroically resisted. (Photo from Vázquez, 1997a: 52.)

and three thousand more were taken prisoner, including eight generals, two of them ex-Presidents of Mexico.[20]

On September 12 Scott decided to attack the final redoubt of Mexican forces, Chapultepec Castle. At dawn on the next day the bombardment of this courtyard commenced, continuing until 7:30 in the morning, when the infantry assault began, opening fire and entering the Castle with bayonets fixed and swords drawn. The steps of the Castle looked like a butcher shop, with the last to fall the young cadets of the Military School, who refused to surrender their flag (fig. 148). The next day, September 14, the invading army captured the National Palace and raised the Stars and Bars over the political heart of the humiliated nation (fig. 149).[21]

On February 2, 1848, the Mexican and North American peace commissioners met in Guadalupe Hidalgo and signed the treaty of the same name, which reduced Mexico's territory to half of what it had been before the invasion. This unjust war was the only thing that could have obliged Mexico to give up territory that it otherwise would never have agreed to surrender. It was a terrible defeat,

Fig. 147. Battle of Churubusco, according to a lithograph of the time. (Photo from Garciadiego, 1997.)

without palliatives, whose direct responsibility fell on the leaders of the army, the heads of the parties, and the governing elite. Unlike the patriotic involvements that characterized most of the troops, the militias, and the popular forces, the generals and leaders of the parties were characterized by their ineptitude at defending the integrity of the territory that they had inherited, and they were incapable of avoiding those blows that humbled the national spirit.

The military and moral collapse that attended the North American invasion shredded the ingenuous optimism of the first years of Independence. The national horizon darkened. A bitter sense of shame overwhelmed any thoughts about the events that led up to that catastrophe. Worried Mexicans asked themselves why the foreign invasion did not elicit a national resistance movement. Why did each of the battles become a victory for the North Americans and a shameful defeat for the Mexicans? Why did the parties continue their factional quarrels when the very existence of the nation was being decided on the battlefield?

These and other questions were the basis for intense debates during the years after the war. The pages of the newspapers became

Fig. 148. Assault on Chapultepec Castle by the North American army, according to an engraving of F. Lehnert. (Photo from Garciadiego, 1997.)

an arena in which arguments about the uncertain destiny of the nation were aired. *El siglo XIX,* the newspaper of the moderate liberals, started up again in 1848 and the notable articles in its pages were immediately debated by radical liberals who wrote for *El monitor republicano* and by the well-entrenched conservatives of *El tiempo* and *El universal.* In these and other newspapers, representatives of the different political currents explained their ideas about the afflictions of the present and the reforms that had to be made to put the future of the nation back on track.[22]

A recurring theme was the identification of those responsible for the catastrophe that had prostrated the nation. Almost all observers declared the army to be partly responsible for the defeat and proposed drastic measures for its reform. The liberals unleashed their most severe criticisms against the church and particularly the leading clerics, whom they described as a foreign entity, indifferent to the fortunes of the nation. These writers

Fig. 149. The invading army, waving the standard of the Stars and Bars over the humiliated nation. (Photo from Christensen et al., 1998: 7.)

indicated that the immoderate accumulation of wealth by the ecclesiastical body, its intolerance of other beliefs, monopolization of education, and fanaticism, were the major obstacles that kept Mexico from moving into modern times and toward democracy. José María Luis Mora, Mariano Otero, and Melchor Ocampo reviewed anticlerical political thought in several writings that later formed the basis of the Reform Laws of 1856.

The conservatives, on the other hand, argued that the Mexicans' adoption of foreign ideas and institutions—that is to say, federalism and liberal principles—and rejection of their Spanish heritage signaled the beginning of the moral and political disintegration of the nation. By repudiating their origins and adopting North American federalism, they argued, Mexico betrayed its destiny. Very soon the debate engendered by the military disaster went beyond immediate reality and asked the anguished questions, could Mexico maintain itself as an independent nation, and did it have a viable future?[23]

In an article marked by disenchantment, Mariano Otero explained that a "nation is nothing more than a large family, and in order for it to be strong and powerful, it is necessary for all its individuals to be intimately bound with the ties of interest and other affections of the heart." On analyzing the very different social groups that made up the population in 1847, Otero stated that those integrating bonds did not exist and made the following terrible statement: "IN MEXICO THERE IS NOT NOR HAS THERE EVER BEEN THAT WHICH IS CALLED A NATIONAL SPIRIT, BECAUSE THERE IS NO NATION." Overcome by that hopeless reflection, Otero foretold for the future a Mexico annexed to the United States or, worse yet, governed by a European monarch.[24]

The uncertainty as to whether Mexico could exist as a nation also permeated the works of conservative writers. José María Gutiérrez de Estrada, Luis G. Cuevas, and Lucas Alamán were witnesses to the political debacle that the country had suffered during the first half of the century, and the three wrote pessimistically about the future. Alamán ended his *Historia de Méjico* with the somber thought that if the Mexican nation were to disappear, "the victim of foreign ambition and internal disorder," at least its actions would serve "to make future generations more careful than the present," and other American nations might take advantage of the sorrowful lesson of the Mexican experience.[25]

Another expression of the depressed national spirit was illustrated by the corrosive language of political caricature. Claudio Linati introduced lithography in Mexico in 1825 and, according to Rafael Barajas, was the creater of the first political cartoon on April 15, 1826. Somewhat later, during the years of the North American invasion, cartoons were among the most effective methods for transmitting messages. Earlier, painting and engraving had been the publicizers of political events, either through the actors themselves or through the symbols and emblems that represented them. The representation of the homeland as a beautiful Indian maiden distinguished by her American raiment became common by the end of the eighteenth century (fig. 128). In those images the homeland

Fig. 150. Representation of the American homeland in the *Calendario liberal de 1859*. The homeland is represented by a beautiful woman in Indian dress, surrounded by exuberant vegetation and animals (as, the crocodile) native to America. (Photo taken from Quiñones, 1994: 109.)

represented the indigenous people and the exuberance of nature in America (fig. 150). When Independence was declared, these images began to be linked with the heroes who shed their blood to free the nation from Colonial dependency (figs. 151–153). Finally, the image of the homeland became the symbol of independence, autonomy, integrity, devotion, and liberty. In a lithograph of 1836, the image represented those values before a Santa Anna who was hastening to defend her (fig. 154).

But between 1821 and 1847 the image of the homeland fell apart. One cartoon showed her rich and splendid in 1821 then knocked about, miserable, and humiliated in 1847 (fig. 155). Other characters, like El Calavera, called for the defense of the homeland against North American invasion or looked on stunned at the shipwreck of the Republic (figs. 156 and 157). The successive defeats

Fig. 151. Funerary monument dated 1823. Two feminine figures flank an urn held up by an eagle, which contains the ashes of the heroes of Independence. The figure on the right represents the American homeland, as indicated by the sorrowful pose and clothing. The other figure seems to be a representation of peace, suggested by the crown of olive branches that she wears on her head. (Photo from *Los pinceles de la historia,* 2000: 140.)

contributed to a feeling of depression and disaster, which was illustrated in an etching that caricatured the coat of arms of the nation. In place of the erect and combative eagle, there was a featherless bird sitting on a crab that, instead of pushing it forward, made it retreat (fig. 158). A cartoon of 1852 presented the nation in ruins, stripped of its wealth by speculators (fig. 159). A lithograph by Constantino Escalante published in *La orquesta* in 1861 showed the Republic beaten by the conservative leaders, staggering and exhausted and on the point of collapsing (fig. 160).

México a través de los siglos, *or the Canon of National History*

So, then, in my town, where there are no monuments to eternalize the memory of heroes and there is little

Fig. 152. *La tumba de Hidalgo,* painting by Felipe Castro, 1859. Here the nation, represented by the goddess of Liberty, leans lovingly over the tomb of Miguel Hidalgo, who has given his life for her. (Photo from *Los pinceles de la historia,* 2000: 241.)

information about them, it is not surprising that the national epic has not flourished. To the contrary, the surprising thing is that there is any history or tradition among the educated classes about who they were.

As concerns the unlettered masses, make your own experiment and ask any man, whether he be one of the illiterate Indians or a Spanish-speaking Mestizo who knows how to read, who the Virgin of Guadalupe is or the patron saint of one village or another, and he will at once give you the story or legend of the miracles. Ask him then who Hidalgo was, who Morelos was, who the Galeanas, Mina, Guerrero, the Bravos, the Rayones, Valerio Trujano, or Pedro Ascencio were and he will shrug his shoulders, not knowing how to answer. Only a vague memory of them remains in the very places where their deeds were carried out!

IGNACIO MANUEL ALTAMIRANO, "PRÓLOGO" TO THE *ROMANCERO NACIONAL* OF GUILLERMO PRIETO (1885)

The establishment of a national State was one of the political obsessions of the nineteenth century. But the construction of a State of national dimensions, with a deterrent force throughout the

Fig. 153. Funerary allegory commemorating the heroes who died for their homeland. (Image provided by the National Museum of Art.)

vast territory and a uniform system of public laws and institutions, instead of promoting balance between the center and the periphery, strengthened the federal system and reduced the spheres of participation of the states and municipalities. The building of a political and administrative machine of that magnitude required many years and was not consolidated under the regime of Porfirio Díaz. It particularly required the confrontations between political, commercial, agrarian, and financial interests entrenched in the capital of the country and the interests of regional groups.

Porfirio Díaz's ambition for power transformed the republican dream into a dictatorship. In just a few years all constitutional liberties and rights, the balance among the three powers, and the autonomy of state and municipal governments were subjugated to the limitless power of the president. It is true that conflicts between regional interests and those entrenched in the capital had begun with the birth of the federal republic, but they were accentuated during the government of Porfirio Díaz.

Fig. 154. Anonymous lithograph published circa 1836. In the foreground is President Antonio López de Santa Anna, pictured gleaming on high, bowing before the homeland and accompanied by three women who symbolize the law (left), progress and business (right), and history (extreme left). Below, three children, representing Indians, Creoles, and Mestizos, are the children of the homeland. Santa Anna seems to be swearing fidelity to the homeland and making the decision to defend her. She is pointing out his destiny: either glory with its laurels to the left or ignominy to the right. (Photo from Barajas, 2000: 134.)

Charles Macune was one of the first historians to discuss the conflict that began in 1824 between the state of Mexico and the federation. At the center of this dispute was the creation of the Federal District, which deprived the state of an immense amount of territory and of the great political and economic power that it had enjoyed until then.[26] From that time until the middle of the century, conflicts ensued between the states and the federation, including disputes over territory, property rights, jurisdictions, economics, and constitutional questions, but with an emphasis on political quarrels. It might be said that after 1824 most of the states adopted federalism as a way to protect their autonomy and

Fig. 155. Lithograph, published in 1848, which shows the opulent homeland, above, later sunk into misery and humiliation by the war of 1847, below. (Photo from Barajas, 2000: 158.)

Fig. 156. The famous character known as El Calavera served as the masthead of several editions of the newspaper of the same name. This image, which anticipates Posada, calls for resistance against the invaders. (Photo from Barajas, 2000: 157.)

Fig. 157. Lithograph from the newspaper *El Calavera,* February 2, 1847. El Calavera witnesses the depressing sinking of the ship of state. (Photo from Barajas, 2000: 156.)

Fig. 158. Engraving from 1829, caricaturing the coat of arms of the Republic, which instead of advancing, retreats like a crab. The eagle looks featherless, with the tips of its wings cut, and, instead of standing on a prickly pear, is standing on a crab, the symbol of retreat. (Photo from Barajas, 2000: 133.)

Fig. 159. Caricature published in the *Calendario de Abrahán López,* 1852. It shows the Republic in ruins, the horn of plenty empty, while the speculators celebrate their personal enrichment.

Fig. 160. Lithograph by Constantino Escalante, published October 16, 1861, in *La orquesta.* Here the conservative presidents of Mexico from 1821 to 1861 are lined up single file, beating the defenceless body of the Republic. (Photo from Barajas, 2000: 201.)

respond to local and regional demands on the part of the citizens and organisms that made up the states.[27] For that reason the greatest and most resented injustice of Díaz's government was the imposition of central authority over the interests of the states of the federation—the crushing of the autonomy that had begun to develop among state and municipal governments. Between 1891 and 1894, a series of state constitutional reforms reduced the states' power in political matters and broadened those of the president. As a consequence of these reforms, the people no longer had the right to establish town councils and the municipal president was no longer elected but became an officer named by the governor of the state or by the President of the Republic himself.[28] The legislators and governors betrayed their local and regional supporters and became pawns in a political chess game played in the National Palace by a solitary player.

This strangling of the power of the states and municipalities restructured the political environment and was reflected in social and cultural circles. The groups and associations that since the middle of the century had promoted the appearance in the states of the first geographies, plans, and maps of their own territory; had supported works of regional history; and had encouraged the cataloging of the local flora, fauna, folklore, and traditions—all those varied affirmations of regional identity were opposed by the centralism and nationalism that was exercised from the capital of the Republic. Just as the nation-state strove to unify language, education, public works, and justice, so too did it support the elaboration of a historiography whose object was to present an ideal of national unity that fatally inhibited the manifestation of local and regional history.

The loss of the territories of California, New Mexico, Arizona, and Texas; the civil wars of the middle of the century; and the moral depression that followed those events all accentuated the feeling of uncertainty that afflicted broad sectors of society. In those years there was no vision of a hopeful future. The past did not support the present, as Indian memory had been denied by the Spanish Conquest and the triumphant insurgent movement blamed the three centuries of the Viceroyalty, with devastating condemnations. In different social groups, the anguish of remembering the nightmares of the past and the uncertainty of living in suspense gave way little by little to the idea of creating a history that could unite the past differences of the nation into one common history. After 1857, in the midst of the war of the Reformation, Manuel Payno criticized those who exclusively favored either Indian or Hispanic roots. Instead of that confusing dichotomy, he proposed a formula that would combine both pasts.[29] Later, in 1865,

Manuel Larráinzar, from the state of Chiapas, insisted on the need for a general history of Mexico "which would embrace each of the different epochs its history could be divided into."[30]

But it was José María Vigil who said that the struggles among the different pasts of the nation were impeding the formation of a common identity among Mexicans. In a text published in 1878, Vigil stated:

> A feeling of hatred for the Colonial system made us include in a common anathema all that came out of that epoch, without considering that whatever one's feelings for their ideas, they contain the seeds of our customs and habits, and their study is consequently indispensible for anyone who wishes to understand current problems. Any other kind of feeling, any idea of contempt as the legacy of the conquistadors toward the conquered races has made us look with supreme disdain on all that concerns those civilizations which were in existence in the New World at the time of the arrival of the Spaniards, without considering that in order to explain the condition of those races, penetrate their character, and resolve their future, it is necessary to go beyond the Colonial period, to study that barbarism which, however much we try to look down on it, lives and persists among us, constituting the most formidable of obstacles for the establishing of peace and the development of favorable elements.[31]

Trained in the classical humanistic tradition, Vigil proposed the incorporation of Náhuatl into university studies, since he considered that it had the same educational value as Greek and Latin. One of the first to recommend "an equally universalist and Mexicanist education," Vigil said:

> We would earnestly desire that our literary and scientific education form an unadulterated and profound Mexican character; that our antiquities be the object of the most exquisite solicitude

on the part of governmemt; that no effort to conserve it and to study it be overlooked; that the Náhuatl language appear beside the learned languages, with the condition that each one of the States pay special attention to its own particular languages and monuments; and in brief that the civilization of our ancestors, more varied, richer, and grander than the bloody barbarism of the ancient tribes of the north, be the basis for our historic and literary studies.[32]

These words of Vigil anticipated the ambitious program undertaken by the government of Porfirio Díaz in the next thirty years (fig. 161). As is known, Díaz was the builder of the first strong, modern State of the nineteenth century. His political ability generated a long period of peace and produced economic growth and wealth. With those resources, the political elite began a program that would have been impossible to imagine earlier, with the goal of making differences disappear by forging a cultural identity shared by the different social groups. The history, including all epochs and themes, that Larráinzar sought and the integrative story of the different roots of the nation that Vigil requested became a reality in *México a través de los siglos.* The title and subtitle of this monumental work, divided into five beautifully published, thick volumes, was the answer to those demands: "Historia general y completa del desenvolvimiento social, político, religioso, militar, artístico, científico y literario de México desde la antigüedad más remota hasta la época actual."[33]

Three successfully employed concepts made this book the outstanding achievement in historiography of the nineteenth century. To begin with, it had the virtue of bringing together past times in a discourse that joined pre-Hispanic antiquity to the Viceroyalty and both of these to the War for Independence, the first years of the Republic, and the Reform movement (figs. 162–165). If the early liberals such as José María Luis Mora had rejected the pre-Hispanic and Colonial past and Lucas Alamán, the head of the conservatives, had only accepted the Hispanic legacy, *México*

Fig. 161. Porfirio Díaz in a photograph included in *México a través de los siglos.*

a través de los siglos built a conciliatory bridge between the conflicted present and the several pasts of the nation for the first time. The title of the work itself gave people to understand that Mexico, the nation, had been able to survive the vicissitudes of history and remain itself in spite of the assaults of the centuries.[34] Edmundo O'Gorman has observed that the inclusion of indigenous antiquities and the Colonial period were the great successes of this work, because they overcame the until then insurmountable antagonisms between Indianism and Hispanism. In place of those irreconcilable pasts, *México a través de los siglos* proposed an integrated vision in which the pre-Hispanic world was "coessentially linked to the evolution of the nation," while the Colonial epoch, considered to be the period in which a new people were formed, "is revealed as the epoch in which an evolutionary process based on the physical and spiritual crossbreeding of conqueror and conquered began and developed. That is, according to O'Gorman, the prime event of our history, which allows us to understand how two foreign pasts are nevertheless our own."[35]

The second concept was the consideration of each one of these periods as part of an evolutionary process whose unfolding was forging the desired national integration and was fulfilling the "immutable laws of progress." The idea of evolution that predominated in this work supported the thesis that proposed a slow fusion of the native and European populations and the progressive integration of the territory and that saw the culmination of those processes in the founding of the Republic. The result of this evolutionary march through history came to be the forging of the new nation.[36]

The third concept was to summarize the knowledge stored up by researchers on each of those periods and explain it in accessible language, accompanied by wonderful illustrations (figs. 166 and 167). The five volumes included something never before seen in history books, two thousand illustrations, half of them specifically requested by the director of the work, Vicente Riva Palacio, and the editor, Santiago Ballescá (figs. 168 and 169). Riva Palacio wanted this new history of Mexico to be saturated with illustrations: "colored prints, engravings, maps, autographic prints, all in abundance and all made by the best artists and taken from the best models; landscapes, cityscapes, buildings, monuments, portraits, drawings of armaments, of objects, art, coins, ancient hieroglyphics and inscriptions, whatever might be necessary for a perfect comprehension of the text." In that way graphic testimonies chosen with very high standards became many more symbols of the historical landscape of the nation.[37] Thus, the graphic element of the work seduced a great many readers, who leafed through its pages fascinated by the beauty of the images.

Fig. 162. Cover of the first volume of *México a través de los siglos*.

Fig. 163. Cover of the second volume of *México a través de los siglos*.

Fig. 164. Cover of the third volume of *México a través de los siglos*.

Fig. 165. Cover of the fourth volume of *México a través de los siglos*.

Fig. 166. Reconstruction of the royal palace of Palenque, *México a través de los siglos.*

The five volumes instantly configured a longed-for past on which to anchor the present and project the future. Suddenly, the young nation turned out to have had a lengthy past, characterized by turbulent epochs but also by memorable deeds. Like the most admired nations of Europe, Mexico had a past that dated back to the most ancient times. For the first time, Mexicans could link the frightening years that had led to the Republic with a remote past that offered them the prestige of antiquity and the glory of civilization. The summation of those virtues made *México a través de los siglos* the work that seemed to restore its diverse pasts to the nation through a cohesive and optimistic discourse.

By bringing together these virtues and the cast of authors that contributed to it, this book established a canon for the publication of historical works. Its five volumes had the effect of captivating a large circle of readers who lived through the experience of submerging themselves in a balanced reading. For the first time the

Fig. 167. Drawing of the pyramid of Xochicalco, *México a través de los siglos.*

reader could survey the complete gamut of a nation beset by serious upheavals and come to the present with the feeling that the long span that had been traveled formed a solid base for the future. *México a través de los siglos* offered its readers a harmonious vision of the contrasting pasts of the nation at a critical time of national rebuilding, when the hope that the nation would endure was in the greatest need of reinforcement.

Standards of balance and restraint were adopted in the group of essays in *México a través de los siglos.* The attitude of considering the stormy past of the nation with moderation was in notable contrast to the historiography of earlier times. The great historical works that had preceded it, beginning with Fray Servando Teresa de Mier's *Historia de las revoluciones de Nueva España* (1813), followed by Carlos María de Bustamante's *Cuadro histórico de las revoluciones de Méjico* (1831), José María Luis Mora's *México y sus revoluciones* (1836), and Lucas Alamán's *Historia de Méjico* (1849–52), on the other hand, were decidedly partisan and polemical works. In those cases historiography, instead of limiting itself to reconstructing the past, transferred to it the struggles that divided

Fig. 168. King Acamapichtli at the moment of his enthronement, *México a través de los siglos.*

Fig. 169. Reproduction of a stela in Copán, *México a través de los siglos.*

political activists in the present and thus became another arena for the ideological conflict of the times. That transferral was also the constant of the historiography of the time of Porfirio Díaz. The early works of that epoch glorified the Reform and the triumph of liberalism over conservatism and imperialism. And in the final stage of the epoch, when Díaz made the error of confusing his person with the destiny of the nation, historiography became an apology for the providential man and an exaltation of peace, prosperity, and material progress. At the same time the "Mestizo, the product of two races [Indians and Europeans] was the great unifier of ethnic, ideological, and class contradictions. The Mestizo was thus the protagonist of Mexican progress, and Porfirio Díaz was the representative and most genuine symbol of this group."[38]

Those works, in addition to exorcizing the past in order to convert it into the devastating armament of the opposing faction or into an instrument for the glorification of the strongman, constructed a historiography obsessed with political change. It was a reflection stressing political crossroads: liberals against conservatives; the Republican state against dictatorship; centralism against federalism; defenders of the homeland against foreign invaders; conflicts between Church and State; educational reform to stress the unity of the nation. And, likewise, it was a meditation on the plans of action that must be developed to achieve peace, stability, economic progress, and national unity.[39] The works of Ignacio Ramírez (*El partido liberal y la reforma religiosa en México*, 1898), Francisco Zarco (*Historia del congreso extraordinario constituyente*, 1857–61), Ignacio Manuel Altamirano (*Historia y política de México*, 1883–84), José María Iglesias (*La cuestión presidencial en 1876*, 1892), Wistano Luis Orozco (*Legislación y jurisprudencia sobre los terrenos baldíos*, 1895), and Francisco Bulnes (*El verdadero Juárez y la verdad sobre la intervención y el imperio*, 1904) and the writings and speeches of a number of politicians, journalists, and historians defined the themes for the citizens' reflection (figs. 170 and 171).[40]

Fig. 170. Portraits of Benito Juárez and Ignacio Manuel Altamirano published in *México a través de los siglos*.

Thus, by debating the crises and political upheavals, considering the defeats, and reflecting on the challenges of the present and the values that should sustain the nation, literature became the arena in which interpretations of the past and future of the nation most frequently came together. Writing made the way in which the nation was formed understandable and served as the spring that nourished the citizens, helping them form their own opinions about the political and social situation of their time. In other words, the historiography of the nineteenth century fulfilled an eminently political function: it participated in the discussion of the national plan; added up the wounds and damages that were obscuring the national horizon; traced the political calvary of the Republic and the plan to found it on the federal agreement; defended the integrity of the territory; and took a stand in favor of national unity. Historiography achieved this to such a degree that, with the assistance of politicians and the strength of the State, it was able to develop a plan that seemed to include the diversity of the populace and a "model identity" for the nation.[41]

Fig. 171. Portraits of Ignacio Zaragoza and Melchor Ocampo published in *México a través de los siglos*.

And there is no doubt that the enthusiasm inspiring those writers was also felt by the authors of *México a través de los siglos*. As has been indicated, this work was an expression of liberal thinking and an exaltation of the principles that inspired that political current. But the erudition of conservative historiographers was also present. Between the middle and the end of the century, José Fernando Ramírez (1804–71), Manuel Orozco y Berra (1816–81), Joaquín García Icazbalceta (1825–94), Juan Hernández y Dávalos (1827–93), and Francisco del Paso y Troncoso (1842–1916) all established the foundations for rigorous historical research. They completed a work that has not so far been equaled: the collection, rescue, and publication of documents on ancient, Colonial, and modern history (figs. 172 and 173).[42]

At a time when there were no academic institutions offering scholarships and grants for the reconstruction of national history, nor professors dedicated exclusively to the study of history, that generation took on the task of gathering the scattered testimonies of the past that had been accumulated in European libraries and archives, ancient church records, and forgotten archives, making of them the best collection of documentary works published in our country. Most of the members of that generation of bibliophiles,

Fig. 172. Family tree of
Motecuzoma that appears in
México a través de los siglos.

Fig. 173. Decree of José María
Morelos abolishing slavery,
México a través de los siglos.

cryptographers, and other learned men took on the same humble task that Joaquín García Icazbalceta defined when he realized at an early age that his vocation "was not to write anything new, but rather to compile materials so that others might do so." He decided to work to the best of his ability, smoothing the road "so that the genius to whom the glory of writing the history of our nation is reserved can move forward with greater speed and fewer problems."[43]

México a través de los siglos had the virtue of bringing together the best of both these traditions. On the one hand, it brought to its pages the liberal desire of basing the nation-state on the values of patriotism, national integrity, republican principles, and the cult of heroes who struggled for Independence and founded the Republic. On the other hand, it adopted the scholarly vocation of conservational historiography, so that in its pages transcriptions of many documents from a variety of different archives appeared,

Fig. 174. Characters from Mexico politics shown in *México a través de los siglos.* Vicente Riva Palacio appears in the lower left.

citing extensive references to sources heretofore ignored and stressing temperance and moderate judgment. These qualities were brought together in a collective work thanks to the talent of its agent and director, Vicente Riva Palacio (fig. 174).

Vicente Riva Palacio was the son on Mariano Riva Palacio, a talented attorney who worked in the ranks of the Liberal party and was a delegate, senator, Secretary of the Treasury, and several times Governor of the state of Mexico. His mother, Dolores Guerrero, was the daughter of Vicente Guerrero, so the child Vicente was born into a family whose lives had contributed to the founding of the Republic. Born on October 16, 1832, Riva Palacio was a distinguished student and later an outstanding attorney, general, poet, journalist, literary critic, novelist, author of stories, orator, politician, and diplomat. To those varied pursuits must be added that of historian, which concerns us here.[44]

The mystery that clouds the origin of *México a través de los siglos* has not yet been cleared up. The official story states that when Manuel González was elected President of the Republic, he decided to give General Vicente Riva Palacio, one of the heroes of the war against Maximilian's Empire, the responsibility for writing a history, with the idea that the general would become absorbed in that task and would abandon the political scene, where he might cast a shadow over the president. A memo from the Minister of War, Jerónimo Treviño, dated February 8, 1881, informed Riva Palacio "that the President of the Republic was pleased to commission him to write the history of the war against the intervention and the empire." Another story maintains that this was not the idea of President González, but rather of Porfirio Díaz, who was continuing to manipulate national politics behind the figure of González. What is known is that Riva Palacio accepted the commission without protest and immediately put his formidable talents to work to carry it out.[45]

Enjoying the protection of the President of the Republic and the support of the Ministry of War, Riva Palacio began to write to all the government agencies; to officials who had commanded troops during the Intervention; to state governors, consulates, and embassies; to the directors of the main archives and libraries of the nation; and to his friends among historians, journalists, and writers. He asked them for all sorts of documents, plans, and reports that would be useful for his history.

Nonetheless, the original mission that had been given to him in February of 1881—to write a history of the war against the French Intervention—was suddenly completely restructured in 1882: the new plan that now occupied Riva Palacio was the writing of a new general history of Mexico, from indigenous antiquity to the triumph of the Reform movement. To complete that ambitious task, he brought together an impressive team and forged new partnerships and alliances. Supported by his own good judgment and his excellent relations with members of the intellectual community, he invited five distinguished writers to collaborate in the daring enterprise: Alfredo Chavero was given the writing of ancient history and the conquest; he himself took on the writing of the history of the Viceroyalty; Julio Zárate was asked to write on the war of Independence; Juan de Dios Arias and Enrique Olavarría y Ferrari were assigned the volume on independent Mexico (1821–55); and José María Vigil was charged with the history of the Reform. Each of these writers had his own fame, body of work, and historiographical credentials, but Riva Palacio had the talent necessary to bring them together in a collective undertaking without the work's losing its equilibrium.

His newest and most important ally was Santiago Ballescá, representative of the Casa Ballescá in Mexico and of the Spanish firm Espasa y Compañía, which together assumed the responsibility for publishing the five large volumes of the work. Riva Palacio's talent becomes clear when we realize that these publishing companies agreed to assume the responsibility for paying the authors and other collaborators on the work as well as the high cost of printing this very luxurious set with a first printing of seven thousand copies. The work initially supported by the government now had its own financing. Ballescá was not only a businessman who resolved the delicate matters of financing, but was also one of Riva Palacio's most effective collaborators in obtaining documents, photographs, plans, and other graphic materials.[46]

It is clear that Riva Palacio had no professional training as a historian; nonetheless, he had cultivated an obsessive passion for the history of his homeland. His interest in the past had begun at home, where both his maternal and paternal ancestry tied him to the past of the Republic and initiated him into the plan for the nation that was then being forged. Years later, the fact that the prodigious archives of the Court of the Holy Inquisition fell into his hands made him a ceaseless reader of old documents, an astounded researcher of the then demonized history of the Viceroyalty, and still later, an enthusiastic promoter of the historical novel. The tragic lives and terrible dramas that he read about in the Inquisition papers gave him the characters, the plot, and the setting for his series of historical novels. Between 1868 and 1872—that is to say, in somewhat less than five years—Riva Palacio wrote seven historical novels. In the fruitful year of 1868, he brought out the first three: *Calvario y Tabor; Monja y casada, virgin y mártir;* and *Martín Garatuza.* These were followed by *Los piratas del Golfo* (1869), *Las dos emparedadas* (1869), *La vuelta de los muertos* (1870), and *Memorias de un impostor: Don Guillén de Lampart, rey de México* (1872). Except for *Calvario y Tabor,* whose plot concerned the deeds of the resistance to the French Intervention in Michoacán, they concerned themselves with episodes and chaacters from the Viceroyalty (fig. 175).[47]

Riva Palacio had not made a specialized study of history, but he was part of that first generation of Mexicans who struggled valiantly to forge a national identity and establish a plan for the nation based on its historical roots. After Guillermo Prieto, Ignacio Ramírez, José Fernando Couto, and other writers founded the Academia de Letrán in 1836, the idea of creating a literature that would express the emotions of the national soul was born, and from that time on that objective became a mandate for cultured Mexicans. Vicente Riva Palacio was no exception.[48]

Following the lead of Ignacio Ramírez and Ignacio Manuel Altamirano, Riva Palacio undertook the building of a national literature, participated in the forming of a native songbook, put together his own gallery of famous Mexicans, made satirical journalism into a popular tribunal, brought the poorest citizens and the dregs of the urban underclass into the national conscience, raised the first statue to Cuauhtémoc and classified him as a national hero, and featured country people as characters in his novels, parading through the novels the full range of society: Indians, urban lepers, Creoles, blacks, mulattos, and Mestizos. Throughout Riva Palacio's works the Mestizos were the physical and moral prototype of the Mexican, the social product of the fusion of native groups with Europeans.[49] *México a través de los siglos,* his great historical work, gathers together those collective symbols and aspirations; the first great mural incorporating the varied pasts of the nation, this work sent Mexicans a message of unity, strength, and optimism (fig. 176).

Fig. 175. Characters from the Colonial Period shown in *México a través de los siglos*: Hernán Cortés, Juan Ruiz de Alarcón, and Juan Vicente de Güemes Pacheco, Count of Revillagigedo.

Inevitably, given the virtues it possessed, *México a través de los siglos* became the historiographic canon of its epoch. Its appearance gave coherence, animation, and prestige to the diffused past, provided the nation with a moving narration of the formation of

Fig. 176. The boy heroes of Chapultepec, *México a través de los siglos*.

the national identity, and elevated historical literature to a pre-eminent position. Its effect on the national conscience was so profound and immediate that eleven years after its publication it generated a masterful summary of Mexican history based on its extensive contents. This summary was the work of Justo Sierra, who first published it as part of the monumental three-volume set, *México: Su evolución social* (ed. J. Ballescá, 1900–1902, 3 vols.). Four decades later Alfonso Reyes had the perspicacity to publish it as a separate work with the title *Evolución política del pueblo mexicano*. Since then it has been reissued several times and is known as one of the best brief histories of Mexico.[50]

The *Evolución política del pueblo mexicano* emphasized the same subjects found in *México a través de los siglos*: pre-Hispanic civilization, the conquest, the Colonial period, Independence, the Republic, and the Reform period, plus a final chapter devoted to the period of Porfirio Díaz. Like Riva Palacio, Sierra adopted

Fig. 177. On the covers of many books of the nineteenth century, following the canonical example of *México a través de los siglos,* the symbols that represented the Mexican nation were reproduced. (Photo from Castillo Negrete, 1875–92.)

an evolutionary focus, his work presenting the history of the Mexican people as an ascending march toward a promising future. It is clear that there were tremendous obstacles on that road, which Sierra was quick to point out, but to the degree that the Mexican people were able to overcome them, their future unfolded (fig. 177).

According to the interpretation of Justo Sierra, after overcoming the stumbling blocks of the war of Independence, the illusions of Iturbide's empire, the struggles with the Church, the battle against conservatism, the tragic years of Santa Anna's reign, foreign invasions, and the amputation of national territory, one of the most difficult trials that the Mexican people had to face was the period of Porfirio Díaz. Sierra stated that the undeniable economic and social advances achieved during those years were in contrast to the weakness of the political process. Although he recognized the merits of Díaz's achievements, Sierra could not deny that the nation was living beneath "the absolute authority of the current head of the Republic."[51] Despite the fact that Sierra was a key man in Díaz's management team, as a historian and critic of his times he could not refrain from concluding his book by pointing out the dilemma that was currently obscuring the future of the nation:

> In summary, the political evolution of Mexico has been sacrificed to other phases of its development; let this obvious, unimpeachable fact suffice to demonstrate it: there is not a single political party, no vital organized group which exists around a program rather than around a single man. Any steps taken along this course have been halted when they came up against governmental suspicion and general apathy. . . . The day on which a political party manages to organize itself and survive, political evolution will begin to move forward again and man, more necessary in democracies than in aristocracies, will follow along. . . . All Mexican social evolution will have been aborted and frustrated if it does not reach that final end: liberty.[52]

This survey of the main historical works of the nineteenth century shows that at the beginning of the century there was a radical change in the conception and writing of history. With the appearance of the *Historia de las revoluciones de Nueva España* by Fray Servando Teresa de Mier in 1813 and *El cuadro histórico de la Revolución de Independencia* by Carlos María de Bustamante in 1823, the cycle of works dominated by the Christian concept of history ended and the epoch of works that recorded national history began. Instead of a concept of historical events dominated by Christian values and the salvation of humanity, the gathering and interpretation of the past now focused on the formation of the nation-state. The old protagonists of historical discourse—the conquistadors, the religious orders, the Church, and the Spanish State—were replaced by patriots who fought for Independence, politicians who struggled to give form to the national State, heroes who offered their lives for the Republic, revolutions that motivated great political and social change, and Mexicans themselves, as the diversity of individuals and groups who constituted the population was henceforth called.

Almost a century after European historiography of the Enlightenment decided to concentrate on questions of government and civil society and the deeds that explained the general march of civilization,[53] Mexican historiography became absorbed by the three political events that changed the image of the nineteenth century in Mexico: Independence, Reform, and the era of Porfirio Díaz. Following in the footsteps of European historiography, Mexicans emphasized descriptions of the nation's formation and of the national identity, as was clearly shown in *México a través de los siglos*. Justo Sierra completed that train of thought, for his *Evolución política del pueblo mexicano* was above all a narration of the political processes that forged the national state, a story that combined individual deeds with sociological generalizations. To his political analysis of the past, Sierra added the most ancient virtue of historical reporting: a well-told story, the gift of literary style. His work can be seen as the most polished expression of historical reporting—an elegant and persuasive narration of the formation of a nation.

IX. The Historical Narrative Coined by the Post-Revolutionary State

From the State that grew out of Mexico's Revolution of 1910–17 came the idea of revolution as an accelerating process of history and a renewing agent for society. It was an idea taken from nineteenth-century liberals, who in turn had received it from the French Revolution, the great movement that favored violent disruption over slow evolutionary processes.[1]

The word *revolution* had a pejorative meaning before the transforming frenzy that erupted in 1910; it evoked political chaos, unbridled action by the masses, the limitless ambition of leaders, and the assumption of power through violent means. Although there is not an informed report explaining the way in which the word *revolution* was changed and affirmed in the history of Mexico, we do know something of its incredible transformation in the nineteenth and twentieth centuries.

From Revolt to Revolution with a Capital R

José María Luis Mora, the founder of Mexican liberalism, considered the Revolution for Independence to be necessary but "pernicious and destructive to the nation." He said that rebellions, before bringing about well-being, had brought on immense evils for the Republic. He saw in them movements that shifted between wantonness and tyranny. For his part, Lucas Alamán, the intelligent leader of the conservative party, dedicated his political life and his talent as a historian to proving that the internal anarchy and external weakness that had led to the debacle of 1847 were consequences of the insurgent movement that forswore its Hispanic heritage and adopted foreign principles. Alamán said that the insurrection led by Hidalgo was not "the heroic effort of a people who struggle for their liberty,"but rather "the uprising of the proletariat class against property and civilization." He also rejected the ideas of Servando Teresa de Mier and Carlos María de Bustamente, who interpreted Independence as the liberation of the ancient indigenous nation from the subjugation of the Spanish yoke.[2]

The repeated condemnation of the radical movements in the first half of the nineteenth century caused Edmundo O'Gorman to say that contrary to the "official Jacobin vision," conservative ideas during those years had greater support than those of liberals.[3] But just when the liberals defeated the conservative party in the Revolution of Ayutla (1854–56), the meaning of the word *revolution* began to change. In 1855 Guillermo Prieto equated that movement to the one begun by Miguel Hidalgo. He argued that the Revolution of Ayutla, like that of Hidalgo, was the selfsame struggle of the people against tyranny. Other liberals, among them Ignacio Ramírez, Ignacio Manuel Altamirano, and Ignacio Vallarta, saw in the Revolution of 1810 the rebirth of Mexico and the beginning of a revolutionary tradition that continued to the present day, when the conservative party was defeated by the Reform movement.[4]

In 1867 Benito Juárez's triumph over French imperialism and native conservatism strengthened the liberal interpretation of history based on disruptive processes. "After 1867, the nineteenth century's liberal vision of history was briefly summarized in a concise form by Justo Sierra. . . . In his book, which has enjoyed great popularity and continuing influence, he declared that 'Mexico has never had more than two revolutions.' The first was the revolution of independence; the second was the great Reform of 1854 to 1867. Both were a part of the same social process for Mexico."[5] The model that affirmed the notion of revolution as the midwife of a new epoch of history was the French Revolution. Ignacio Manuel Altamirano expressed this frankly in the following words: "We are the direct offspring of that glorious revolution of 1789, and our ideas are those which were proclaimed in the Constituent Assembly, which, lighting the world like a great torch, crossed the Atlantic and came to illuminate our people, sunk in the shadows of Colonial servitude."[6]

The French Revolution, with its affirmation of popular sovereignty, its declaration of the Rights of Man, the preeminence it placed on democratic principles, and its aura as the founding event of modern times and of republican legitimacy, was the political model that inspired liberal Mexicans.[7] Beneath these banners, the liberals revalued the history of their homeland.

David Brading has emphasized the new interpretation of the concepts of homeland and nation made by the intellectuals of the Reform movement. After examining the works of Ignacio Ramírez and Ignacio Manuel Altamirano, he observed that both considered their homeland "to be a federal republic, heir not of Anáhuac or New Spain, but of the French Revolution and of the Insurgency of 1810." Ramírez and Altamirano interpreted the pre-Hispanic past as an epoch governed by barbarism and saw in the Viceroyalty a long night dominated by religious obscurantism. They believed that a liberal Republic could not be based on such roots, and they proclaimed other origins: "We," they said, "came from the town of Dolores; we are descendents of Hidalgo."[8]

By tying the insurgent movement to the Revolution of Ayutla, liberals supported the myth of a continuous revolutionary process whose tremors revealed successive steps in national development. The regime of Porfirio Díaz formalized this interpretation of the past in its great historical works such as *México a través de los siglos,* in the civic calendar that was instituted at that time, in the museums, and in the sumptuous ceremonies celebrating the hundredth anniversary of the insurgent movement. Independence, Reform, and the Porfirian present thus formed a single sequence, a historic block set in the great moments that had defined the course of the nation.

The Myth of the Unity and Continuity of the Nation

The Reform generation, beset by civil wars, foreign invasions, and the treasury crisis that had dislocated the country, embraced the myth of national unity beyond political quarrels and social antagonisms. One of Juárez's goals in the years following the war of the Reform was to stanch the wounds created by political confrontations. His amnesty law of 1870 was the first step in that crusade. Later, the inclusion of former collaborators with Maximilian's Empire in the cabinets of Benito Juárez, Sebastián Lerdo de Tejada, and Porfirio Díaz ratified that effort at conciliation.

But it was not until the electoral victory of Porfirio Díaz in 1876 that Díaz invited his old enemies, the supporters of Benito Juárez, Sebastián Lerdo de Tejada, and José María Iglesias, to form part of his government. Thus, in 1887, when another anniversary of the death of Benito Juárez was commemorated, the old enemy of Díaz was elevated to the rank of national hero and, in effigy, received the homage of his most recalcitrant enemies. The idea of unifying the nation through the cult of heroes gained strength during the regime of Porfirio Díaz. The pantheon of heroes venerated in the civic calendar was created at that time, including Cuauhtémoc, Hidalgo, Morelos, Melchor Ocampo, Benito Juárez, Ignacio Zaragoza, and Porfirio Díaz. Among that group were the heroes who proclaimed Independence, reestablished the Republic, and defended the integrity of the nation.

The presence of such patriots in different stages of the formation of the nation expressed unity and continuity despite the vicissitudes of history. Even when, at the end of the Porfirian era, the governing elite and the "scientists" traded their admiration of the Revolution for the idea of gradual evolution, they maintained their belief in the historic continuity of the nation.[9] In *México a través de los siglos* and in *México: Su evolución social,* the reader was presented with the long journey of the homeland as an evolutionary progression joining the ancient indigenous past with the Viceroyalty, Independence, and the Reform, finally illuminating the Porfirian present with its light of optimism.

Madero's Revolution of 1910

In *La bola,* the novel of Emilio Rabasa published in 1887, there is an exaltation of revolution as a regenerative act of society and a condemnation of the numberless revolts that stunned the nation during the nineteenth century. But the event that changed the meaning of the word *revolution* was the revolt led by Francisco I. Madero against Porfirio Díaz. Even though Madero's following at first used the terms *revolution, insurrection,* and *revolutionary movement* indiscriminately, little by little the word *revolution* acquired a meaning it had not had earlier.

Guillermo Palacios, the first to scrutinize the meanings of the word *revolution* in the twentieth century, observed that Madero gave it an essentially political connotation (fig. 178). In April of 1911, José María Pino Suárez, who later would be Vice President, declared: "Revolution is progress." Then, when the Madero movement overthrew Porfirio Díaz, the latter's government came to be "the Old Regime" and Madero's triumph was proclaimed as the dawning of democracy. In that same year of 1911, Luis Cabrera made his famous statement: "the Revolution is the Revolution," by which he meant that revolution was not merely a change of government, but a profound social shake-up, a wave capable of knocking down the strongest parapets.[10] In the years that followed, the word *revolution* acquired the meaning of an autonomous process, independent of human action—a sort of hurricane that seemed to have been born from the foundations of history.

Between 1911 and 1913 the spokesmen for the Madero movement tied that rebellion to two earlier revolutionary dates: 1810 and 1855–57, the war of Reform. According to their interpretation, the

Fig. 178. Francisco I. Madero.
(Photo from Casasola, 1973.)

Revolution of 1910 was part of the same historical process that had driven the formation of the nation. Madero's supporters equated their hero to the figures of Hidalgo and Juárez. In those years of political effervescence, in the process of "reification," the tendency was to make the Revolution a movement independent of human actors, created by mechanical forces and autonomous purposes, beyond the will of humankind. The Revolution, said one Madero supporter, "is not a man or a group of men, but the national spirit in action!"[11]

Madero insisted on clarifying the ties between the Revolution of 1910 and its two prestigious ancestors. He affirmed that the first revolution, started by Hidalgo, broke with Colonial subjugation. The second, "the glorious Revolution of Ayutla," restored the rights of the people and wrote the rights of man into the Constitution of 1857. And the third, he argued, indelibly engraved on the national conscience the principles of Effective Suffrage and No Re-Election.[12] This was a revolution with a personal drive more imperative than the actions of its own leaders. As one of his spokesmen stated, "The Revolution had a beginning, then developed its transforming course, and continues alive in the present thanks to the united spirit of the numberless popular masses who support it.[13]

The Revolution Divided: Supporters of Villa, Zapata, and Carranza

The assassination of Francisco I. Madero in 1913 once again unleashed civil war and new interpretations of the word *revolution*. In 1915 Adolfo de la Huerta was defeated, triumphant revolutionary forces promulgated a new Constitution in 1917, and Venustiano Carranza was elected president.

The tragic death of Madero made him the first martyr of the revolutionary movement. The legitimacy that he had not enjoyed during his lifetime was granted after his death. In the years after the fall of Huerta, the tomb of Madero was an obligatory pilgrimage site for Venustiano Carranza, Álvaro Obregón, Francisco Villa (fig. 179), and other revolutionary chiefs. November 20, the date chosen by Madero to begin the Revolution, became a civic celebration commemorated every year.[14]

With Carranza's ascent to power, the meaning that Madero had given to the revolutionary movement began to change. One of Carranza's spokesmen declared that the purpose of the movement was not the simple continuation of the rebellion begun in 1910. Carranza followers began to refer to Madero's movement as purely political and argued that what was necessary was a social revolution. They adopted the idea that the Revolution of 1910 was a continuation of those popular struggles begun in 1810 and 1855. They maintained that the constitutional movement headed by the First Chief (Carranza) had attached an economic and social significance to the initial revolution that changed it into a transcendent reform.[15]

At the time of his greatest power, Carranza defined the revolution as the "reconstruction of Mexico," dividing it into three periods.

Fig. 179. Francisco Villa. (Photo from Brenner, 1971.)

The first period was defined by the struggle against Huerta, the second concentrated on the conflict against Emiliano Zapata and Pancho Villa, and the third had the goals of reestablishing constitutional order and reconstructing the nation. But despite his capable handling of propaganda and the means of communication, Carranza never achieved the heroic heights of Villa or Zapata (fig. 180), nor was he considered a true revolutionary during his lifetime.[16]

Later, the break of Villa and Zapata supporters with Carranza divided the revolutionary forces and made it more difficult to discern the distinction between each of the groups calling themselves revolutionaries. Villa partisans believed themselves to be the legitimate followers of Madero's ideals and accused Carranza of being a traitor. To them Villa was the man predestined to free the masses and champion true democracy. During his life and after his assassination, in the hearts of the poor, Pancho Villa maintained the image of a hero, the aura of a brave revolutionary, and the charisma of a leader of men.[17]

Zapata's followers put forward similar arguments against Carranza (fig. 181). They never shared the fervor of Villa's supporters toward Madero, and they considered Carranza a traitor to the social principles of the Revolution. Together with followers of Ricardo Flores Magón, Zapata's people made up the radical wing of the Revolution; their demands reflected the social and political aspirations of the most dispossessed of the groups, the Indians and the peasants.[18]

The First Buds of Nationalism

The vast social and political shake-up that the Revolution of 1910 unleashed was accompanied by an unfamiliar feeling: the sense of discovering the hidden visage of a country. Several members of the generation that lived through the tornado of the Revolution pointed to the year 1915 as the mythic date that initiated the uncovering of the hidden nation. Its appearance occurred in isolated cases and in different ways, through the voices of poets, anthropologists, painters, teachers, authors, musicians, and cinematographers who proclaimed, as Ramón López Velarde stated canonically (fig. 182), the *Novedad de la patria*. López Velarde was referring to the intimate vitality that was enriching life in the provinces day after day.[19] As José Luis Martínez has said, Ramón López Velarde "summed up and crystalized our modern meaning and spirit of nationality."[20]

Fig. 180. Emiliano Zapata. (Photo from Brenner, 1971.)

Fig. 181. Venustiano Carranza. (Photo from Brenner, 1971.)

A few years earlier, the generation of the Ateneo de la Juventud (1909), which brought together a bright cast of characters including Alfonso Reyes (fig. 183), Pedro Henríquez Ureña, Julio Torri, Enrique González Martínez, Antonio Médiz Bolio, Martín Luis Guzmán, Carlos González Peña, José Vasconcelos, Antonio Caso, Federico Mariscal, Diego Rivera, Roberto Montenegro, Manuel Ponce, Julián Carrillo, and others, broke with the Porfirian past and adopted new forms of expressing reality.[21] The members of the Ateneo were "direct precursors of the Revolution. Through

Fig. 182. Ramón López Velarde.
(Photo from Sheridan, 1989: 134.)

all-encompassing criticism, they condemned the Porfirian epoch, which they characterized as lacking in humanitarian or Christian values, rigid in educational policies . . . turning a deaf ear to human misery and obsessively colonial."[22]

Manuel Gamio (fig. 184), the first professional anthropologist to graduate abroad, stated in 1916—one year before the Constituent Congress of 1917—that the Constitution in force did not represent the majority of the population. Alarmed by the "character [of that Constitution,] foreign in origin, form, and foundation," he demanded that the Latin American republics in which Indian populations predominated revise their constitutions "in order to respond to the nature and needs of all the elements which constitute the populace." And Gamio went beyond the Utopian thinkers of the nineteenth century. He proposed the incorporation of the native population into the concept of national identity, rejecting the Western canons in order to value pre-Hispanic art and to create an aesthetic that viewed native creations within the framework of

Fig. 183. Portrait of Alfonso Reyes by David Alfaro Siqueiros. (Photo from *Alfonso Reyes: Homenaje nacional,* 1981: 52.)

their own historical and cultural categories. Gamio was the first to demand that the process forging the Revolution include the Indian, European, and Mestizo legacies in a new Mexican identity.[23]

After 1913 in the field of music, Manuel M. Ponce left the established canon for Italian and French music and suggested the rescue of popular music.[24] In 1915 Carlos González Peña, one of the founders of the Ateneo de la Juventud, published an interview with painter Saturnino Herrán that described the nationalistic spirit that overcame that generation:

> You are completely correct to tell me that in order to create a national painting movement, first we have to do something which is uniquely ours; to observe what is here, to feel it—I have never understood why Mexicans go off to paint coquettes in Paris, village scenes in Britain, quiet canals in Bruges, or desolate plains in La Mancha. . . . Hasn't Manuel Ponce already

pointed the way, harmonizing the songs that you and I and all the peasants wanted to hear the blind beggars sing as they played the harp, or the maids that sang in their plaintive voices as darkness fell . . . ? To turn to what is ours alone, observing it; that is our salvation![25]

Recent studies on the origins of the cinema reveal the presence of these nationalistic ideas in the first documentaries that showed Mexican landscapes, customs, traditions, celebrations, and events. These sentiments were also present in the first films, whose settings, characters, and plots visualized the past and present through the lens of nationalism. In the decade from 1910 to 1920, picturesque reportage was replaced by surprising documentaries (fig. 185) that one after another, with a force never before seen, transmitted the spectacular images of *Viaje triunfal del jefe de la revolución, don Francisco I. Madero* (1911), *Insurrección en México* (1911), *Asalto y toma de ciudad Juárez* (1911), *La revolución orozquista* (1912), *La revolución en Veracruz* (1912), *La invasión norteamericana* (1914), *La revolución zapatista* (1914), and films showing the dazzling victories of Francisco Villa in the north of the country.

Thanks to this great display of images (fig. 186), the Revolution was the first historical event of the modern epoch to have an immediate, profound and emotional national dissemination. (The projection of the North American preparations for the invasion of Veracruz caused uproars and outbursts of nationalistic fervor.) The appearance of the first films, done by private companies, was also characterized by a notable weight of effusive nationalism. According to Aurelio de los Reyes, two sources fed this nationalism: the desire to present, as writers already had, an "authentic" image of what was truly Mexican—of its men, women, landscapes, and values; and the decision to counteract the devalued image of the nation transmitted by the press and by North American films, which showed Mexicans as savage bandits, jealous he-men, and quintessentially primitive people.[26]

Fig. 184. Photograph of Manuel
Gamio, around 1920. (Photo from
González Gamio, 1987.)

Fig. 185. Advertisement for a
documentary on the Mexican
Revolution.

Preceding those nationalistic outbreaks in anthropology, poetry, music, and film, the novel was the first mirror of characters born of the revolutionary process. Contemporary with the nationalistic witness earlier mentioned in poetry, music, and movies, these characters appeared in the works of Mariano Azuela: *Los fracasados* and *Mala yerba* in 1909; *Andrés Pérez maderista* in 1911; *Los de abajo* in 1915; and *Los caciques* in 1917. In those stories Azuela (fig. 187) presented a turbulent world in which the citizenry in arms clashed with their ancient exploiters and with the new

Fig. 186. Advertisement for *Memorias de un mexicano,* which collected the works of Salvador Toscano on the main events of the Revolution of 1910.

Fig. 187. Mariano Azuela. (Photo from Azuela, 1958.)

lords of power—the military, the educated elite, and the politicians formed by the torrent of revolution. Azuela's novels were characterized by violence, opportunism, betrayal of popular ideals, and the fatalistic view that such an immense social upheaval would end in betrayal by those newly in power.

In a literary sense, Carlos Monsiváis has observed, Azuela's prose was the means by which "the national prose was renewed, words were legitimized, and modes of expression were standardized throughout all the regions of the nation."[27] Socially, that literature "generated a market of readers avid to recognize themselves in the national symbols, legends and sagas." In the revolutionary novel, "a formidable and primitive mythology" appeared, which located the popular heroes, such as Pancho Villa, in the foreground and condemned the villains, symbolized by the uncouth figure of Victoriano Huerta. Politically, "the image of the Revolution was prepared and adjusted as otherness: something that happened in another time and to other people, strange and foreign."[28]

The Break with the Conciliatory Interpretation of History and the Argument over the Past, 1916–1935

Madero's triumph over the Porfirian government in 1911 disseminated the conviction that the Revolution had brought down a corrupt regime and the idea that a new national plan had been born out of it—a future of liberty and progress that would benefit the most oppressed sectors: Indians and peasants, workers, the middle classes. This prospect unleashed a compulsive reinterpretation of the past and an appraisal of the Revolution in the historical trajectory of the nation. The revision of the past that then began demanded the incorporation into the historical account of "those social and ethnic groups which traditional history . . . had marginalized, and likewise [demanded the consideration of] an array of events . . . that had not been included in the elaboration of old official accounts."[29] Manuel Gamio proposed in 1916 that our indigenous and Hispanic roots be united in one vessel that could contain all their components. He stated: "It now falls on Mexico's revolutionaries to take up the maul, tie on the blacksmith's apron, and forge on this miraculous anvil a new nation made of iron and bronze conmingled."[30]

The revolutionary Félix Palavicini found from reading done while he was in jail "that in the history of Mexico very little importance was attached to the efforts of civilians, who were completely ignored by historians in their descriptions of wars and battles." This discovery later led Palavicini, when he held a high position in the Secretary of Public Education, to prepare a book that he called *Diez civiles notables de la historia patria* (1914), which was one of the first works that attempted to overcome the common fascination with military leaders.[31]

Martín Luis Guzmán (fig. 188), who had participated in the revolutionary upheaval that began in 1910, delved into history in 1915 to discern the failures and disorders of the present. His study concentrated on bitter and disenchanted pages, where instead of great men there were lists of political tyrants, caricature-like events, lies, venality, baseness, and abjectness. After that depressing survey, he concluded that Mexicans lacked the most elemental political virtues: education, moderation, patience, respect for law, loyalty, justice.[32] In that same year of 1915, other observers discovered an unexpected Mexico. Manuel Gómez Morín stated that

> in 1915, when revolutionary failure seemed most certain, when the most shameful and hidden defects of Mexicans were commented on with the greatest ostentation and the men of the Revolution hesitated and were losing faith . . . , suddenly a new direction started to become clear. And in an optimistic stupor we understood unsuspected truths. Mexico existed. Mexico, as a nation with capacities, aspirations, life, and problems of its own. . . . And the Indians and mestizos and creoles [were] living realities, men with every human attribute.[33]

The revolutionary uproar provoked an avalanche of books and essays on the past and future of the nation, national identity, and the role of education in national destiny. Between 1910 and 1920, the analyses of the historical bases of the nation were led by militants of the various revolutionary factions. To them was added a contingent of professors and intellectuals who emphasized the themes of national identity and unity and the means for achieving them: history books. This discussion intensified old antagonisms between liberals and conservatives, Indianists and Hispanists, traditionalists and revolutionaries. The division was so great that each author and each group defended its own historical origins, traditions, heroes, and founding dates: "So while some

Fig. 188. Martín Luis
Guzmán. (Photo from
Guzmán, 1970.)

tried to extract the historical tradition from the heroic . . . figure of
Cuauhtémoc, others supported the foundation of nationality on
the conquering general Hernán Cortés. Followers of Hidalgo
abominated Iturbide. . . . Even the spelling of the name of the
nation became a rallying flag for division. Some wrote México,
others Méjico."[34]

There is no study that rises above the opposition between liberals
and conservatives or between Indianists and Hispanists to discover
the class antagonisms, ideological contradictions, and party affili-
ations that underlay that debate. The fact is that the discussion
changed when the Secretary of Public Education was reestablished
in 1921 and the different revolutionary groups joined in the Partido
Nacional Revolucionario in 1929. After that time, the deliberation
over national identity and the historical foundations of the homeland was concentrated in the Department of Public Education and
was manipulated by State institutions and the Partido Nacional
Revolucionario.

1920–1928: The Revolution Becomes the Government

The rebellion in Agua Prieta in 1920 resulted in the death of Venustiano Carranza and raised the Sonora group to power under the leadership of Álvaro Obregón, Adolfo de la Huerta, and Plutarco Elías Calles. According to Thomas Benjamin, the Sonorans introduced two semantic revisions into the concept of revolution. On the one hand, they transformed revolutionary action into government, and on the other hand, they made an effort to cover the deep differences between revolutionary groups with a protective umbrella: the "revolutionary family" (fig. 189).[35]

As far as the Sonorans were concerned, this family had many offshoots, but it was united by common principles. Thus, the rebellion of Agua Prieta was presented as a continuation of the popular movement initiated by Madero. And very soon Presidents Álvaro Obregón and Plutarco Elías Calles developed a politics of conciliation toward their ancient rivals. Zapatism, for example, ceased to be a movement of savage hordes led by the "Atilla of the South" and was incorporated into the official memory of the Revolution in the decade of the 1920s.[36] In 1922 Congress honored the memory of anarchist Ricardo Flores Magón, arranged for the return of his remains, and elevated him to the rank of precursor of the Mexican Revolution. Like his predecessors, Obregón affirmed that his government was a continuation of the process begun in 1810 and celebrated the hundred-year anniversary of the Revolution of Independence with great splendor.[37]

With both Obregón and Calles, the commemoration of the revolutionary movement ceased to be an activity of the spokesmen and leaders of the factions that were contending for power and became a first priority of the State. During Calles's presidency, from 1924 to 1928, the government assumed the responsibility for commemorating and presiding over the celebration of great revolutionary deeds. The rifts caused by the assassination of Obregón, the Cristero Rebellion from 1926 to 1929, and the

Fig. 189. Part of the "revolutionary family" in Diego Rivera's mural on the stairway of the National Palace: José María Pino Suárez, Francisco Madero, and Francisco Villa above. José Guadalupe Posada, José Vasconcelos, Venustiano Carranza, and Luis Cabrera in the midground. (Photo from Folgarait, 1998.)

power struggles within the "revolutionary family" encouraged a movement for "revolutionary unity" led from within State institutions. This campaign for the unity of the revolutionary group was also extended into the past in an effort to cure wounds opened during the armed struggle.

In this manner the "Revolution-made government" was changed into a succession of recollections, rites, monuments, and celebrations that invaded the most far-flung spheres of public life (fig. 190). The Revolution, Calles declared in his last speech in September of 1928, must cease to be a movement of caudillos and must transform itself into a regime of institutions and laws. The revolutionary family, he said, had to unite in order to save itself and the nation. The next year, the different groups and factions agreed to join in what they called the Partido Nacional Revolucionario, or PNR. After 1927, said one of Calles's critics, the Revolution began to exercise excessive influence not only on politics, but on all aspects of life, including the economy, science, and art.[38]

The Executors of the Program of National Integration

Perhaps the greatest achievement of the Revolution-made government was to ascribe the plan of integrating the nation through education and culture to an institution of the State. The new

Fig. 190. *La maestra rural,* mural by Diego Rivera on the building of the Secretary of Public Education, 1923–24. (Photo from Folgarait, 1998: plate VI.)

Secretary of Public Education was created by a decree of Congress on September 28, 1921. In contrast to the Porfirian department, this department had jurisdiction throughout the country; it was a Federal institution that had the support of the President of the Republic himself from its beginning. The integration of the diverse pieces of the ethnic, social, and cultural mosaic into a plan of national unity, led by a homogeneous educational system, was the ideal of José Vasconcelos (fig. 191) and Moisés Sáenz, the two political actors who defined the programs of the Secretary between 1921 and 1930.

With clairvoyant vision, Vasconcelos perceived that the educational program would have to include the education of Indians to make them a part of the nation, of peasants to improve the terrible conditions under which they languished, and of technical and advanced students to match the progress of the nation with that of better developed countries, as well as including the diffusion of culture to forge a citizenry sure of its identity and engaged in a national plan. In addition to the full-scale reorganization and modernization of teaching, Vasconcelos's program implied a "true cultural plan."[39]

Fig. 191. José Vasconcelos.
(Photo from Blanco, 1997.)

Instead of promoting elitist education, Vasconselos saw in the educational process a plan for social integration, the elevation of the common citizen, and the strengthening of the national identity. Educational reforms that he undertook embraced the totality of the Mexican people. With uncommon vigor he visited the most far-flung places, interviewed rural and Indian teachers, held meetings with educators and directors of a variety of educational centers, gave speeches, and established dialogues with the most diverse groups, bringing together a distinguished team of teachers, writers, educators, architects, painters, anthropologists, musicians, and experts in the popular arts. Thus, he created the illusion in the nation that all of these people were working together in a national crusade with the goal of morally redeeming the Mexicans. The concept of teaching staff as apostolate in service to the nation grew out of this crusade.[40]

The vision that Vasconcelos had of education led him to conjoin it with culture, an idea that bore fruit at the time and continues in force in the Secretary of Education today. As Vasconcelos said, "a ministry of education which limited itself to founding schools would be like an architect who sticks to building the cells without thinking of the battlements, without putting in windows, without raising the towers of a vast edifice." He never tired of repeating that an artistic production "which was rich and elevated would bring with it the rebirth and exaltation of the national spirit."[41]

Seen through the perspective of time, the work achieved by Vasconcelos in the brief period between the end of September 1921 and July 1924 assumes enormous proportions. He built schools at a dizzying pace; formed a new generation of teachers, educators, and rural professors; reformed the techniques of teaching and designed new study programs, diminishing the gap between rural and urban schools; made educational sites into areas for meetings, recreation, sports, and spiritual uplifting; raised the teacher to the rank of forger of citizens; and conceived of cultural activities as regenerative forces for society and as builders of national identity. Vasconcelos said that "knowledge and art" must serve to "improve the condition of mankind." But by making this enormous work fall on the State that grew out of the Revolution, he inevitably, as observed Claude Fell, "elaborated and promoted a cultural model of the State which . . . tended to become dominant."[42]

In contrast with the artistic and cultural beginnings that had made their appearance in various places between 1910 and 1917, which were isolated and incidental in nature, cultural creations following Vasconcelos's promotion of his cultural model of the State tended to be increasingly absorbed and manipulated by the State. As will be seen, historical reporting would be one of the most sought-after methods through which the post-revolutionary State could legitimize itself and transmit its message of unity and national identity.

History Captured on Painted Walls

Art in Mexico is political . . .
All life in Mexico is political[43]

José Vasconcelos, the Secretary of Education under Álvaro Obregón from 1921 to 1924, changed the violent face of the revolution through a plan for the rebirth of society. When he accepted his position, he said: "Let us then organize the army of educators which will replace the army of destroyers."[44] His program was sustained by education and moral values, and one of the means for achieving his objectives was to make use of the walls of public buildings to transmit the program's message. Between 1921 and 1940, a new generation of artists portrayed the decisive moments in Mexico's history in bright images, glorifying its heroes and denigrating its villains, painting the Revolution as a movement of social redemption. A plastic plan stressing historical landscapes, faces, and deeds, its distinctive features were popularizing the interpretation of the past that had been developed in the nineteenth century and exalting episodes of the Revolution of 1910.

The first works of mural painting were done on the walls of the old Colegio de San Pedro y San Pablo and the Escuela Nacional Preparatoria (San Ildefonso) by artists Roberto Montenegro, Jean Charlot, Adolfo Best Maugard, Xavier Guerrero, Doctor Atl, David Alfaro Siqueiros, and Diego Rivera (fig. 192). José Vasconcelos stated that the only restrictions on these novice painters was that they paint Mexican themes and that their work be of high quality.[45] Thus, at the beginning of the decade of the 1920s, before the embarrassed eyes of students and teachers, the walls of the buildings began to be populated with scenes, historical episodes, and the faces of Mexican men and women (fig. 193). The obsession of the muralists at that time was to transfer to the walls the great historical deeds of the past and what was then considered to be an identifying feature of the Mexican soul: popular traditions (fig. 194). As Octavio Paz has pointed out, "Mexico, its history and its landscape, its heroes and its people, its past and its future, these were the central theme of our painters."[46]

Between 1920 and 1940, the artisans of muralism presented their own version of the past; they painted on walls the faces of the heroes who had transformed the course of history and the

Fig. 192. Diego Rivera painting. (Photo from Folgarait, 1998: 31.)

changes that had been introduced by the collective catharses. But none of them—not even Diego Rivera or José Clemente Orozco, the most radical in their interpretation of the past—modified the historiographic canon established by *México a través de los siglos* and the works of Justo Sierra. In general, they accepted and reproduced the traditional historical stages: the pre-Hispanic epoch, the Colonial Period, Independence, and Reform, which were crowned by the unexpurgated episode of the Revolution of 1910.

Diego Rivera was the painter with the greatest sensitivity to historical narration expressed in images. He considered the murals of the National Palace, especially those in the stairwell, to be his most innovative work. This painting, he said proudly, "is the only effort throughout the history of art, to represent in one continuous wall mural the history of a people from their remote past to their foreseeable future."[47] With his Pantagruelian appetite, he compressed that immense past into three frescoes packed with historical characters and events: *El México antiguo,* painted in 1929; *De la conquista a 1930,* painted in 1929–31; and

Fig. 193. The Tlatelolco market in a famous painting by Diego Rivera in the National Palace. (Photo from Tibol et al., 1997.)

Fig. 194. The *Jarabe tapatío* (a well-known regional dance from Jalisco, often called the Mexican Hat Dance in the United States). Stained glass by Roberto Montenegro in the ex-convent of Saints Peter and Paul, 1921–22. (Photo from Folgarait, 1998: 35.)

México de hoy y mañana, painted in 1934–35 (figs. 195–197). He filled that space with hundreds of historical figures and deeds, "so much so that the wall . . . looks like it is going to explode from the pressure of the beings that teem within it."[48]

Themes and Characters in the
Murals of the National Palace

Diego Rivera did not alter the historical process imagined by Justo Sierra in *La evolución política del pueblo mexicano*. But he gave a different twist to the themes and personalities of his history and used other tools to explain the course of its development. The triptych in which he summarized the history of Mexico expressed his concept of its historical development.

His great canvas begins on the right side of the stairwell and unfolds horizontally to the opposite side. This narration at times is conjoined to the other story, which ascends vertically from the lower floor, so that when the narrative planes cross, they create different perspectives from which to read the events and tie together the characters who make up the whole.

The scene painted on the right wall refers to the pre-Hispanic epoch and has a simple composition. The horizontal axis of the upper part is dominated by the volcanoes that form the mountain-ringed amphitheater of the Valley of Mexico, the cradle of Mexica culture. The central vertical axis is occupied by the figure of Quetzalcóatl as high priest, patron of the arts, and founder of civilization. At his right several scenes represent the development of agriculture, arts, and science. The figures on the left, on the other hand, express the payment of tribute, the oppression of the peasants, and the wars for domination. Above, an image of the myth of Quetzalcóatl crosses the sky, fleeing in his serpent canoe toward his final immolation, from which he will be reborn as the morning star. It is a simplified vision of the indigenous world, reduced to the central highlands and the myth of the cultural hero Quetzalcóatl (fig. 195).

The central wall covers the longest period, from the Conquest to the governments of Álvaro Obregón and Plutarco Elías Calles, and the largest number of historical events and characters. The lower horizontal plane narrates the sequence of the Conquest, dramatized by the horses, armor, shields, steel lances, and swords

Fig. 195. *El México antiguo,* in the stairwell of the National Palace. (Photo from Tibol et al., 1997.)

and the exploding cannons and arquebuses of the Spanish invaders. On the other side are the indigenous defenders, with their beautiful war costumes and weak armament, impotent to contain the debacle that is overcoming them.

Above, in a second horizontal plane that also runs from right to left, a succession of images crowds together to narrate the establishment of European dominion: the slavery of the Indians, the conflict of Fray Bartolomé de las Casas with Cortés and the landlords, the baptism of the natives, the noble figure of Fray Bernardino de Sahagún collecting the history of the ancient civilization that was beginning to disintegrate, the Inquisition, the figures of Malinche and Cortés giving birth to the first Mestizo, and the construction of the new society, based on the enslavement of the Indians. The central part features the emblem of the founding of México-Tenochtitlán—the royal eagle digging his claws into the prickly pear.

The five arches in the upper part frame the seminal episodes of the modern history of Mexico. Those on the ends tell of tragic

Fig. 196. *De la conquista a 1930*, fragment of the mural of Diego Rivera in the National Palace. (Photo from Tibol et al., 1997.)

Fig. 197. *México de hoy y mañana*, fragment of the mural of Diego Rivera in the Palacio Nacional. (Photo from Tibol et al., 1997.)

foreign interventions, the one on the right describing the North American invasion, the one on the left the French invasion and imposition of the empire of Maximilian. The second from the left describes civil wars and the Reform and is divided into two parts: on the right, Antonio López de Santa Anna and the conservatives; on the left, the liberals, especially Benito Juárez, Ignacio Manuel Altamirano, Ignacio Ramírez, and Melchor Ocampo. The third arch, which is the central axis, shows the heroes of Independence: Miguel Hidalgo, José María Morelos, Vicente Guerrero, Leona Vicario, and above them, Emiliano Zapata and the forgers of the post-revolutionary State: Alvaro Obregón and Plutarco Elías Calles.

The fourth arch brings together characters from the end of the nineteenth century—Guillermo Prieto, Gabino Barreda, Justo Sierra, Porfirio Díaz, José Yves Limantour, with the pioneers of the Revolution of 1910—Francisco I. Madero, Emiliano Zapata, Francisco Villa, Luis Cabrera, Venustiano Carranza, José Vasconcelos, and engraver José Guadalupe Posada. In this section, as in all the frescos, the dynamism of the images is based on the opposition between historical good and evil, between the argument of force (the unsheathed swords of the soldiers) and the inscriptions that summarize the revolutionary plans and principles: the Plan of Ayala, the Plan of San Luis, Land and Liberty, Social Revolution, the Constitution of 1917. On one side are the characters who represent the revolutionary movement, on the other the exploiters and partisans of retrocession (fig. 196).

The last part takes up the south wall of the staircase and is divided into three axes that run diagonally. On the lower border there are scenes of peasants and workers, exploited and absorbed in their devotion to the Virgin of Guadalupe. In contrast, a professor and several teachers are instructing students in the doctrine of socialism. The second horizontal level shows the causes of the social ills. An enormous pipe drains the wealth of the people, diverting it to the politicians and the wealthy classes. Finally, the third level describes the struggle of the proletariat against capitalistic oppressors. A worker harangues his companions, waving the Russian flag, and the upper section shows the imposing figure of Karl Marx with the Communist Manifesto in his hands. The message of this painting promotes the triumph of the proletariat and the establishment of a Communistic utopia, the Mexico of tomorrow (fig. 197).[49]

The Interpretation of History Confirmed on the Walls of the National Palace

To tell a story that lasted for more than two millenia relatively briefly, Diego Rivera chose to return to the ancient indigenous traditions. Just as the Mexicas and Mixtecs used images to tell the history of their people, so Rivera used characters and events to tell a history that was long in time and dense in content. Instead of detailing the origin, development, and meaning of each deed, he decided, like his Indian ancestors, to represent each one with the image that personified that event or the character who had brought it about.[50]

Diego Rivera's murals are a tumultuous succession of images, organized in vertical and horizontal planes that, like the ancient codices, tell the history of a people. In contrast to the Mexica and Mixtec pictographs, Rivera's images lack dates and texts to locate each character or event precisely, except for the few texts and slogans that are dated. To overcome these limitations, Rivera had to select characters and events whose identity and historical significance did not allow the slightest doubt. That is to say, he used figures confirmed by the traditions and official histories of his time. He began a large-scale use of what historians contemptuously called the "history of bronze," a history centered on the great men and deeds canonized by official cant.

Rivera publicly proclaimed his support of Marxist doctrine and considered himself to be a communist. And certainly, the paintings of the National Palace show the intent to illustrate some passages through the dialectic of class struggle, a conflict between working men and their exploiters: conquistadors, landlords, the Church, estate holders, capitalists. But in most cases this plan dissolves into rhetoric, since the telling never convinces the observer that the workers or the people ever really made history. In several scenes the people appear as simple spectators or as a passive retinue, not as agents of historical transformation.

The observer of these paintings perceives that it is the great characters who dominate the scene, converted into generators of social progress. The painter's obsession with dividing the protagonists of his story into two antagonistic groups is also evident: on one side are the good peasants and workers; on the other is the crowd of exploiting politicians, estate holders, capitalists, and intellectuals. By emphasizing the deeds that led to the Revolution of 1910, Rivera was one of the first diffusers of the Manichean idea of history and one of the most important creators of the mythology of the Revolution disseminated by the post-revolutionary State.[51]

Octavio Paz has indicated that the governments of those times considered themselves to be "the heirs and continuants of the Mexican Revolution. Therefore, from the very beginning they proposed to use to the extent possible the paintings of the muralists, closing their eyes—or better said, semi-closing them—to certain infringements on dogma and doctrine. They looked on mural painting as a public art which, going beyond this or that ideological inclination, expressed the nature of our people and their revolution."[52]

The Integration of the Peasant into Post-Revolutionary Nationalism, 1930-1934

The importance of the Secretary of Public Education in the building of nationalism that flourished between 1920 and 1934 was less visible than painting or music, but it was decisive in the integrative plan that developed for Indians and peasants at that time. In addition to the Cultural Missions that visited the indigenous areas of the nation, Vasconcelos established the Department of Indigenous Culture in 1922 to promote the founding of rural schools in those areas that had earlier been neglected. Claude Fell maintains that with the founding of this Secretary, "the work of national unification which so many political leaders hoped to complete began in a concrete and practical manner."[53]

Ten years later, in March of 1932, authorities of the Secretary of Public Education (SEP) began the publication of *El maestro rural* (fig. 198), a journal that was to be the means of appropriate communication between the SEP and rural teachers and between the teachers and the peasants. As proven by Guillermo Palacios in a brilliant analysis of the content of *El maestro rural,* this journal fully took on the problem of national integration. In its pages the rural teachers and their peasant students were the central characters in the plan for modernization undertaken by post-revolutionary governments; they represented the popular aspirations that contributed to the nationalistic ideal.[54]

The educational and cultural plans of the governments that followed the Revolution were based on the unification of programs and the implantation of a Federal policy that would include all the varied territories. A 1933 article defended the federalization of education as "the basic, indispensible condition for solving the entire national problem: the integration of all different ethnic groups into a broad and coherent unit, within which racial differences and oppositions can be reconciled; where the isolation of small communities can be totally overcome; where traditional regionalism can be everywhere erased; and where all are brought into a profound nationalistic spirit."[55]

That is to say, the plan of these governments was to make ethnic, regional, and local identities disappear, molding them into a homogeneous unity imposed from the center of the Federation. To socialize these orders, *El maestro rural* made the teacher and the school into the fulcrum of that civilizing odyssey. The good news that the Cultural Missions and the rural schools were to spread to the four corners of the land was that the moment had arrived for the nation to move "toward the unification of its elements, toward the equalization of its aspirations and toward a uniformity

Fig. 198. *El maestro rural,*
from a drawing by Diego
Rivera. (Photo from Palacios,
1999.)

of feelings and of ideas." The rural school thus acquired a transcendent political mission. As one teacher said, the "rural school
has taken on the colossal task of bringing the people to their feet,
of showing them a new life, of showing them the straight road
that leads them away from slavery, misery, and humiliation."[56]

Through the perspective opened up by the rural school,
"democracy will come about through education [fig. 199] rather
than politics, and it will be the teachers, not the politicians . . . who
will implant it." This adventure changed humble rural teachers
into Promethean figures. They not only assumed the enormous
educational task but also strove to create a new man:

"Our task is to civilize, and nothing less; to elevate the level of
the masses, to make the Indian one of us; to organize the nation;
to improve the quality of life; to improve the economic state of
the laborer and the peasant; to convert ethnic, social and political
elements of Mexico into a single nation."[57]

Fig. 199. Illustration from *La maestra rural*, drawing by Diego Rivera. (Photo from *Los maestros y la cultura nacional*, 1987.)

Immersed in the rhetoric distributed by the government, rural teachers came to believe themselves to be "true apostles of the sacred mission given them by the Department of Public Education." First, they accepted that "the mission of Rural Teacher was rare, unique, and apostolic." Then they agreed to "give themselves completely to the salvation of the small Indian community entrusted to them, without considering riches nor honors, but rather the improvement of the community."[58]

And just as teachers, when they tried to transform the indigenous communities, created a new image of themselves, in like manner they forged a different image of the object of their action: the peasants (fig. 200). Upon examining these explanations of reciprocity, Guillermo Palacios discovered three ways of describing the peasant: the bucolic vision; the vision showing him to be an imperfect social being; and the vision picturing him as a revolutionary agent. The bucolic image was disseminated in many articles in *El maestro rural* and in small theatrical works called "Peasant Theatre," which were in fact works created by teachers and professors of the Secretary of Public Education, to be learned and put on by the peasants. These works provided a romantic and moralistic image of the rural environment in contrast to the vice-filled image of modern urban life. This discourse praised the Arcadian rural life and rejected the corrupting industrialization of ancient values.

Fig. 200. Peasant man. (Photo from Brenner, 1971.)

The second image painted the peasant before the Revolution as an imperfect, incomplete being who would have to receive instruction from a teacher in order to become a dynamic agent of the renewal movement unleashed by the Revolution. This was a paternalistic image that submitted the peasant to the tutelage of his political and intellectual mentors.

The third image proposed "the need to construct a new peasant who would not only be a revolutionary, both in the sense of his social origin and in his ideological . . . affiliation, but who would above all constitute an efficient unit of production, open to modern technology." It was believed that by constructing this new peasant, the teachers would at the same time build a nation of "free men, of true citizens, who would be masters of their destiny, and from whose common action, responsible and well directed, the great strong homeland we all desire would result." That new peasant, "materially constructed by agrarian reform, was the one who had to be prepared by the rural school."[59]

Through these different images, a passive relationship was built between the peasants and the Revolution. According to this interpretation, the former were reborn thanks to the Revolution and were its direct beneficiaries. As Palacios has stated, in that manner a sort of "social debt" was created between the revolutionary regime and the peasants, which would finally have to be repaid by the rural school. "The school in truth is the only and best offering which the nation can give in payment to the generous peasant for the great anguish with which the Revolution was accomplished."[60]

The Revolution Frozen in a Monument

Politicians of the Porfirian period, inspired by the Capitol in Washington, D.C., wanted to build a monument that would serve as the seat of legislative power. The fall of Díaz frustrated the completion of that project, and for more than two decades the residents of the capital were accustomed to seeing the unfinished skeleton of iron foreshadowing that building. Nevertheless, during the 1930s this ruin was converted into a great triumphal arch dedicated to celebrating—in iron, stone, and bronze—the unity of the Revolution.

A 1937 report indicated that the Monument to the Revolution was conceived by "the Revolutionary family" to "perpetuate the memory of the Mexican social revolution." Historians indicate, however, that its objective was to unify various groups who argued over the revolutionary heritage and to deny others the legitimacy needed to assume that legacy. Between 1915 and 1930, followers of Madero, Zapata, and Villa, together with the constitutionalists, strove to celebrate their own movements; some of them established a special calendar of celebrations and raised grand monuments to their leaders. As Thomas Benjamin has said, the revolutionary past itself became a battleground. Against those factional inclinations, the "revolutionary family" demanded unity and obedience to "our common mother, the Revolution."[61]

On June 15, 1933, President Abelardo Rodríguez, former President Plutarco Elías Calles, and architect Carlos Obregón Santacilia dedicated the building of a monument to symbolize the triumph of the Revolution over the old regime. As Calles and Alberto Pani, then Secretary of the Treasury, wrote, this "should be the greatest [monument] in the capital of the Republic," a structure whose beauty and magnitude would radiate an extraordinary commemorative strength. Obregón Santacilia designed the building sustained by four strong pillars and crowned with a tall cupola (fig. 201). As proposed by Calles and Pani, the monument would express the historical process the Revolution went through in three stages. The first, "Political Emancipation," would symbolize the War for Independence. The second, "Spiritual Emancipation," would signify the Reform and the struggle against the French Intervention. And the last, "Economic Emancipation," would express the struggle of the proletariat for economic equity that had begun in 1910.

The Monument to the Revolution was to render homage to those struggles in four sculptural groups. Its execution was given to Oliverio Martínez, who had earlier made an equestrian statue of Zapata in Cuautla. The group on the southeast corner symbolized national Independence, represented by stoic Indian figures. The group on the northeast corner celebrated the Reform. On the southwest corner several peasants expressed the triumphs of their class, holding up their property titles in their hands. The final group, on the northwest corner, symbolized the advances achieved by the workers. According to the slogan written on the monument, it was intended to render homage to "the Revolution of yesterday, today, tomorrow, and forever." As stated by Calles and Pani, the monument was not intended to glorify any hero in particular, but the Revolution itself, as manifested in the secular battles undertaken by the proletariat.[62]

Nevertheless, more than celebrating the popular struggles, the task of the Monument to the Revolution was to legitimize the governments that emanated from that process. Year after year its

Fig. 201. The Monument to the Mexican Revolution.

generous arched roof has sheltered official ceremonies promoted in turn by the government: the anniversaries of Madero's rebellion; homages to the martyrs of the Revolution, the Constitution of 1917, the petroleum expropriation of 1938. Years later the Congress assigned it another purpose that would refine its character as a unifying monument: guarding the mortal ashes of revolutionary leaders. In January of 1942, the ashes of Carranza were deposited inside one of its pillars, in 1960 those of Madero, in 1969 those of Calles, in 1970 those of Lázaro Cárdenas, and in 1976 those of Francisco Villa. That is to say, the integrative purpose of the "revolutionary family" made the monument into a tomb for the revolutionaries who in life fought among themselves or defended opposing programs.[63]

The Revolution Made Official History

The final transformation of the movement begun in 1910 was its conversion into official history sanctioned by the State. Just as since 1920 the revolutionary group had turned to the formula of the "revolutionary family" to limit internal discord and strengthen the orthodoxy of the movement, so also, after the creation of the PNR, a primary objective was to bring together the different versions of the origin and historical development of the Revolution. In May of 1930, one year after the founding of the PNR, Emilio Portes Gil announced the creation of an archive, a museum, and a history of the Revolution. El Archivo Histórico de la Revolución, founded at that time and directed by Jesús Silva Herzog, was to be the seedbed where those chosen to write the history of the Revolution would be nourished. The task of unifying and appeasing the "revolutionary family," outlined in an accord of the Chamber of Deputies in July of 1931, proposed to write in gold letters on the walls of that space the names of Venustiano Carranza and Emiliano Zapata, who were added to those earlier canonized: Madero in 1925; Álvaro Obregón in 1929, and Felipe Carrillo Puerto in 1930. Thus, in an act of posthumous reconciliation, the Revolution brought together on the altar of the homeland those who in life had been the bitterest of enemies.

The politics of unity became an irrepressible compulsion on the part of the governmental party. In 1930 the Calendario Nacionalista appeared, celebrating the deeds and anniversaries of the numerous revolutionary chiefs and showing portraits of the founders of the "revolutionary family." In 1934 *La revolución mexicana*, the first journal dedicated to collecting and exalting the deeds of that movement, was published. The next year the first *Diccionario biográfico revolucionario* came out, and in 1936 the *Historia de la revolución mexicana*, coordinated by José T. Meléndez, was published, and for a number of years was the best collection of that type. Later, outstanding intellectuals such as Andrés Molina Enríquez, Miguel Alessio Robles, Alfonso Teja

Zabre, Félix F. Palavicini, and Jesús Romero Flores published books reviewing the avatars of the Revolution. Among the landmark works of that type was the monumental graphic testimonial compiled by Agustín Casasola: *Historia gráfica de la revolución mexicana.*

The literary commemoration of the Revolution culminated in the work of Alberto Jiménez Morales, *Historia de la revolución mexicana,* which won a prize given by the Partido Revolucionario Institucional (PRI) in a contest held to honor that event. Jiménez Morales's book is the prototype of official history, a story that makes the Revolutionary movement sacred, exalts its heroes, erases internal contradictions, and converts the slogans and banners of the fighting revolutionary groups into paradigmatic goals of the governments that grew out of that conflict. It brings together the characteristics that Arnaldo Córdova identified as archetypical traits of the ideology of the Mexican Revolution: popular, nationalistic, and democratic revolution; the deux ex machina of the Mexican identity; and the apotheosis of the revolutions that began with the war for Independence.

X. History Constructed by Historical Professionals

As the reader will have noted, ever since the origins of historical narration the forces that have changed the interpretations of the past have been external to the office of the historian. Since the appearance of human beings, the milestones that have signaled new directions in the understanding of the past have been the invention of language and writing, the advent of printing, and the constituting of national States.

During the course of most of human history, the conservators of collective memory were heads of families, tribal leaders, the Church, the city, or the State, and the transmission of memory was by means of rituals, oral reporting, and the annals compiled by the leaders of kingdoms. Throughout those centuries, historical recollection was linked to oral memory, the depositary of ancestral wisdom.

Historical narration in those times concentrated on the events that knit together the collective life of the people and the deeds that gave unity and identity to the group. History was an egocentric story, built around the tribe, the city, the dynasty, the kingdom, or the nation. It was a story based on the authority of its tellers and the credibility of its listeners and readers, as it lacked proof of veracity to support its content. Its composition and transmission depended on oral memory, with moral authority resting on traditions maintained from generation to generation, the recipients of ancient wisdom.[1] The possession of this knowledge, not its authenticity, conferred authority on historical reporting. Its highest expression was the art of narration.

From the Art of History to Scientific Discipline

History as an art dedicated to delight, instruction (*magistra vitae*), and maintaining the memory of origin was suddenly transformed by the accelerated expansion of printing. After the end of the fifteenth century, written documents replaced oral memory as a worthy witness of the past, and the study of history became the office of learned men.[2] The split between the Reform and Catholic churches unleashed a battle over the bases of the true religion, which was expressed through a confrontation among memories, doctrines, and theologies printed in documents and books. Even the oldest texts and the most respected doctrines were submitted to critical examination to establish their veracity. Herodotus, Thucydides, and the Bible itself ceased to be unimpeachable authorities and became only additional testimonials whose legimacy had to be demonstrated with persuasive arguments (figs. 202 and 203). Every page, affirmation, or thesis had to prove its date of elaboration, origin, and authorship; clarify its interpolations or contradictions; and clearly establish its internal coherence.

Printing, by bearing texts to distant and diverse publics, brought about an unaccustomed exchange of points of view and an alert criticism dominated by polemic and permanent refutation (figs. 204 and 205).[3] Thus, to the degree that historical reporting gave priority to the authenticity of the written document, it distanced itself from literary art. Similarly, by depending increasingly on written records, it withdrew itself from the fragile memories of contemporary witnesses of the events. Those changes in sources, content, and analyses of historical events caused profound changes in the writing of history: inexorably, written documents overshadowed oral memory, and reports based on text prevailed over memories based on observation and the fickleness of subjective recall.[4]

Fig. 202. Allegory representing Herodotus as the historian of the wars of the Greeks against the Persians. (Photo from Hartog, 1980.)

Fig. 203. Allegory of the "birth of history." Double bust of Herodotus and Thucydides. (Photo from Hartog, 1980.)

Changes Driven by Academic History

In the eighteenth century historians of the Enlightenment, led by Voltaire (1697–1778), began an unusual battle for the autonomy of history. Like Voltaire, other historians of the Enlightenment were members of the middle class who wrote their reports free of the control of the princes of the Church. In his *Essai sur les moeurs et le esprit des nations,* Voltaire abandoned the theological interpretation of history and for the first time attempted to write a universal history—a report based on laws, arts, and sciences, on the great achievements of humanity rather than the trivial triumphs of kings.[5] Voltaire's desire was to make a "universal history" that would illuminate the long road of civilization, and in that sense

353

Fig. 204. Cover of the *Biblia Sacra,*
published in 1624. (Photo from
Grañen Porrúa, 1996: 64.)

Fig. 205. Photograph of *Doctrina cristiana en lengua mixteca,* by Benito
Hernández, published in 1568. The book is one of the first printed in
Mexico. (Photo from Grañen Porrúa, 1996: 25.)

he was an innovator, one of the first to take arts and sciences as certain signs of historical development.[6]

The History of the Decline and Fall of the Roman Empire (1776–78), the masterpiece of Edward Gibbon (1734–94), did not have the scientific repercussions of Voltaire's writing but from its appearance was proclaimed a classic, admired by successive generations of readers. The seduction this work has exercised on the public can be attributed in large part to the hypnotic attraction of its central theme, the rise and fall of the most powerful empire of antiquity; it was a summation of civilization, conquering epic, and political perfection. Gibbon considered the Roman Empire to be one of the greatest creations of humanity. His book, supported by a broad panoply of sources, was the first to trace the origins of Christianity, the ascent of Islam, and the contributions of Byzantine culture.

Gibbon's book also regained one of the qualities of ancient historical reporting—literary virtue. J. B. Blake, a student of history as art, reviews the prose of *The Decline and Fall of the Roman Empire* in this manner:

The sobriety and dignity, the quality and propriety of expression, run parallel to the greatness of the theme. . . . Gibbon does not tell the events just as he perceives them. To the contrary, he passes them through a series of complex and mysterious screens to polish, refine and enrich them, until they finally emerge bejeweled and splendid. . . . The force and elegance of his style had the quality of making into fluid narrations themes as abstruse as the endless Persian wars, the theological arguments of the early church, or the technical aspects of the legal reforms of Justinian.[7]

A taste for aesthetic form and the rigorous management of sources reached a high point in the work of German historian Leopold von Ranke (1795–1886). His *Historia de Alemania en la época de la Reforma* (1839–47) and the *Historia de los papas*

Fig. 206. Leopold von Ranke. (Photo from Barnes, 1963.)

(1878) earned him the title of the "greatest master of philological criticism" and prestige as a fine analyst of the psychology of historical characters (fig. 206).[8]

Among Ranke's most notable merits were his internal critical methods concerning documents. In Ranke the rigorous management of the diverse phases of investigation merged with "his critical treatment of a wide range of sources unused before that time," "the volume of his productivity," and his interest in developing a seminar for the training of academics. In all of those tasks, Ranke "had no precedent nor was he ever surpassed." To that must be added his well-known harping on the objective treatment of past matters, as summarized in the following sentence: "The office of judging the past and of teaching its contemporaries about the experiences of the past for the benefit of future years has been attributed to history; the present essay does not pretend to such exalted intentions: it only wishes to show what has really happened."[9]

Ranke's critics point out that the influence he exercised as a teacher of new generations was probably more decisive than the

Fig. 207. Portrait of Alejandro de Humboldt, the German traveler who wrote the first general book on New Spain. (Photo from Labastida, 1999.)

influence of his own works. In 1833 Ranke founded the first seminary of historical studies, an innovative academic institution that trained a large number of historians from throughout Europe, who in turn diffused the methods and teachings of the master and promoted the development of the German school of history, at that time perhaps the most influential in the world (figs. 207 and 208).[10]

The history seminary founded by Ranke and the schools for historians that cropped up throughout Germany, England, France, and Italy between the middle and end of the nineteenth century foretold the conversion of the old artisan of history into the university professor, a professional exclusively dedicated to teaching, studying, and spreading historical knowledge. During this time the first history departments were founded in universities, archives and libraries were formed to gather the knowledge of the past and put it in order, and history's epistemological rating changed

Fig. 208. Drawing of Eduard Seler, the great German historian who restored Mesoamerican studies in Mexico. (Photo from Seler, 1990.)

once again; from a branch of fine arts, it was reborn as a discipline related to the humanities and social sciences.[11]

Thus, through carefully examining historical remnants and submitting reports to rigorous proofs of authenticity, historical research was transformed into critical knowledge, a positive awareness of human experience. Historical investigation of the time established the rule that "no statement may be made unless it can be proved" and advised that "among all the poisons capable of contaminating testimony, the most virulent is false attribution."

To the degree that a historian intensified his critical analysis and selection of sources, improving his analytical methods and taking advantage of the methodologies of science and the humanistic disciplines, he challenged the concepts of historical development founded on myths, religion, providential heroes, nationalisms, and ideologies of any kind. Thus, instead of being a search for transcendent meaning for human acts, a legitimizing of power, or a placing of oneself at the service of ideologies, the practice of history became a critical and demystifying exercise, a "reasoned business of analysis," as Marc Bloch has stated.[12]

The Revolution Promoted by French Historiography

From the end of the nineteenth century until the years after the Second World War, as a result of the formation of national States, the study of history became inescapable in primary, secondary, and advanced education in nations of the Western world. The education of new citizens and the need to strengthen national identity gave the study of history a place of privilege.

Under these auspices, between 1960 and 1980 in France a radical transformation of forms of investigating, considering, and writing history occurred and within a few years had expanded to most university campuses. The French school, called the Annales after the name of the journal that spread its ideas on the task of the historian (figs. 209 and 210), initiated an approach to the methods developed by the social sciences (economics, demography, geography, sociology, anthropology). Within a few years this had caused a renovation of academic historiography, a harvest of master works, and a reconsideration of the writings and purposes of history.[13]

Under the influence of the social sciences, history began to change both its face and its vestments. Suddenly historical investigation was filled with crises, cycles, and economic, demographic, social, and political opportunities and transformations. Historians took over quantitative techniques and with those tools reconstructed an impressive series of production, price, salary, and commercial and demographic changes that illuminated the structures on which preindustrial societies rested and the lines of force that drove their dynamics. What had earlier been unknown territory became a persuasive reading of economic and social structure, economic fluctuations, and the lack of equality among social classes.

Fig. 209. Fernand Braudel, leading representative of the French Annales school.

Fig. 210. Ruggiero Romano, a representative of the Annales school who allied himself closely with Latin American historians and has written important books about this movement.

The past acquired an unexpected dynamism and complexity. Suddenly, the political chronology constructed by the old historians was challenged because of the extended periods of time marking the slow formation of demographic structures and economic systems over centuries; the convulsive tenor of demographic, agricultural, and commercial cycles and crises; and the fleeting nature of daily events.[14] These new registers of temporality shed light on other contradictions in social development. The historical dynamic ceased to be a linear trajectory occasionally altered by political changes and acquired the profile of an uneven flow, continually interrupted by different forces that intervened in the formation of the social fabric.

The success that greeted those new methods extended to other fields concerned with the past and to other countries. Historical analysis, based on sophisticated techniques, included the examination of both antiquity and modern and contemporary times. It included the study of representations of the collective conscience ("mentalities") as well as the analysis of religion, myths, power, urban development, the discourses of historians, educational and nutritional systems, the body, insanity, sexuality . . . new themes that in turn stimulated the appearance of other methods and new questions about the past.[15]

Upon reviewing the scope of these achievements, Peter Burke has commented that in the last generation "the universe of historians has expanded at a dizzying rate."[16] The conquering march of history through fields until then ignored did not fail to surprise the cultivators of Clio themselves. Almost all of them celebrated the inclination toward the study of religion, literature, sciences, politics, and art to explain a wider world through the in-depth consideration of global concepts: the sacred, the text, the code, the power, the monument. Others pointed out the audacity of a discipline that dared to incorporate themes and subjects that until then had been outside their orbit. The numerous publications that inundated the university market showed that historians were proud of the extraordinary spread of their discipline and their advantageous relationship with the social sciences.[17]

The New History

It is, then, a matter of a new history that modified the canons of traditional history. In contract with the history that favored the analysis of institutions and political life, the new history was interested in almost all realms of the past. If traditional history was committed to the narration of events, its new counterpart emphasized the analysis of structures and preferred explanations. While the old history was centered on the deeds of great men and spectacular happenings, the new history was interested in the popular sectors, the forgotten corners of daily life, and delved successfully into the history of the marginalized and the "people without a history."[18]

Faced with the pretensions of the positivist school, which desired to tell history "as it really happened," since the end of 1940 and especially in the decade of the 1960s a current gained strength that slowed the optimistic march of history toward objectivity and real knowledge. In the last third of the twentieth century, the winds began to blow in another direction, threatening the old ideal of objectivity with unprecedented strength.[19]

The loss of internal unity among historians, doubts as to the most appropriate instruments for accomplishing their task, and the relativism that invaded their once-firm territory undermined the very foundations of the old discipline of history. In earlier times individual interests—whether national, regional, ethnic, religious, or ideological—were seen as the enemies of objective truth. But by the end of the 1960s, the discipline of history had lost its true north and fragmented into "study areas" and specializations. By the end of the century, the tendency that began with Black studies and gender studies had shattered historical research. According to one North American observer, the cultivators of this discipline were "little more than a jumble of groups, some of them very small . . . who can only communicate imperfectly with one another." "Around 1980, there were more and more professionals who, to their regret, believed that, even after applying the most generous of definitions, history was no longer a coherent discipline; not only was the whole less than the sum of the parts, but the whole did not exist, only the parts." Thomas Bender, another North American historian, "described the historical discipline as fragmented into a great number of self-sufficient boxes, where each area is 'studied on its own terms, with its own network of knowledge and its own discourse.'"[20]

Another devastating blow to the ancient fortress of history was that which attacked the idea of objectivity. As Peter Novick has commented, in the second half of the twentieth century it stopped "being axiomatic that the work of the researcher or of the scientists was to represent correctly what was 'there.'" The notion of a "determinate and unitary truth of the physical or social world . . . , came to be considered by more and more researchers as a chimera." The so-called "new criticism," anthropology, postmodern analysis, philological and literary studies, and historians themselves, with Hayden White as their leader, became spokesmen for radical "nihilistic relativism." White maintained that it was possible "to imagine not only one or two stories, but many about any . . . event which had cultural significance, all of them equally plausible and authorized by virtue of their conformity to the generally accepted norms of historical construction." In a word, as Peter Novick has stated, the discipline of history had ceased to exist as "a community of broad discourse, as a community of researchers united by common goals, criteria, and intentions."[21]

These and other revisions of the task of the historian were transferred to Mexico and had their own unique incarnations here.

Mexican Academic Institutions and the New Canon for Reporting the Past

In the second half of the nineteenth century, the lengthy Mexican historiographic tradition grew to a level of excellence in the critical evaluation and selection of basic sources for reconstructing the fragmented past of the nation. A small group of both conservative and liberal historians, under the influence of the French and German schools, made an effort to acclimatize the paradigms of European historiography in this country (fig. 211) and to support a recovery of the past that would be less inclined to back the political groups in conflict.[22] In the first half of the twentieth century that tradition joined with new historiographic currents from Europe and North America and with the nation's establishment of academic institutions dedicated to the support of historical studies.

The founding of institutes, schools, majors, master's degrees, doctorates, and seminars intended to shape professionals for teaching

Fig. 211. Justo Sierra, eminent
educator and author of one of the
best syntheses of Mexican history.
He introduced French concepts
of history in Mexico. (Photo from
Cárdenas, 1979: III, 416.)

and specialists for historical research changed the form, content,
and purposes of historical reporting (figs. 212 and 213). From
then on, in order to be a professor or to dedicate oneself to historical research it would be necessary to have that specialization and
to be accredited with the proper degree. Soon the professionali-
zation of historical studies confronted the professorial ranks, in
turn composing the academic colleges, the normative organizations
that defined a total separation between the accredited specialist
and the hobby historian. Thus, by creating a physical space in academic institutions where economic and administrative resources,
professors, researchers, students, libraries, and distribution media
all came together, a powerful establishment was born that from
that time on had the capacity to generate its own interpretations
of history, just as earlier the polis [the city], the Prince, and the State
had fomented interpretations of the past that became the longest
lasting and most influential.[23]

Fig. 212. The Archivo General de la Nación at the beginning of the twentieth century.

The concentration of these resources in the academic institutions caused them to create a model for historical reporting and gave them the means to reproduce and expand it in an accumulative form through teaching, research, the publication of journals and books, and conferences and colloquia dedicated to the analysis of historiographic products and trends. In the construction of that paradigm, Mexican institutions imitated the model that was already proved in European institutions.

The prescriptions of European academic life were transferred to Mexican universities through the educational system and research methods. The steps required for the training of professors and researchers were the undergraduate, masters, and doctoral programs instituted long ago in Old World universities. The paradigm in which the various aspects of that tradition came together was to be found in the preparation of a thesis, article, or book that brought together a lengthy training whose ultimate aim was to make an important contribution, reviewing the past or illuminating

Fig. 213. Photo of the Archivo General de la Nación in 1980.

a hidden detail of that heritage (figs. 214 and 215). In addition to demonstrating the professional talents acquired, the thesis was to be based on unknown archives, documents not previously investigated, refutations of older interpretations, or updates of the understanding of a character, theme, or epoch considered decisive in the historical unfolding of the nation. The framework of that research was the nation itself. National history came to be the special preserve of academic historiography.

The Division between Professional
Historiography and Collective Memory

This model of interrogating the past, based on the scrutinizing of unpublished documents, refined methods, and theories of human development, caused a fatal rupture between academic historiography and the collective memory. That memory which recalled

Fig. 214. Daniel Cosío Villagas, accompanied by his wife. Cosío Villegas was a cultural impresario who created institutions, reviews, seminars, and books that transformed historical studies in Mexico. (Photo from Cosío Villagas, 1999.)

Fig. 215. Portrait of Edmundo O'Gorman by his father, Cecil O'Gorman. (Photo from Ortega y Medina, 1968.)

the past in the form of myths, legends, rituals, oral traditions, and beliefs derived from a remote past fell into disfavor and was relegated to the casket of reported fantasy. Historians who graduated from academic institutions decreed that the only competent and unimpeachable sources for the scientific recovery of the past were documents, textual materials, and writing.

Josef Yerushalmi, the historian who has most widely studied the opposition between the collective memory of the Jewish people and modern historiography, indicates that the break occurred when those traditions began to be analyzed using the paradigms of Western historiography. Yerushalmi maintains that the basis of Jewish collective memory is The Book, the Torah, the collection of religious beliefs, traditions, myths, and avatars that forged the identity of the Jewish people, continuously transmitted by the social and religious institutions that were an organic part of Jewish society. When this tradition was put in doubt by Western historiography, academic research turned against what had been until that moment the most deeply held historical foundation of the Jewish people—their millennial tradition. According to Yerushalmi, "Only in the modern era can we find, for the first time, a Jewish historiography divorced from the collective Jewish memory, and, in some crucial aspects, totally contrary to it."[24]

A similar process occurred in Mexico when the canon of Western history was imposed in academic centers. The oral tradition was then replaced by research founded on documents. The myths, rituals, and traditions transmitted by collective memory were classified as legends or were defined as testimonies without scientific support, and in like manner the teller of the deeds of the people, the collector of local and regional memories, was rejected by academic standards that decreed that only an investigator trained within their walls had the qualifications to objectively rescue the past.

The Distortions of the Academic Canon

Nonetheless, the period between 1980 and the end of the century, instead of seeing a progressive ascent of the followers of Clio, witnessed a fall from the high levels established by professional historiography, an alarming deterioration of institutions, failures in the training of professors and researchers, and a loss of the intellectual vigor that had animated the founding of those centers. The first indicator of the debacle was the absence of leadership in those institutions dedicated to the teaching, research, and dissemination of historical knowledge. Unlike the effervescent period of four or five decades earlier, when those institutions led great research undertakings as well as the development of professors and research plans, now that drive had disappeared. In most of these centers a mistaken idea of scientific obligations separated research from teaching to such a degree that the former neither supported nor rejuvenated the latter, while research was set adrift without programs or goals, abandoned to the personal initiatives of individual researchers.[25]

Another negative sign that grew in the decades of the 1970s and 1980s was the loss of the former standards of rigor and academic excellence, which were replaced by populist, ideological, unionist, and bureaucratic practices. Most alarming was not the appearance of those currents, but the absence of criticism of their suggestions and the subsequent imposition of their ideological contents on research and teaching.[26]

The work of the historian is a faithful mirror of the changes taking place both in the system that produced him and in the profession itself. From 1940 to the present, more works have been published than in all pervious times as a result of the multiplication of institutions, journals, and publishing houses dedicated to the distribution of academic production. History theses have increased in a similar proportion, as have meetings, conferences, and symposia. But as it happens, most of this production is represented by specialized studies read only by the history professionals themselves and by their students. That is to say, though more is produced, it is not for the sake of more people or more readers, as proved by the disastrous fact that Mexican academic institutions hold the world record for storage of books: hundreds of thousands (some speak of millions) of books stacked up in warehouses!

In the route followed by historical research during the past twenty years, there is no recognizable program, nor are precise goals pursued. Rather, this route resembles a map drawn of individual adventures, containing abundant side trips without continuity, isolated explorations, fortuitous intersections, and zigzagging routes. The early initiative of the founders of the academic institutions (figs. 216–219), who in the 1940s and 1950s tried to channel

Fig. 216. Silvio Zavala, dean of Mexican historians. A historian of institutions and of the American Colonial world, he was a master of restraint and historical rigor. (Photo from Zavala, 1982.)

the goals of the institutions through seminars with short- and mid-length programs, was destroyed by the personal interests of the investigators. In the 1970s and 1980s these researchers managed to impose their different individual projects as the equivalent of institutional programs. What is now recognized is in fact the sum of the investigations proposed by each researcher, defined by his own training or by fashions from overseas. Since that time there has not been a common plan developed by researchers or tailored to the needs of the institution, the situation of the nation, or the demands of the immediate future.

Under the banner of "freedom of teaching and research"— principles that had earlier defended freedom of opinion and the plurality of academic thought—corporate interests that oppose any effort to rationalize teaching and research are now protected. Their academic cloistering into increasingly autonomous and impenetrable groups has resulted in an almost total lack of communication between researchers and the diverse currents and institutions that

Fig. 217. Alfonso Caso. Archaeologist, founder of institutions, and outstanding figure in Mesoamerican studies in the twentieth century. (Photo courtesy of INAH.)

Fig. 218. Gonzalo Aguerri Beltrán, eminent anthropologist and reformer of the theory and practice of the discipline of anthropology. (Photo from *Homenaje a Gonzalo Aguirre Beltrán*, 1973.)

come together in the field of Mexican history. Those specializing in one epoch are unaware of what is happening in others; experts dedicated to ethnology almost never read what is being done in social, economic, political, or psychological historiography, and conversely, specialists in the prehistoric Nahua world know nothing of the studies investigating the mysteries of the Zapotec,

Fig. 219. Luis González, author of *Pueblo en vilo,* masterwork of Mexican historiography. (Photo from Cosío Villegas, 1999.)

P'urhépecha, Maya, or Totonac cultures. Although today there are more institutions, schools, and researchers than there were fifty years ago, the profession is completely disarticulated. We live, as the last verse of the Book of Judges states, in autarchy: "In those days there was no king in Israel; every man did that which was right in his own eyes."[27]

Perhaps the greatest intellectual crisis facing the field of history is its inability to offer the nation a history of the nation. Divided as it is into as many units as there are historians or historiographic currents, it seems impossible that any one of them could bring that myriad of specializations into a single coherent whole, meaningful and accessible to the common reader.

Isolation and fragmentation ("each group makes its own history,") join with the resounding decline of criticism and self-criticism. While in Europe and the United States the latest and most specific transformations of the discipline have been carefully recorded, to the point that veritable mountains of analysis in favor of and against the recent evolutions of Clio have been recorded, in our country the exercise of evaluation has virtually disappeared or has become a sham. We lack dependable indicators of the main variables of historiographic production: the number of students who enroll and are accepted; the number of professors per area, specialization, and university; the relationship between salary and productivity; the relationship between research undertaken and research completed, and so forth. And even more troubling, the collective responsibility for facing the challenges of the profession has evaporated. Professors and researchers join together only to approve salaries and loans, not to strengthen their institutions or to encourage productivity, quality, and the competitive system—the main engine that has driven creativity in the Western world.

But perhaps the main drama facing the Mexican academic institution is its aging and obsolescence. Because of a disastrous combination of economic crises, a continuing growth of student population accompanied by a progressive decrease of funds, and a lack of foresight in programming, the public university and the cultural apparatus of the State dedicated to research are aging establishments. The Universidad Nacional Autónoma de México (UNAM), the Instituto Nacional de Antropología e Historia (INAH), the Colegio de México, and most of the state universities are working with a staff that is more than forty-five to fifty years of age. And although this situation could have been predicted two decades ago, neither their directors nor the corresponding governmental departments have developed retirement programs appropriate for professors and researchers followed by hirings directed toward the new generations. The result is ominous: our most important and prestigious scientific institutions are fatally threatened in the short term, because the evil that corrodes them is making their personnel and their knowledge obsolete.

The generation that could and should replace our old professors and researchers is here, but outside the classrooms and laboratories of the public universities, unemployed or working in positions that they have never before considered.

NOTES

*I. The Origins of the Story of the Creation of the Cosmos, the
Beginning of the Kingdoms, and the Deeds of the Rulers*

1. Enrique Florescano, 1999.

2. See David Freidel, Linda Schele, and Joy Parker, 1993: 59–75.

3. An English translation of this text appears in Linda Schele and David Freidel,
1990: 245–55. A summary of this text in Spanish can be seen in Florescano, 1999:
18–22.

4. Donald Robertson, 1959: 62.

5. William F. Rust and Barbara W. Leyden say that in the La Venta area
between 1150 and 500 B.C. there is evidence of "larger *Zea* pollen as well as substan-
tial increases in the presence of charred maize. Recovered quantities of both charred
maize kernels and cupoles and metates show their sharpest rise in late La Venta
Period (ca. 800–500 B.C.), when local riverine population was at a maximum and La
Venta reached its apogee as a regional Olmec center." See Rust and Leyden, 1994:
181–201. See also Barbara L. Stark, 2000: 31–53.

6. Karl Taube, 2000a: 297–337.

7. Peter David Joralemon, 1971; Karl Taube, 1985: 171–81; Karl Taube, 1996:
39–81; and Taube, 2000a.

8. See the study of Rust and Layden, 1994.

9. Taube, 1996: 76.

10. See the studies cited by Peter David Joralemon, 1971, 1976. In the description of the Joven Gobernante, I have followed the text of Joralemon published in
Elizabeth Benson and Beatríz de la Fuente, eds., 1996: 212–16. See also the studies
of John E. Clark, Ann Cyphers, David C. Grove, Jorge Angulo, and Kent F. Reilly,
in John E. Clark, ed., 1994; and Michael D. Coe, ed., 1996, especially Kent F.
Reilly: 27–47.

11. Florescano, 1999: chap. 1.

12. See the studies of Rene Millon: 1981: 198–243; 1992: 241–310; and 1993. See also
the important study of Clemency Chase Coggins, 1996; and Esther Pasztory, 1997.

13. See David Stuart, 2000: 465–513; Karl Taube, 2000b; and Simon Martin and
Nikolai Grube, 2000: 28–31 and 191–96.

14. This is the image that the Nahuas of Mexico-Tenochtitlán transmitted to Bernardino de Sahagún, 2000.

15. Sahagún, 2000: I, vol. I, chap. V.

16. Coggins, 1996; Florescano, 1999.

17. When *cipactli* is joined with the number one, "it is the first day of the Tonalpohualli or divinatory cycle of 20 days." See Alfredo López Austin, Leonardo López Luján, and Saburo Sugiyama, 1961: 35–52; Karl Taube, 1992: 53–87; Coggins, 1996: 24–26.

18. Florescano, 1999: 121.

19. See the *Leyenda de los soles en Códice Chimalpopoca: Anales de Cuauhtitlán y leyenda de los soles* (Legend of the suns in the Chimalpopoca Codex: Annal of Cuauhtitlán and legend of the suns), 1945; *La historia de los Mexicans por sus pinturas* (The history of Mexicans through their paintings), and the *Histoire du Mechique* (History of Mexico), in Ángel María Garibay K., 1965.

20. See Doris Heyden, 1975: 131–47; and Karl Taube, 1986: 51–82.

21. Florescano, 1999.

22. See Bernardino de Sahagún's descriptions of the Toltecs and Quetzalcóatl in Sahagún, 2000: vol. I, book one, chap. V; book three, chaps. III–XIV. The image that the Aztecs had of ancient Tollán and the Toltecs can be seen in Miguel León-Portilla, 1980.

23. Sahagún, 2000: vol. I, chap. III, 308–9.

24. Garibay, 1965: 38.

25. *Códice Chimalpopoca*, 1945: 7–8, 121, and 124–25.

26. Cited by Miguel León-Portilla, 1996: 135.

27. Pedro Armillals, René Millon, Michael D. Coe, George L. Cowill, and the epigraphist Karl Taube. See Karl Taube, 1992: 53–87.

28. Saburo Sujiyama, 2000: 117–43.

29. See Jacques Cauvin, 1997: 43–55, 100–105; Claude Lévi-Strauss, 1989.

30. See Christine Niederberger Betton, 1987: vol. I, fig. 167, 355.

31. Florescano, 1999: 113–15.

32. See, for example, Linda Schele and Mary Ellen Miller, 1992.

33. Only recently have the roles of architecture and urban design begun to be evaluated in the transmission of visual messages. See, for example, Carolyn E. Tate, 1992; William Fash and Barbara Fash, 1996: 127–47; Linda Schele and Peter Matthews, 1998; Jeff K. Kowalski, ed., 1999; and Flora S. Clancy, 1999.

34. Enrique Florescano, 1995a: chaps. I, II, and III.

35. See Joyce Marcus, 1992; and Joyce Marcus and Kent V. Flannery, 1996.

II. The Canon of the Post-Classic Period, 1100–1521

1. On the formation of the kingdom of Tula see Nigel Davies, 1977; and Dan M. Healan, comp., 1989. A comparison between Tula and Chichén Itzá can be seen in Lindsay Jones, 1995. On Chichén Itzá see also Linda Schele and David Freidel, 1999.

2. *Popol Vuh*, 1950.

3. Florescano, 1999: chap. I.

4. Ibid.: 34; and Florescano, 1995b.

5. Michael D. Coe was the first to advise that the images recorded on Maya ceramics of the Classic Period represented characters from the *Popol Vuh*. See Michael D. Coe, 1973.

6. The best analysis of the Divine Twins is that of Michael D. Coe, 1989: 161–84; see also Florescano, 1995b.

7. Florescano, 1995b: 211–17 and 288–90.

8. Florescano, 1999: 40.

9. Bruce E. Byland and John M. D. Pohl, 1994: chap. 4: 209–29.

10. Florescano, 1999: 22–30; Elizabeth H. Boone, 2000: 89–96.

11. Ronald Spores, 1967: 13–14.

12. Alfonso Caso, 1977.

13. The best studies of the *Códice de Viena* are found in Jill Leslie Furst, 1978; and Ferdinand Anders, Maarten Jansen, and Gabina Aurora Pérez Jiménez, 1992.

14. Michel Graulich, 1974: 311–54.

15. Juan de Torquemada, 1975–83: vol. I, 49; *Relaciones geográficas del siglo XVI: Tlaxcala*, 1985: vol. II, 35–36; John M. Pohl, 1994: 145.

16. *Relaciones geográficas del siglo XVI: Tlaxcala*, 1985: vol. I, 130.

17. See Paul Kirchhoff, Lina Odena Güemes, and Luis Reyes García, 1976.

18. Luis Reyes García, 1988; Dana Leibsohn, 1994: 161–67; Keiko Yoneda, 1991.

19. Pohl, 1994: 150–53.

20. Boone, 2000: 184.

21. See a detailed description of the pages of this codex in Charles E. Dibble, 1980.

22. Fernando de Alva Ixtlilxóchitl, 1972: vol. I, 295–96.

23. See a study of the political and cultural development of Texcoco in Jerome A. Offner, 1983.

24. Reyes García, 1988: 76.

25. Ibid.: 119–22.

26. *La Leyenda de los soles* (The legend of the suns) and *La historia de los mexicanos por sus pinturas* (The history of the Mexicans through their paintings), texts that relate the formation of the Mexica Fifth Sun, are collected in Garibay K., 1965.

27. See an analysis of the *Mapa Sigüenza* and of the *Aubin, Boturini, Azcatitlán, Mendoza*, and *Mexicanus* codices, which relate the Mexico migration, in Boone, 2000: 166–73 and 197–213.

28. Christian Doverger, 1987.

29. Enrique Florescano, 1998.

30. Florescano, 1999: 53–63.

31. Ibid.: 173.

32. Boone, 2000: 213.

33. Rudolf Von Zantwijk, 1985: 27–28; and Enrique Florescano, 1995a (new ed., 2001): chap. IV.

34. Alva Ixtlilxóchitl, 1972: vol. I, 270.

35. See Paul Kirchhoff, Lina Odena Güemes, and Luis Reyes García, eds., 1989. The best critical edition of the *Relación de Michoacán* is the one coordinated by Moisés Franco Mendoza in Jerónimo de Alcalá, 1980.

36. See the excellent study in Marcus, 1992.

37. On the reconstruction of this surprising political biography, see Zelia Nuttall, 1902; James Cooper Clark, 1912; Herbert Spinden, 1935: 429–51; Nancy Troike, 1974; Byland and Pohl, 1994; and *Códice Alfonso Caso: La vida de 8-Venado, Garra de Tigre* (The life of 8-Deer, Jaguar Claw), 1996.

38. See Boone, 2000: 68–70. As stated by Henry B. Nicholson (1971: 38–81), the best-known annals are those of the Mexica group: The *Aubin, Mendoza, Telleriano-Remensis,* and *Azcatitlán* codices, and so forth.

39. Charles E. Dibble, 1951; see also the enlightening analysis of this story genre in Boone, 2000: 79–86.

40. See, for example, Mary Elizabeth Smith, 1973; and Yoneda, 1991.

41. Alva Ixtlilxóchitl, 1972: 527.

III. The Western Canon versus the Mesoamerican Canon

1. Joaquín García Icazbalceta, 1941: 204.

2. Juan Ginés de Sepúlveda, 1979. See also David Brading, 1991b: 107–8; and Carmen Bernard and Serge Gruzinski, 1991: 538–39.

3. On this topic see Brian Stock, 1983.

4. Elizabeth L. Eisenstein, 1993; and David R. Olson, 1998: 78–79.

5. Jack Goody, 2000: 155.

6. Juan Bautista Pomar, 1941: 37–39. Italics mine.

7. Elio Antonio de Nebrija, 1492.

8. Shirley B. Heath, 1972: 24–25.

9. On this topic see Walter D. Mignolo, 1995; Heath, 1972; Gonzalo Aguirre Beltrán, 1982; and Dorothy Tanck de Estrada, 1999.

10. Cited by Miguel León-Portilla, 1961: 52. Italics mine. Fray Bernardino de Sahagún (2000: vol. II, 929), the Franciscan who best knew the ancient Indian traditions, wrote that their ways of recording were as follows: "These people did not have any letters nor characters, nor did they know how to read or write. They communicated through images and pictures, and all their relics and the books which they had were painted with figures and images, so that they knew and had the memory of things that their ancestors had done and had left in their annals for more than a thousand years back, before the Spaniards came to this land."

11. Fray Toribio de Motolinía, 1969: 2.

12. Mignolo, 1995.

13. José de Acosta, 1962.

14. "Letter from Father Joseph de Acosta to Father Juan de Tovar, of the Company of Jesus," in Joaquín García Icazbalceta, 1947: vol. IV, 89–93. An excellent explanation of the historical tangle caused by the text sent by Tovar to Acosta, who used it extensively in his *Historia natural y moral de las Indias,* causing him to be accused of plagiarism, can be found in the prologue of O'Gorman to the latter work and in the appendices thereto, 1962: XIV–XXI and LXXVII–LCV. See also *Manuscrit Tovar: Origines et croyances des Indiens du Mexique,* 1972.

15. Francisco de Burgoa, 1934a: 210.

16. Bartolomé de las Casas, 1967: vol. II, 34. Italics mine.

17. Antonio de Herrera, 1945: vol. III, 165.

18. Sahagún, 2000: vol. I, 63.

19. Fernando de Alva Ixtlilxóchitl, 1972: vol. I, 263 and 420. "And it is found in the history of the Tultecs that this age and first world, as they call it, had lasted for 1,716 years" and "they used the pictures and the characters with which which they had painted all those things which had happened from the creation of the world until their times."

20. Michael D. Coe, 1993: 190.

21. Alva Ixtlilxóchitl, 1972: vol. II, 7; Walter D. Mignolo, 1995: 98.

22. Michael D. Coe and Justin Kerr, 1997: 101–10.

23. Alva Ixtlilxóchitl, 1972: vol. I, 527–28.

24. Cited by Coe and Kerr, 1997: 222.

25. Cited by Maarten Jansen in the introduction to Anders, Jansen, and Reyes García, eds., 1994: 14.

26. Robert Ricard, 1986: 397. Italics mine.

27. David Tavárez, 2000: 19–27.

28. Ibid.: 20.

29. Ibid.: 21. See José Alcina Franch, 1993: 25–26.

30. Alcina Franch, 1993: 71–75.

31. Burgoa, *Geográfica descripción*, 1934: vol. I, 340–41. Italics mine.

32. Mignolo, 1995: chap. III.

33. Cited by Mignolo, 1995: 127.

34. Torquemada, 1975–83: vol. I, book one, chap. XI, 47. Italics mine.

35. The best study of the impact the ideas mentioned had on America is that of Antonello Gerbi, 1960.

36. See I. J. Gelb, 1963: V; and Michael D. Coe, 1993: 26.

37. In *Memoria indígena* (Indigenous memory), 1999, I present a more complete explanation of the principal vehicles that transmitted and continue to transmit that memory.

38. Josef Hayim Zakhor Yerushalmi, 1996: 15. The posthumously published work of Roy A. Rappaport, 1999, is the best study of rituals and their effectiveness in transmitting values and practices essential to the formation of peoples.

39. Florescano, 1999: chap. II.

40. I have developed these ideas in *Memoria indígena,* chap. II.

41. See Catherine Bell, 1997: 102–3; and the great work of Rappaport, 1999.

42. Enrique Florescano, 1995b.

43. Jan Vansina, 1985: 27–28.

44. Diego Durán, 1984: vol. I, XXXI.

45. See Robertson, 1959; John B. Glass, 1964; Joaquín Galarza, 1990; Joyce Marcus, 1992; Smith, 1973; and Elizabeth P. Benson, comp., 1973.

46. The main references to the life of Lorenzo Boturini and his Mexican museum can be found in Lorenzo Boturini Benaduci, 1974: IX–LXXII; and Lorenzo Boturini Benaduci, 1990: IX–LIV.

47. Boturini Benaduci, 1974: 32. Italics mine.

48. Ibid.

49. Ibid.
50. See Walter Mignolo's analysis of the historic concepts of Boturini and of his relationship to the ideas of Vico in Mignolo, 1995: 143–63; see also Álvaro Matute, 1976.
51. Isaiah Berlin, 1983: 181–87.
52. Rappaport, 1999: 1920.
53. Friedrich Meinecke, 1943: 53–67.
54. Boone, 2000: 4–5.
55. Ibid.: 5.
56. Ibid.

IV. The Conquest and the Imposition of the Christian Canon on History

1. See Antonello Gerbi, 1978.
2. Rómulo D. Carbia, 1940: 76 and 91–92.
3. Michel de Certeau refers to a colonization of the American body accomplished by the discourse of power and the conquering writing of Western man. See Certeau, 1978: 3–5. On the interpretation of the land and people of America by Europeans, see Barbara E. Mundy, 1996; Duccio Sacchi, 1997; Jerry M. Williams and Robert E. Lewis, eds., 1993; and John F. Moffitt and Santiago Sebastian, 1966.
4. Juan López de Velasco, 1971.
5. Acosta, 1962. See the study by Edmundo O'Gorman, which precedes Acosta's text.
6. In this section I reproduce and summarize substantive parts of chapter V, "La conquista y la elaboración de un nuevo discurso histórico" (The conquest and elaboration of a new historical discourse), from *Memoria mexicana* (Memory, Myth, and Time in Mexico), 1995b.
7. Arnaldo Momigliano, 1966: 18–19. See the detailed analysis of the Hebrew concept of historical development and time by S. G. F. Brandon, 1965: 106–40.
8. Ibid.: 184–87.
9. J. H. Plumb, 1974: 184–87.
10. Norman Rufus Colin Cohn, 1972: 28.
11. Brandon, 1965: 95 and 104–5.
12. See Oscar Cullman, 1962: 111. Jacques le Goff, 1979: 49.
13. Plumb, 1974: 65–66.
14. Le Goff, 1979: 48 and 51.
15. Brandon, 1965: 196; and Lewis Munford, 1977: 30–31.
16. Cohn, 1981. This work deals broadly with messianic movements.
17. Ibid.
18. For the ideas of Joaquín de Fiore, see Cohn, 1981: 108–10. See also Karl Lowith, 1958: 207–28 and 299–307. Lowith studied the influence of Fiore on the philosophy of modern history. Delmo C. West and Sandra Zimdars-Swartz (1986) offer a global treatment of his interpretation of history.
19. See the introductory study of Edmundo O'Gorman in Casas, 1967: LVIII–LXXIX.

20. See Pedro Mártir de Anglería, 1964; Gonzalo Fernández de Oviedo, 1972; Francisco López de Gómara, 1971: 156, 168, and 194.

21. John Leddy Phelan, 1972: 32.

22. Ibid.: 82-98.

23. Ricard, 1986: 192–94.

24. Constantino Reyes Valerio, 1989: 93. See also Serge Gruzinski, 1988: chap. I.

25. Esteban J. Palomera, 1962: 137; Reyes Valerio, 1989: 103.

26. Diego Valadés, 1989: 237; Esteban J. Palomera, 1962: 66–67.

27. Reyes Valerio, 1989: 112–19.

28. Gruzinski, 1988: 45.

29. Gruzinski, 1994b: 12–13.

30. Ramón A. Gutiérrez, 1993: 118–19.

31. Robert Ricard, 1947: 268.

32. On the diffusion and function of painting in New Spain, see (only a sample, due to the length of the bibliography): Manuel Toussaint, 1965; Guillermo Tovar de Teresa, 1979; Mariano Monterrosa, ed., 1990; Reyes Valerio, 1989; Jeanette Favrot Peterson, 1993; and Gruzinski, 1994b.

33. Constantino Reyes Valerio, 1978; Guillermo Tovar de Teresa, 1992.

34. See Othón Arróniz, 1979: 15–16, 37, 42, and 120–22; Fernando Horcasitas, 1974: 72–73 and 170–73; and Armando Partida, ed., 1992: 38–47.

35. Gutiérrez, 1993: 127. James Lockhart (1992: 407) also describes the pedagogical nature of the theater: "Though thus strongly naturalized, the predominant themes of the plays remain Spanish, with emphasis on teaching the audience the principal personages, doctrines and morality of Christianity."

36. Florescano, 1999: 248–49.

37. Ibid.: 248–52.

V. *The First European Versions of the American World and the Origin of the Mestizo Chronicle*

1. See these citings and commentaries in David A. Brading, 1991a: 29–30.

2. Anglería, 1964.

3. Brading, 1991a: 30–33.

4. Edmundo O'Gorman, 1951; and Edmundo O'Gorman, 1977.

5. See Hernán Cortés, 1963; and Bernal Díaz del Castillo, 1983.

6. Francisco Esteve Barba, 1992: 159–60.

7. José Luis Martínez, 1990: 844–45.

8. Enrique Florescano, 1995a: 298–99.

9. See Edmundo O'Gorman, 1972; and Gonzalo Fernández de Oviedo, 1971: 156–57.

10. Francisco López de Gómara, 1971: 156, 168, and 294.

11. See some of the characteristics that distinguished the chroniclers of the Indies in Carbia, 1940; and Esteve Barba, 1992.

12. Florescano, 1995a: 314–20.

13. Sahagún, 2000: vol. I, 61. On the methods and the works of Sahagún, see J. Jorge Klor de Alva, H. B. Nicholson, and Eloise Quiñones Keber, eds., 1988; and the more recent book of Miguel León-Portilla, 1999.

14. Motolinía, 1969; and Fray Toribio de Motolinía, 1996.

15. Angel María Garibay K., 1954.

16. Jerónimo de Mendieta, 1997: vol. I, 179–80. Italics mine.

17. Durán, 1984.

18. Ibid., XXVII–XXXV.

19. J. Eric S. Thompson, 1959: 46.

20. Alfredo López Austin, 1976: 9–56; and Munro S. Edmonson, ed., 1974.

21. Ibid.: 18; see also Ellen T. Baird, 1993: chap. 2.

22. Bernardino de Sahagún, 1997.

23. Sahagún, 2000: vol. I, 130–31.

24. Garibay K., 1954: vol. II, 67–69; Alfredo López Austin, 1976: 21–22; Donald Robertson, undated: vol. IX, no. 3, 617–28; Miguel León-Portilla, 1980: 101–35; Walden Browne, 2000: 93–99. In reference to the title of the *Historia general,* Jesús Bustamante García, in his study on Fray Bernardino de Sahagún (1990), convincingly proved that the original title was *Historia universal de las cosas de Nueva España.*

25. Sahagún, 2000.

26. *Códice florentino,* 1979. Earlier (1950–70, 12 volumes), an excellent edition was published in English, but it did not include all the illustrations.

27. Bernardino de Sahagún, 1956: vol. I, "Proemio general," 10–77.

28. Sahagún, 2000: vol. I, "Estudio introductorio," 41 and 129.

29. Ibid., 62–63.

30. Sahagún, 2000, "Prólogo": vol. II, book VI, 473.

31. Sahagún, 2000: vol. III, book XII, 1161–62.

32. Ibid.: 1174 and 1182.

33. See the studies of this story and other native testimonies on the conquest in Miguel León-Portilla, 1959b; and Georges Baudot and Tzvetan Todorov, eds., 1990.

34. Eloise Quiñones Keber, 1988b: 199–210; and Eloise Quiñones Keber, 1997: 15–37; see also Baird, 1993.

35. Sahagún, 2000: vol. I, 130.

36. Quiñones Keber, 1988b: 207–9.

37. Quiñones Keber, 1988a: 269; Jeanette Favrot Peterson, 1988: 273–93; Baird, 1993: chap. VI.

38. Quiñones Keber, 1988a: 255–72; Eloise Quiñones Keber, 1997: 15–37.

39. Quiñones Keber, 1988b: 207.

40. Tzvetan Todorov, 1982: 234–35.

41. Robertson (undated: 625) says, with reference to this polemic: "The usual manner of writing by Canon Garibay and Doctor León-Portilla about the various texts of Sahagún, they tend to give the authorship credit, especially in the earlier texts, the *Primeras memoriales* and the *Códices matritenses,* to 'Sahagún's informants.' Even though they should receive some credit, they are in fact being credited as 'assistants in the investigation' with the composition of the final work, something which is not done in normal bibliographical practices. . . . What is being overlooked by giving credit for the work to Sahagún's informants is the fact that it was he himself who

established the design of the work, conceiving a type of true encyclopedia, and he, with his questions, obtained the information through the answers of the informants, who simply followed the patterns that he proposed to them to present the materials that he judged should be brought to light."

42. Sahagún, 2000: vol. I, 112–17.

43. Ibid.: 423–25.

VI. The Canon of Memory Wrought by the Títulos primordiales

I would like to express my gratitude for the valuable comments and suggestions on this chapter that I received from Rodrigo Martínez, Sergio Pérez Cortés, Ruggiero Romano, María de los Angeles Romero Frizzi, Xavier Noguez, Hans Roskamp, Mario Humberto Ruz, Juan Pedro Viqueira, and Stephanie Wood.

1. See Joaquín Galarza, 1972; Joaquín Galarza, 1980; James Lockhart, 1982: 367–93; and Lockhart, 1992.

2. Donald Robertson, 1975: vol. 14, 253–80; H. R. Harvey, 1986: 153–84.

3. Lockhart, 1982; Lockart, 1992.

4. See. for example, the excellent analysis of the *Títulos* by Serge Grozinski, 1988: 141–88; Stephanie Wood, 1998: 167–207; and the more recent study of Margarita Menegus Bornemann, 1999: 137–61.

5. Galarza, 1972.

6. Luis Reyes García and Marcelo Díaz de Salas, 1968: 283–92.

7. Lockhart, 1982; Lockhart, 1992.

8. Lockhart, 1982. Gruzinski observed these features in many *Títulos* from the region of the Valley of Toluca and central Mexico (1988: 160–70).

9. Lockhart, 1982: 385–86; Danièle Dehouve, 1995: 111–21; see also the founding acts described by Marion Oettinger, 1983: 25–26.

10. Lockhart, 1982.

11. Lockhart, 1992: 415–16.

12. Lockhart, 1982: 376–81.

13. Ibid.

14. Ibid.: 391.

15. Lockhart, 1992: 417.

16. Hans Roskamp, 1998; Hans Roskamp, 2003: 305–60.

17. Roskamp, 1998: 213–18 and 231.

18. Ibid.: 231–45.

19. Ibid.: 246–63 and 283–87.

20. Harvey, 1986: 153–54.

21. Nadine Béligand, 1993.

22. Ibid.: 61–120.

23. Stephanie Wood, 1989: 245–85; see also Alberto Castillo, 1991: 187–210.

24. Stephanie Wood, 1987: 472–85.

25. Harvey, 1986: 162–64.

26. Fernando Horcasitas and Wanda Tommasi de Magrelli, 1975: 243–72; Harvey, 1986: 156–57; Galarza, 1980: 23.

27. Galarza, 1980: 23.

28. Gruzinski, 1988; Enrique Florescano, 1997a: 318–29; Menegus Bornemann, 1999: 153. Bornemann states: "In summation, in my opinion the Títulos primordiales were created by the community itself to conserve the memory of the origin and borders of its property."

29. Torquemada, 1975–83: vol. IV, 334, italics mine; Boone, 2000: 126–27. An analysis of the characteristics of the Mixtec canvases can be seen in Víctor de la Cruz, 1997: vol. II, 193–212.

30. Smith, 1973: 169.

31. Boone, 2000: 126–27.

32. Alfonso Caso pointed out the presence of these gods and sacred symbols in the founding of Coixtlahuaca, Ihuitlán, Tlapiltepec, and other Mixtec cities. See Caso, 1954; Caso, 1958: vol. I, 373–93; and Caso, 1961: 237–74. See also the analysis of Ross Parmenter, 1982; and Boone, 2000: 136–39.

33. María de los Ángeles Romero Frizzi, 1988: 16–20.

34. See Caso, 1954; Caso, 1958; Caso, 1961; see also his analysis of the *Códice Selden* in Caso, 1964.

35. Caso, 1964. See also the interpretation of this foundational scene in the work of Boone, 2000: 152–61. The *Códice Selden II* can be consulted in José Corona Núñez's edition in the *Antigüedades de México,* 1964: vol. II, 101–13.

36. Smith, 1973: 10; see also Smith and Parmenter, 1991: 20 and 32. On the *Lienzo de Tequixtepec I,* see Parmenter, 1982; and Luis Reyes García, 1998: 21–23.

37. See Smith, 1973: 62; Parmenter, 1982: 63–64; Kevin Terraciano and Lisa M. Sousa, 1992: 8–90; and Boone, 2000: 128–30 and 145.

38. Smith, 1973: 180.

39. Ibid.: 181. Italics mine.

40. Enrique Florescano, 1976b: 42–45; see also Menegus, 1999: 140–43.

41. Smith, 1973: 122–147 and 170. Another case of transformation and reuse of an ancient canvas as a map to outline lands is described by Manuel A. Hermann Lejarazo, 2000: 15–18.

42. Alfonso Caso, 1966: 131–37; Smith, 1973: 336–37.

43. Michel R. Oudijk, 2003. Another canvas, very similar to the one from Tabáa, is the *Lienzo de Tiltepec,* discussed in Jorge Guevara Hernández, 1991.

44. See María de los Ángeles Romero Frizzi, 2000: 4–11; in the *Memorias de la Academia Mexicana de la Historia,* vol. XLIII, 2000: 141–60, there is a more extensive edition of this study; see also María de los Angeles Romero Frizzi, 2003. See also Lejarazo, 2000: 15–18.

45. Terraciano and Sousa, 1992: 74.

46. Ibid.: 69.

47. See, for example, Florescano, 1999; and Johanna Broda and Félix Báez-Jorge, comps., 2001, in which Alfredo López Austin, Johanna Broda, Andrés Medina, and other authors point out the unity of the Mesoamerican cosmovision.

48. M. de Charencey, 1885; and Adrián Recinos, 1950.

49. Robert M. Carmack and James L. Mondloch, 1983; and Robert M. Carmack and James L. Mondloch, 1989.

50. Carmack and Mondloch, 1983: 14–16.

51. In making this comparison, I used the structural analysis that I made earlier of the *Popol Vuh* and other Mesomerican cosmogonic myths. See Florescano, 1999: chap. 1.

52. Carmack and Mondloch, 1983: 16.

53. Ibid.: 17.

54. Ibid.: 17–18.

55. Florescano, 1999: chaps. 3–5.

56. Taube, 2000b.

57. *Memorial de Solalá: Anales de los Cakchiqueles,* 1950: 212. The *Título de Pedro Velasco* (1592) in Carmack and Mondloch, 1989: 139–92, is also based on the *Popol Vuh* and the *Título de Totonicapán.*

58. The *Fragmento* introduces into the ancient chronicle the inventory of lands and a list of witnesses related to the Yax lineage who, "all old principals together," confirmed "the validity of this title" and affirmed it to be legally these . . . lands ever since the arrival of the above-mentioned Yaxes." Carmack and Mondloch, 1989: 16, 129–33. See also the *Título de Cristóbal Ramírez* in Carmack and Mondloch, 1989.

59. Adrián Recinos, 1984: 23–67. The *Títulos de la Casa Ixquin-Nehaib,* probably written in the sixteenth century, likewise offer a story of the ancient history of Quetzaltenango, written by its headmen, which is presented as "the titles and verification of this town of Quetzaltenango and the conquests that our ancestors and great-grandfathers carried out which they left to us until Judgment Day." One of the arguments made by the headmen to legitimize their titles was that their ancestors were baptized and collaborated with the first conquistadors and Spanish authorities (Recinos, 1984: 71–94). Another document that repeats these arguments and shows the strength of the chiefs is the so-called *Título real de don Francisco Izquin Nehaib,* in Recinos, 1984: 91–117. See also Matthew Restall, 1998: 105–28.

60. Recinos, 1984: 121–29 and 172–81. Carmack and Mondloch, 1989: 203–10 and 211–19, include the *Título de Paxtocá* (1557) and the *Título de caciques* (1544), which are additional proof of the intervention of the chiefs in the manufacture and legalization of the *Títulos.* See also the curious *Título* of the region of Acalán-Tixchel, signed by Pablo Paxbolón, in France V. Scholes and Ralph L. Roys, 1996: 289–305.

61. Carmack and Mondloch, 1989: 192.

62. Recinos, 1984: 152–69. See other examples in which the will and testament was used to transmit the property of the heads of the lineage and the chiefs in Juan Dubernard Chauveau, 1991.

63. Restall, 1998: 34.

64. Florescano, 1997a: 187–88, in which I provide an ample bibliography of the application of this program in different areas of New Spain.

65. Enrique Florescano, 1976b: 52–53.

66. Gruzinski, 1988: 155.

67. This information and that in table 5 show the presence of substantive changes in the political, social, and cultural order between 1530 and 1560 that are not reflected in James Lockhart's analysis of the changes experienced in the Náhua world during those years. See Lockhart, 1992: table 10.1, 428–36.

68. Roskamp, 2003, equates the community chests where the *Títulos* were kept to the cult of the "sacred bundle" among prehispanic peoples. For his part Robert

Haskett, 1996: 99–126, shows that the *Títulos* became a type of political shield of the towns.

VII. From the Creole Homeland to the History of the Nation

1. The program of congregation of peoples and the creation of the Repúblicas de Indios and the Fundo Legal together meant a reassignment of lands, a redistribution of the indigenous population, and the growth of new towns. All of this was expressed in new boundaries, land registries, maps, canvases, and land descriptions that were developed between 1530 and 1570. See chapter 6.

2. Alejandra Moreno Toscano, 1968; Mundy, 1996; Sacchi, 1997.

3. Enrique Florescano and Isabel Gil Sánchez, eds., 1976.

4. Manuel Orozco y Berra, 1973: 326–34.

5. Ibid.: 341.

6. Ibid.

7. Boturini Benaduci, 1974: 31.

8. Gerbi, 1960.

9. Agustín Millares Carlo, 1957.

10. Villoro, 1950: 96.

11. Clavijero, 1958–59: vol. I, 71.

12. Villoro, 1950: 98.

13. Ibid.: 96.

14. Trabulse, 1988: 29.

15. Villoro, 1950: 99–101.

16. Francisco Javier Clavijero, 1958–59: vol. IV, 205–6.

17. José Emilio Pacheco, 1976: 43.

18. Ibid.: 32.

19. David A. Brading, 1973: 54 and 57–58.

20. Ibid.

21. Ignacio Bernal, 1979: 86; José Alcina Franch, 1995.

22. See Alejandro de Humboldt, 1966; José Miranda, 1962; and Jaime Labastida, 1999.

23. I develop these ideas extensively in Florescano, 1998.

24. See Jaime Cuadriello, 1984; Jaime Cuadriello, 1994: 91–96; and Jaime Cuadriello, 1995.

25. Florescano, 1998: chap. II.

26. Luis Villoro, 1986: 80.

27. Ibid.

28. Ibid.: 98–99.

29. Ibid.: 101.

30. Carlos Herrejón Morelos, 1985.

31. Florescano, 1998: 106; Ernesto Lemoine Villicaña, 1985: 560–61.

32. Florescano, 1995a: 511–14.

33. Servando Teresa de Mier, 1922: vol. II, 166–67. An excellent analysis of the political allegation of Teresa de Mier can be seen in Servando Teresa de Mier, 1978.

34. Teresa de Mier, 1922: vol. II, 197–99; David A. Brading, 1980: 72.

35. Teresa de Mier, 1922: vol. II, 314–18.

36. Luis Villoro, 1981: 150–52, 153–65.

37. In addition to studies on Teresa de Mier by Villorio, O'Gorman, and Brading, see the excellent novel of Reinaldo Arenas on Fray Servando, *El mundo alucinante,* 1981.

38. Ernesto Lemoine Villicaña, 1984: IX–X. Other biographical information on Bustamante is available in the preliminary study done by Ernesto Lemoine for the edition of the *Abeja* of Chilpancingo; see also Roberto Castelán Rueda, 1997.

39. The book bears the title *Cuadro histórico de la revolución de la América Mexicana, comenzada el quince de septiembre de mil ochocientos diez por el ciudadano Miguel Hidalgo y Costilla, dedicada al ciudadano José María Morelos.* The second edition, corrected and augmented by the author, was published in 1843–46. See Lemoine Villicaña, 1984: XII.

40. Ibid., XIV; and Juan A. Ortega y Medina, "El historiador don Carlos María de Bustamante ante la conciencia histórica mexicana," 1970.

41. Carlos María de Bustamante, 1835–36.

42. On the historical nationalism of Bustamante, see Josefina Zoraida Vázquez de Knauth, 1970: 32–33; Brading, 1980: 118–19; Castelán Rueda, 1997: 127–34.

43. Vásquez de Knauth, 1970: 32–33; and Brading, 1980: 118–19.

44. A list of the publications and editions of Bustamante can be found in Bartolomé de las Casas, 1967.

45. Ocampo, 1969: 16.

46. Ibid.

47. Bustamante, 1985: vol. V, 328–29.

48. Ibid.: 333.

49. See Ocampo, 1969. Another source, Vicente Riva Palacio, ed., 1884–89, vol. IV, 18 and 24, stated: "While in the capital of the new Empire they marked . . . [the celebrations of Independence], the provinces, which were already anxious for Independence, marked it with the most expressive manifestations of joy when the news came of the entrance of the Army of the Three Guarantees into the city of Mexico." And in another section, he adds: "Despite Independence having been declared and sworn to in a solemn fashion in almost all the cities and towns of the Empire, the same had not been done in the capital itself, and the Regency therefore decreed that such an act be carried out in the city of Mexico and in such places where the oath had not been taken." Another version (Ocampo, 1969: 39) indicated that the number of people who witnessed the oath of Independence in the main plaza of the city of Mexico exceeded sixty thousand.

50. Riva Palacio, 1884–89: vol IV, 24; Ocampo, 1969: 15–16.

51. In one example of such plans, an author proposed to demolish the Parián market to open up the main plaza of the city of Mexico. "In the center of this great plaza would be a magnificent pyramid with the statue of the liberator of the Mexican Empire." Ocampo, 1969: 101.

52. On the use of time and the calendar for revolutionary events, see Mona Ozouf, 1976: chap. VIII.

53. Ocampo, 1969: 157–60.

54. *La bandera de México*, 1985: 106.

55. Florescano, 1995a: 520–22.

VIII. Oblivion and Memory: From the Collapse of the Republic to the History of the Nation

1. Prologue to José María Roa Bárcena, 1971: vol. I, IX.

2. Nettie Lee Benson, 1955; Michael P. Costeloe, 1975; Jaime E. Rodríguez, ed., 1989.

3. Timothy E. Anna, 1998.

4. Costeloe, 1975: 60–61; Michael P. Costeloe 2000: 29–30.

5. Costeloe, 1975: 115.

6. Ibid.: chap. VI.

7. Ibid.

8. Ibid.: chap. VIII; Barbara E. Tenenbaum, 1985.

9. Costeloe, 1975: chap. IX.

10. Mora (cited by Costeloe, 1975: 219) defines this change as follows: "The administration of General Vicente Guerrero was for Mexico a period of crisis in which the elements of the parties, which for two years had upset the country, ended up dissolving themselves to take on new forms, acquire a new composition, and present social questions again in the guise of regression and progress."

11. Ibid.: chaps. XIV and XV; Costeloe, 2000: II.

12. Pablo Mijangos y González, 2001; Costeloe, 2000: 30–51 and 361–65.

13. Costeloe, 2000: 379–80.

14. Josefina Zoraida Vázquez, 2000: 571–77; and Josefina Zoraida Vázquez, 1997: chaps. 6 and 7.

15. John S. D. Eisenhower, 2000: chap. VI; Vázquez, 1997: chap. 9.

16. Eisenhower, 2000: chap. VI; Vázquez, 1997: chap. 12.

17. Eisenhower, 2000: 191–203.

18. Ibid.: 215 and chaps. XVII–XIX.

19. Vázquez, 1997: chap. 13.

20. Eisenhower, 2000: 391–409.

21. Ibid.: 422–27. Other studies of the war done by North Americans include Robert W. Johannsen, 1985; and Pedro Santoni, 1996. This North American vision of the war has begun to be balanced in recent years by interpretations by Mexican authors. See the studies cited above by Josefina Zoraida Vázquez, 1997; Josefina Zoraida Vázquez, 2000; Josefina Zoraida Vázquez, ed., 1997; and Laura Herrera Serna, comp., 1997.

22. See Charles Hale, 1957: 153–73; and Jesús Velasco Márquez, 1975.

23. Hale, 1957: 161–69.

24. Mariano Otero, 1967: vol. I, 127–37.

25. Lucas Alamán, 1986: vol. I. Works of other authors cited include José María Gutiérrez de Estrada, 1848; and Luis G. Cuevas, 1954.

26. Charles W. Macune, Jr., 1978. See also Jesús Gómez Serrano, 1994, chap. 6.

27. These conflicts were recorded in several studies. See, for example, Josefina Zoraida Vázquez, ed., 1994; and Marcelo Carmagnani, 1994. The book that best describes these early conflicts is *Anna*, 1998.

28. Carmagnani, 1994: 173–76; François-Xavier Guerra, 1985: vol. I, 256 and 275–305.

29. Manuel Payno, 1987.

30. Juan A. Ortega y Medina and Rosa Camelo, eds., 1996: 161–66. Even though before *México a través de los siglos* there had not been any general works that included historical development from antiquity until the present, there were manuals, collections, and lessons on the history of the homeland published from that perspective. See, for example, Epitacio de los Ríos, 1852; José María Roa Bárcenas, 1862; Manuel Payno, 1883; Luis Pérez Verdía, 1883; Guillermo Prieto, 1886. See an analysis of some of these works in Guy Rozat, 2001.

31. See Ortega y Medina, 1970: 268; Josefina Zoraida Vázquez, 1960: 1–3.

32. Vigil, "Necesidad y conveniencia de estudiar la historia patria": 267. See a biographical sketch of Vigil and an appreciation of his work in José Luis Martínez, 1993: 331–38.

33. Riva Palacio, 1884–89.

34. See José Ortiz Monasterio, 1999b: 226–27 and 235.

35. O'Gorman, 1960: 213–16; and Vicente Riva Palacio, 1997: 32–33.

36. Ortiz Monasterio, 1999a: 434, 448, 470, and 522–23.

37. Ibid.: 297 and 502–8.

38. Thomas Benjamin and Marcial Ocasio-Meléndez, 1984: 323–64.

39. Ibid.; see also Moisés González Navarro, 1970.

40. See María de la Luz Parcero, 1971: 443–47; and Álvaro Matute Aguirre, 1999: 20–31.

41. This was also the function of history in nineteenth-century France. See Antoine Prost, 1996: 293–95; and Howard F. Cline, 1973: vol. 13, 370–427.

42. An account of the contributions of those historians can be seen in Howard F. Cline, comp., 1972–75.

43. Luis González, ed., 1961–62: vol. I, XXXIII.

44. For the biography of Vicente Riva Palacio, see the introductory studies of Clementina Díaz y de Ovando, 1976; and Vicente Riva Palacio, 1968. See also José Ortiz Monasterio, 1993.

45. For the origins of this work, see Daniel Cosío Villegas, 1970: 660–66; Riva Palacio, 1976; and Riva Palacio, 1968.

46. Ortiz Monasterio, 1999a: 295 and 305.

47. See Ortiz Monasterio, 1993. Antonio Castro Leal, Clementina Díaz y de Ovando, and Carlos Monsiváis have made interesting evaluations of these novels in prologues to different editions.

48. Martínez, 1993: 45–47; and Nicole Girón, 1976.

49. See Ortiz Monasterio, 1993, and Clementina Díaz y de Ovando, 1985.

50. Justo Sierra, 1940. There are other recent editions of this work; see, for example, the edition of Edmundo O'Gorman in Justo Sierra, 1984, vol. XII; and that of Álvaro Matute, 1993.

51. The best studies of Justo Sierra can be found in the prologues to his works and in his biographies. Outstanding among these is the work of Claude Dumas, 1986. See also Andrés Lira, 1995: 22–40.

52. Sierra, 1984: Vol. XII, 396 and 399.

53. See the excellent book by J. G. A. Pocock, 2000.

IX. The Historical Narrative Coined by the Post-Revolutionary State

I am grateful for the comments and suggestions on this chapter by José Antonio Aguilar, Rita Eder, Guillermo Palacios, and Aurelio de los Reyes.

1. Dorothy Tanck de Estrada, 1991: 65–80; and Andrés Lira, 1991: 65–80 and 179–214.

2. Lucas Alamán, 1985: vol. I, 83, 346; vol. IV, 722–24; vol. V, 352. See also Charles H. Hale, 1972: 19–25.

3. Edmundo O'Gorman, 1954: 174–75.

4. Thomas Benjamin, 2000: 39–40.

5. Hale, 1972: 6.

6. Cited by Nicole Girón, 1991: 201–14. See also Jacqueline Covo, 1988: 69–78.

7. Alberro et al., 1993: 210–11.

8. Brading, 1991b: 714.

9. Hale, 1997: 821–37.

10. Guillermo Palacios, 1969: 2–3; Luis Cabrera, 1972: vol. III, 255–74.

11. Cited by Benjamin, 2000: 45. See Palacios, 1969: 5.

12. Benjamin, 2000: 44.

13. Ibid.: 46–47.

14. See the excellent study by Irene V. O'Malley, 1986: 19–39.

15. Palacios, 1969: 22; Benjamin, 2000: 52.

16. Benjamin, 2000: 65–67. See the public images of Carranza in O'Malley, 1986: 71–86.

17. Benjamin, 2000: 53. The best biography of Villa is that of Friedrich Katz, 1998.

18. John Womack, Jr., 1969.

19. Ramón López Velarde, 1971: 232–34.

20. Ibid.: 10.

21. Carlos Monsiváis, 2000: 959–1076, 970–71.

22. Ibid.: 971.

23. Manuel Gamio, 1960: 5–6, 30, 41–46, 72–73, 76,n>77.

24. Julio Estrada, ed., 1984: 11–13, 44–46.

25. Cited by Enrique Krauze, 1976: 62–63.

26. Aurelio de los Reyes, 1987; and Aurelio de los Reyes, 1973; Carlos J. Mora, 1982.

27. Monsiváis, 2000: 1007.

28. Ibid.: 1007–8.

29. Ibid.: 112.

30. Gamio, 1960: 183.
31. Félix F. Palavicini, 1914; Vázquez de Knauth, 1970: 7–44.
32. This devastating analysis is in Martín Luis Guzmán, 1970: 7–44.
33. Manuel Gómez Morín, 1973: 20.
34. Cited by Vásquez de Knauth, 1970: 125–30.
35. Benjamin, 2000: 68–72.
36. O'Malley, 1986: 42–70.
37. Benjamin, 2000: 68–72.
38. Ibid.: 93–95.
39. Claude Fell, 1989: 56; Mary Kay Vaughan, 1982: chaps. 4 and 8.
40. See Fell, 1989: chaps. II and III.
41. Ibid.: 365–66.
42. Ibid.: 665–66.
43. Betty Kirk, 1942: 20, 306. Cited by Leonard Folgarait, 1998: 27.
44. Cited by Raquel Tibol et al., 1997: 30.
45. Folgarait, 1998: 38.
46. Octavio Paz, 1994: 183.
47. Cited by Raquel Tibol et al., 1997: 35. On another occasion he said: "My mural at the Palacio Nacional is the only plastic poem which I know of which includes in its composition the complete history of a people." Cited in Itzel Rodríguez Mortellaro, in Raquel Tibol et al., 1997: 57.
48. Paz, 1994: 185.
49. A more detailed description of this painting can be seen in Tibol et al., 1997; see also Folgarait, 1998: 87–99; and Alicia Azuela, 1987.
50. See Boone, 2000: 33–63.
51. Florescano, 1976a: II–VI; Rodríguez Mortellaro, 1997: 68–69; Folgarait, 1998: 99–102, 195-203.
52. Paz, 1994: 209.
53. Ibid.: 267.
54. Guillermo Palacios, 1999.
55. Ibid.: 37–38.
56. Ibid.: 39.
57. Ibid.: 48.
58. Ibid.: 49.
59. Ibid.: 74–105.
60. Ibid.: 144.
61. Benjamin, 2000: 117–19, 124–27.
62. Ibid.: 129–33.
63. Ibid.: 133–35.

X. *History Constructed by Historical Professionals*

1. Krzytof Pomian, 1999: 263–313.
2. Walter J. Ong, 1987: 117–36; Eisenstein, 1993; Mignolo, 1995.
3. Pomian, 1999: 312.

4. Ibid.: 320–21.

5. Eduard Fueter, 1953: vol. II, 12–35.

6. Meinecke, 1943: 73–74 and 78.

7. Cited by Barnes, 1963: 160. The best book on Gibbon and his work is Pocock, 2000.

8. Fueter, 1953: vol. II, 153–54, says: "He had to a surprising degree the talent for penetrating, as he used to say, into the thoughts and feelings of others." These qualities joined forces with his aesthetic concept of historical works. According to Fueter, "Few historians have polished their style so conscientiously."

9. The first citation comes from Peter Novick, 1997: vol. I, 39–40; the second is from Fritz Wagner, 1958: 239; Meinecke, 1943: 497–511.

10. Barnes, 1963: 246.

11. Pomian, 1999: 322–31.

12. Marc Bloch, 1952: 65–73.

13. See Peter Burke, 1990; and Robert W. Fogel and G. R. Elton, 1989.

14. For an analysis of the times of history, see the classic study of Fernand Braudel, 1984, 60–106; and Michel Vovelle, 1988: 359–86.

15. As examples of these historiographic currents, see Marc Bloch, 1952; Ernest Labrousse, 1962; Fernand Braudel, 1976; Pierre Goubert, 1960; Pierre Vilar, 1962; Emmanuel Le Roy Ladurie, 1969; Michel de Certeau, 1975; Michel Foucault, 1961; François Furet, 1978.

16. Peter Burke et al., ed., 1994: 11.

17. See, for example, the introduction to the collected work that reviews these tendencies in French historiography, Jacques Le Goff and Pierre Nora, eds., 1974.

18. For example, Edward Palmer Thompson, 1965: E. J. Hobsbawm, 1963; Cohn, 1972; Carlo Ginzburg, 1981; Mijail Bajtín, 1974.

19. Novick, 1997: vol. II, 623.

20. Ibid., 682–83, 687, and 688–89. Farther on (699), Novick says that "When the subcommunities of historians began to express themselves in the languages of statistics, the psychology of the unconscious, Marxist structuralism, and semiotics, the result was not only that they communicated less effectively with the uninitiated . . . , but that they had more and more difficulty communicating with each other."

21. Ibid.: vol. II, chap. 16. The work of Hayden White perhaps best summed up these tendencies and was the most influential among the newer generation of historians. See White, 1993.

22. See Ortega y Medina, 1970.

23. Florescano, 1997b: 41–43.

24. Josef Hayim Yerushalmi, 1989.

25. Enrique Florescano Mayet, 1991: 173–74.

26. Ibid.: 160–61.

27. Cited by Novick, 1997: vol. II, 746.

Bibliography

Acosta, José de. 1962. *Historia natural y moral de las Indias.* Edited by Edmundo O'Gorman. Fondo de Cultura Económica.

Aguirre Beltrán, Gonzalo. 1982. *Lenguas vernáculas: Su uso y desuso en la enseñanza.* Casa Chata.

Alamán, Lucas. 1985. *Historia de Méjico desde los primeros movimientos que prepararon su independencia en el año de 1808, hasta la época presente, 1849–1852.* Facsimile ed. 5 vols. Fondo de Cultura Económica.

———. 1986. *Historia de Méjico.* 5 vols. Editorial Jus.

Alberro, Solange et al. 1991. *La revolución francesa en México.* El Colegio de México.

Alcalá, Jerónimo de. 1980. *La relación de Michoacán.* Paleographic version, separation of texts, colloquial ordering, preliminary study, and notes by Francisco Miranda. Fimax Publicistas Editores.

———. 2000. *Relación de las ceremonias y ritos y población y gobernación de los indios de la provincia de Michoacán.* Edited and preliminary study coordinated by Moisés Franco Mendoza. El Colegio de Michoacán and Government of the State of Michoacán.

Alcina Franch, José. 1993. *Calendario y religión entre los zapotecos.* Universidad Nacional Autónoma de México.

———. 1995. *Arqueólogos o anticuarios: Historia antigua de la arqueología en la América española.* Ediciones del Serbal.

Alfonso Reyes: Homenaje nacional. 1981. Instituto Nacional de Bellas Artes.

Alva Ixtlilxóchitl, Fernando de. 1972. *Obras históricas.* Edited, with introduction and documented appendix, by Edmundo O'Gorman. 2 vols. Universidad Nacional Autónoma de México.

Anders, Ferdinand, Maarten Jansen, and Gabina Aurora Pérez Jiménez. 1992. *Origen e historia de los reyes mixtecos: Libro explicativo del llamado Códice Vindobonensis.* Fondo de Cultura Económica.

———, ———, and Luis Reyes García, eds. 1994. *La gran familia de los reyes mixtecos: Libro explicativo de los códices llamados Egerton y Becker II.* Fondo de Cultura Económica.

Anglería, Pedro Mártir de. 1964. *Décadas del Nuevo Mundo.* Analysis and appendix by Edmundo O'Gorman. Editorial Porrúa.

Anna, Timothy E. 1998. *Forging Mexico, 1821–1835.* University of Nebraska Press.

Arenas, Reinaldo. 1981. *El mundo alucinante.* Montesinos Editor.

Arróniz, Othón. 1979. *Teatro de evangelización en Nueva España.* Universidad Nacional Autónoma de México.

Azuela, Alicia. 1987. *Imagen de México: La aportación de México al arte del siglo XX.* Instituto Nacional de Bellas Artes.

Azuela, Mariano. 1958. *Los de abajo.* Fondo de Cultura Económica.

Baird, Ellen T. 1993. *The Drawings of Sahagún's Primeros Memoriales: Structure and Style.* University of Oklahoma Press.

Bajtín, Mijail M. 1974. *La cultura popular en la edad media y el renacimiento: El contexto de François Rabelais.* Barral.

Barajas, Rafael. 2000. *La historia de un país en caricatura.* Conaculta.

Barnes, Harry Elmer. 1963. *A History of Historical Writing.* Dover Publications.

Baudot, Georges. 1977. *Utopie et histoire au Mexique: Les prémiers chroniqueurs de la civilization mexicaine (1520–1569).* Editions Privat.

———, and Tzvetan Todorov, eds. 1990. *Relatos aztecas de la conquista.* Editorial Grijalbo.

Béligand, Nadine. 1993. *Códice de San Antonio Techialoyan.* Instituto Mexiquense de Cultura.

Bell, Catherine. 1997. *Ritual: Perspectives and Dimensions.* Oxford University Press.

Benavente, Fray Toribio de (Motolinía). 1969. *Historia de los indios de la Nueva España.* Introduction, appendices, notes, and index by Edmundo O'Gorman. Editorial Porrúa.

———. 1989. *El libro perdido: Ensayo de reconstrucción de la obra histórica extraviada de fray Toribio.* Consejo Nacional para la Cultura y las Artes.

———. *Memoriales.* 1996. Introduction, appendices, notes, and index by Nancy Joe Dyer. El Colegio de México.

Benitez, Fernando. 1982. *Historia de la Ciudad de México.* Salvat.

Benjamin, Thomas. 2000. *Mexico's Great Revolution in Memory, Myth and History.* University of Texas Press.

———, and Marcial Ocasio-Meléndez. 1984. "Organizing the Memory of Modern Mexico: Porfirian Historiography in Perspective, 1880s–1980s." *Hispanic American Historical Review* 64 (2): 323–64.

Benson, Elizabeth P., ed. 1973. *Mesoamerican Writing Systems.* Dumbarton Oaks Research Library and Collections.

———, and Beatríz de la Fuente, eds. 1996. *Olmec Art of Ancient Mexico.* National Gallery of Art.

Benson, Nettie Lee. 1955. *La diputación provincial y el federalismo mexicano.* El Colegio de México.

Berlin, Isaiah. 1983. *Contra la corriente: Ensayos sobre la historia de las ideas.* Fondo de Cultura Económica.

Bernal, Ignacio. 1979. *Historia de la arqueología en México.* Editorial Porrúa.

Bernard, Carmen, and Serge Gruzinski. 1991. *Histoire du Nouveau Monde.* Fayard.

Blanco, José Joaquín. 1977. *Se llamaba Vasconcelos.* Fondo de Cultura Económica.

Bloch, Marc. 1952. *Introducción a la historia.* Fondo de Cultura Económica.

Boone, Elizabeth H. 2000. *Stories in Red and Black: Pictorial Histories of the Aztecs and Mixtecs.* University of Texas Press.

Boturini Benaduci, Lorenzo. 1974. *Idea de una historia general de la América Septentrional.* Preliminary analysis by Miguel León-Portilla. Editorial Porrúa.

———. 1990. *Historia general de la América Septentrional.* Edited, with analysis, notes, and documented appendix, by Manuel Ballesteros Gaibrois. Universidad Nacional Autónoma de México.

Brading, David A. 1973. *Los origenes del nacionalismo mexicano.* SepSetentas.

———. 1980. *Los orígenes del nacionalismo mexicano.* Editorial Era.

———. 1991a. *The First America: The Spanish Monarchy, Creole Patriots and the Liberal State, 1492–1867.* Cambridge University Press.

———. 1991b. *Orbe indiano: De la monarquía católica a la república criolla.* Fondo de Cultura Económica.

Brandon, S. G. F. 1965. *History, Time and Deity.* Manchester University Press.

Brenner, Anita. 1971. *The Wind That Swept Mexico.* Harper.

Braudel, Fernand. 1976. *El Mediterráneo y el mundo mediterráneo en la época de Felipe II.* Fondo de Cultura Económica.

———. 1984. *La historia y las ciencias sociales.* Alianza.

Broda, Johanna, and Félix Báez-Jorge, comps. 2001. *Cosmovisión ritual e identidad de los pueblos indígenas de México.* Fondo de Cultura Económica.

Browne, Walden. 2000, *Sahagún and the Transition to Modernity.* University of Oklahoma Press.

Burgoa, Francisco de. 1934a. *Geográfica descripción.* 2 vols. Talleres Gráficos de la Nación.

———. *Palestra historial.* 1934b. Talleres Gráficos de la Nación.

Burke, Peter. 1990. *La revolucion historiografica francesa: La escuela de los Annales, 1929–1989.* Gedisa.

———, et al., eds. 1994. *Formas de hacer historia.* Alianza.

Burrus, Ernest J., S.J. 1973. "Religious Chroniclers and Historians: A Summary with Annotated Bibliography." In *Handbook of Middle American Indians,* vol. 12, *Guide to Ethnohistorical Sources,* edited by Howard F. Cline, 138–85. University of Texas Press.

Bustamante, Carlos María de. 1835–36. *Mañanas de la Alameda de México: Publicadas para facilitar a las señoritas el estudio de la historia de su país.* 2 vols. Valdés.

———. 1976. *La abeja de Chilpancingo.* Preliminary study by Ernesto Lemoine Villicaña. PRI.

———. 1985. *Cuadro histórico de la Revolución mexicana.* Facsimile ed. of ed. of J. Mariano Lara. 5 vols. Fondo de Cultura Económica.

Bustamante García, Jesús. 1990. *Fray Bernardino de Sahagún: Una revisión crítica de los manuscritos y de su proceso de composición.* Universidad Nacional Autónoma de México.

Byland, Bruce E., and John M. D. Pohl. 1994. *In the Realm of 8 Deer: The Archaeology of the Mixtec Codices.* University of Oklahoma Press.

Cabrera, Luis. 1972. *Obras completas.* 4 vols. Ediciones Oasis.

———. *Cacaxtla.* 1987. Ediciones Citicorp.

Carbia, Rómulo D. 1940. *La crónica oficial de las Indias Occidentales.* Ediciones Buenos Aires.

Cárdenas de la Peña, Enrique. 1979. *Mil personajes en el México del siglo XIX.* Banco Mexicano Somex.

Carmack, Robert M., and James Mondloch, eds. 1983. *El Título de Totonicapán.* Facsimile ed. Universidad Nacional Autónoma de México.

——, and ——, eds. 1989. *El Título de Yax y otros documentos Quichés de Totonicapán, Guatemala.* Facsimile ed. Universidad Nacional Autónoma de México.

Carmagnani, Marcelo. 1994. "Territorios, provincias y estados: Las transformaciones de los espacios políticos en México, 1750–1850." In *La fundación del Estado mexicano,* coordinated by Josefina Zoraida Vásquez. Nueva Imagen.

Casas, Bartolomé de las. 1967. *Apologética historia sumaria.* Edited by Edmundo O'Gorman. 2 vols. Universidad Nacional Autónoma de México.

Casasola, Gustavo. 1973. *Historia gráfica de la Revolución Mexicana.* Trillas.

Caso, Alfonso. 1954. *Interpretación del Códice Gómez de Orozco.* Talleres de Impresión de Estampillas y Valores.

——. 1958. "Comentario al Códice Baranda." In *Miscelánea Paul Rivet, Octogenario Dicata,* 2 vols., vol. I, 373–93. Universidad Nacional Autónoma de México.

——. 1961. "Los lienzos mixtecos de Ihuitlán y Antonio de León." In *Homenaje a Pablo Martínez del Río,* 237–74. Instituto Nacional de Antropología e Historia.

——. 1966. "Mapa de Santo Tomás Ocotepeque, Oaxaca." In *Summa anthropológica en homenaje a Roberto J. Weitlaner.* Instituto Nacional de Antropología e Historia.

——. 1977. *Reyes y reinos de la Mixteca.* 2 vols. Fondo de Cultura Económica.

Castelán Rueda, Roberto. 1997. *La fuerza de la palabra impresa: Carlos María de Bustamante y el discurso de la modernidad.* Fondo de Cultura Económica.

Castillo, Alberto. 1991. "Chiquisnaquis un indio escribano, artífice de títulos primordiales." *Relaciones* XII, no. 48: 187–210.

Castillo Negrete, Emilio de. 1875–92. *México en el siglo XIX.* El Neve Editor.

Cauvin, Jacques. 1997. *Naissance des divinités: Naissance de l'agriculture.* Flammarion.

Certeau, Michel de. 1978. *L'ecriture de l'histoire.* Gallimard.

Charencey, M. de, trans. 1885. *Título de los Señores de Totonicapán (Titre Généalogique des Seigneurs de Totonicapan).* Bulletin de la Societé de Philologie. E. Renaut de Broise.

Christensen, Carol et al. 1998. *The U.S.–Mexican War.* Bay Books.

Clancy, Flora S. 1999. *Sculpture in the Ancient Maya Plaza: The Early Classic Period.* University of New Mexico Press.

Clark, James Cooper. 1912. *The Story of "Eighth Deer" in Codex Colombino.* Taylor and Francis.

Clark, John E., ed. 1994. *Los olmecas en Mesoamérica.* El Equilibrista.

Clavijero, Francisco Javier. 1958–59. *Historia antigua de México.* Introduction and prologue by Mariano Cuevas. 4 vols. Porrúa.

——. 1976. *Antología.* Introduction by Gonzalo Aguirre Beltrán. Secretaría de Educación Pública.

Cline, Howard F., ed. 1972–75. *Handbook of Middle American Indians,* vol. 12, *Guide to Ethnohistorical Sources.* 4 vols. University of Texas Press.

———. 1973. "Selected Nineteenth-Century Mexican Writers on Ethnohistory." *Handbook of Middle American Indians*, vol. 13, edited by Robert Wauchope, 370–427. University of Texas Press.

Códice Alfonso Caso: La vida de 8-Venado, Garra de Tigre. 1996. Introduction by Miguel León-Portilla. Patronato Indígena AC.

Códice Azcatitlán. 1995. Introduction by Michel Graulich. Bibliotheque Nacional de France, Societé des Americanistes.

Códice Chimalpopoca: Anales de Cuautitlán y leyenda de los soles. 1945. Edited and translated by Primo Feliciano Velázquez. Universidad Nacional Autónoma de México.

Códice de Tepetlaoztoc. 1994. El Colegio Mexiquense.

Códice Tlatelolco. 1994. Preliminary study by Perla Valle. Instituto Nacional de Antropología e Historia.

Códice de Yanhuitlán. 1994. INAH–Universidad Autónoma de Puebla.

Códice florentino: El Manuscrito 218–220 de la colección Palatina de la Biblioteca Medicea Laurenziana. 1979. Facsimile Edition. 3 vols. Archivo General de la Nación–Giunti Barbera.

Códice Techialoyan de San Pedro Tototepec. 1999. El Colegio Mexiquense.

Códice Techialoyan García Granados. 1992. Gobierno del Estado de México.

Códice Xiquipilco-Temoaya y Títulos de tierras otomies. 1999. El Colegio Mexiquense.

Coe, Michael D. 1973. *The Maya Scribe and His World.* Grolier Club.

———. 1989. "The Hero-Twins: Myth and Image." In *The Maya Vase Book,* edited by Justin Kerr, 161–84. Kerr Associates.

———. 1993. *The Maya.* Thames and Hudson.

———, ed. 1996. *The Olmec World: Ritual and Rulership.* Art Museum, Princeton University.

———, and Justin Kerr. 1997. *The Art of the Maya Scribe.* Thames and Hudson.

Coggins, Clemency Chase. 1996. "Creation Religion and the Numbers at Teotihuacan and Izapa." *RES* 29–30 (Spring–Fall): 17–38.

Cohn, Norman Rufus Colin. 1972. *En pos del milenio: Revolucionarios milenaristas y anarquistas místicos de la edad media.* Barral.

Corona Núñez, José. 1964. *Antigüedades de México.* Secretaría de Hacienda y Crédito Público.

Cortés, Hernán. 1963. *Cartas y documentos.* Introduction by Hernández Sánchez Barba. Editorial Porrúa.

Cosío Villegas, Daniel. 1970. *Historia moderna de México: El Porfiriato, Vida política interior.* Part 1. Editorial Hermes.

———. 1999. *Obras completas de Daniel Cosío Villegas.* 1961. Clío.

Costeloe, Michael P. 1975. *La primera República Federal de México (1824–1835).* Fondo de Cultura Económica.

———. 2000. *La República Central en México (1835–1846).* Fondo de Cultura Económica.

Covarrubias, Miguel. 1961. *Arte indigena de México y Centroamérica.* Universidad Nacional Autónoma de México.

Covo, Jacqueline. 1988. "La idea de la Revolución francesa en el Congreso Constituyente de 1856–1857." *Historia mexicana* XXXVIII (July–September): 69–78.

Cruz, Víctor de la. 1997. "Lienzos y mapas mixtecos." *Historia del arte de Oaxaca.* Gobierno del Estado de Oaxaca.

Cuadriello, Jaime. 1984. *Maravilla americana: Variantes de la iconografía guadalupana.* Patronato Cultural de Occidente.

———. 1994. "Los jeroglíficos de Nueva España." In *Juegos de ingenio y agudeza: La pintura emblemática de la Nueva España.* Museo Nacional de Arte.

———. 1995. "Visiones en Patmos Tenochtitlán: La mujer águila." *Artes de México,* no. 29: 10–22.

Cuevas, Luis G. 1954. *Porvenir de México.* Editorial Jus.

Cullman, Oscar. 1962. *Christ and Time.* SCM Press.

Davies, Nigel. 1977. *The Toltecs until the Fall of Tula.* University of Oklahoma Press.

Dehouve, Danièle. 1995. *Hacia una historia del espacio en la montaña de Guerrero.* Centro de Estudios Mexicanos y Centroamericanos.

Díaz, Gisela, and Alan Rodgers. 1993. *The Codex Borgia: A Ful-Color Restoration of the Ancient Mexican Manuscript.* Dover Publications.

Díaz del Castillo, Bernal. 1983. *Historia verdadera de la conquista de la Nueva España.* Edited, with indexes and prologue, by Carmelo Sáenz de Santa María. Editorial Patria.

Díaz y de Ovando, Clementina. 1985. *Vicente Riva Palacio y la identidad nacional.* Universidad Nacional Autónoma de México.

Dibble, Charles E. 1980. *Códice Xolotl.* Universidad Nacional Autónoma de México.

Dubernard Chaureau, Juan, comp. 1991. *Códices de Cuernavaca y unos títulos de sus pueblos.* Miguel Angel Porrúa Editor.

Dumas, Claude. 1986. *Don Justo Sierra y su tiempo.* 2 vols. Universidad Nacional Autónoma de México.

Durán, Fray Diego. 1984. *Historia de las Indias de Nueva España e Islas de la Tierra Firme.* Edited by Angel María Garibay. 2 vols. Editorial Porrúa.

———. 1995. *Historia de las Indias de Nueva España e Islas de la Tierra Firma.* Preliminary study by Rosa Camelo and José Rubén Romero. Consejo Nacional para la Cultura y las Artes.

Duverger, Christian. 1987. *El origen de los aztecas.* Grijalbo.

Edgerton, Samuel Y. 2000. *Theaters of Conversion: Religious Architecture and Indian Artisans in Colonial Mexico.* University of New Mexico Press.

Edmonson, Munro S., ed. 1974. *Sixteenth-Century Mexico: The Work of Sahagun.* University of New Mexico Press.

Eisenhower, John S. D. 2000. *Tan lejos de Dios: La guerra de Estados Unidos contra México, 1846–1848.* Fondo de Cultura Económica.

Eisenstein, Elizabeth L. 1993. *The Printing Revolution in Early Modern Europe.* Cambridge University Press.

El Título de Totonicapán. 1983. Facsimile edition. Transcription, translation, and notes by Robert M. Carmack and James L. Mondloch. Universidad Nacional Autónoma de México.

El Título de Yax y otros documentos Quichés de Totonicapán, Guatemala. 1989. Facsimile edition. Transcription, translation, and notes by Robert M. Carmack and James L. Mondloch. Universidad Nacional Autónoma de México.

El territorio mexicano. 1982. Instituto Mexicano del Seguro Social.

Esteve Barba, Francisco. 1992. *Historiografía indiana.* Ed. Gredos.

Estrada, Julio, ed. 1984. *La música de México: Período nacionalista.* Universidad Nacional Autónoma de México.

Fane, Diana. 1996. *Converging Cultures: Art and Identity in Spanish America.* Harry N. Abrams.

Fash, William, and Barbara Fash. 1996. "Building a World-View: Visual Communication in Classic Maya Architecture." *RES* 29–30 (Spring–Fall): 127–47.

Fell, Claude. 1989. *José Vasconcelos: Los años del águila.* Universidad Nacional Autónoma de México.

Fernández de Oviedo, Gonzalo. 1971. *Historia general y natural de las Indias.* Centro de Estudios de Historia de México.

———. 1972. *Sucesos y diálogos de la Nueva España.* Sep-Setentas.

Florescano, Enrique. 1976a. "La historiografía del poder (1920–1976)." *La cultura en México.* Supplement to *Siempre!* September 14: II–VI.

———. 1976b. *Origen y desarrollo de los problemas agrarios de México, 1500–1821.* Editorial Era.

———. 1991. *El nuevo pasado mexicano.* Cal y Arena.

———. 1995a. *Memoria mexicana.* Fondo de Cultura Económica.

———. 1995b. *El mito de Quetzalcóatl.* Fondo de Cultura Económica.

———. 1997a. *Etnia, Estado y Nación.* Editorial Aguilar.

———. 1997b. *La historia y el historiador.* Fondo de Cultura Económica.

———. 1998. *La bandera mexicana: Breve historia de su formación y simbolismo.* Fondo de Cultura Económica.

———. 1999. *Memoria indígena.* Taurus.

———, and Isabel Gil Sánchez, eds. 1973. *Descripciones económicas generales de Nueva España.* Instituto Nacional de Antropología e Historia.

———, and ———, eds. 1976. *Descripciones económicas regionales de Nueva España,* Instituto Nacional de Antropología e Historia.

Florescano Mayet, Enrique. 1991. *El nuevo pasado mexicano.* Cal y Arena.

Fogel, Robert William, and G. R. Elton. 1989. *¿Cuál de los caminos al pasado? Dos visiones de la historia de Eric Herran Salvatti.* Fondo de Cultura Económica.

Folgarait, Leonard. 1998. *Mural Painting and Social Revolution in Mexico, 1920–1940: Art of the New Order.* Cambridge University Press.

Foucault, Michel. *Histoire de la folie á l'age classique.* Plön.

Freidel, David, Linda Schele, and Joy Parker. 1993. *Maya Cosmos: 3000 Years of the Shaman's Path.* William Morrow.

Fuente, Beatríz de la, coord. 1995. *La pintura mural prehispánica en México: Teotihuacán.* Universidad Nacional Autónoma de México, Instituto Nacional de Antropología e Historia, Consejo Nacional para la Cultura y las Artes.

Fueter, Eduard. 1953. *Historia de la historiografía moderna.* 2 vols. Editorial Nova.

Furet, François. 1978. *Penser la revolution française.* Gallimard.

Furst, Jill Leslie. 1978. *Codex Vindobonensis Mexicanus I: A Commentary.* Institute for Mesoamerican Studies–State University of New York.

Galarza, Joaquín. 1972. *Lienzo de Chiepetlan.* Mission Archéologique et Ethnologique Française au Mexique.

———. 1980. *Codex de Zempoala: Techialoyan e 705 manuscrit pictographique de Zempoala, Hidalgo, Mexique.* Mission Archéologique et Ethnologique Française au Mexique.

———. 1990. *Amatl, Amoztli.* Tava.

Gamio, Manuel. 1922. *La población del Valle de Teotihuacan.* 3 vols. Dirección de Talleres Gráficos.

———. 1960. *Forjando patria.* Editorial Porrúa.

García Icazbalceta, Joaquín. 1941. *Nueva colección de Documentos para la historia de México: Códice Franciscano.* Editorial Salvador Chávez Hayhoe.

———. 1947. *Don fray Juan de Zumárraga, primer obispo y arzobispo de México.* Edited by Rafael Aguayo Spencer and Antonio Castro Leal. 4 vols. Porrúa.

García Zambrano, Ángel J. 1994. "Early Colonial Evidence of Pre-Columbian Rituals of Foundation," in *Seventh Palenque Round Table, 1989,* edited by Merle Greene Robertson, 217–27. The Pre-Columbian Art Research Institute.

Garciadiego, Javier. 1997. *En defensa de la patria, 1847–1997.* Secretaria de Gobernación, Archivo General de la Nación.

Garibay K, Ángel María. 1954. *Historia de la literatura náhuatl.* 2 vols. Editorial Porrúa.

———. 1965. *Teogonía e historia de los mexicanos: Tres opúsculos del siglo XVI.* Editorial Porrúa.

Gelb, I. J. 1963. *A study of Writing.* University of Chicago Press.

Gerbi, Antonello. 1960. *La disputa del Nuevo Mundo: Historia de una polémica, 1750–1900.* Fondo de Cultura Económica.

———. 1978. *La naturaleza de las Indias Nuevas.* Fondo de Cultura Económica.

Ginzburg, Carlo. 1981. *El queso y los gusanos: El cosmos según un molinero del siglo XVI.* Muchnik.

Girón, Nicole. 1976. "La idea de cultura nacional en el siglo XIX." In *En torno a la cultura nacional,* edited by Héctor Aguilar Camín. Instituto Nacional Indigenista.

———. 1991. "Ignacio M. Altamirano y la Revolución francesa: Una recuperación liberal." In *La Revolución francesa en México,* edited by Solange Alberro et al. El Colegio de México: 201–14.

Glass, John B. 1964. *Catálogo de la colección de códices.* Instituto Nacional de Antropología e Historia.

Gómez Morín, Manuel. 1973. *1915 y otros ensayos.* Jus.

Gómez Serrano, Jesús. 1994. *La creación del estado de Aguascalientes (1786–1857).* Consejo Nacional para la Cultura y las Artes.

González, Luis, ed. 1961–62. *Fuentes para la historia contemporánea de México: Libros y Folletos.* El Colegio de México.

González Gamio, Ángeles. 1987. *Manuel Gamio: Una lucha sin final.* Universidad Nacional Autónoma de México.

González Navarro, Moisés. 1970. *Sociología e historia en México (Barreda, Sierra, Parra, Molina Enríquez, Gamio, Caso).* El Colegio de México.

Goody, Jack. *The Logic of Writing and the Organization of Society.* Cambridge University Press.

———. 2000. *The Power of the Written Tradition.* Smithsonian Institution Press.

Goubert, Pierre. 1960. *Beauvais et le Beauvaisis de 1600 à 1730 contribution à l'histoire sociale de la France du xviie siècle.* Sevpen.

Grañen Porrúa, María Isabel. 1996. *Las joyas bibliográficas de la Universidad Autónoma Benito Juárez de Oaxaca: La Biblioteca Francisco de Burgoa.* Fomento Cultural Banamex.

Graulich, Michel. 1974. "Las peregrinaciones aztecas y el ciclo de Mixcóatl." *Estudios de Cultura Náhuatl* XI: 311–54.

Gruzinski, Serge. 1988. *La colonisation de l'imaginaire: Societés Indigenes et occidentalisation dans le Mexique espagnol, XVIe et XVIIIe Siécle.* Gallimard.

———. 1994a. *El águila y la síbila: Frescos indios de México.* M. Moleiro Editor.

———. 1994b. *La guerra de las imágenes: De Cristóbal Colón a "Blade Runner."* Fondo de Cultura Económica.

Guerra, François-Xavier. 1985. *Le Mexique de l'Ancien Régime à la Révolution.* 2 vols. L'Harmattan.

Guevara Hernández, Jorge. 1991. *El lienzo de Tiltepec: Extinción de un señorío zapoteco.* Instituto Nacional de Antropología e Historia.

Gutiérrez, Ramón A. 1993. *Cuando Jesús llegó, las madres del maíz se fueron.* Fondo de Cultura Económica.

Gutiérrez de Estrada, José María. 1848. *México en 1840 y en 1847.* Andrade y Escalante.

Guzmán, Martín Luis. 1970. *La querella de México: A orillas del Hudson, otras páginas.* Compañía General de Ediciones.

Hale, Charles H. 1957. "The War with the United States and the Crisis of Mexican Thought." *The Americas* XIV (October): 153–73.

———. 1972. *El liberalismo mexicano en la época de Mora, 1821–1853.* Siglo Veintiuno Editores.

———. 1997. "Los mitos políticos de la nación mexicana: El liberalismo y la revolución." *Historia mexicana* XLVI (April–June): 821–37.

Hartog, François. 1980. *Le miroir d'Herodote: Essai sur la répresentation de l'autre.* Gallimard.

Harvey, H. R. 1986. "Techialoyan Codices: Seventeenth-Century Indians Land Titles in Central Mexico." In Ronald Spores (comp.), *Handbook of Middle American Indians,* vol. 4, *Supplement,* edited by Ronald Spores, 153–84. University of Texas Press.

Haskett, Robert. 1996. "Paper Shields: The Ideology of the Coats of Arms in Colonial Mexican Primordial Titles." *Ethnohistory* 43, no. 1: 99–126.

Healan, Dan M., comp. 1989. *Tula of the Toltecs.* University of Iowa Press.

Heath, Shirley B. 1972. *La política del lenguaje en México: De la colonia a la nación.* Instituto Nacional Indigenista.

Hellmuth, Nicholas. 1987. *The Surface of the Underwaterworld.* Foundation for Latin American Anthropological Research.

Herrejón, Carlos. 1985. *Morelos, Antología documental.* Secretaría de Educación Pública.

Herrera, Antonio de. 1945. *Historia general de los hechos de los castellanos en las islas y tierra firme del mar Océano.* 5 vols. Editorial Guaranía.

Herrera Serna, Laura, comp. 1997. *México en guerra (1846–1848): Perspectivas regionales.* Consejo Nacional para la Cultura y las Artes.

Heyden, Doris. 1975. "An Interpretation of the Cave Underneath the Pyramid of the Sun in Teotihuacan, Mexico." *American Antiquity* 40: 131–47.

Hobsbawm, E. J. 1963. *Primitive Rebels Studies in Archaic Forms of Social Movement in the 19th and 20th Centuries.* Manchester University.

Homenaje a Gonzalo Aguirre Beltrán. 1973. Instituto Indigenista Interamericano.

Honour, Hugh. 1975. *The European Vision of America.* Cleveland Museum of Art.

Horcasitas, Fernando. 1974. *El teatro náhuatl: Epocas novohispana y moderna.* Universidad Nacional Autónoma de México.

———, and Wanda Tommasi de Magrelli. 1975. "El Códice de Tzictepec: Una nueva fuente pictórica indígena." *Anales de Antropología del Instituto de Investigaciones Antropológicas* 12.

Humboldt, Alejandro de. 1966. *Ensayo político sobre el reino de la Nueva España,* edited by Juan A. Ortega y Medina. Porrúa.

Jiménez Codinach, Guadalupe. 1997. *México: Su tiempo de nacer, 1750–1821.* Fomento Cultural Banamex.

Johannsen, Robert W. 1985. *To the Halls of the Moctezumas: The Mexican War in the American Imagination.* Oxford University Press.

Jones, Lindsay. 1995. *Twin City Tales: A Hermeneutical Reassessment of Tula and Chichen Itza.* University Press of Colorado.

Joralemon, Peter David. 1971. "A Study of Olmec Iconography." *Studies in Pre-Columbian Art and Archaeology,* no. 7.

———. 1971. "The Olmec Dragon: A Study in Pre-Columbian Iconography." In *Origins of Religions Art and Iconography in Pre-Classic Mesoamerica,* edited by M. B. Nicholson, 29–71. Latin American Publications, University of California at Los Angeles.

Katz, Friedrich. 1998. *Pancho Villa.* Editorial Era.

Kerr, Justin. 1980–92. *The Maya Vase Book.* 3 vols. Kerr Associates.

Kirchhoff, Paul, Lina Odena Güemes, and Luis Reyes García. 1989. *Historia tolteca-chichimeca.* Instituto Nacional de Antropología e Historia.

Kirk, Betty. 1942. *Covering the Mexican Front: The Battle of Europa versus America.* University of Oklahoma Press.

Klor de Alva, Jorge, H. B. Nicholson, and Eloise Quiñones Keber, eds. 1988. *The Work of Bernardino de Sahagún: Pioneer Ethnographer of Sixteenth-Century Aztec Mexico.* University of Albany.

Kowalski, Jeff K., ed. 1999. *Mesoamerican Architecture as a Cultural Symbol.* Oxford University Press.

Krauze, Enrique. 1976. *Caudillos culturales de la revolución mexicana.* Siglo Veintiuno Editores.

La bandera de México. 1985. Miguel Ángel Porrúa Editor.

Labastida, Jaime. 1999. *Humboldt, ciudadano universal.* Siglo Veintiuno Editores.

Labrousse, Ernest. 1962. *Fluctuaciones económicas e historia social.* Tecnos.

Ladurie, Emmanuel Le Roy. 1969. *Les paysans de Languedoc.* Flammarion.

Landa, Diego de. 1959. *Relación de las cosas de Yucatán.* Introduction by Ángel María Garibay. Porrúa.

Le Goff, Jacques. 1979. "Au Moyen Age: Temps de l'eglise et temps du marchand." In *Pour un autre Moyen Age: Temps, travail et culture en Occident,* 49. Gallimard.

———, and Pierre Nora, eds. 1974. *Faire de l'histoire.* 3 vols. Gallimard.

Leibsohn, Dana. 1994. "Primers for Memory: Cartographic Histories and Nahua Identity." In *Writing Without Words: Alternative Literatures in Mesoamerica and the Andes,* edited by Elizabeth H. Boone and Walter D. Mignolo, 161–67. Duke University Press.

Lejarazo, Manuel A. Hermann. 2000. "Continuidades y transformaciones mixtecos: El caso del Códice Muro." *Acervos* 4 (July–September): 15–18.

Lemoine Villicaña, Ernesto. 1984. *Carlos María de Bustamante y su apologética historia de la revolución de 1810.* Universidad Nacional Autónoma de México.

———. 1985. *Morelos: Su vida revolucionaria a través de sus escritos y de otros testimonios de la época.* Universidad Nacional Autónoma de México.

León-Portilla, Miguel. 1959a. *Relaciones indígenas de la conquista.* Universidad Nacional Autónoma de México.

———. 1959b. *Visión de los vencidos: Relaciones indígenas de la conquista.* Universidad Nacional Autónoma de México.

———. 1961. *Los antiguos mexicanos a través de sus crónicas y cantares.* Fondo de Cultura Económica.

———. 1980. "La investigación integral de Sahagún." In *Toltecáyotl: Aspectos de la cultura náhuatl,* 101–35. Fondo de Cultura Económica.

———. 1996. "Literatura en náhuatl clásico y en las variantes de dicha lengua hasta el presente." In *Historia de la literatura mexicana,* vol. 1, edited by Beatríz Garcia Cuarón and Georges Baudot, 135. Siglo Veintiuno Editores.

———. 1999. *Bernardino de Sahagún: Pionero de la antropología.* Universidad Nacional Autónoma de México.

Le Roy Ladurie, Emmanuel. 1969. *Les paysans de Languedoc.* Flammarion.

Lévi-Strauss, Claude. 1989. *Des symboles et leurs doubles.* Plön.

Linati, Claudio. 1956. *Trajes civiles, militares y religiosos de México.* Introduction by Justino Fernández. Universidad Nacional Autónoma de México.

Lira, Andrés. 1991. "La Revolución francesa en la obra de Justo Sierra." In *La Revolución francesa en México,* edited by Solange Alberro et al., 179–214. El Colegio de México.

———. 1995. "Justo Sierra: La historia como entendimiento responsable." In *Historiadores de México en el siglo XX,* edited by Enrique Florescano and Ricardo Pérez Monfort, 22–40. Fondo de Cultura Económica.

Lockhart, James. 1982. "Views of Corporate Self and History in Some Valley of Mexico Towns: Late Seventeenth and Eighteenth Centuries." In *The Inca and Aztec States, 1400–1800,* edited by George A. Collier, Renato I. Rosaldo, and John D. Wirth, 367–93. Academic Press.

———. 1992. *The Nahuas after the Conquest: A Social and Cultural History of the Indians of Central Mexico, Sixteenth through Eighteenth Centuries.* Stanford University Press.

Logan Wagner, Eugene. 1997. *Open Spaces as a Tool of Conversion: The Syncretism of Sacred Courts and Plazas in Post-Conquest Mexico.* Ph.D. diss., University of Texas at Austin.

López Austin, Alfredo. 1976. "Estudio acerca del método de investigación de fray Bernardino de Sahagún." In *La investigación social de campo en México,* edited by Jorge Martínez Ríos, 9–56. Universidad Nacional Autónoma de México.

———. López Luján, Leonardo, and Saburo Sugiyama. 1991. "El Templo de Quetzalcóatl en Teotihuacán: Su posible significado ideológico." *Anales del Instituto de Investigaciones Estéticas* 62: 35–52.

López de Gómara, Francisco. 1971. *Hispania Victrix: Primera y segunda parte de la historia general de las Indias.* Biblioteca de Autores Españoles.

López de Velasco, Juan. 1971. *Geografía y descripción universal de las Indias.* Atlas.

López Velarde, Ramón. 1971. *Obras.* Fondo de Cultura Económica.

Los maestros y la cultura nacional. 1987. Secretaría de Educación Pública, Museo Nacional de Culturas Populares.

Los pinceles de la historia: De la patria criolla a la nación mexicana, 1750–1860. 2000. Museo Nacional de Arte.

Lowith, Karl. 1958. *El sentido de la historia: Implicaciones teológicas de la filosofía de la historia.* Editorial Aguilar.

Macune, Charles W., Jr. 1978. *El estado de México y la federación mexicana.* Fondo de Cultura Económica.

Manuscrit Tovar: Origines et croyances des indiens du Mexique. 1972. Edited by Jacques Lafaye. Academische Druck-u. Verlagsanstalt.

Marcus, Joyce. 1992. *Mesoamerican Writing Systems: Propaganda, Myth and History in Four Ancient Civilizations.* Princeton University Press.

———, and Kent V. Flannery. 1996. *Zapotec Civilization: How Urban Society Evolved in Mexico's Oaxaca Valley.* Thames and Hudson.

Martin, Simon, and Nikolai Grube. 2000. *Chronicle of the Maya Kings and Queens: Deciphering the Dynasties of the Ancient Maya.* Thames and Hudson.

Martínez, José Luis. 1990. *Hernán Cortés.* Fondo de Cultura Económica.

———. 1993. *La expresión nacional.* Consejo Nacional para la Cultura y las Artes.

Martínez Donjuán, Guadalupe. 1981. "Teopantecuanitlán, Guerrero: Un sitio olmeca." *Revista Mexicana de Estudios Antropológicos,* no. 28.

Matute, Álvaro. 1976. *Lorenzo Boturini y el pensamiento histórico de Vico.* Universidad Nacional Autónoma de México.

———. 1993. *La revolución mexicana: Actores, escenarios y acciones.* Instituto Nacional de Estudios Históricos de la Revolución Mexicana.

———. 1999. *Pensamiento historiográfico mexicano del siglo XX: La desintegración del positivismo (1911–1935).* Fondo de Cultura Económica.

Meinecke, Friedrich. 1943. *El historicismo y su génesis.* Fondo de Cultura Económica.

Memorial de Sololá: Anales de los cakchiqueles, Título de los Señores de Totonicapán. 1950. Edited by Adrián Recinos. Fondo de Cultura Económica.

Memorias de la Academia Mexicana de la Historia. 2000. Academia Mexicana de la Historia, vol. XLIII.

Mendieta, Jerónimo de. 1997. *Historia eclesiástica indiana.* Introduction by Joaquín García Icazbalceta. Preliminary analysis by Antonio Rubial García. 2 vols. Consejo Nacional para la Cultura y las Artes.

Menegus Bornemann, Margarita. 1999. "Los títulos primordiales de los pueblos indios." In *Dos décadas de investigación en historia económica comparada en*

América Latina: Homenaje a Carlos Sempat Assadourian, edited by Margarita Menegus, 137–61. El Colegio de México.

Mignolo, Walter D. 1995. *The Darker Side of the Renaissance: Literacy, Territoriality, and Colonization.* University of Michigan Press.

Mijangos y González, Pablo. 2001. *El primer constitucionalismo conservador: Las Siete Leyes de 1836.* Undergraduate thesis, Instituto Tecnológico Autónomo de México.

Millares Carlo, Agustín. 1957. *Don Juan José de Eguiara y Eguren y su Bibliotheca mexicana.* Universidad Nacional Autónoma de México.

Millon, René. 1981. "Teotihuacan: City, State and Civilization." In *Handbook of Middle American Indians, Archaeology Supplement,* edited by Jeremy A. Sabloff, 198–243. University of Texas Press.

———. 1992. "Teotihuacan Studies: From 1950 to 1990 and Beyond." In *Art, Ideology and the City of Teotihuacan,* edited by Catherine Berlo, 241–310. Dumbarton Oaks Research Library and Collections.

———. 1993. "The Place Where Time Began." In *Teotihuacan: Art From the City of The Gods,* edited by Kathleen Berrin and Esther Pasztory. Thames and Hudson.

Miranda, José. 1962. *Humboldt y México.* Universidad Nacional Autónoma de México.

Moffitt, John F., and Santiago Sebastián. 1966. *Brave New People: The European Invention of the American Indian.* University of New Mexico Press.

Momigliano, Arnaldo. 1966. "Time in Ancient Historiography." *History and Theory* 6: 18–19.

Monsiváis, Carlos. 2000. "Notas sobre la cultura mexicana del siglo XX." In *Historia general de México,* 959–1076. El Colegio de México.

Monterrosa, Mariano, ed. 1990. *La pintura mural de los conventos franciscanos en Puebla: Estudio iconográfico.* Gobierno del Estado de Puebla.

Mora, Carlos J. 1982. *Mexican Cinema: Reflections of a Society.* University of California Press.

Moreno Toscano, Alejandra. 1968. *Geografía económica de México, siglo XVI.* El Colegio de México.

Motolinía, Fray Toribio de. *See* Benavente, Fray Toribio de.

Mundy, Barbara E. 1996. *The Mapping of New Spain: Indigenous Cartography and the Maps of the Relaciones Geograficas.* University of Chicago Press.

Munford, Lewis. 1977. *Técnica y civilización.* Alianza Editorial.

Muñoz Camargo, Diego. 1981. *Descripción de la ciudad y provincia de Tlaxcala.* Universidad Nacional Autónoma de México.

Nebrija, Elio Antonio de. 1492. *Gramática de la lengua castellana.* Salamanca.

Nicholson, Henry B. 1971. "Pre-Hispanic Central Mexican Historiography." In *Investigaciones contemporáneas sobre historia de México: Memoria de la Tercera Reunión de Historiadores Mexicanos y Norteamericanos,* 38–81. Universidad Nacional Autónoma de México.

Niederberger Betton, Christine. 1987. *Paleopaysage et archéologie pré-urbaine du bassin de Mexico.* Centre d'Études Mexicaines et Mesoamericaines.

Novick, Peter. 1997. *Ese noble sueño: La objetividad y la historia profesional norteamericana.* 2 vols. Instituto Mora.

Nuttall, Zelia. 1902. *Codex Nuttall.* Peabody Museum of American Archaeology and Ethnology.

Ocampo, Javier. 1969. *Las ideas de un dia: El pueblo mexicano ante la consumación de su independencia.* El Colegio de México.

Oettinger, Marion. 1983. *Lienzos coloniales: Guía de la Exposición de Pinturas de Terrenos Comunales de México (siglos XVI–XIX).* Universidad Nacional Autónoma de México.

Offner, Jerome A. 1983. *Law and Politics in Aztec Mexico.* Cambridge University Press.

O'Gorman, Edmundo. 1951. *Idea del descubrimiento de América.* Universidad Nacional Autónoma de México.

———. 1954. "Precedentes y sentido de la revolución de Ayutla." In *El Plan de Ayutla.* Universidad Nacional Autónoma de México.

———. 1960. *Seis estudios históricos de tema mexicano.* Universidad Veracruzana.

———. 1972. *Cuatro historiadores de Indias.* Secretaría de Educación Pública.

———. 1977. *La invención de América.* Fondo de Cultura Económica.

Olson, David R. 1998. *El mundo sobre el papel: El impacto de la escritura y la lectura en la estructura del conocimiento.* Gedisa.

O'Malley, Irene V. 1986. *The Myth of the Revolution: Hero Cults and the Institutionalization of the Mexican State.* Greenwood Press.

Ong, Walter J. 1987. *Oralidad y escritura tecnologías de la palabra.* Fondo de Cultura Económica.

Orozco y Berra, Manuel. 1973. *Apuntes para la historia de la geografía en México.* Edmundo Aviña Levy, Editor.

Ortega y Medina, Juan A. 1968. *Conciencia y autenticidad históricas: Escritos en homenaje a Edmundo O'Gorman.* Universidad Nacional Autónoma de México.

———. 1970. *Polémicas y ensayos mexicanos en torno a la historia.* Universidad Nacional Autónoma de México.

———, and Rosa Camelo, eds. 1996. *En busca de un discurso integrador de la nación (1848–1884).* Universidad Nacional Autónoma de México.

Ortiz Monasterio, José. 1993. *Historia y ficción: Los dramas y novelas de Vicente Riva Palacio.* UNAM—Instituto de Investigaciones Dr. José María Luis Mora.

———. 1999a. *La obra historiográfica de Vicente Riva Palacio.* Ph.D. diss., Universidad Iberoamericana.

———. 1999b. *"Patria," tu ronca voz me repetía: Biografía de Vicente Riva Palacio y Guerrero.* UNAM—Instituto de Investigaciones Doctor José María Luis Mora.

Otero, Mariano. 1967. *Obras.* Introduction and commentaries by Jesús Reyes Heroles. 2 vols. Editorial Porrúa.

Oudijk, Michel R. 2003. "Espacio y escritura: El lienzo de Tabáa I." In *Escritura zapoteca, 2500 años de historia,* coordinated by María de los Angeles Romero Frizzi. Instituto Nacional de Antropología e Historia/Centro de Investigaciones y Estudios Superiores en Antropología Social.

Ozouf, Mona. 1976. *La fête révolutionnaire, 1789–1797.* Gallimard.

Pacheco, José Emilio. 1976. "La patria perdida (notas sobre Clavijero y la cultura nacional)." In *En torno a la cultura nacional,* edited by Héctor Aguilar Camín. Instituto Nacional Indigenista.

Palacios, Guillermo. 1969. *La idea oficial de la "Revolución Mexicana."* Master's thesis, El Colegio de México.

———. 1999. *La pluma y el arado: Los intelectuales pedagogos y la construcción sociocultural del "problema campesino" en México, 1932–1934.* El Colegio de México–Centro de Investigación y Docencia Económicas.

Palavicini, Félix F. 1914. *Diez civiles notables de la Historia Patria.* Secretaría de Instrucción Pública.

Palomera, Esteban J. 1962. *Fray Diego de Valadés, evangelizador humanista de la Nueva España: Su obra.* Editorial Jus.

Parcero, María de la Luz. 1971. "El liberalismo triunfante y el surgimiento de la historia nacional." In *Investigaciones contemporáneas sobre historia de México,* 443–47. Universidad Nacional Autónoma de México.

Parmenter, Ross. 1982. *Four Lienzos of the Coixtlahuaca Valley.* Dumbarton Oaks Research Library and Collections.

Partida, Armando, ed. 1992. *Teatro mexicano, Historia y dramaturgia: II Teatro de evangelización en náhuatl.* Consejo Nacional para la Cultura y las Artes.

Pasztory, Esther. 1997. *Teotihuacan: An Experiment in Living.* Prologue by Enrique Florescano. University of Oklahoma Press.

Payno, Manuel. 1987. *La reforma social en España y México: Apuntes históricos y principales leyes sobre desamortización de bienes eclesiásticos.* Instituto Nacional de Estudios Históricos de la Revolución Mexicana.

Paz, Octavio. 1994. *Obras completas: Los privilegios de la vista II.* Fondo de Cultura Económica.

Peterson, Jeanette Favrot. 1988. "The Florentine Codex Imaginery and the Colonial Tlacuilo." In Klor de Alva, Jorge, H. B. Nicholson and Eloise Quiñones Keber, (eds.), *The Work of Bernardino de Sahagún: Pioneer Ethnographer of Sixteenth Century Aztec Mexico,* edited by Jorge Klor de Alva, H. B. Nicholson, and Eloise Quiñones Keber, 273–93. University of New York at Albany Press.

———. 1993. *The Paradise Garden Murals of Malinalco.* University of Texas Press.

Phelan, John Leddy. 1972. *El reino milenario de los franciscanos en el nuevo mundo.* Universidad Nacional Autónoma de México.

Plumb, J. H. 1974. *La muerte del pasado.* Barral Editores.

Pocock, J. G. A. 2000. *Barbarism and Religion.* 2 vols. Cambridge University Press.

Pohl, John M. 1994. "Mexican Codices, Maps and Lienzos as Social Contracts." In *Writing Without Words: Alternative Literatures in Mesoamerica and the Andes,* edited by Elizabeth Hill Boone and Walter D. Mignolo, 137–60. Duke University Press.

Pomar, Juan Bautista. 1941. "Relación de Tezcoco." In *Nueva colección de Documentos para la Historia de México: Pomar-Zurita-Relaciones antiguas (siglo XVI),* edited by Joaquín García Icazbalceta. Editorial Salvador Chávez Hayhoe.

Pomian, Krzysztof. 1999. *Sur l'histoire.* Gallimard.

Popol Vuh. Las antiguas historias del Quiché. 1950. Translated from the original text with an introduction and notes by Adrián Recinos. Fondo de Cultura Económica.

Proskouriakoff, Tatiana. 1946. *An Album of Maya Architecture.* Institute of Washington.

Prost, Antoine. 1993. *Douze leçons sur l'histoire.* Éditions de Seuil.

Quiñones, Isabel. 1994. *Mexicanos en su propia tinta.* Instituto Nacional de Antropología e Historia.

Quiñones Keber, Eloise. 1988a. "Deity Images and Texts in the Primeros Memoriales and Florentine Codex." *The Work of Bernardino de Sahagún: Pioneer Ethnographer of Sixteenth Century Aztec Mexico,* edited by Jorge Klor de Alva, H. B. Nicholson, and Eloise Quiñones Keber, 255–72. University of New York at Albany Press.

———. 1988b. "Reading Images: The Making and Meaning of the Sahaguntine Ilustrations." In *The Work of Bernardino de Sahagún: Pioneer Ethnographer of Sixteenth Century Aztec Mexico,* edited by Jorge Klor de Alva, H. B. Nicholson, and Eloise Quiñones Keber, 255–72. University of New York at Albany Press.

———. 1997. "An introduction to the Images, Artists, and Physical Features of the Primeros Memoriales," In *Primeros memoriales,* by Bernardino de Sahagún, with paleography of the Náhuatl text and translation to English by Thelma Sullivan, 15–37. University of Oklahoma Press.

Rabasa, José. 1993. *Inventing America: Spanish Historiography and the Formation of Eurocentrism.* University of Oklahoma Press.

Rappaport, Roy A. 1999. *Ritual and Religion in the Making of Humanity.* Cambridge University Press.

Recinos, Adrián. 1984. *Crónicas indígenas de Guatemala,* 23–67. Academia de Geografía e Historia de Guatemala.

———, ed. 1950. *Memorial de Sololá; Anales de los cakchiqueles; Título de los Señores de Totonicapán.* Fondo de Cultura Económica.

Reilly, Kent F. 1996. "Art, Ritual, and Rulership in the Olmec World." In *The Olmec World: Ritual and Rulership,* edited by Michael D. Coe, 27–47. Art Museum, Princeton University.

Relaciones geográficas del siglo XVI: Tlaxcala. 1985. Edited by René Acuña. 2 vols. Universidad Nacional Autónoma de México.

Restall, Matthew. 1998. *Maya Conquistador.* Beacon Press.

Revel, Jacques. 1999. *Fernand Braudel et l'histoire.* Hachette.

Reyes, Aurelio de los. 1973. *Los orígenes del cine en México (1896–1900).* Universidad Nacional Autónoma de México.

———. 1987. *Medio siglo de cine mexicano (1896–1947).* Editorial Trillas.

Reyes, Luis. 1998. "Las mojoneras antiguas en el Lienzo I de Tequixtepec." *Acervos* 2 (April–September): 21–23.

Reyes García, Luis. 1988. *Cuauhtinchan del siglo XII al XVI: Formación y desarrollo histórico de un señorío prehispánico.* Fondo de Cultura Económica.

———, and Marcelo Díaz de Salas. 1968. "Testimonio de la fundación de Santo Tomás Ajusco." *La Palabra y el Hombre* 46 (April–June): 283–92.

Reyes Valerio, Constantino. 1978. *Arte indocristiano: Escultura del siglo XVI en México.* Instituto Nacional de Antropología e Historia.

———. 1989. *El pintor de conventos: Los murales del siglo XVI en Nueva España.* Instituto Nacional de Antropología e Historia.

Ricard, Robert. 1986. *La conquista espiritual de México.* Fondo de Cultura Económica.

Riva Palacio, Vicente. 1884–89. *México a través de los siglos.* 5 vols. Ballescá y Cía. Editores.

———. 1968. *Cuentos del General.* Editorial Porrúa.

———. 1976. *Antología.* Universidad Nacional Autónoma de México.

———. 1997. *Obras escogidas: IV, Ensayos históricos.* Compiled by José Ortiz Monasterio. Consejo Nacional Para la Cultura y las Artes.

Roa Bárcena, José María. 1971. *Recuerdos de la invasión norteamericana (1846–1848).* 3 vols. Editorial Porrúa.

Robertson, Donald. 1959. *Mexican Manuscript Painting of the Early Colonial Period.* Yale University Press.

———. 1975. "Techialoyan Manuscripts and Paintings with a Catalog." In *Handbook of Middle American Indians,* vol. 14, *Guide to Ethnohistorical Sources,* edited by Howard F. Cline, 253–80. University of Texas Press.

———. Undated. "The Sixteenth Century Mexican Encyclopedia of Fray Bernardino de Sahagún." *Cuadernos de historia mundial,* 9, no. 3: 617–28.

Robicsek, Francis, and Donald Hales. 1981. *The Maya Book of the Dead: The Ceramic Codex.* University of Virginia Museum.

Rodríguez, Jaime E. 1994. *Mexico in the Age of Democratic Revolutions.* Lynne Reinner Publications.

———, ed. 1989. *The Independence of Mexico and the Creation of a New Nation.* University of California Press.

Rodríguez Mortellaro, Itzel. 1997. "La nación mexicana en los murales de Palacio Nacional (1929–1935)." In *Los murales de Palacio Nacional,* edited by Raquel Tibol et al. Instituto Nacional de Bellas Artes.

Romero Frizzi, María de los Angeles. 1988. "Los lienzos de San Miguel Tequixtepec." *Acervos* 2 (April–September): 16–20.

———. 2000. "Los cantos de los linajes en el mundo colonial." *Acervos* 4 (July–September): 4–11.

———, coord. 2003. "Memoria y escritura: La memoria de Juquila." In *Escritura zapoteca, 2500 años de historia,* 393–448. Centro de Investigaciones y Estudios Superiores en Antropología Social.

Roskamp, Hans. 1998. *La historiografía indígena de Michoacán: El lienzo de Jucutácato y los títulos de Carapan.* Leiden University, Research School CNWS.

———. 2003. "Los 'Títulos primordiales' de Carapan: Legitimación e historiografía en una comunidad indígena de Michoacán." In *Autoridad y gobierno indígena en Michoacán a través de su historia,* edited by Carlos Paredes Martínez and Marta Terán. 2 vols. El Colegio de Michoacán.

Rozat, Guy. 2001. *Los orígenes de la nación: Pasado indígena e historia nacional.* Universidad Iberoamericana.

Rust, William F., and Barbara W. Leyden. 1994. "Evidence of Maize Use at Early and Middle Preclassic La Venta Olmec Sites." In *Corn and Culture in the Prehistoric New World,* edited by Sissel Johannessen and Christine E. Hastorf, 181–201. Westview Press.

Sacchi, Duccio. 1997. *Mappe dal Nuovo Mondo: Cartografie locali e definizione del territorio in Nuova Spagna (secoli XVI–XVII).* Franco-Angeli.

Sahagún, Bernardino de. 1950–70. *Florentine Codex, General history of the things of New Spain.* Translation from Náhuatl to English, notes, and illustrations by Arthur J. O. Anderson and Charles E. Dibble. 12 vols. School of American Research and the University of Utah.

———. 1956. *Historial general de las cosas de Nueva España.* Edited by Angel María Garibay K. 4 vols. Editorial Porrúa.

———. 1974. *Primeros memoriales.* Text in Náhuatl, translation, prologue, and commentaries by Wigberto Jiménez Moreno. Instituto Nacional de Antropología e Historia.

———. 1993. *Primeros memoriales.* Facsimile edition. Photographs by Ferdinand Anders. University of Oklahoma Press.

———. 1997. *Primeros memoriales.* Paleography of Náhuatl text and translation to English by Thelma Sullivan. University of Oklahoma Press.

———. 2000. *Historia general de las cosas de la Nueva España.* Introduction, paleography, and notes by Alfredo López Austin and Josefina García Quintana. 3 vols. Consejo Nacional para la Cultura y las Artes.

Santoni, Pedro. 1996. *Mexicans at Arms: Pure Federalists and the Politics of War, 1845–1848.* Texas Christian University Press.

Schatten vit de Nieuwe Wereld. 1992. Museo Real de Arte e Historia de Bruselas.

Schele, Linda, and David Freidel. 1990. *A Forest of Kings: The Untold Story of the Ancient Maya.* William Morrow.

———, and ———. 1999. *Una selva de reyes: La asombrosa historia de los antiguos mayas.* Fondo de Cultura Económica.

———, and Peter Matthews. 1998. *The Code of Kings: The Language of Seven Sacred Maya Temples and Tombs.* Scribner.

———, and Mary Ellen Miller. 1992. *The Blood of Kings: Dynasty and Ritual in Maya Art.* Thames and Hudson.

Scholes, France V., and Ralph L. Roys. 1996. *Los Chontales de Acalán-Tixchel.* Universidad Nacional Autónoma de México–CIESAS.

Sebastián, Félix de, S.J. 1988. *Vida de Francisco Zavier Clavijero.* Introduction by Elías Trabulse. Novus Orbis.

Segundo Calendario de Pedro de Urdinales para el año bisiesto de 1858. 1858. Biblioteca Nacional de Antropologia e Historia.

Seler, Eduard. 1990. *Collected Works in Mesoamerican Linguistics and Archaeology.* Labyrinthos.

Sepúlveda, Juan Ginés de. 1979. *Tratado sobre las justas guerras de la guerra contra los indios.* Fondo de Cultura Económica.

Sheridan, Guillermo. 1989. *Un corazón adicto: La vida de Ramón López Velarde.* Fondo de Cultura Económica.

Sierra, Justo. 1940. *Evolución política del pueblo mexicano.* Prologue by Alfonso Reyes. Ediciones de la Casa de España.

———. 1984. *Obras completas,* edited by Edmundo O'Gorman. Universidad Nacional Autónoma de México.

Smith, Mary Elizabeth. 1973. *Picture Writing from Ancient Southern Mexico: Mixtec Place Signs and Maps.* University of Oklahoma Press.

———, and Ross Parmenter. 1991. *The Codex Tulane.* Tulane University Press.

Spinden, Herbert. 1935. "Indian Manuscripts of Southern Mexico." In *Annual Report of the Smithsonian Institution 1933.* Smithsonian Institution.

Spores, Ronald. 1967. *The Mixtec Kings and Their People.* University of Oklahoma Press.

Stark, Barbara L. 2000. "Framing the Gulf Olmecs." In *Olmec Art and Archaelogy in Mesoamerica,* edited by John E. Clark and Mary E. Pye, 31–53. National Gallery of Art.

Stock, Brian. 1983. *The Implications of Literacy: Written Language and Models of Interpretation in the Eleventh and Twelfth Centuries.* Princeton University Press.

Stuart, David. 2000. "The Arrival of Strangers: Teotihuacán and Tollan in classic Maya History." In *Mesoamerica's Classic Heritage. From Teotihuacan to the Aztecs,* edited by David Carrasco, Lindsay Jones, and Scott Sessions, 465–513. University Press of Colorado.

Stuart, George E. 1993. "The Carved Stela from La Mojarra." *Science* 259 (March): 1700–1701.

Sugiyama, Saburo. 2000. "Teotihuacan as an Origin for Postclassic Feathered Serpent Symbolism." In *Mesoamerica's Classic Heritage: From Teotihuacan to the Aztecs,* edited by David Carrasco, Lindsay Jones, and Scott Sessions. University Press of Colorado.

Tanck de Estrada, Dorothy. 1991. "Los catecismos políticos: De la Revolución francesa al México Independiente." In *La Revolución francesa en México,* edited by Solange Alberro et al., 65–80. El Colegio de México.

———. 1999. *Pueblos de indios y educación en el México colonial, 1750–1821.* El Colegio de México.

Tate, Carolyn E. 1992. *Yaxchilan: The Design of a Maya Ceremonial City.* University of Texas Press.

Taube, Karl. 1985. "The Classic Maya Maize God: A Reappraisal." In *Fifth Palenque Round Table,* edited by Merle Greene Robertson, 171–81. Pre-Columbian Art Research Institute.

———. 1986. "The Teotihuacan Cave of Origin: The Iconography and Architecture of Emergence Mythology in Mesoamerica and the American Southwest." *RES* 12 (Fall): 51–82.

———. 1992. "The Temple of Quetzalcoatl and the Cult of Sacred War at Teotihuacan." *RES* 21 (Spring): 53–87.

———. 1996. "The Olmec Maize God." *RES* 29–30 (Spring–Autumn): 39–81.

———. 2000a. "Lightning Celts and Corn Fetishes: The Formative Olmec and the Development of Maize Symbolism in Mesoamerica and the American Soutwest." In *Olmec Art and Archaelogy in Mesoamerica,* edited by John E. Clark and Mary E. Pye, 297–337. National Gallery of Art.

———. 2000b. *The Writing System of Ancient Teotihuacan.* Center for Ancient American Studies.

Tavárez, David. 2000. "De cantares Zapotecas a 'libros del demonio': La extirpación de discursos doctrinales híbridos en Villa Alta, Oaxaca, 1702–1704." *Acervos* 17 (July–September): 19–27.

Tenenbaum, Barbara E. 1985. *México en la época de los agiotistas, 1821–1857.* Fondo de Cultura Económica.

Teresa de Mier, Servando. 1922. *Historia de la Revolución de Nueva España, antiguamente Anáhuac, o verdadero origen y causas de ella con la relación de sus progresos hasta el presente año de 1813.* 2 vols. Imprenta de la Cámara de Diputados.

———. 1978. *Ideario político.* Prologue, notes, and chronology by Edmundo O'Gorman. Biblioteca Ayacucho.

Terraciano, Kevin, and Lisa M. Sousa. 1992. "The 'Original Conquest' of Oaxaca: Mixtec and Nahua History and Myth." UCLA *Historical Journal* 12: 8–90.

Thompson, Edward Palmer. 1965. *The Making of the English Working Class.* Gollancz.

Thompson, J. Eric. 1959. *Grandeza y decadencia de los mayas.* Fondo de Cultura Económica.

Tibol, Raquel, et al. 1997. *Los murales del Palacio.* Instituto Nacional de Bellas Artes.

Todorov, Tzvetan. 1982. *La conquêt de l'Amérique: La question de l'autre.* Editions du Seuil.

Torquemada, Juan de. 1975–83. *Monarquía Indiana.* Edition prepared by the Seminary for the Study of Sources of Indigenous Tradition under the coordination of Miguel León-Portilla. 7 vols. Universidad Nacional Autónoma de México.

Toussaint, Manuel, 1965. *Pintura colonial en México.* Universidad Nacional Autónoma de México.

Tovar de Teresa, Guillermo. 1979. *Pintura y escultura del Renacimiento en México.* Instituto Nacional de Antropología e Historia.

———. 1992. *Pintura y escultura en Nueva España (1557–1640).* Grupo Azabache.

Trabulse, Elías. 1988. *Los manuscritos perdidos de Sigüenza y Góngora.* El Colegio de México.

Troike, Nancy. 1974. *The Codex Colombino-Becker.* Ph.D. diss., University of London.

Valadés, Diego. 1989. *Retórica cristiana.* Introduction by Esteban J. Palomera. Universidad Nacional Autónoma de México, Fondo de Cultura Económica.

Vansina, Jan. 1985. *Oral Tradition as History.* University of Wisconsin Press.

Vaughan, Mary Kay. 1982. *The State, Education and Social Class in Mexico, 1880–1928.* Northern Illinois University Press.

Velasco Márquez, Jesús. 1975. *La guerra del 47 y la opinión pública (1845–1848).* SepSetentas.

Vilar, Pierre. 1962. *La Catalogne dans l'Espagne moderne: Recherches sur le fondaments économiques des structures nationales.* Sevpen.

Villoro, Luis. 1950. *Los grandes momentos del indigenismo en México.* El Colegio de México.

———. 1986. *El proceso ideológico de la revolución de independencia.* Secretaría de Educación Pública.

Vovelle, Michel. 1988. "La historia y la larga duración." In *La nueva historia*, edited by Le Goff et al, 359–86. Mensajero.

Wagner, Fritz. 1958. *La ciencia de la historia*. Universidad Nacional Autónoma de México.

Wauchope, Robert, ed. 1973. *Handbook of Middle American Indians*. University of Texas Press.

West, Delmo C., and Sandra Zimdars-Swartz. 1986. *Joaquín de Fiore: Una visión espiritual de la historia*. Fondo de Cultura Económica.

White, Hayden. 1993. *Metahistoria: La imaginación histórica en la Europa del siglo XIX*. Fondo de Cultura Económica.

Womack, John, Jr. 1969. *Zapata y la Revolución mexicana*. Siglo Veintiuno Editores.

Wood, Stephanie. 1987. "Pedro Villafranca y Juana Gertrudis Navarrete: Falsificador de títulos y su viuda." In *La lucha por la supervivencia en la América colonial*, edited by David G. Sweet and Gary B. Nash, 472–85. Fondo de Cultura Económica.

———. 1989. "Don Diego García de Mendoza Moctezuma: A Techialoyan Mastermind?" *Estudios de Cultura Náhuatl* 19: 245–485.

———. 1998. "El problema de la historicidad de los Títulos y los códices del grupo Techialoyan." In *De tlacuilos y escribanos*, edited by Xavier Noguez and Stephanie Wood. El Colegio Mexiquense–El Colegio de Michoacán.

Yerushalmi, Josef Hayim. 1996. *Zakhor: Jewish History and Jewish Memory*. Foreword by Harold Bloom. University of Washington Press.

Yoneda, Keiko. 1991. *Los mapas de Cuauhtinchan y la historia cartográfica prehispánica*. Fondo de Cultura Económica.

Zantwijk, Rudolf Von. 1985. *The Aztec Arrangement: The Social History of Prehispanic Mexico*. University of Oklahoma Press.

Zavala, Silvio. 1982. *Datos biográficos y profesionales del Dr. Silvio Zavala*. El Colegio Nacional.

Zoraida Vázquez, Josefina. 1960. "La historiografía romántica en México." *Historia Mexicana* X (July–Sept.).

———. 1970. *Nacionalismo y educación de México*. El Colegio de México.

———. 1994. "De la difícil constitución de un Estado: México, 1821–1854." In *La fundación del Estado mexicano*, coordinated by Josefina Zoraida Vázquez, 9–37. Nueva Imagen.

———. 1997a. *La intervención norteamericana 1846–1848*. Secretaría de Relaciones Exteriores.

———. 2000. "Los primeros tropiezos." In *Historia general de México*, 9–37. El Colegio de México.

———, ed. 1997b. *México al tiempo de su guerra con los Estados Unidos (1846–1848)*. Fondo de Cultura Económica.

Index